The Colossus of Rhodes

The Colossus of Rhodes

Archaeology of a Lost Wonder

NATHAN BADOUD

Translated in collaboration with
JASON R. HARRIS

Great Clarendon Street, Oxford, OX2 6DP,
United Kingdom

Oxford University Press is a department of the University of Oxford.
It furthers the University's objective of excellence in research, scholarship,
and education by publishing worldwide. Oxford is a registered trade mark of
Oxford University Press in the UK and in certain other countries

© Nathan Badoud 2024

The moral rights of the author have been asserted

All rights reserved. No part of this publication may be reproduced, stored in
a retrieval system, or transmitted, in any form or by any means, without the
prior permission in writing of Oxford University Press, or as expressly permitted
by law, by licence or under terms agreed with the appropriate reprographics
rights organization. Enquiries concerning reproduction outside the scope of the
above should be sent to the Rights Department, Oxford University Press, at the
address above

You must not circulate this work in any other form
and you must impose this same condition on any acquirer

Published in the United States of America by Oxford University Press
198 Madison Avenue, New York, NY 10016, United States of America

British Library Cataloguing in Publication Data
Data available

Library of Congress Control Number: 2023920962

ISBN 978–0–19–890373–4

DOI: 10.1093/oso/9780198903734.001.0001

Printed and bound by
CPI Group (UK) Ltd, Croydon, CR0 4YY

Links to third party websites are provided by Oxford in good faith and
for information only. Oxford disclaims any responsibility for the materials
contained in any third party website referenced in this work.

For Salomé and Lucien

ἁβρὸν ἀδουλώτου φέγγος ἐλευθερίας.

Preface

This book started twenty-two years ago as a letter to the French anthropologist Jean-Pierre Vernant. I was then a student at the University of Neuchâtel, where my professor of archaeology, Denis Knoepfler, had convinced me to devote my master's thesis to Greek amphora stamps, small marks that cities impressed into the clay of their containers for taxation purposes. A number of these marks, from Rhodes, included a device that archaeologists defined (and still define, I am afraid) as a 'symbol of Helios'. It seemed to me that this figure rather was a *kolossós*, a type of statue with magical powers that Jean-Pierre Vernant had placed at the centre of his research on the psychology of the ancient Greeks. I began to write a letter describing my modest discovery, but I dared not send it, my admiration for its intended recipient being too great.

The years passed. When Juliette de la Genière and Denis Knoepfler invited me to present a sample of my research to the Académie des Inscriptions et Belles-Lettres, I decided to return to the *kolossós* that I had identified a decade earlier on Rhodian amphora stamps. The lecture, given in 2011, was destined to form the first part of a larger study on the most famous *kolossós*, the Colossus of Rhodes. Already in 2012, the Académie provided me with the opportunity to study the place of this statue in Western imagination. It remained for me to examine several other topics related to the Colossus. The occasion presented itself in 2017: during my fellowship at Harvard University's Center for Hellenic Studies, I became acquainted with Jason Harris, who suggested that he could translate into English the comprehensive study that I should dedicate to the statue. The result is the present book. The second and seventh chapters are based on the articles published in the *Comptes rendus de l'Académie des Inscriptions et Belles-Lettres* and in the *Monuments et mémoires de la fondation Eugène Piot*, but they contain numerous additions and some corrections; it goes without saying that the English version is now the authoritative work. The remainder of the book is entirely unpublished.

I wish to warmly thank the Ephorates of Antiquities for having allowed me to pursue my research on Rhodes and in Thebes from 2010, as well as the Académie des Inscriptions et Belles-Lettres for having permitted me to use the studies published under its auspices in 2011 and 2012. I also wish to express my gratitude to all those who have contributed to the results of my research, by providing me with sources, by responding to my questions, or by suggesting topics for reflection. I think especially of Pascal Arnaud, Richard Ashton, Gilbert Dagron, Catherine Dobias-Lalou, Jean-Bernard de Vaivre, Jean-Louis Ferrary,

Anne Jacquemin, Jacques Jouanna, Charalampos Kritzas, Didier Laroche, John Lund, Silvia Marengo, Marco Masseti, Oscar Mei, Benoît Mille, Viki Pandit, Francis Prost, Miguel Quintana, Jaimee Uhlenbrock, and Riet van Bremen. Nor can I forget my dear colleagues and Italian friends who, in 2012, invited me to present my research as part of a 'Grand Tour' that took me from Rome to Pisa, from Pisa to Perugia, and would have taken me from Perugia to Bologna if a train strike had not changed my plans: they are Carmine Ampolo, Alice Bencivenni, Lucia Criscuolo, Donatella Erdas, Roberta Fabiani, Enzo Lippolis, Anna Magnetto, and Massimo Nafissi.

Finally, I should like to highlight the contributions of Fabrice Delrieux and Myriam Fincker, the creators of Figures 1.1, 2.9, 2.17 (b–c), and 5.1, and to recognize the skill and dedication of my translator, Jason Harris, who welcomed all of my suggestions with equal kindness and checked all sections that I directly wrote in English. My last words will be for Richard Ashton (again) and Elisabeth Dutton, who carefully read the text before submission to Oxford University Press.

Geneva, Spring 2022

Contents

List of Illustrations   xiii
List of Abbreviations   xxi

    Introduction   1

1. The Rise of Helios   6
    The Reign of Zeus   6
    A New God for a New City   9
    Correcting the Past   10
    Ialysian Motivations   12
    Rhodian Acceptance   14

2. The *Kolossoí*   16
    The Etymology of the Word   16
    The Meaning of the Word   17
        The Terms of the Debate   17
        A Reappraisal of the Debate   24
    The First *Kolossoí*   27
        A Review of the Evidence   27
        Dorian Statues   33
    The *Kolossoí* of Rhodes   35
        The Colonization of Cyrene   35
        Rhodian Amphora Stamps   42
        Posidippus *On the Making of Statues*   43
        A First Glance at the *Alexandra* of Lycophron   44
        Polybius and His Rhodian Source   46
    A Base from Thespiae   47
    A Short History of the *Kolossoí*   49

3. The Artist   52
    The Origin of Chares   52
    The Pupil of Lysippus   54
        Chares in Tarentum?   55
        Lysippus on Rhodes   56
    The Works Attributable to Chares   61
    The End of Chares   63

4. The *Kolossós* of Rhodes   64
    Chronology   64
        Construction, Completion, and Destruction   64
        Alleged Reconstructions   67
        The Myth of Muʿāwiya   69

The Height of the Statue	73
Seventy Cubits	73
The Base	74
The Original Project	76
The Highest Statue of the Ancient World	77
Building the Statue	79
The Casting Process and the Signature of Chares	79
The Internal Structure	87
A Huge Mound of Earth	88
The Materials and the Cost of the Statue	89
The Appearance of the Colossus	92
The Evidence	92
Becoming a Wonder	94
5. Over the Seas and on the Land	**96**
The Dedicatory Epigram of the Colossus	96
The Text	96
Historiographical Analysis	97
In Defence of *Anth. Pal.* 6.171	101
The Aim of the Colossus	103
Rhodes and Macedonia	105
The Shadow of the Helepolis	106
The Nike of Samothrace Revisited	107
Rhodes and Rome	108
Illuminating the *Alexandra*	108
A Common Struggle against Piracy	116
Imperialism and Propaganda in the Mediterranean	120
6. The Location of the Colossus	**121**
The Port	121
The Medieval Myth	121
The Origin of the Myth	126
The Perpetuation of the Myth	128
The *Deîgma* and the Agora	131
The Soichan-Minetou Plot	134
The Pythion	139
A Sanctuary of Apollo-Helios?	140
A Sanctuary of Helios Only?	142
A Sanctuary of Apollo and Helios?	144
A Sanctuary of Apollo and Artemis	144
The Top of the Acropolis	151
The Palace of the Grand Master and Its Environs	152
Prior Arguments	152
New Arguments	157

7. The Image of the Statue	163
The Most Ancient Representations	163
Byzantine Iconography	163
Western Colossi	164
The Colossus as a Column	165
The *Nuremberg Chronicle*	165
Nicetas of Heraclea and Cyriac of Ancona	167
The Colossus Spanning the Port of Rhodes	168
A Landscape by Heemskerck	168
A Lost Manuscript and an Alexandrine Legend	170
The First Numismatic Colossi	173
The Hidden Gods	175
Heemskerck's Triumph	182
A Lonesome Colossus on a Lonely Base	184
Theme and Variations	186
Japanese Imagery and Colossal Genitals	191
Artists and Archaeologists	195
Two Statuettes	195
The Liberty Enlightening the World	198
A Relief from Rhodes and a Painting by Salvador Dali	202
A Statue from Santa Marinella and a Painting by William Blake	205
Additional Numismatic Colossi	210
Spaghetti Archaeology	213
'Casting' the Colossus	213
Reconstructing the Colossus	215
Conclusion	219
The Tradition	219
The Sources	221
References	225
Indexes	
Literary Sources	253
Papyri	257
Other Manuscripts	258
Inscriptions	259
Greek Index	261
General Index	262

List of Illustrations

1.1	Map of the island of Rhodes.	8
	Map by Fabrice Delrieux and the author.	
2.1	Stele from Cyrene bearing a sacred law and an account about grain supplies.	18
	From Oliverio (1933) pl. 8, fig. 9.	
2.2	Decrees of Cyrene for the citizenship of the Therans.	20
	From Oliverio (1928) pl. X.	
2.3	Hippodrome of Constantinople, with the 'walled obelisk' in the foreground.	25
	Personal collection.	
2.4	Drawing of the inscription *IG* XII, 3, 1015, from Thera.	28
	From the original publication.	
2.5	Attestations of the original meaning of *kolossós*, prior to the construction of the Colossus of Rhodes.	28
2.6	The temple of Ptah at Gerf Hussein.	30
	Victoria and Albert Museum.	
2.7	Statuettes from the Cairo Museum.	31
	From Borchardt (1911), nos. 223, 225, 228.	
2.8	*Perirrhantḗrion* from Isthmia.	32
	From Sturgeon (1987) pl. 1.	
2.9	Distribution of *kolossoí* before the construction of the Colossus of Rhodes.	34
	Map by Fabrice Delrieux and the author.	
2.10	Silver tetradrachm from Cyrene depicting the devices of three different cities.	37
	The Trustees of the British Museum.	
2.11	Fragment of a Rhodian (?) mould-made figurine found in Cyrene.	38
	Photograph by Jaimee Uhlenbrock, reproduced with permission.	
2.12	Fragment of a calyx from Chios with dedication to the Dioscuri, found in Cyrene.	39
	Missione Archeologica Italiana dell'Università di Urbino a Cirene.	
2.13	The graffito *IGCyr* 118100.	40
	Photograph and drawing by Catherine Dobias-Lalou; the drawing has been slightly modified by the author.	

xiv   LIST OF ILLUSTRATIONS

2.14 Lindian decree concerning suppliants.   41
      Photograph by the author, with permission of the Ephorate of Antiquities
      of Dodecanese.

2.15 Rhodian amphora stamps with the device of the *kolossós* of Helios.   43
      Photographs by the author, with permission of the Ephorate of Antiquities
      of Athens / American School of Classical Studies at Athens / Gerald Finkielsztejn,
      Tania Panagou (a, b, d); by Gonca Şenol (c).

2.16 Rhodian amphora stamp with the device of the herm of Helios.   43
      Photograph by Craig Mauzy, American School of Classical Studies at Athens.

2.17 Base of a *kolossós*, found at Thespiae in 1891.   49
      Photograph by the author, with permission of the Ephorate of Antiquities
      of Boeotia. Drawing by Myriam Fincker. Reconstitution by Myriam Fincker
      and the author.

3.1   View of the Palace of the Grand Master in 1826.   57
      From Rottiers (1830) pl. XVIII, photograph by Jean-Bernard de Vaivre.

3.2   Base of a statue signed by Lysippus (?).   58
      Photograph by John Lee, National Museum of Denmark.

3.3   Reconstruction of the Rhodian pillar at Delphi.   60
      From Jacquemin and Laroche (1986) 305, updated by the authors.

3.4   Base for a statue offered by Publius Cornelius Lentulus.   62
      Photograph by the author, with permission of the Ephorate of Antiquities
      of Dodecanese.

4.1   Detail from ms. *Bambergensis class*. 42, f. 57r.   67
      Photograph by Gerald Raab, Staatsbibliothek Bamberg.

4.2   Medallion depicting the Flavian Amphitheatre and the Colossus of Nero.   74
      The Trustees of the British Museum.

4.3   Base of the Colossus of Nero in front of the Flavian Amphitheatre.   75
      Gabinetto Fotografico Nazionale. Reproduced with permission of the
      Istituto Centrale per il Catalogo e la Documentazione MiBACT.

4.4   Silver tetradrachm from Apollonia Pontica depicting a statue sculpted by Calamis. 76
      From the website www.cngcoins.com.

4.5   Reconstruction of the casting by stages of the Buddha of Nara.   83
      From Katori (1981) 28–29.

4.6   Buddha of Kamakura.   84
      Photograph by Viki Pandit.

4.7   Foundry no. 1 from the Mylonas plot at Rhodes.   85
      Photograph by the author, with permission of the Ephorate of Antiquities
      of Dodecanese.

4.8	Statue being cast 'in parts' in Mylonas' Foundry no. 1.	85
	From Zimmer and Bairami (2008) 48.	
5.1	Map of the Rhodian territory.	106
	Map drawn by Fabrice Delrieux and the author.	
5.2	Winged Victory of Samothrace in the Louvre.	109
	Photograph by Philippe Fuzeau, Musée du Louvre/RMN-Grand Palais.	
5.3	Reconstruction of the column of Philip V at Samothrace.	110
	Drawing by Leah Solk, American Excavations Samothrace.	
5.4	Map of the Sanctuary of the Great Gods at Samothrace.	111
	Map by the American Excavations Samothrace, modified by the author.	
5.5	Skyphos belonging to the Berthouville Treasure.	114
	Photograph by Tahnee Cracchiola. J. Paul Getty Trust/Bibliothèque nationale de France.	
5.6	Inscription alluding to diplomatic relations between Rhodes and Rome.	117
	Photograph by the author, with permission of the Ephorate of Antiquities of Dodecanese.	
5.7	Epitaph of three brothers killed while fighting pirates.	119
	Photograph by Klaus Hallof, Berlin-Brandenburgische Akademie der Wissenschaften.	
6.1	Proposed locations for the Colossus of Rhodes, from 1394 to 1856.	123
	Map from Newton (1865) pl. 4, modified by the author.	
6.2	Illumination in the *Gestorum Rhodiae obsidionis commentarii* of Guillaume Caoursin.	125
	Bibliothèque Nationale de France.	
6.3	Fort Saint Nicholas.	127
	Photograph by the author.	
6.4	Ancient block reused in the entrance of Fort Saint Nicholas.	128
	Photograph by the Ephorate of Antiquities of Dodecanese; drawing from Gabriel (1932) 355.	
6.5	Naturalistic base *TC* 31.	130
	Photograph by the author, with permission of the Ephorate of Antiquities of Dodecanese.	
6.6	So-called 'hand of the Colossus'.	132
	Photograph by the author, with permission of the Ephorate of Antiquities of Dodecanese.	
6.7	Street map of Rhodes illustrating several proposed locations for the Colossus.	134
	Map provided by the Ephorate of Antiquities of Dodecanese, modified by the author.	

6.8	Peristyle structure discovered in the Soichan-Minetou plot. The Archaeological Society at Athens.	135
6.9	Restitution of the structure plan by Grigoris Konstantinopoulos. From Konstantinopoulos (1975) 239–240 (παρένθετος πίναξ ζ), reworked by Hoepfner (2003) 46.	136
6.10	Interpretation of the structure plan by Wolfram Hoepfner. From Hoepfner (2003) 47.	137
6.11	Base of a statue dedicated by the priest of Helios Archokrates. Photograph by the Ephorate of Antiquities of Dodecanese.	138
6.12	Plan of the sanctuary of Pythian Apollo. Scuola Archeologia Italiana di Atene, Fondo Paolini, PD183.	140
6.13	Sanctuary of Apollo-Helios, as imagined by Wolfram Hoepfner. From Hoepfner (2003) 39.	141
6.14	Inscription mentioning Apollo Pythios, as copied by Johan Hedenborg. From Badoud (2017c) pl. 43.	143
6.15	Inscription mentioning the hippodrome (*NSER* 3). From the original publication.	144
6.16	The sanctuary of Artemis, viewed from the south-west. Photograph by the author.	146
6.17	Fragments of the elevation of temple B. Photograph by the author.	147
6.18	Terracotta figurine discovered in a votive deposit near temple B. From Laurenzi (1939) pl. XVI, 1.	148
6.19	Four Rhodian funerary altars decorated with deer skulls. a, b, d: photograph by the author, with permission of the Ephorate of Antiquities of Dodecanese. c: from Jacopi (1932a) 14.	149
6.20	Fallow deer of Rhodes. Photograph by Marco Masseti.	150
6.21	The so-called 'lower acropolis' and the Monte Smith. As seen on the British Admiralty chart no. 1667 (1862).	152
6.22	Palace of the Grand Master. Photograph by the author.	154
6.23	Head of Helios, from the 'Inn of Provence'. Photograph by the author, with permission of the Ephorate of Antiquities of Dodecanese.	154
6.24	The island of Rhodes, as seen from the fortress of Loryma. Photograph by the author.	158

LIST OF ILLUSTRATIONS xvii

6.25 Catalogue of the priests of Helios. 159
      From Badoud (2015) 308 and 310.

6.26 Base of a statue dedicated by the priest of Helios Antisthenes. 160
      From Badoud (2015) 396.

7.1   Detail from the illumination in the *Scholia mythologica* of Pseudo-Nonnus. 164
      From Weitzmann (1984²) pl. XI.

7.2   Illumination in the *Miroir historial* of Jean de Vignay, by Perrin Remiet. 165
      Bibliothèque nationale de France.

7.3   Illumination in the *Chroniques de Hainaut* of Jean Wauquelin. 165
      Bibliothèque royale de Belgique.

7.4   Hand-coloured woodcut printed in the *Buch der Croniken* of Hartmann Schedel. 166
      Bayerische Staatsbibliothek.

7.5   Engraving from the *Cosmographia* of Sebastian Münster. 167
      Bayerische Staatsbibliothek.

7.6   Detail from the *Panorama with the Abduction of Helen Amidst the Wonders of the Ancient World*, by Maerten van Heemskerck. 169
      The Walters Art Museum.

7.7   Drawing of the Capitoline Hercules by Maerten van Heemskerck. 169
      Staatliche Museen zu Berlin.

7.8   Detail from an engraving by Franz van Aelst, printed in *Li sette miracoli del' mondo* by Orazio Tigrini. 172
      Bibliothèque nationale de France.

7.9   Engraving from the *Cosmographie de Levant* of André Thevet. 174
      Bibliothèque de Genève.

7.10 Rhodian coins reproduced by Guillaume du Choul, *Discours de la religion des anciens Romains*. 175
      Bibliothèque nationale de France.

7.11 Drawing by Antoine Caron for *L'Histoire de la Royne Arthemise* of Nicolas Houel. 177
      Bibliothèque nationale de France.

7.12 Tapestry belonging to the 'Tenture d'Artémise' by François de Comans and Marc de la Planche. 178
      Photograph by Lawrence Perquis, Mobilier national/Les Gobelins.

7.13 Engraving of the Apollo Belvedere from the *Speculum Romanae Magnificentiae* of Antoine Lafrery. 180
      Institut national d'histoire de l'art.

7.14 Drawing by Maerten van Heemskerck, from the collection of the
     Octo mundi miracula. 181
     Courtauld Institute Gallery.

7.15 Drawing of the Apollo Belvedere by Maerten van Heemskerck. 181
     Staatliche Museen zu Berlin.

7.16 Engraving from the *Cosmographie universelle* of André Thevet. 182
     Staats- und Stadtbibliothek Augsburg.

7.17 Engraving by a Chinese artist for the *Explanation of the World Map*
     [*Kunyu tushuo*] of Ferdinand Verbiest. 183
     Biblioteca Apostolica Vaticana.

7.18 Print from the series *Septem orbis miracula* by Antonio Tempesta. 185
     The Trustees of the British Museum.

7.19 Engraving by Matthäus Merian published in the *Historische Chronica* of
     Johan Ludwig Gottfried. 186
     Bibliothèque publique et universitaire de Neuchâtel.

7.20 *Teagene*, engraving by Gilles Rousselet and Abraham Bosse, after
     Claude Vignon. 187
     The Trustees of the British Museum.

7.21 Engraving from the *Description de l'univers* of Allain Manesson Mallet. 188
     Bibliothèque de Genève.

7.22 Engraving from Johann Bernhard Fischer von Erlach, *Entwurf einer
     historischen Architectur*. 188
     Bibliothèque de Genève.

7.23 Engraving by Simon Fokke for the Dutch version of the *Histoire ancienne*
     of Charles Rollin. 189
     Personal collection.

7.24 Engraving by Pierre-Joseph Witdoeck from the *Description des
     monuments de Rhodes* of Bernard-Eugène-Antoine Rottiers. 190
     Bayerische Staatsbibliothek.

7.25 Engraving from the *Cyclopaedia of Universal History* of John Clark Ridpath. 191
     New York Public Library.

7.26 Photograph of the right arm of the Statue of Liberty, exhibited
     at Philadelphia. 192
     New York Public Library.

7.27 A marble copy of the Apollo Citharoedus. 192
     Musei Capitolini.

7.28 Antonio Muñoz Degraín, *El Coloso de Rodas*. 193
     Real Academia de Bellas Artes de San Fernando.

LIST OF ILLUSTRATIONS   xix

7.29 Utagawa Kunitora, *Dutch Ships Entering the Port of the Island of Rhodes*. 194
Art Institute of Chicago.

7.30 Anonymous flyer depicting the *Dutch World Map of Genitalia*. 194
Fine Arts Museums of San Francisco.

7.31 Reconstitution of the Colossus of Rhodes by Louis Bernier for the
Voyage aux Sept merveilles du monde of Augé de Lassus. 195
Musée d'art et d'histoire de Genève.

7.32 Bronze statuette of Sol discovered at Chalon-sur-Saône. 196
Bibliothèque nationale de France.

7.33 František Kupka, *The Colossus of Rhodes*. 197
Národní Galerie.

7.34 Reconstitution of the Colossus of Rhodes by Wolfram Hoepfner. 197
From Hoepfner (2003) 80.

7.35 Bronze statuette of Sol discovered at Montdidier. 198
Photograph by Hervé Lewandowski, Musée du Louvre/RMN-Grand Palais.

7.36 Auguste Bartholdi, *The Liberty Enlightening the World*. 199
Photograph by Norbert Nagel.

7.37 Project of Auguste Bartholdi for *The Liberty Enlightening the World*. 199
Photograph by Christian Kempf, Musée Bartholdi Colmar.

7.38 Bronze Rhodian coin depicting the nymph Rhodos. 200
Photograph by Rikke Margrete Mølvig Sekkelund, National Museum
of Denmark.

7.39 Rhodian amphora stamp of the manufacturer Nysios depicting the
nymph Rhodos. 201
From Nilsson (1909) pl. II.

7.40 Reconstruction of the Colossus of Rhodes by Albert Gabriel. 202
From Gabriel (1932) 337.

7.41 Reconstruction of the Colossus of Rhodes by Herbert Maryon. 203
From Maryon (1956) 72.

7.42 Hellenistic relief in the museum of Rhodes. 203
From Jacopi (1932a) pl. II.

7.43 Salvador Dali, *The Colossus of Rhodes*. 204
Kunstmuseum Bern.

7.44 Reconstruction of the Apollo from Santa Marinella by Paolino Mingazzini. 206
From Mingazzini (1974) 53.

7.45 Reconstruction of the Colossus of Rhodes by Paolo Moreno. 207
From Moreno (1994b) 138.

LIST OF ILLUSTRATIONS

7.46 Terracotta head of Helios, found in Rhodes.   208
Photograph by the Ephorate of Antiquities of Dodecanese.

7.47 William Blake, *The Angel of Revelation*.   209
The Metropolitan Museum of Art.

7.48 Bronze statuette of Alexander with a lance discovered in Orange.   212
The Trustees of the British Museum.

7.49 Large bronze coin from Epiphaneia, in Cilicia.   213
Bibliothèque nationale de France.

7.50 Silver didrachm from Rhodes depicting a head of Helios in profile.   214
The Trustees of the British Museum.

7.51 The bust of Sergio Leone's *Colossus* during construction at Laredo in 1960.   214
Personal collection.

7.52 The Strangford Apollo.   215
The Trustees of the British Museum.

7.53 A project for a reconstruction of the Colossus of Rhodes.   216
From the deleted website www.colossusrhodes.com.

List of Abbreviations

The abbreviations used are those of the *Oxford Classical Dictionary*, supplemented by those of the *Année philologique* (for the bibliography) and those of the *Association internationale d'épigraphie grecque et latine* (for the inscriptions). Other abbreviations are limited to:

AER II	Kontorini (1989), inscriptions.
AOM	Archives of the Order of Malta, National Library of Malta, Valletta.
ASCSA	American School of Classical Studies at Athens.
BnF	Bibliothèque nationale de France, Paris.
Brodersen	Brodersen (1992).
Greg. Naz.	Gregorius Nazianzus.
HTC	Bresson et al. (2001).
IK	*Inschriften griechischer Städte aus Kleinasien.*
Lindos	Blinkenberg (1941).
NESM	Jacopi (1932b).
NS	Maiuri (1925).
NSER	Pugliese Carratelli (1955–1956).
Pérée	Bresson (1991).
PSA	Pugliese Carratelli (1939–1940).
SER	Pugliese Carratelli (1952–1954).
TC	Segre and Pugliese Carratelli (1949–1951).
TRI	Badoud (2015), inscriptions.

Introduction

At the beginning of a book dealing with archaeology or any other science, it is wise for the authors to describe the state of knowledge when they commenced their work. This information will allow readers to follow step by step the arguments presented. Upon finishing the book, they will be able to appreciate the path travelled and, perhaps, to open new avenues for research.

When I began this book, the consensus among archaeologists regarding the—now lost—Colossus of Rhodes was limited to a few facts. In 304 BC, after the Rhodians had resisted the siege inflicted upon them for nearly an entire year by the Macedonian Demetrius Poliorcetes ('the Besieger'), they decided to build an extraordinarily large bronze statue representing the god Helios. Entrusted to the sculptor Chares of Lindos, the construction lasted no less than twelve years. The monument had only been completed for several decades and was already included in the Seven Wonders of the World when an earthquake destroyed it. Its ruins were still visible in the first century AD. All of this information can be found in (or deduced from) Pliny the Elder's *Natural History*, whose Book 34 is largely dedicated to sculpture in bronze.[1]

The exact date of the Colossus' construction by Chares and destruction by the earthquake, among other aspects of Pliny's testimony, remained controversial. Narratives about the Colossus spanning the harbour of Rhodes and its destruction by the Arabs, transmitted by later sources, were either accepted as authentic or reduced to a so-called 'kernel of truth'.

Does the exact correspondence between the knowledge agreed upon by archaeologists and the information already provided by Pliny signify that research on the Colossus of Rhodes has not progressed since the death of the latter author in AD 79? Numerous scholars have attempted to clarify certain aspects of the *Natural History* for which a consensus had not been established and, above all, to resolve two questions for which Pliny offered only scarce and indirect evidence: the location of the Colossus and its appearance. The first of these scholars was the Count of Caylus in his commentaries on the *Natural History*, published in 1759,[2] on which the short thesis of Carl Ferdinand Lüders (thirty-six pages), defended in 1865, heavily relies.[3] Neither was however able to add any information to the literary sources. In two monographs published in 2003 and 2015 respectively,

---

[1] Plin. *HN* 34.41 (below, pp. 64–65).   [2] De Pestels [Caylus] (1759) 360–367.
[3] Lüders (1865).

2   INTRODUCTION

Wolfram Hoepfner[4] and Ursula Vedder[5] turned to the location and the appearance of the statue by using material evidence. Unfortunately, their conclusions cannot be accepted, since unsubstantiated views on the Colossus were used to interpret non-relevant structures or artefacts. The pages devoted to the statue by Paolo Moreno between 1973 and 2013 have suffered from the same issues.[6]

More specific studies have been dedicated to the statuary type of the *kolossós*,[7] to the process of construction employed by Chares,[8] and to the epigram inscribed on the base of the Colossus,[9] with some brilliant results. Nevertheless, these directions of research were pursued independently of one another, without a comprehensive approach to the problems posed by the Colossus. In addition, regardless of their direction, the most recent studies compare unfavourably with the previous state of research, as they return to the most conventional ideas about the statue, whose fame has worsened the situation by generating much substandard literature.[10] As a result, the Colossus of Rhodes has become a minor and almost negligible object, which the best specialists of Greek sculpture hardly mention.[11] Yet the Colossus is of outstanding interest, and this book aims to restore the monument to its original grandeur. Its purpose is not only to provide the reader with a holistic approach to the statue, but also with an example of how methodology can change our perception of virtually any topic.

For the general public and for many specialists, archaeology is a science whose progress is dependent on field discoveries. This conception is not inexact but doubly reductive, since excavation is only one way of investigation at the archaeologist's disposal and since this way is not sufficient by itself (for instance, the Parthenon has been studied profitably before and after the excavations completed in the 1880s, while the discoveries made in these excavations are, even today, the object of differing interpretations). As a rule, archaeology is based on a body of

---

[4] Hoepfner (2003); cf. Hoepfner (2000) 129–153; Hoepfner (2007) 69–119.
[5] Vedder (2015); cf. Vedder (1999–2000) 23–40; Vedder (2003) 131–149; Vedder (2006a) 151–153; Vedder (2006b) 361–370.
[6] Moreno (1973–1974) 453–463; Moreno (1977) 424–426, 432; Moreno (1990) 343–344; Moreno (1994a) 240–242; Moreno (1994b) 126–147; Moreno (1999) 193–200; Moreno (2013) 51–53.
[7] Chantraine (1931) 449–452; Benveniste (1932) 118–135, 381; Roux (1960) 5–40; Vernant (1965) 251–264; Ducat (1976) 239–251; Vernant (1990) 31–82; Dickie (1996) 237–257.
[8] Gabriel (1932) 331–359; Maryon (1956) 68–86; Haynes (1957) 311–312; Haynes (1992) 121–128; Vedder (2017) 21–27.
[9] Benndorf (1876) 45–48; Edson (1934) 220–222; Momigliano (1942) 55; Walbank (1942) 134–145; Accame (1947) 95–99; K. R. Jones (2014a) 136–151.
[10] In academic scholarship, see Kebric (2019a) 11–32; Kebric (2019b) 1–40; and Kebric (2019c) 83–114; these works constitute an unusual offence against the most elementary principles of historical research. Beyond academic scholarship, see Kaplun (2015), who suggests that the statue did not exist. A better command of the evidence and a better understanding of the historiography are displayed by fiction-writers, including Bertheroy [Le Barillier] (1909); Durrell (1953) 80–93; and Sprague de Camp (1960).
[11] Stewart (1990) 200; Sismondo Ridgway (2001) 210; Queyrel (2020) 139–142; no mention in Smith (1991).

evidence that grows only slightly in certain areas, and not at all in others. Its ability to progress therefore does not depend as much, quantitatively, on the body of evidence at its disposal as, qualitatively, on the lines of thinking about this evidence. From that point of view, the Colossus constitutes an especially interesting case, since the statue disappeared many centuries ago without leaving the slightest trace. The idea that the progress of knowledge necessarily must advance through an increase of documentation is precisely the reason why various archaeologists wrongly convinced themselves that they had discovered remains of the statue (or at least of its pedestal). The present work, on the contrary, is based on the premise that progress lies in reasoning. This certainly does not exclude progress in documentation, but the latter will stem from the heuristic power of the method developed here.

Let us begin with the following question: in the absence of any remains, is a study of the Colossus of Rhodes possible, and even desirable? No, if we look at the works of the most well-regarded specialists of Greek sculpture who, from the eighteenth century to the present day, either have ignored the statue or have reproduced (with a few questionable additions) the description offered by Pliny two millennia ago. Yes, if we assume that archaeology must embrace all technical works of a given civilization, whether preserved, mutilated, or lost; that it must comprehend their historical significance without limitation to the most traditional tasks of the discipline, which are dating and restoring; and that it must use all relevant sources to this effect, without regard for the borders established between disciplines and periods. As it adheres to this conception of archaeology, the present work will break in two ways with the studies devoted so far to the Colossus of Rhodes.

The first break concerns interdisciplinarity. While the Colossus poses strictly archaeological problems, including its technique of construction, its appearance, and its location, these problems cannot be solved and the statue cannot be properly understood without mobilizing a large array of scholarly disciplines. Three reasons lie behind this assertion. First, in the absence of physical remains, the Colossus may only be understood through indirect evidence, mainly written sources pertaining to linguistics and philology. Second, the Colossus should be seen as a complex cultural phenomenon, where technical skills were employed for religious and political purposes, which must be subject to proper historical study. Third, the impact of the Colossus on art and literature has been so powerful that the statue must also be considered from the viewpoint of reception studies.

The last two reasons are linked to a second break, which regards chronology. A major challenge of this book is to demonstrate that the history of the Colossus begins well before its construction and ends long after its destruction. On one hand, we cannot understand the statue without placing it within its cultural context, the roots of which date back to the eighth century BC. During this period, the island of Rhodes was settled by a people who would adopt Helios as their patron deity and would later decide to dedicate to him a statue of a very special type: the *kolossós*, from which the Colossus would take its name. On the other hand, an uninterrupted chain of testimonies and studies has spanned the twenty-three centuries that separate us from the destruction of the statue, so that there is neither a gap in the tradition between us and the ancients nor (it would seem) a need for a critical approach to the monument. The epistemological consequences of this situation should not be underestimated: until the present day, scholars have selected and interpreted the ancient sources in accordance with a tradition whose development is due to the fact that it cannot be compared with any remains of the monument. In this context, the remains allegedly identified by archaeologists have functioned as the secular equivalent of relics whose exhumation strengthens the faith of believers without being able, by definition, to add anything to it. It is here that a history of research, or more broadly a history of reception, makes sense. Its goal is not only to define a 'state of the art' to distinguish tradition from innovation (as I have done in the first part of this introduction); it is also to bring to light the determinisms which affect, synchronously, our knowledge and, diachronically, its construction by taking into account not only the scientific bibliography, but also all of the literary and artistic works that may have informed the imagination of researchers. This intellectual excavation through the layers of tradition will allow us to uncover the original meaning of the ancient sources previously discussed and to look with fresh eyes for new documents that may reveal the true nature of the Colossus.

The wide range of sources used in this work is the most immediate consequence of the two breaks—disciplinary and chronological—described above. The sources are not limited to sculpture and architecture but include literary evidence, inscriptions, papyrus, coins, and amphora stamps. They are not limited to antiquity but include later periods, with manuscript illuminations, engravings, paintings, tapestries, statues, films, and even video games. They go beyond the traditional borders of Classical Studies to include Pharaonic Egypt, the Near East, and Japan.

The book is divided into seven chapters. As the Colossus represented Helios, Chapter 1 will be devoted to this god: to understand his importance, we shall search for the first traces of his cult on the island of Rhodes. Chapter 2 will go a step further by analysing the type of the statue. We shall create a definition of the *kolossós* by exploring sculptures prior to the Colossus, which will allow us to check (in Chapters 4 and 5) whether the latter met this definition. Chapter 3 will be devoted to the creator of the monument, Chares of Lindos. Although his life remains little known, it seems possible to illuminate some of its aspects, among which his relationship with his master Lysippus, who was himself famous for the gigantic Zeus he had cast in Tarentum.

Chapter 4 will first deal with the history of the statue and debunk the myths which it contains. It will then discuss the height of the Colossus and of several other oversized statues, the most important of which was erected by the emperor Nero in Rome. The technique of construction used by Chares and the appearance of the Colossus will be examined thereafter. Chapter 5 will address this fundamental yet never asked question: why did the Rhodians decide to erect such a statue? We shall explore the political meaning of the monument within the context of the period 305–200 BC, marked by their rivalry with the Antigonid monarchy and by the coming of Rome in the eastern Mediterranean.

The question of the meaning will turn out to be closely tied to the location of the statue, which will serve as the focus of Chapter 6. We shall evaluate the hypotheses formulated from the Middle Ages to discover the most likely, and shall incidentally discuss several problems of topography related to the cult of Helios. By considering the period from the ninth century AD to the present, Chapter 7 will demonstrate both the ways in which artists have created the image of the Colossus and how this image has influenced archaeologists looking for a copy or the location of the statue.

The Conclusion will assemble the main results of the inquiry and place them into a chronological perspective. It will first address the tradition of the Colossus by going back in time; it will then restart from the sources to reconstruct the history of the statue. The Colossus of Rhodes will thus appear as what it was: the most extraordinary statue in antiquity.

1
The Rise of Helios

At the beginning of the eighth century BC, the Aegean world emerged from the period of decline that followed the collapse of Mycenaean civilization. From this time, the island of Rhodes already was inhabited by Dorians, one of the major Greek-speaking peoples. Having settled in the Peloponnese, they had progressively colonized the southern part of the Cyclades, Crete, and the Dodecanese, and finally reached the eastern coast of the Aegean Sea (further to the north, the Ionians and Aeolians had followed a parallel trajectory). The Greeks themselves, beginning with Homer in the eighth century BC, attributed the colonization of the island of Rhodes to the hero Tlepolemos, one of the sons of Heracles. According to legend, this Tlepolemos had been forced to flee the Peloponnesian city of Argos after having killed Licymnios, an elderly uncle of his father.[1] The historians Thucydides[2] and Polybius[3] held the Argive origin of the Rhodians as certain, as did the Rhodians[4] and the Argives themselves.[5] They were correct: evidence from their language and customs allows us to establish that the Rhodians indeed were related to the Argives.[6]

The Reign of Zeus

The *Iliad* recounts that the Rhodians were among the Greeks who set out to conquer Troy. Under the command of Tlepolemos, their squadron consisted of nine ships, provided by Lindos, Ialysos, and Kamiros,[7] the three cities of the island whose foundation the poet attributes to the three tribes from Argos (Fig. 1.1).[8] In the aftermath of the Persian Wars (probably from 479 BC), Lindos, Ialysos, and Kamiros came under the command of Athens.[9] They only managed to escape its control in 411 BC, with the military aid of the Spartans.[10] In order to protect their

---

[1] Hom. *Il.* 2.657–670.   [2] Thuc. 7.57.6.   [3] Polyb. 21.24.10.
[4] Pind. *Ol.* 7.19 and Aristid. 24.27 (Behr) (both authors rely on Rhodian material and write for a Rhodian audience).
[5] Badoud (2019a) 80, l. 5; cf. Stroud (1984) 195, ll. 4–7 with Polyb. 21.24.10.
[6] Badoud (2019a) 81–83.   [7] Hom. *Il.* 2.653–656; cf. *Lindos* 2, B, l. 54–61.
[8] Hom. *Il.* 2.669 ('they settled in three divisions by tribes'); cf. Kontorini (1975) 99–103, A I, l. 8–9; *SER* 18, l. 8; *Lindos* 222, l. 5; *Lindos* 707, l. 3 ('Lindian tribe'); Kontorini (1975) 99–103, B I, l. 26–27; *NS* 19, l. 6; *TC* 63, l. 21, 25–26 ('Ialysian tribe'); *SER* 19, l. 6; *IGUR* I, 227, l. 4 ('Kamirean tribe').
[9] *PMG* 727 (a poem of Timocreon, cited by Plut. *Vit. Them.* 21) with the commentary of McMullin (2001) 56–57; Thuc. 1.94, with the commentary of Bresson (1994) 54.
[10] Thuc. 8.44; Diod. Sic. 13.38.5.

independence, they decided to join forces in a confederation, within which each city preserved its sovereignty.[11] In 408 BC, they went one step further: through a procedure known as synoecism (*sunoikismós*, literally 'living together'), they merged into a single city represented by a new town, constructed on the northernmost tip of the island (Fig. 1.1).[12] This city (*pólis*) and this town (*ástu*) both took the name of Rhodes. Within the new state, the former cities of Ialysos, Kamiros, and Lindos were no more than 'communities' (*koiná*), stripped of all rights with regard to foreign relations.

The new state required its own institutions, whose creation could not damage any of its constituent communities in political, economic, or religious terms.[13] The choice of the patron deity, who would preside over the future of the city, was clearly crucial. For centuries, the Lindians, Ialysians, and Kamireans had gathered together on the summit of Mount Atabyron, the highest point on the island of Rhodes, to worship Zeus.[14] This was still their practice in the third century BC, according to an inscription that mentions a delegation composed of three groups of men 'from Lindos', 'from Ialysos', and 'from Kamiros'.[15] Several scholars believe

---

[11] *Lindos* 16, with the commentary of Kinch *apud* Blinkenberg and Kinch (1905) 6/34–20/48.
[12] Diod. Sic. 13.75.1 with the commentary of Kinch *apud* Blinkenberg and Kinch (1905) 18/46–19/47; Badoud (2015) 23.
[13] Badoud (2019a) 89–92.
[14] Pind. *Ol.* 7.87–88 stresses the importance of Zeus Atabyrios for the Rhodians (cf. Hom. *Il.* 2.668–670). Diod. Sic. 5.59.2–3; Strabo 14.2.12; [Apollod.] 3.2.1; Lactant. *Div. inst.* 1.22; Timaeus *FGrH* 566 F39a = Steph. Byz. s.v. Ἀταβύριον; Steph. Byz. s.v. Κρητινία refer to him and to his sanctuary. *Scholia in Pind. Ol.* 7.160b (Drachmann) and Tzetz. *Chil.* 4.392–396, 703–705 describe the bronze oxen that began to bellow when Rhodes was in danger; cf. Isigonus *FHG* IV, p. 435, no. 4 = Cyrill. *Adv. Iul.* 3.22 (Brüggemann, Kinzing, and Riedweg; *PG* LXXVI, 636A). See also Polyb. 5.70.6, who calls Mount Tabor 'Atabyrion' (the mountains of Galilee and Rhodes have a similar name and appearance). The results of recent excavations are discussed by Triantafyllidis (2017) 553–563, who also presents offerings not included in the preliminary report of Jacopi (1928) 88–91; Triantafyllidis, Rocco, and Livadiotti (2017) 275–289; Rocco and Livadiotti (2023) 220–231. For the inscriptions, the earliest of which has been attributed to the sixth century BC by Jeffery (1990) 356, no. 11, see *NESM* 144–217; Pugliese Carratelli (1950) 80, no. 17; *SER* 8. Several associations worshipped the divinity (*PSA* 19, l. 25; *IG* XII, 4.2, 654 ['wandering stone' found on Kos]; *SER* 17, ll. 2–6; *IG* XII, 1, 161, l. 5; *IG* XII, 1, 937, ll. 3–4, 13–14; *Lindos* 391, ll. 31–32; *Lindos* 392 a, ll. 12–13, and b ll. 15–16), who also had a sanctuary in the city of Rhodes (App. *Mithr.* 103–104) that probably was served by public slaves (*IG* XII, 1, 31; cf. Konstantinopoulos [1969] 482, β, 1), in spite of the contrary opinions of Van Gelder (1900) 300–301 and Boyxen (2018) 264–265; cf. Badoud (2017b) 105–115. For other attestations of the cult of Zeus Atabyrios in Rhodian territory, whose organization is illustrated in Fig. 5.1 and briefly described in Badoud (2015) 1, see *IG* XII, 1, 891, l. 7; *Lindos* 339 (Lindos); Papachristodoulou (1989) 197, no. 8 (Ialysos); Held (2003) 55–58, nos. 1–2 (Integrated Peraea); *HTC* 20 (Subject Peraea); cf. Bean (1962) 7, no. 5 (Sura, dating perhaps to the years 188–167, when Lycia was under Rhodian domination). The mention of Zeus Atabyrios in *IG* XII, 1, 786 (*TC* 38) l. 7 is unlikely for both grammatical and historical reasons. On *IOSPE* I², 670 (a dedication found at Scythian Neapolis), see the bibliography gathered by Avram, *BE* 2007, 412. See also below, n. 15.
[15] *TRI* 66, with the corrections of Bresson (2021b) 670, whose restoration of l. 2 nevertheless cannot be accepted: the participle [ἱερατεύσας] would imply that the magistrate named in l. 3 was outgoing, but he was certainly named in the performance of his functions, as all of the individuals named following him.

8 THE RISE OF HELIOS

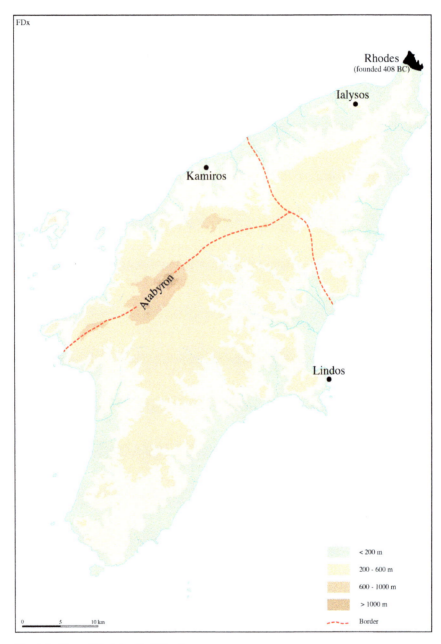

Fig. 1.1 Map of the island of Rhodes.

that Athena Lindia also was a panrhodian divinity,[16] but their opinion is based on the misinterpretation of a document from the Hellenistic period;[17] it is further contradicted by the absence of any trace of action jointly undertaken by the Rhodians in the sanctuary of the goddess and, conversely, by the absence of any trace of her cult within the territories of Ialysos and Kamiros.

A New God for a New City

Until 408 BC, Zeus Atabyrios had reigned as the sole ruler on the island of Rhodes, and we would thus expect him to be the patron deity of the city founded that year. Nevertheless, it was one of his cousins, Helios (the Sun, called Halios in Dorian dialect), son of the Titan Hyperion and grandson of Ouranos,[18] who was chosen. Several historians have seen here the expression of ancient religious practices, to which they have attributed a Mycenaean[19] or Asianic[20] origin. Others have argued that, before 411 BC, the cult of Helios had been an indication of the cultural (and even political) unity of the Rhodians.[21] Both of these hypotheses face two obstacles: on one hand, unlike Zeus Atabyrios,[22] Helios did not appear in the pantheon of the colonies founded by the Rhodians in the seventh and sixth centuries BC; on the other hand, unlike the city of Rhodes, neither Kamiros nor Lindos ever had a priest of Helios[23] (I shall discuss the case of Ialysos later).[24] There are also difficulties specific to both hypotheses. First, the cult of Helios is not documented during the Mycenaean period. Second, its attestations in Asia Minor are not only later

---

[16] Momigliano (1936) 49–51, followed by Pugliese Carratelli (1951) 81; Morelli (1959) 82; Cordano (1974) 181; Bresson (1980) 307–308 [(2000) 37–38]; Lippolis (1988–1989) 119; Gabrielsen (2000) 182; Nielsen and Gabrielsen (2004) 1196; Cairns (2005) 88 n. 96; Constantakopoulou (2005) 16; Kowalzig (2007) 264; Coppola (2008–2011) 27 n. 5; Parker (2009) 205–206; Malkin (2011) 86; Filimonos-Tsopotou and Marketou (2014) 75; Paul (2015); Monaco (2023) 127; cf. Ringwood Arnold (1936) 433.

[17] *TC* 105. See Badoud (2020b) 161–162.   [18] Hes. *Theog.* 956–957; [Apollod.] 1.2.2.

[19] Bouzek (1969) 97; Dignas (2003) 37–38.

[20] Von Wilamowitz-Möllendorff (1931) 84; Nilsson (1933) 142; Pugliese Carratelli (1951) 81; Morelli (1959) 95; cf. Becker (1883) 113; Farnell (1930) 40.

[21] Heffter (1833) 7; Dittenberger (1886–1887) 4; Van Gelder (1900) 14–15, 290; Jessen (1912) 66; Bresson (1979) 156, with the clarification provided by Bresson (1994) 121 ('prior to the synoecism, the cult of Helios assumed a panrhodian aspect'); Gabrielsen (2000) 183; Nielsen and Gabrielsen (2004) 1196; Filimonos-Tsopotou and Marketou (2014) 75. The hypothesis of an early union of Rhodian cities, also endorsed by Coppola (2008–2011) 27–50, owes its popularity to the works of Gabrielsen; it has been definitively refuted by Moggi (2009) 52–57. One may add that Hom. *Il.* 2.669 (passage cited above, p. 6, n. 8) explicitly and uniquely refers to the way in which the Argives were established at Rhodes, without the island appearing 'politically unified', as Pugliese Carratelli (1951) 78 seems to have first suggested.

[22] Timaeus *FGrH* 566 F39a = Steph. Byz. *s.v.* Ἀταβύριον; Polyb. 9.27; *Scholia in Pind. Ol.* 7.159g (Drachmann).

[23] An altar of Helios exists at Kamiros (*TC* 147), but this altar, certainly dating later than the synoecism, was established under the aegis of the demiurge and the hieropes (*TRI* 67).

[24] See below, pp. 13–14.

than 408 BC, but also concentrated in the regions at one time subject to or integrated into the city of Rhodes.²⁵ Third, despite their common insularity, origin, and destiny, the Rhodians were not united politically before 411. In the Archaic and Classical periods, Lindos, Ialysos, and Kamiros remained distinct members of the league known as the Dorian Hexapolis;²⁶ it is true that, as administrators of the Hellenion of Naucratis, they shared the same vote, but this arrangement was due to the wish of Pharaoh Amasis II (570–526 BC) to maintain a balance between Dorian and Ionian cities in the managing of this trade port on the Canopic branch of the Nile.²⁷

Nevertheless, a bronze hydria discovered by looters working for the art market has been interpreted as proof of the existence of a panrhodian cult of Helios prior to the synoecism. An inscription specifies that it was 'a prize (coming) from Rhodes (and obtained) from Helios' (ἆθλον ἐγ 'Ρόδō παρ' Ἀλίō),²⁸ namely a prize from an athletic competition organized during the *Halíeia*, the great festival celebrated by the Rhodians in honour of their patron deity. While the countless attestations of this festival are all subsequent to the synoecism of 408 BC,²⁹ archaeologists and epigraphists generally have dated the hydria to the middle or second half of the fifth century.³⁰ If the competition had been organized before 408 BC, however, it would have been by one of the three original cities (Ialysos, Kamiros, or Lindos)—or 'the Rhodians' at the very least—but certainly not by 'Rhodes' as an island. 'Rhodes' necessarily is mentioned as a city, which encourages us to date the inscription after 408 BC; the palaeography suits this conclusion,³¹ as does the typology of the vase.³² Thus, nothing prevents the argument that the cult of Helios was established at the moment of the synoecism. It remains for us to understand how and why.

Correcting the Past

To do so, let us turn our attention towards an eminent family from Ialysos, the Eratids, whose name indicates that they claimed descent from the legendary

---

[25] Fraser and Bean (1954) 130–131, followed by Laumonier (1958) 683; cf. Wiemer (2002) 258.
[26] Hdt. 1.144.   [27] Hdt. 2.178 with the comment of Bresson (1980) 308–309 [(2000) 38–39].
[28] *SEG* XXVII, 481.   [29] Most attestations are collected by Morelli (1959) 17–19.
[30] Frel (1975) 77–78; Johnston (1975) 157–158; Zervoudaki (1975) [1983] 20; Angeli Bernardini (1977) 1–3; Nielsen and Gabrielsen (2004) 1196; Cairns (2005) 78; Kowalzig (2007) 244 n. 64, who wrongly mentions a 'disc'; cf. Robert and Robert, *BE* 1976, 513. Parker (2009) 207 rightly speaks of a 'late-fifth century bronze kalpe' and notes that it is 'natural' to date it after 408 BC. The editor of the vase, Jiří Frel, who has played a major role in art trafficking, neither indicates where the vase was discovered nor how he had the opportunity to study it. According to Ernst Langlotz (cited by Zervoudaki), it was found in 'Ionia' and kept in Bonn, but we should give no credence to the information about its find spot, whose vagueness and/or incorrectness are meant to hide the true location of the looting (Rhodes itself should not be excluded).
[31] Cf. the drawing of the inscription with the photograph of *Lindos* 16.
[32] Konstantinopoulos (1969) 473 places a similar hydria, without inscription and discovered at Rhodes, 'around the end of the 5th century'. The connection between the two hydriae was made by Zervoudaki (1975) 20.

kings of Argos.³³ According to Pausanias, the family itself ruled at Ialysos in the distant past.³⁴ When the Athenians took over the island of Rhodes (around 479 BC, as noted above),³⁵ it firmly sided with their political, and then military, opponents.

In 464 BC, one of the Eratids, Diagoras, won the boxing competition at Olympia, after having triumphed in several other games (the list of victories included the *Tlapolémeia* organized on his birth island, but not the *Halíeia*, which confirms that these games did not yet exist).³⁶ Tasked with composing the ode that glorified the victor, Pindar proposed a new version of the origins of Rhodes. He writes that, when the gods were dividing up the world, Helios was absent; having refused the offer of a redistribution, he remained without a lot (*láchos*) of his own, until Rhodes rose up from the sea to become his bride. The three cities of the island were founded by heroes named Ialysos, Kamiros, and Lindos (Ialysos being the oldest). Their father was Kerkaphos, son of Helios and the nymph Rhodos, the personification of the island bearing the same name.³⁷ A divine genealogy thus was superimposed on the heroic genealogy inherited from Homer. It would be a mistake to use the Pindaric text to argue for the existence of a cult of Helios on the island of Rhodes *as a whole* before the synoecism.³⁸ By stressing the necessity to 'correct' the foundation myth,³⁹ Pindar himself has broken with the tradition embodied by the great epic poems of the eighth century (which mention Tlepolemos⁴⁰ but ignore entirely the liaison between Helios and Rhodos).⁴¹ The scholiasts who endeavoured to clarify the meaning of his ode have themselves underlined its novelty⁴² without understanding its programmatic character.⁴³ Let us therefore consider the aftermath of Diagoras' triumph at Olympia.

By the end of the fifth century BC, other Eratids had won numerous victories in boxing or the pankration.⁴⁴ The most famous and respected of them was Dorieus,

---

[33] Paus. 2.36.4.   [34] Paus. 4.24.2.   [35] Above, p. 6.
[36] Pind. *Ol.* 7.15–17, 80–87, with scholia; Paus. 6.7.2; *I. Olympia* 151.
[37] Pind. *Ol.* 7.13–14, 39–76. Bresson (1979) provides a ground-breaking commentary of the ode, whose conclusions have gained only late acceptance due to their Marxist—or simply historical—orientation. Cairns (2005) 63–91 makes insightful additions and corrections. Kowalzig (2007) 224–266 relies on the same study but is flawed with factual errors and incorrect assumptions. This is also the case with Monaco (2023) 126–134, whose views on synoecism and Rhodian cults cannot be accepted. See also Konstantinopoulos (1997) and Hornblower (2004) 131–145.
[38] Such is the case of the authors cited above, p. 9, n. 21, with the exception of Dittenberger.
[39] Pind. *Ol.* 7.21.   [40] Above, p. 6.
[41] The *Iliad* says nothing of the liaisons of Helios, unlike the *Odyssey* and the *Theogony*. For Perse(is), see Hom. *Od.* 10.135–139 and Hes. *Theog.* 956–957. For Neaira, see Hom. *Od.* 12.132–133.
[42] *Scholia in Pind. Ol.* 7.101 (Drachmann).
[43] *Scholia in Pind. Ol.* 7.36c, 146a–b, 147b (Drachmann), misinterpreted in various ways by Boeckh (1821) 174; Farnell (1932) 56; and Angeli Bernardini (1977) 1–3; but well understood by Von Wilamowitz-Möllendorff (1922) 366, followed by Morelli (1959) 98.
[44] *Scholia in Pind. Ol.* 7 inscr. b–c. (Drachmann) = Arist. frag. 569 (Rose); *P. Oxy.* 2.222, col. II. (*FGrH* 415 F2); Paus. 6.7.1–3; *I. Olympia* 152 and 159. The monuments commemorating the Eratids at Olympia were the object of a renovation at the end of the fourth or beginning of the third century: at that time, the family had regained at least part of its importance, since one of its members had re-obtained the priesthood of Helios in c.320 BC (*TRI* 1, II, l. 13).

son of Diagoras, who won three times in a row at Olympia (in 432, 428, and 424 BC), and triumphed in all other sacred games of the Greek world (organized at Nemea, Isthmia, and Delphi).[45] This Dorieus, condemned to death by the Athenians and forced into exile by their supporters who came into power at Ialysos,[46] obtained the intervention of the Spartans in 411 BC,[47] which launched the process of unification concluding with the synoecism of 408 BC.[48]

The ode celebrating the victory won by Diagoras in 464 BC reveals the programme achieved by Dorieus in 408 BC (it has been rightly argued that the name of the latter, meaning the 'Dorian' and thus the 'non-Athenian', was 'a political manifesto in itself').[49] The span of time separating the two dates should not be surprising. When Pindar delivered his poem (at a date perhaps later than 464 BC),[50] the failure of revolts at Naxos[51] and Thasos[52] had shown to the Rhodians that they had not only to unite, but also to wait for the right opportunity to liberate themselves from the yoke of the Athenians. This opportunity only presented itself in 411 BC, when the Spartans helped Dorieus to seize control of Rhodes. Consequently, there is no question that the choice of Helios as the patron deity of the unified state, which was supported in 464 (or later) and realized in 408 BC, must be attributed to the Eratids.[53] This choice was justified by geographical and historical reasons.

Ialysian Motivations

Mount Atabyron (on which Pindar himself, while lauding the victory of Diagoras, places the realm of Zeus)[54] was shared between the territories of Kamiros, to the west, and Lindos, to the east. The territory of Ialysos, on which the city of Rhodes would be built, was located at a distance further to the north (Fig. 1.1). For this simple reason, Zeus was out of place at the moment of the synoecism. A comparable argument may be made concerning Tlepolemos. While this Homeric hero would have played a unifying role as a common ancestor of the Rhodians, the myth narrated by Pindar relegates him to the background. The reason probably lies

---

[45] Paus. 6.7.2, 4, and Thuc. 3.8.1. Dorieus has been suggested as the honorand of *Syll.*[3] 82 (from Delphi) and *I. Olympia* 153 (from Olympia), with no definitive argument in the first case, wrongly in the second. See Moretti (1953) 51–56, no. 21; 57–60, no. 23; Moretti (1957) 56, no. 201; 73, no. 322.
[46] Paus. 6.7.4; Xen. *Hell.* 1.5.19.
[47] Thuc. 8.44 (cf. Thuc. 8.35.1 and Thuc. 8.84.2); Diod. Sic. 13.38.5.
[48] Diod. Sic. 13.45.1 notes that, in 410, Dorieus 'had fixed the trouble on Rhodes' (cf. Xen. *Hell.* 1.1.2). *Hell. Oxy.* (*P. Oxy.* 5.842) 15.2 (Bartoletti; *FGrH* 66 F1.1) describes the violent end of the 'Diagorians' in power in 395/4 BC; absent at the moment of the events, Dorieus was killed a bit later (Androtion *FGrH* 324 F46 = Paus. 6.7.6). Although no source affirms explicitly that the Eratids were responsible for the synoecism, this fact is not in doubt.
[49] Cairns (2005) 69.   [50] Currie (2011) 271 n. 9 and 287 n. 75.   [51] Thuc. 1.98.4.
[52] Thuc. 1.100–101.   [53] As already noted by Pugliese Carratelli (1951) 80.
[54] Pind. *Ol.* 7.87–88.

in the fact that the tomb of the hero,[55] close to which were held the *Tlapolémeia*[56] where Diagoras was victorious,[57] was located at Kamiros or Lindos,[58] and not at Ialysos.

Following the Rhodian historian Zenon, Diodorus Siculus further recounts that the seven sons of Helios and Rhodos, including Kerkaphos, as well as their only daughter Elektryone (Alektrona in Dorian dialect), had grown up within the territory of Ialysos. The settlement in which they lived, before the sons of Kerkaphos divided the island into three cities, was called Achaia Polis[59] (a toponym also attested in Rhodian epigraphy during the Hellenistic period, where it designates the acropolis of Ialysos).[60] Like Pindar, Zenon insists on the primacy of Ialysos,[61] but he alone underlines its exclusive links with the children of Helios. We would nevertheless be wrong to consider this as a literary creation of the Hellenistic period. A votive deposit discovered at Trianta, in the territory of Ialysos, contained a series of jugs produced in the sixth century BC and the first half of the fifth century BC. Two of these jugs were inscribed with the name of Kerkaphos,[62] which suggests that the neighbouring altar (?) belonged to this son of Helios.[63] It is therefore likely that the sanctuary that Elektryone possessed on the slopes of Achaia Polis was also founded before the synoecism, although we know it only from a sacred law from the third century BC.[64] Under these circumstances, it is plausible that Helios was honoured in the territory of Ialysos before 408 BC; to be more precise, the inverse hypothesis is difficult to accept, since Kerkaphos and Elektryone owed not only their existence, but also their importance, to Helios. The silence of Pindar[65] on this point is easily explained: connecting the god (with his lineage) to Ialysos would have compromised his adoption by all Rhodians. Instead, the poet took care to stress that Helios was opposed to the idea of land redistribution after the division that, until the epiphany of Rhodes, had left him without a domain of his own. Known as *anadasmós*, this redistribution was a typical claim of the democrats whom the Athenians put in power within their empire. Helios' opposition to *anadasmós* thus made him the representative, not of the Ialysians, but of the aristocrats who, in all three Rhodian cities, would organize the synoecism that would liberate them from Athenian domination.[66]

---

[55] *Scholia in Pind. Ol.* 7.36c (Drachmann).
[56] Still mentioned in the Hellenistic inscription *IK* 38-*Rhodische Peraia* 555 = *Pérée* 5, l. 8.
[57] Pind. *Ol.* 7.77–80.
[58] No trace of Tlepolemos has remained at Kamiros (where Althaimenes was the main local hero), but he and his companions are mentioned in the so-called *Lindian Chronicle* (*Lindos* 2, B I, ll. 37–40, 54–61). As the inscription cited in n. 56 was also discovered in a deme of Lindos, it is possible that the sanctuary of Tlepolemos was located in the territory of this city (then a community).
[59] See Diod. Sic. 5.55–56, with the commentary of Wiemer (2001) 207–218 and Wiemer (2013) 284–298.
[60] *IG* XII, 1, 677, l. 18; *PSA* 15, l. 1; *Lindos* 441, l. 5; *Lindos* 482, l. 1.   [61] Becker (1883) 113.
[62] *SEG* XLVI 989.   [63] Filimonos-Tsopotou and Marketou (2014) 70.   [64] *IG* XII, 1, 677.
[65] On silence as a literary tool in Pindar *Olympian* 7, see Cairns (2005) 82–85.
[66] Bresson (1979) 19–21.

14   THE RISE OF HELIOS

Let us now return to the position occupied by Ialysos. It is certain that Helios was not the poliad deity of the city, since this position had been reserved for Athena, as at Lindos and Kamiros.[67] Nevertheless, we know that, from remote times, 'the god who sees all and hears all'[68] was the object of private, and occasionally public, worship in the Greek world,[69] especially in the Peloponnese.[70] It is thus quite likely that the Eratids began by establishing a cult to Helios as the leading (or even royal) family of Ialysos.[71]

Rhodian Acceptance

By choosing Helios as their patron deity during the synoecism of 408 BC, the Rhodians definitively transferred him from the private to the public sphere. The priest responsible for his cult was the highest magistrate in the city. Each year, he was selected by lot (*láchos*) in one of the three communities: first at Ialysos, then at Kamiros, and finally at Lindos.[72] We recognize here the birth order of the three sons of Kerkaphos,[73] as defined by Pindar on behalf of Diagoras[74] (the grandson of the latter, who commanded the Rhodian fleet during the Battle of Aigospotami in 405 BC,[75] incidentally was the third Ialysian to become priest of Helios, in 398 BC);[76] the process of selection, which was certainly limited to a few candidates, is itself reminiscent of the fact that, according to the poet, Rhodes was the lot

---

[67] Pind. *Ol.* 7.35–53 stresses the importance of Athena for the cities of Rhodes and places her cult 'on the top of the acropolis', which is consistent for each of them. On the sanctuaries and their votive deposits, see Martelli (1996) 46–50; Rocco (1996a) 43–46 (Ialysos); Caliò (2001) 86–107; Bernardini (2006) (Kamiros); Blinkenberg (1931); Dyggve (1960); and Lippolis (1988–1989) 97–157 (Lindos). For the catalogues of priests (all subsequent to the synoecism), see Badoud (2019c) 49, no. 1 (Ialysos), *TRI* 9 (Kamiros), *Lindos* 1 (Lindos), and *TRI* 12 (Lindos).
[68] Hom. *Od.* 11.109.   [69] Jessen (1912) 58–93.   [70] Larson (2007) 68.
[71] Pugliese Carratelli (1951) 81, followed by Morelli (1959) 95, already attributed to the cult of Helios a familial and Ialysian origin, but by drawing his argument from the existence of familial groups (*pátra*, *diagonía*) named after Helios. The inscriptions which mention these groups, however, all date later than the synoecism, and they have no relationship either to Ialysos or with the cult of Helios. See *NS* 18, l. 20; *Lindos* 183, l. 1; *Lindos* 219.
[72] Badoud (2015) 154.
[73] Apart from the inscriptions mentioned on p. 13, n. 62, traces of the sons of Kerkaphos are rare. See the epigraphical attestations collected by Morelli (1959) 20 (Alka, daughter of Kamiros), 60 (Kamiros, son of Kerkaphos), 59 (Lindos, son of Kerkaphos), and 60 (Lindos and other heroes). As is often the case, Ialysos has provided no inscriptions, but we know of one Ialysian statesman whose father was named Kerkaphos: Hiller von Gaertringen (1895) 228, no. 2, l. 9. Furthermore, a painting by Protogenes (fourth century BC) representing Ialysos is mentioned by Plin. *HN* 35.104 (cf. Plin. *HN* 7.126); Plut. *Vit. Demetr.* 22; and Aul. Gell. 15.31. According to Mnaseas of Patara (third century BC), the daughter of Ialysos, born from his liaison with Dotis, was named Syme (*FHG* III, p. 151, no. 12 = Ath. 7.47). This evidence, mentioned by Blinkenberg (1913) 240 but since ignored, might call into question that the island of Syme belonged to the Lindian deme of Kasara, as suggested since Fraser and Bean (1954) 140, the more so as Bresson (2021a) 19–24 provides numismatic arguments for a link between Ialysos and Syme. A part of the answer lies in *IG* XII, 3, suppl. 1269, ll. 4–5, which makes the proponent of this Symian decree a man from the deme of Kasara. If the reading and the restitution of these lines hold true, Syme would arguably have been disputed by Ialysos and Lindos.
[74] Pind. *Ol.* 7.73–74.   [75] Paus. 10.9.9.   [76] *TRI* 1, I, l. 11.

(*láchos*) of Helios.[77] Before being 'corrected' by Pindar, the Homeric myth had placed the ships of Lindos, Ialysos, and Kamiros under the command of Tlepolemos. In an unfortunately lone inscription (slightly prior to 270 BC), the delegations dispatched to Mount Atabyron by the communities which succeeded to the three ancient cities are mentioned in the same order.[78] Even if Zeus was still honoured in the sanctuary that he possessed on top of this mountain, the Rhodians had denied him the position of patron deity of their city. This rejection explains why, from 408 BC, by way of compensation, a cult of Zeus Polieus was joined to that of Athena on the acropoleis of Ialysos, Kamiros, and Lindos;[79] founded the same year, the city of Rhodes also created a common sanctuary for the two divinities on the top of its acropolis.[80]

For the Rhodians, Helios thus was not a god who would have come through the ages and who would have been the object of popular devotion. Helios was essentially a political god. By uniting the Ialysians, the Kamireans, and the Lindians, he succeeded where his cousin Zeus had failed. He embodied the city founded in 408 BC.

---

[77] Pind. *Ol.* 7.58.   [78] *TRI* 66. See above, p. 7, n. 15.
[79] Badoud (2015) 45–46 (Lindos); Badoud (2015) 116 (Kamiros); *IG* XII, 1, 786, ll. 2–3, 5–6, 6–7 (Lindos, Ialysos, Kamiros).
[80] For the sanctuary: Kontis (1952) 553–559; Konstantinopoulos (1986) 217–219. For the inscriptions that mention Athena Polias and Zeus Polieus: *IG* XII, 1, 61; *NESM* 9; *NESM* 10.

2
The *Kolossoí*

In Greek, the Colossus that the Rhodians decided to build for Helios was a *kolossós*. Asking why the statue was called by this name may seem unnecessary: common opinion would suggest that the Colossus received its name 'because it was a gigantic statue'. The reality is not only quite different, but also much more interesting.

The Etymology of the Word

The etymology of the word *kolossós* has been the object of a long debate among scholars. In an article published in 1931, Pierre Chantraine stressed that the suffix *–ssos* appeared in a certain number of words, including *nárkissos* (narcissus) or *kupárissos* (cypress), that were defined as 'pre-Hellenic' or 'pre-Indo-European', since the Greeks, on their arrival in the Aegean world likely at the end of the third millennium BC, had borrowed them from populations already settled there. For him, *kolossós* belonged to the same group of words and, in the light of a city named *Kolossaí* (Colossae) in Anatolia, more precisely had an 'Asianic' origin.[1] In an article published one year later, Émile Benveniste argued that several other Anatolian toponyms, such as *Kolophṓn*, designated cities built in prominent locations, so that *kolossós* should have expressed the idea of a 'set-up object' or an 'erected image', just as the Latin *statua* had: 'This is to say that the Greeks possessed no name for the statue, and that the people who established the most complete canons and models in sculpture for the Western world had borrowed from native populations the very concept of figural representation.'[2] As brilliant as it was, this theory raised serious difficulties, the most evident of which was posed by the Latin *collis* (hill), which seemed to be based on the same root as the Greek *kolossós* and appeared itself to express the idea of elevation without having been considered as pre-Indo-European, let alone Asianic. The problem was resolved by Brent Vine, who demonstrated that both words derived from an Indo-European root (*$kelh_3$), which described an erected object; the ending of *kolossós* was not borrowed from a pre-Hellenic substratum, such as that which produced other words in *–ssos*, but most probably resulted from a phenomenon

---

[1] Chantraine (1931) 449–452.
[2] Benveniste (1932) 118–135, 381, followed by Chantraine (1970) 558 and Beekes (2010) 739–740 (with erroneous reference to a paper published in 1929).

known as 'second palatalization', which occurred in the Proto-Greek language during the third millennium BC.[3] Thus, *kolossós* is a Greek word, with no 'Asianic' or pre-Indo-European background.[4]

The Meaning of the Word

A second debate, of both historical and archaeological significance, has not yet found a satisfactory solution. What did a *kolossós* evoke in the minds of the ancient Greeks? Did this term always indicate a statue of enormous size, or was this meaning established only after the construction of the Colossus of Rhodes, due to the dimensions of the monument created by Chares?

The Terms of the Debate

These questions emerged after the discovery of a fascinating stele in 1922, during excavations at Cyrene in Libya (Fig. 2.1). Dated to *c*.325 BC (prior to the construction of the Colossus, which began in 295 BC),[5] it contains an account about grain supplies as well as a sacred law that mainly discusses rites of purification. The final lines of the latter text concern suppliants, namely strangers constrained by certain circumstances to plead for aid and accommodation. The law of Cyrene distinguishes among three categories of suppliants, only the first of which is relevant here. Facing a 'suppliant sent against the house' (most probably a spirit sent by a dead person),[6] the head of the household must summon the sender by name for three days. If he does not know this third party, the sacred law requires him to make two *kolossoí* of wood or clay, one male and one female, which we may assume represent the spirit. After inviting these two statues to eat at his table and serving them part of each dish, he must transport them into the forest and plant them in the ground, together with the meal. With this rite completed, the suppliant then comes under his authority. The text reads as follows:

110   ἱκεσίων.
        ἱκέσιος ἐπακτός, αἴ κα ἐπιπεμφθῆι ἐπὶ τὰν
        οἰκίαν, αἰ μέγ κα ἰσᾶι ἀφ' ὅτινός οἱ ἐπῆνθε, ὀ-
        νυμαξεῖ αὐτὸν προειπὼν τρὶς ἀμέρας· αἰ δ[ὲ]
        κα τεθνάκηι ἔγγαιος ἢ ἄλλη πη ἀπολώλη[ι],

---

[3] Vine (2006) 499–515; cf. Garnier (2006) 355–356.
[4] On the phonetic aspects of this word, see Chantraine (1970) 558; Dobias-Lalou (2011) 352.
[5] Chapter 4, p. 66.   [6] On this point, see Jakubiec (2016) 96–100.

18 THE KOLOSSOÍ

Fig. 2.1 Stele from Cyrene bearing a sacred law and an account about grain supplies.

115 αἰ μέγ κα ἰσᾶι τὸ ὄνυμα, ὀνυμαστὶ προερεῖ, αἰ
δέ κα μὴ ἰσᾶι, 'ὦ ἄνθρωπε, αἴτε ἀνὴρ αἴτε γυνὰ
ἐσσί, κολοσὸς ποιήσαντα ἔρσενα καὶ θήλεια[ν]
ἢ κάλινος ἢ γάϊνος, ὑποδεξάμενον παρτιθ[έ]-
μεν τὸ μέρος πάντων· ἐπεὶ δέ κα ποιῆσες τὰ
120 νομιζόμενα, φέροντα ἐς ὕλαν ἀεργὸν ἐρε-
ῖσαι τὰς κολοσὸς καὶ τὰ μέρη.

About suppliants.—Suppliant sent against the house: if it has been sent against such a house, if one knows from whom it came against him, one shall summon him by name for three days; if he is dead and buried or if he disappeared in some other way, if one knows his name, one shall summon him by name and if one does not know, one shall say: 'Oh creature, whether you be man or woman' and, after having made male and female *kolossoí* out of wood or clay, one shall entertain them and set out their share of everything; once one will have made the customary rites, bringing them to an uncultivated grove, set them up, *kolossoí* and shares.[7]

The *kolossoí* reappear in another inscription of Cyrene, inscribed in the early fourth century BC and also found in 1922 (Fig. 2.2). This document contains two decrees. The first, contemporary with the engraving, provides for 'the giving back of city-rights' to the people of Thera, in the Cyclades, in accordance with a previous agreement. This 'agreement'[8] is the object of the second decree, said to have been issued when the colonists who founded Cyrene in c.631 BC departed from Thera in c.638 BC.[9] Finally, a narrative section (probably borrowed from a local historian, like the second decree) contains an excerpt of the oath by which the citizens of Thera commit to respect the agreement, which concerns those who will depart for Africa and those who remain on the island:

      κηρίνος πλάσσαντες κολοσὸς κατέκαιον ἐπα-
45   ρεώμενοι πάντες συνενθόντες καὶ ἄνδρες καὶ γυναῖκ-
      ες καὶ παῖδες καὶ παιδίσκαι· τὸμ μὴ ἐμμένοντα τούτοις
      τοῖς ὁρκίοις ἀλλὰ παρβέωντα καταλείβεσθαί νιν καὶ κα-
      ταρρὲν ὥσπερ τὸς κολοσός, καὶ αὐτὸν καὶ γόνον καὶ χρή-
      ματα.

Having formed waxen *kolossoí*, [the Therans] burnt them, all together, men, women, boys and girls, while uttering these curses: 'Whoever will not abide by the clauses [of the agreement], but will transgress against them, should melt away and flow down like the *kolossoí*, himself, his offspring, and his belongings.'[10]

---

[7] *IGCyr* 016700, ll. 110–121, with bibliography and translation. The term 'figures' has been replaced here by '*kolossoí*'.
[8] On the translation of ὅρκιον as 'agreement' rather than as 'oath', see Graham (1960) 104.
[9] On the foundation date, see Hdt. 4. 150–158 and Euseb. *Chron.* II pp. 87–88 (Schoene), with the commentary of Chamoux (1953) 121. On the authenticity of the treaty, see Graham (1960) 94–111; cf. Meiggs and Lewis (1969) 7–9; R. Osborne (2009) 8–17; and Malkin (2018) 96. On the participation of the Rhodians in the colonization of Cyrene, see below, pp. 35–42.
[10] *IGCyr* 011000, ll. 44–49, with bibliography and translation, slightly modified here.

20 THE KOLOSSOÍ

Fig. 2.2 Decrees of Cyrene for the citizenship of the Therans.

In the terms of the first decree, all expatriates from Thera henceforth will be considered as citizens of Cyrene. Nevertheless, it is expected that those 'living at Cyrene [in the fourth century BC] should make the same oath as the one once sworn by the others [in c.631 BC]'.[11] This re-enactment probably implied the making of new *kolossoí* of wax.

According to Ulrich von Wilamowitz-Möllendorf, who (like his two immediate successors, Chantraine and Benveniste) knew the text of the sacred law regarding suppliants but not that of the Theran founders' oath, *kolossós* initially was synonymous with *andriás* (a statue of human form). In his opinion, the term designated an 'oversized statue' only after the construction of the Colossus of Rhodes. Indeed, Diodorus used the term in this sense during the first century BC,[12] while, a century before, Polybius still spoke of 'the great *kolossós*' (τὸν κολοσσὸν τὸν μέγαν)[13] when describing the statue of Chares.[14]

Although conceding that the sacred law of Cyrene did not provide for the use of 'colossal statues', Chantraine argued against Wilamowitz that Book II of Herodotus, dedicated to the description of Egypt, contained several mentions of *kolossoí* that, in his opinion, always referred to works of 'gigantic' size.[15] While denying any value to the testimony of Polybius, three centuries later, he drew attention to a difficult passage within the *Agamemnon* of Aeschylus,[16] in which Menelaus, haunted by the ghost of Helen, his unfaithful wife who has followed Paris to Troy, begins to despise the *kolossoí* standing in the palace of the Atreidae.[17]

Benveniste objected that Herodotus clarified the size of the *kolossoí* when they were extraordinarily large, with the result that other statues of the same kind mentioned in Book II could very well have been smaller. The comparison between the law of Cyrene and the text of Aeschylus enabled him to discover what he considered the original sense of *kolossós*, namely 'funerary statues, ritual substitutes, or "doubles" that continue the earthly existence of the dead by taking their place'. For Benveniste, the construction of the Rhodian Colossus effectively added new value to this term and allowed it to break free from the Dorian world in which it had previously been confined (its use by Herodotus being motivated by comparison between Greek and Egyptian cultures and thus not relevant here).[18]

Georges Roux judged the definition of Benveniste 'not erroneous but insufficient', as it could not apply to several works, beginning with the Colossus of Rhodes itself. According to Pseudo-Philo of Byzantium, this statue was identifiable only by its attributes,[19] while for Nicetas of Heraclea, author of a commentary on Gregory of Nazianzus in the 1080s, it was a *kíōn*, a term that normally designated a column or pillar.

---

[11] Ibid., ll. 13–15.   [12] Diod. Sic. 1.67.1; cf. 1.46.1, 2.34.5, 11.72.2, 16.33.1.
[13] Polyb. 5.88.1 (below, pp. 46–47); cf. Euseb. *Chron.* II pp. 122–123 (Schoene).
[14] Wilamowitz-Möllendorf (1927) 169; cf. Wilamowitz-Möllendorf (1925) 39.
[15] Hdt. 2.130–131, 2.143, 2.149, 2.153, 2.175, 2.176.   [16] Aesch. *Ag.* 404–419.
[17] Chantraine (1931) 449–452.
[18] Benveniste (1932) 118–135, 381; cf. Gernet (1948–1949) 65.
[19] [Philo Byzantius] p. 30, ll. 11–12 (Brodersen; below, pp. 80–82, §1). On the authorship of this text, see Chapter 4, pp. 79, 82.

τινὲς δέ φασι κίονα τοῦτον εἶναι χαλκοῦν καὶ μεγέθη πάνυ ὑψηλόν, πηχῶν κατὰ Ἀριστοτέλην ἑξακοσίων.

Some people state that [the Colossus] was a bronze *kíōn* of great height, 600 cubits according to Aristotle.[20]

Roux believed that this last piece of evidence, cited from Overbeck's collection of ancient texts on the history of Greek fine arts (without precise identification of its author),[21] possessed the merit of a *lectio difficilior* preserved in a recent manuscript. For him, it also made possible the definition of *kolossós* as a statue-pillar or a statue with legs joined together, comparable (if not always identical) to a herm. Evidence other than Book II of Herodotus seemed to agree with this hypothesis. Indeed, a Delian account dated to 302 BC mentioned a *kolossós*,[22] a work identified by Fernand Courby as the cult statue of Tektaios and Angelion once installed in the Archaic temple of Apollo[23] and represented on coins with legs joined together.[24] Furthermore, an *Idyll* of Theocritus referred to a boxer 'hammered out like a *kolossós*'.[25] In the fifth century AD, the lexicographer Hesychius defined *kolossoí* as the *á-bantes*, 'those who do not walk'.[26] For Roux, while the construction of the Colossus of Rhodes certainly created the meaning of 'gigantic statue', that of 'statue-pillar' or 'statue with legs joined together' was preserved in Asia Minor even until the Imperial period, as revealed by epigraphic evidence.[27] This result was entirely consistent with the works of Chantraine and Benveniste, which had previously supported the Asianic origin of the term *kolossós*.

Jean Ducat observed that the theory of Roux, marked by constant uncertainty regarding the definition of *kolossós*, accounted neither for the religious character of the statue apparent in the inscriptions of Cyrene nor for the motif of 'double' found in the *Agamemnon* of Aeschylus. As Jean Servais had remarked, this theory additionally omitted one of the oldest occurrences of *kolossós*: the dedication of the Cypselids in Olympia,[28] cited word for word by Theocritus in his *Idylls*.[29] Moreover, the account of Delos did not refer to a statue by Tektaios and Angelion

---

[20] Nicetas Heracleensis *Commentarii in XVI orationes Greg. Naz.* 67, ll. 17–19 (Constantinescu; Brodersen 20), about Greg. Naz. *Orationes* 43.63 (Bernardi; *PG* XXXVI, 577C–579B; Brodersen 9); cf. Greg. Naz. *Epigrammata* 1 (*PG* XXXVIII, 81–82), with Cosmas Hierosolymitanus, *Commentarii in Greg. Naz. carmina*, p. 216 (Lozza; *PG* XXXVIII, 534), and 50 (*PG* XXXVIII, 109–110; Brodersen 8), with Cosmas Hierosolymitanus *Commentarii in Greg. Naz. carmina*, p. 226 (Lozza; *PG* XXXVIII, 545; Brodersen 17). On the importance of Gregory of Nazianzus, see Chapter 7, p. 163. On Cosmas of Jerusalem, see Chapter 4, p. 71.

[21] Overbeck (1868) 293, no. 1551, with reference to the edition of (Pseudo-)Philo by Orelli, where Nicetas is not identified either. On the latter author and his writings, see Roosen (1999) 119–144.

[22] *IG* XI, 2, 145, l. 24.   [23] Courby (1921) 201–202 and Courby (1931) 226.

[24] Bruneau (1970) 54–60. The documents published in Boussac (1982) 427–446 have since shown that the statue did not have legs joined together.

[25] Theoc. *Id.* 22.47.   [26] Hesych. *s.v.* Ἄβαντες.   [27] Roux (1960) 5–40.

[28] Photius *s.v.* Κυψελιδῶν ἀνάθεμα ἐν Ὀλυμπίᾳ, collects the mentions of the statue, the earliest of which is Pl. *Phdr.* 236b.

[29] Servais (1965) 144–174.

displayed in the Archaic temple, but to what Jacques Tréheux and Philippe Bruneau considered an unknown work housed in an unidentified building.[30] In Ducat's opinion, the term *kolossós* originally had multiple meanings. From the Archaic period, it variously designated statues of large size, statues serving as 'doubles' in a ritual, or hieratic statues. In these three cases, however, the term could well apply to the type of statue that archaeologists name the kouros,[31] motionless enough, according to Ducat, to satisfy the definition provided by Hesychius for *kolossós*, since its forward leg only served to render the statue 'more stable and immobile'. Furthermore, the stele of the Argive Seers, which described the fitting-out of the sanctuary of Apollo, alluded to the moving of *kolossoí*.[32] Did this stele not precisely refer to 'kouroi (and korai?), whose presence was natural with Apollo?'[33]

In the 1960s and 1970s, Jean-Pierre Vernant was also interested in the *kolossós*, which he placed at the core of his *Mythe et pensée chez les Grecs*[34] and of several lectures at the Collège de France.[35] His conception of the statuary type conformed to the works of his predecessors, but also to his own conception of the history of Greek psychology. In its origin, the *kolossós* would have been the aniconic *double* of the dead or the absent, as in the inscriptions of Cyrene. It then would have given way to the *image* of the dead, realized by the kouros; the term *kolossós* nevertheless would have continued to apply to anthropomorphic images with legs joined together that embodied the absence of the person represented, as in the *Agamemnon* of Aeschylus.

The theory of Vernant experienced success equal to the renown of its author.[36] In 1996, however, the philologist Matthew Dickie defended the idea that the term *kolossós* always and everywhere designated oversized statues. The ritual described in the sacred law of Cyrene, which Benveniste had already compared to the banquet for the Spartan dead and to the Roman *lectisternum*,[37] also resembled the ritual of *theoxenía*, where a meal was offered to a divinity represented by its image. One therefore would have expected greater sculptures, as apparently confirmed by the verb *ereídō*, which, according to Dickie, implied some effort in the act of erecting the statues mentioned in the sacred law (ll. 120–121). As Dickie argued, because the oath of the founders referred to a public act, it likewise excluded the use of simple, small statues. Moreover, despite earlier research, the *kolossoí* to which Herodotus alluded in Book II, but also in Book IV, were larger than life.[38] The Delian account almost certainly alluded to the older temple of Apollo, as Roux argued, but the term *kolossós* used here meant nothing other than

---

[30] Bruneau (1970) 53–54, from the then unpublished thesis of Tréheux, defended in 1959: see now Tréheux (2023) 12–14.
[31] Cf. E. Fraenkel (1950) 219 and Aesch. *Ag.* 416.   [32] Piérart (1990) 329–330, no. 1.
[33] Ducat (1976) 246–251.   [34] Vernant (1965) 251–264. Cf. already Van Hall (1941).
[35] Vernant (1990) 17–30 (lectures of 1975–1976: 'le symbole plastique') and 31–59 (lectures of 1976–1977: 'la figure des morts I').
[36] In the field of classical studies, see D'Onofrio (1982) 135–137 and Steiner (2001) *passim*; in other fields, see for instance Ginzburg (1991) 1225–1226; Didi-Huberman (1993) 219; and Mason (2013) 11.
[37] Benveniste (1932) 119 (not acknowledged by Dickie).   [38] Hdt. 4.152.

a monumental statue. Finally, the mysterious epithet *kolossobámōn*, attributed by Lycophron to Diomedes in his *Alexandra* (already noticed by Wilamowitz but hardly studied after him) also related to the great size of the hero.[39] Other evidence previously used in the debate had little merit: Theocritus for merely reproducing the dedication of the Cypselids, (Pseudo-)Philo for copying an earlier paradoxographer, and Polybius by virtue of his emphasis, which led him to describe a 'great *kolossós*', just as the poet Sopater of Paphos[40] and Herodotus[41] had before him.[42]

Several archaeological hypotheses concerning the meaning of *kolossós* have appeared on the margin of this mostly philological debate. In 1933, Charles Picard linked the 'statues menhirs' of the Mycenaean cenotaph at Midea to the *kolossoí* mentioned by Aeschylus in the palace of the Atreidae.[43] In 1936, he proposed the same type of interpretation for the stelae with human-like heads dedicated to Zeus Melichios at Selinus,[44] and in 1966 for third millennium BC metal figurines allegedly found in Dorak,[45] of which a drawing had just been published by the fraud and smuggler James Mellaart[46] (the origin of the figurines remains unknown and their very existence uncertain).[47] Likewise, Pierre Guillon recognized a *kolossós* in the 'stele of Agamedes' at Lebadeia;[48] Elise van Hall went further by presenting the Greek stele as the Nordic (!) successor of the *kolossós* and by comparing the latter to statues from Indonesia and China.[49] Nikolaos Faraklas then suggested that the free-standing columns of Minoan sanctuaries were also *kolossoí*,[50] and Giovanni Pugliese Carratelli proposed the same identification for the busts representing a deity of the Underworld found in the tombs of Cyrene, with each deity's face either absent, idealized, or veiled; in his opinion, they had the same function as the stelae from Selinus.[51] All of these theories extend the ideas of Benveniste without supporting them. While some attempt to date the use of *kolossoí* to several centuries prior to the appearance of the word, the last supposes an assimilation of the dead of both sexes to a divinity who is always feminine at Cyrene but masculine at Selinus. Finally, Christopher Faraone has proposed incorporating some *kolossoí* into the immense group of 'voodoo' dolls.[52] As legitimate as this hypothesis may be, it says no more about the form and the function of these statues than its predecessors.

A Reappraisal of the Debate

Although Ducat rightly stressed the limits of the arguments developed by Roux, themselves founded on an insightful critique of his predecessors, he did not tackle

---

[39] Lycoph. *Alex.* 615.　[40] Sopater frag. 1 (Kaibel).　[41] Hdt. 2.175.
[42] Dickie (1996) 237–257.　[43] Picard (1933) 341–354.　[44] Picard (1936) 206–207.
[45] Picard (1960) 106–108.　[46] Mellaart (1959) 754–757.
[47] On Mellaart's personality and activity, see Zangger (2018) 125–188.
[48] Guillon (1936) 209–235.　[49] Van Hall (1941).　[50] Faraclas (1968) 210.
[51] Pugliese Carratelli (1987) 29–32.　[52] Faraone (1991) 165–205; cf. Carastro (2012) 36–39.

Fig. 2.3 Hippodrome of Constantinople, with the 'walled obelisk' in the foreground. Postcard sent in 1931.

the most important question: was the Colossus of Rhodes a statue-column? Far from demanding such a hypothesis, the testimony of Pseudo-Philo actually excludes it, since it mentions the feet and ankles of the statue.[53] We can search for an explanation of the comparison made by Nicetas between *kíōn* and *kolossós* on the two obelisks in the Hippodrome of Constantinople (Fig. 2.3).[54] The first, imported from Egypt by Theodosius I (AD 379–395), was properly called a *kíōn* in the dedication carved on its pedestal.[55] The second was not imported but built on site during the Imperial period with ordinary blocks and is thus currently known as the 'walled obelisk': 32 m tall, it was restored, adorned with bronze plates (now lost), and named the 'second Colossus' by Constantine VII Porphyrogennetos (AD 913–959).[56] As he was living in Constantinople, Nicetas certainly referred to the latter monument in his description of the statue of Chares, without taking it for granted (as the words τινὲς δέ φασι, 'some say', make clear). Nevertheless, unaware that the comparison made by the emperor was justified by the height of the monument and the metal of its adornment, he concluded that the Colossus of Rhodes itself was a *kíōn*—that is, an obelisk and not a column. His testimony thus

---

[53] [Philo Byzantius] p. 32, ll. 2–3 (Brodersen; below, pp. 80–82, §3). Cf. below, p. 42.
[54] Feissel (2003) 506.   [55] *Anth. Pal.* 9.682.   [56] *CIG* IV, 8703; cf. Janin (1964) 192–194.

does not have the merit of the *lectio difficilior* attributed to it by Roux. Furthermore, the herm, which appeared in Attica at the end of the sixth century BC to celebrate the tyrant Hipparchus,[57] has no chronological, geographic, or functional relationship with the *kolossós*, used in magic rituals in Dorian cities one century prior to his rule, with the result that the identification of the two types, as proposed by Roux, is not relevant. Finally, the inscriptions from Asia Minor suggested as proof of his theory by Roux do not preserve what he considered the original meaning of *kolossós* (at a time when scholars generally but erroneously considered the term as 'Asianic')[58] and all refer instead to oversized statues.[59]

While we must therefore dismiss the thesis of Roux, this dismissal does not imply that the thesis of Ducat, which is itself a refutation of Roux, holds true. Indeed, if the term *kolossós* originally possessed substantially different meanings, we would have to account for the extreme rarity of its use before the Hellenistic period. Moreover, a constant opposition exists in Archaic statuary between the kouros, with one of his legs forward, and the kore, with her legs joined together. The relative mobility of the former is thus incompatible with the definition of the *kolossós* provided by Hesychius. In addition, the inscriptions carved on kouroi never define them as *kolossoí* and we have no reason to suppose, following Ducat, that the *kolossoí* of the Argive stele were what the archaeologists call kouroi.[60]

The works of Vernant give rise to the same difficulties as those of Benveniste, Roux, and Ducat, which they extend. Moreover, they account for only a small portion of the available documentation and suppose a radical change of the *kolossós*, which, from an aniconic 'double', would have become an anthropomorphic 'image'.

The theory of Dickie, which omits the evidence from Hesychius and neglects the verses of Aeschylus, does not deduce the meaning of *kolossós* from the texts: the latter are instead interpreted in accordance with the meaning traditionally attributed to the word, which Dickie takes for granted (both a factual and methodological error). Moreover, we must dismiss the sole philological argument introduced to support his theory, as the verb *ereídō* indicates the action of setting up not only the *kolossoí* of Cyrene, but also the portions of their meal. The verb is not associated with a sense of effort but rather with a sense of stability. Furthermore, whatever uncertainty surrounded the etymology of *kolossós*, it has always been clear that the term did not derive from a root expressing an idea of size.[61] Consequently, how could this idea have been associated with the original meaning of the word? Archaeological data relating to *theoxenía* does not confirm the

---

[57] Siebert (1990) 375–376.   [58] Above, p. 16.
[59] For these examples, see the list of inscriptions below, p. 51, n. 184.
[60] See Richter (1960) 337 and Richter (1968) 324 for a collection of inscriptions on kouroi and korai.
[61] Above, pp. 16–17.

use of oversized statues in the ritual;[62] the wrong identification of the Delian *kolossós* by Roux has not been corrected according to the suggestion of Ducat,[63] and the text of Pseudo-Philo has been discarded with no thought for the studies which confirmed its value.[64] Nevertheless, the theory put forward by Dickie is now dominant,[65] because it repeats one of the most widespread misbeliefs about the Colossus of Rhodes (and because it was not published in French, like most of the relevant literature, but in English).

The First *Kolossoí*

A Review of the Evidence

In order to understand the true meaning of *kolossós*, we must return to its earliest attestations in the Greek language by stopping first in the period before the construction of the Colossus of Rhodes. After formulating a general definition of the term, we then shall compare this definition with all information at our disposal about the statue constructed by Chares.[66]

First of all, however, an inscription that I once considered as possibly the earliest attestation of the word *kolossós*[67] should be discarded (Fig. 2.4). Discovered on Thera, it was engraved on a stone with dimensions of 43 × 32 cm and a thickness of 110 cm. While noting that the first and the third letters were dubious, Friedrich Hiller von Gaertringen suggested reading it as *kolos(s)ós*.[68] His hypothesis was all the more attractive because it had been formulated before the discovery of the stone containing the Theran founders' oath in Cyrene. Yet Catherine Dobias-Lalou has made it clear that the inscription from Thera was not as ancient as it would seem, as the first letter apparently was not the Archaic koppa (Ϙ) but the Classical kappa (K).[69] A photograph of Hiller von Gaertringen's squeeze then left little doubt about the fact that the third letter was not a lambda (Λ) but a rho (Ρ).[70] What the inscription said remains uncertain, but the reading *kolos(s)ós* may reasonably be excluded. Let us now consider the remaining evidence (Fig. 2.5).

The earliest sources noted in Fig. 2.5 state that the *kolossoí* were fashioned from varied materials: wax on Thera (1), clay or wood at Cyrene (2), sheets of gold at

---

[62] Nercessian (2004) 438–439.
[63] One may add that Ducat is incorrectly presented as a follower of Roux, whose thesis is criticized with arguments taken from Ducat himself. Cf. Sève *BE* (1998) 59; Baker and Thériaut (2005) 306 n. 16.
[64] Chapter 4, p. 82.
[65] See for instance Johnston (1999) 59; Neudecker (1999) 670; Strocka (2007) 333 n. 4; Neils (2010) 264–265; Bresson (2012) 211; cf. Ma (2013) 251 n. 61; Keesling (2017) 838 n. 3.
[66] Chapter 4, pp. 92–94 (appearance of the statue); Chapter 5, pp. 103–105 (function and origin of the statue).
[67] Badoud (2011a) 131–132.   [68] Hiller von Gaertringen, *IG* XII, 3, 1015.
[69] Dobias-Lalou (2011) 352.
[70] In a personal communication (4 March 2020), C. Dobias-Lalou kindly let me know that a rhotacism (*koros(s)ós* for *kolos(s)ós*) was excluded.

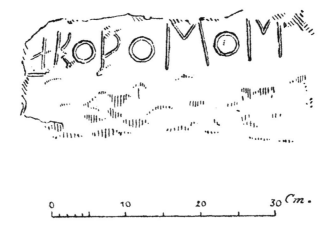

Fig. 2.4 Drawing of the Theran inscription *IG* XII, 3, 1015, fifth century BC (?).

	Source		Kolossoí			
No.	Reference	Date	Location	Material	Appearance	Size
1	*IGCyr* 011000	400–375 (seventh century)	Thera (Cyrene)	wax	—	[manoeuvrable]
2	*IGCyr* 016700	325–300 (Archaic Period)	Cyrene	wood or clay	men and women	[manoeuvrable]
3	[Colossus of the Cypselids]	before 585/530 (?)	Olympia (Corinth)	gold leaf	—	—
4	Piérart (1990) 329–30, no. 1	325–250	Argos	—	—	portable
5	*IG* XI, 2, 145, l. 24	302	Delos	—	—	—
6	Aesch. *Ag.* 416	458	Argos	—	eyes	—
7	Hdt. 2.130–1	*c.* 445	Egypt	wood	nude women, hands	[≤ 1:1]
8	Hdt. 2.143			wood	priests of Zeus	[≤ 1:1]
9	Hdt. 2.149			stone	[Amenemhat III]	[*c.* 12 m]
10	Hdt. 2.153			[stone]	architectural supports	*c.* 5.3 m
11	Hdt. 2.175			stone	—	large
12	Hdt. 2.176			stone	(Osiris, Isis, and Nephtys)	*c.* 5.9 and 22.2 m
13	Hdt. 4.152		Samos [Cyrene-Thera/Argos]	bronze	supports for a krater	*c.* 3.1 m

Fig. 2.5 Attestations of the word *kolossós* before the construction of the Colossus of Rhodes.

Olympia (3), and bronze on Samos (13). In addition, the Egyptian statues identified by Herodotus as *kolossoí* are built of wood and of stone (7–12).

The *kolossoí* mentioned in the stele of the Founders must be made of wax and thrown into the fire (1), while their male and female counterparts, whose use the sacred law commands, must be created by the citizens themselves and abandoned in the forest (2). It seems reasonable to conclude that all of them had a crude appearance and were small in size.

In Book II of his *Histories*, written in the middle of the fifth century BC, Herodotus uses the term *kolossós* nine times to identify six Egyptian statues or groups of statues, described as standing, seated, or lying down. Although all of these statues have disappeared, we can estimate their dimensions quite easily and can envisage their appearance in at least two cases. As Benveniste has noted,[71] Herodotus only identifies the size of the 'great' *kolossoí* (10–12; cf. 13). The twenty statues meant to represent the concubines of Mykerinos (7) must have been comparable in height to the daughter of the pharaoh, whose body lay in repose in a wooden cow with the dimensions of a large animal.[72] Judging by their number, the statues of the 345 priests of Zeus (Amon) which Herodotus saw at Thebes erected together in the same building surely had nothing 'colossal' about them (8).

The stone *kolossoí* that served as pillars in the propylaea of the Temple of Ptah at Memphis (10) were comparable to the pillars of Osiris frequently used in Egyptian architecture, which themselves did not replace architectural supports, as Herodotus affirms, but leaned against them:[73] the temple of Ptah, built at Gerf Hussein (Fig. 2.6) and now submerged under Lake Nasser, provides perhaps the best parallel to the text of the historian.[74] Also at Memphis, but in the Palace of Amasis II, Herodotus states that he saw approximately twenty wooden *kolossoí* representing nude females, some of which had lost their arms[75] due to a state of disrepair. Some Egyptians led Herodotus to believe that these statues dated back to the time of Mykerinos and thus were nearly 2,000 years old. As no 'colossal' statues of naked women seemingly existed in Egypt, authors of commentaries generally assume that Herodotus did not recognize the thin garments in which the *kolossoí* of Memphis were clothed.[76] Nevertheless, disregarding any preconception about the size of the *kolossoí*, we should note that several objects stored in the Cairo Museum correspond to the description of Herodotus (Fig. 2.7). These wooden statues, representing nude women, have lost one or both arms.[77] Between these objects, tens of centimetres in size, and the statues of Osiris leaning against

---

[71] Benveniste (1932) 120–121.
[72] Hdt. 2.132.   [73] Cf. Leblanc (1980) 70.   [74] El-Tanbouli (1975).
[75] Hdt. 2.131 says that, according to a 'foolish tale', the 'hands' (*cheîras*) of Mykerinos' attendants were cut by his wife, who inflicted the same treatment on their statues. Nothing prevents us from admitting that the latter actually had lost their arms.
[76] How and Wells (1912) 231, followed by P.-E. Legrand (1936) 157 n. 2; cf. Asheri (2007) 335.
[77] Borchardt (1911) 148–150 n. 223, 225, and 228.

Fig. 2.6 The temple of Ptah at Gerf Hussein photographed by Francis Frith during the years 1850–1870 (Victoria and Albert Museum, E.208:1457-1994).

the pillars of Egyptian temples, there is a similarity (underlined by Roux)[78] made only more striking by the difference in size and material: all of them have legs joined together or at least carved on the same plane. If we take the testimony of Herodotus at face value, his text regarding the statues of Memphis therefore confirms that the *kolossós* was not, by definition, a statue of great size. Thus, through Egyptian artefacts we begin to understand the Greek conception of the *kolossós*.

While the debate concerning the meaning of *kolossós* since the time of Chantraine has partially focused on the description of Egypt left by Herodotus (7–12), the father of history (as Dickie has correctly emphasized)[79] also uses the term *kolossós* when describing an offering erected in one of the most important sanctuaries of the Greek world, the Heraion of Samos (13). In Book IV of his *Histories*, he describes a monumental Argolic krater of bronze that rested on three kneeling *kolossoí*, each measuring 7 cubits (more than 3 m) in height. Although the identification of potential copies of the krater is risky,[80] another type of vase may offer a clue to the supports mentioned by Herodotus. The *perirrhantērion*, an ablution vessel frequently dedicated, like the krater, in sanctuaries during the Archaic

---

[78] Roux (1960) 20–21, who refers to parallels less convincing than the statues in the Cairo Museum.
[79] Dickie (1996) 239, who cites Donohue (1988) 27 n. 65.
[80] See the studies cited by Chamoux (1953) 103 n. 3.

Fig. 2.7 Statuettes from the Cairo Museum. a. Sixth Dynasty or later (height 43 cm). b. Second Intermediate period (height 35.5 cm). c. Second Intermediate period (height 54 cm).

period, was supported either by a central column or by anthropomorphic figures with legs joined together (Fig. 2.8). This probably was the case with the *kolossoí* that supported the krater in the Samian sanctuary.[81] Be that as it may, the diversity of positions generally attributed by Herodotus to *kolossoí* (kneeling, standing, sitting on a throne, or lying down), and their crude form on Thera and at Cyrene, all prove that *kolossoí*, in the eyes of the Greeks, were nothing more than statues that represented some immobile being. The imposing dimensions that they occasionally (but not always) possessed only reinforced their lack of mobility.

Let us now return to Aeschylus (6). The verses of the *Agamemnon* in which the *kolossoí* appear are marked by a double opposition: between presence and absence on one hand, between movement and immobility on the other.[82] Menelaus is both

---

[81] For discussion of the *perirrhantḗrion*, see Sturgeon (1987) 14–61. For other parallels no less convincing, see Rolley (1981) 323–326.
[82] This latter opposition is highlighted well by Steiner (1995) 177–179; cf. Steiner (2001) 49–50, 137. Bollack (1981) 432–436 adopts the definition of *kolossós* as 'double'.

Fig. 2.8 *Perirrhantḗrion* from Isthmia, c.660–650 BC.

present and motionless in the palace, while Helen, kidnapped by Paris, is both absent and on the move. Aeschylus recounts that she abandons the army of the Greeks, brings death to the Trojans, and passes speedily through the gates. This double opposition culminates in the last verses, when the poet juxtaposes the image of the ghost of Helen with the 'beautiful *kolossoí*', whose grace is hateful to Menelaus.

If this analysis of Aeschylus confirms, or at least agrees with, the immobile nature of the *kolossós*, it also allows us to better understand the exact function of the statue. The *kolossoí* of Aeschylus, like those of Cyrene, clearly maintain a close relationship with the idea of 'double'. Even so, however, the *kolossós* was not a double. While it occasionally functioned as such, it did so, as Vernant has rightly argued,[83] through its ability to fixate. In magic rituals described by the inscriptions from Cyrene, the power of the *kolossós* appears most fully as the statue fixes the dead in the world of the living or sends the living into the world of the dead. In the *Agamemnon* of Aeschylus, however, the power of the *kolossós* fails to fix the ghost of Helen to the palace of Menelaus, the cause of his despair. In other words, the source of misfortune here is not the effectiveness of the *kolossós*, as Benveniste and Vernant have argued, but its ineffectiveness.

---

[83] Vernant (1965) 263; cf. Roux (1960) 35.

From a figurative point of view, the *kolossós* was the representation of immobility. From a functional point of view, it served to enclose whatever it represented, a form of agency that explains its appearance in magic rituals and as an offering or representation of power. For this latter reason, the Cypselids, tyrants of Corinth, decided to erect a *kolossós* at Olympia to place their reign under the protection of Zeus.

Dorian Statues

Before returning to Rhodes (or precisely so that we may return to Rhodes), we must define the relationship between the examples of *kolossoí* earlier than the *magnum opus* of Chares and the Dorian world. This area included a large part of the Peloponnese, inhabited from the end of the second millennium BC by a Greek people speaking its own dialect, with additional areas colonized further to the east and south between the seventh and sixth centuries BC. As Book II of Herodotus is not relevant to this discussion, only two pieces of evidence may dissuade us from following the hypothesis of Benveniste, who was the earliest to consider *kolossós* as a Dorian word.[84] First, Aeschylus is an Attic author (6), and the observation that his *kolossoí* were set up at Argos, in the very centre of the Peloponnese, would perhaps not be sufficient to prove that the word must be interpreted as a Doricism. However, Aeschylus did use lexical borrowings to give foreign colour to other passages of the *Agamemnon*,[85] and the same explanation should hold true for his description of the Atreid palace.[86] Second, a dedication by Dorians of the *kolossós* appearing in the Delian account dated to 302 BC (5) seems unlikely.[87] The term may rather designate the *xóanon*[88] whose installation was attributed to the legendary king Erysichthon[89] in Athenian tradition and which likely served as the cult image of Apollo before Peisistratus substituted for it the statue made by Tektaios and Angelion,[90] itself incorrectly identified by several archaeologists as the *kolossós* of the inscription or even as the so-called 'Colossus of the Naxians' (a kouros which owes its misleading modern appellation to its size).[91] If correctly interpreted, the Delian account becomes a document of prime

---

[84] Benveniste (1932) 122, who mistakenly links the island of Cyprus to the Dorian world.
[85] Aesch. *Ag.* 689 (*helénas* = a Doricism) and 282 (*ággaros* = a Persian word). For these two passages, see respectively Judet de la Combe (1982) 31 and Judet de la Combe (2001) 120.
[86] As a point of comparison, see Colvin (1999).
[87] For Dorian presence in the sanctuary, see Chankowski (2008) 18–19.
[88] Donohue (1988) remains the reference work on this type of statue (carved, of wood).
[89] Plut. *De daedalis Plataeensibus* frag. 10 and Paus. 3.23.2-5, with the commentary of Bruneau (1970) 62.
[90] Badoud (forthcoming 1).
[91] Above, pp. 22–23, for the identification with the statue by Tektaios and Angelion. See Hermary (1994) 26 and Coarelli (2016) 63 for the identification with the so-called 'Colossus of the Naxians'.

importance. On the one hand, it becomes the only example that names a (decommissioned) cult statue as a *kolossós*; for its Delian writer, the simple wooden pole of the *xóanon* evoked—formally if not functionally—what the Dorians called a '*kolossós*'. On the other hand, after Aeschylus and Herodotus in the fifth century BC, it provides a third case of diffusion of this word beyond the Dorian realm, a phenomenon that is thus unrelated to the construction of the Rhodian Colossus undertaken seven years later.

Nevertheless, the earliest attestations of the term are indisputably Dorian (Fig. 2.9). The *kolossós* at Olympia was erected by the tyrants of Corinth (Fig. 2.5, 3), a major city of the Dorians, as was Argos, where other *kolossoí* appeared (4). Beyond the Peloponnese (yet still in Dorian territory), we find *kolossoí* on Thera and at Cyrene (1–2). This pairing of sites is no coincidence, since Thera was the metropolis of Cyrene, and because *kolossoí* played a key role in the oath taken by the colonists upon their embarkation for Africa. Finally, another group of *kolossoí* supports the krater seen by Herodotus on Samos. It is true that Samos was an Ionian city, but the krater in question was dedicated by a Samian crew who had made their fortune by providing help during the colonization of Cyrene by Thera. Upon return to their homeland, the Samians had decided to dedicate a

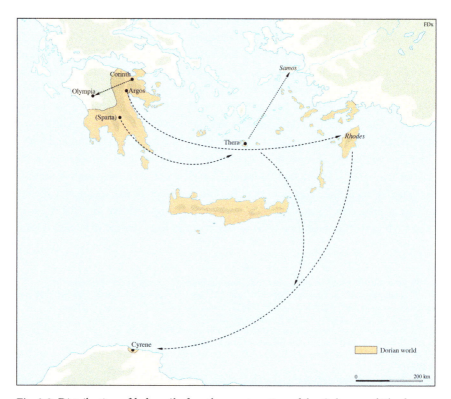

Fig. 2.9 Distribution of *kolossoí* before the construction of the Colossus of Rhodes.

monumental krater to Hera, their guardian divinity. Immediately after noting that this krater was supported by 7-cubit-tall *kolossoí*, Herodotus adds, 'this act was the foundation of the great friendship that the Cyrenaeans and Therans had entered into with the Samians'.[92] Although the conclusion of the Herodotean narrative has seemed disconcerting to modern scholars,[93] it is not, if the choice of the Samians to erect their offering on *kolossoí* (or *kolossoí*-like supports) derived from their desire to honour Thera and Cyrene, the two cities at the root of their fortune. The history of these *kolossoí* is thus intimately tied to Dorian colonization, even more so after Herodotus ethnically defines the krater as 'Argolic'.[94]

The *Kolossoí* of Rhodes

The Colonization of Cyrene

Rhodes was colonized (or rather settled) by the Argives in the early Archaic period.[95] The inhabitants of the island thus were natives of one of the few cities where traces of *kolossoí* remain. Furthermore, the so-called *Lindian Chronicle*[96] recounts that the Rhodians themselves—more precisely the Lindians guided by the children of Pankis—participated in the colonization of Cyrene:

XVII   Λινδίων τοὶ μετὰ τῶν Πάγκιος παίδων
110   Κυράναν οἰκίξαντες σὺν Βάττωι Π[α]λλά-
         δα καὶ λέοντα ὑ[πὸ] Ἡρακλεῦς πνιγόμ[ενον],
         ταῦτα δ' ἦν λώτ[ι]να, ἐφ' ὧν [ἐ]πεγ[έ]γρα[πτο]·
         'Λινδίων τοὶ μ[ε]τὰ τῶν Πάγκιος παίδων
         Κυράναν κτίσαντες σὺν Βά[τ]τω[ι] Ἀθαναί-
115   αι καὶ Ἡρακλεῖ [δ]εκά[ταν ἀπὸ] λαίας ἂν ἔλ[α]-
         βον ἀ[πὸ . . . .]Ι[. . . .]Σ[. . . .]Ιων', ὥς φατι Ξενα-
         γόρας [ἐ]ν [τᾶι α' τᾶς] χρονικᾶς συντάξιος.

Those of the Lindians who, with the children of Pankis, colonized Cyrene with Battos (dedicated) a lion being strangled by Heracles. These were of lotus wood, on which had been inscribed: 'those of the Lindians who, with the children of Pankis, founded a colony on Cyrene with Battos (dedicated) to Athena and to

---

[92] Hdt. 4.152.   [93] Chamoux (1953) 107–108.
[94] This type of vase appears in the inventories of the Parthenon, including *IG* II², 1424a, I, ll. 150 (369/8 BC) and 1425, B, l. 359 (368/7 BC).
[95] Chapter 1, p. 6.
[96] On the purpose of the inscription, misunderstood by Higbie (2003) and her followers, see Bresson (2006) 531–544 and Badoud (2018a) 254–255.

Heracles a tenth of the booty which they took from [...]' as Xenagoras states in the first book of his *Annalistic Account*.[97]

Blinkenberg dated this event to *c*.570 BC,[98] two generations after the arrival of the Therans, in order to reconcile the evidence of the inscription with that of Herodotus, who writes that, during the rule of Battos II, third king of Cyrene, 'an oracle of the Pythia invited all Greeks to join the Cyrenaeans in Libya, who offered land to the new arrivals'.[99] Nevertheless, this hypothesis, of which Blinkenberg himself was at first hardly convinced (as opposed to his successors),[100] does not agree with the text of the *Chronicle*, which does not refer to an act taken 'under the king Battos', but 'with Battos' (σὺν Βάττωι, ll. 110, 114), and does not present this act as the consolidation of a pre-existing settlement, but as the foundation of a new city (οἰκίξαντες l. 110; κτίσαντες l. 114). Nor does it agree with the structure of the document, in which the Lindian colonization of Cyrene (ch. XVII) occurs largely prior to the reign of the tyrant Cleobulus (ch. XXIII), thus most probably before *c*.570 BC. Hence François Chamoux could speak of a confusion[101] and Irad Malkin of a 'usual exaggeration'.[102]

Apart from the authority of Blinkenberg,[103] nothing forces us to discredit the *Chronicle* and, *a fortiori*, its source, namely the (Lindian?) historian Xenagoras, seemingly contemporary with the establishment of relations between Rhodes and Rome at the end of the fourth century BC.[104] While the major role of the Rhodians in the foundation of Cyrene, dated to *c*.631 BC, is not mentioned in the Theran or Cyrenaean accounts collected by Herodotus during the fifth century BC, this fact is hardly surprising, since both accounts focus on the oecist Battos. On the other hand, a tetradrachm also cited by Blinkenberg, dating to the first period of coinage in Cyrene (*c*.525–480 BC), connects silphium, the emblem of the city, to the symbols of Lindos and Ialysos: the head of a lion facing right on the obverse and an eagle eating a snake on the reverse (Fig. 2.10).[105] This very specific iconography confirms that the Rhodians did not come to populate Cyrene by responding to the invitation that Battos II had offered to 'all Greeks', as Blinkenberg

---

[97] *Lindos* 2, B, ll. 109–117, with the translation of Higbie (2003) 29–31, modified; cf. *Lindos* 44 (dedication by the Cyrenaean descendants of Pankis, fourth century BC) and *PSA* 19, l. 21 (crowns offered by a long series of associations, among which were the *Pagkiádai patriōtai*, second century BC). Several Rhodian inscriptions also mention Cyrenaeans: *IG* XII, 1, 437; *IG* XII, 1, 438; *NS* 174; Berges (1996) 144, no. 224; *TC* 105 (see below, p. 42, n. 126); *IK* 38-*Rhodische Peraia* 8 (= *Pérée* 195, l. 2) and 155 (= *Pérée* 128, l. 6).

[98] Blinkenberg (1912) 354/38; Blinkenberg (1915) 19; and Blinkenberg (1941) 168–170.

[99] Hdt. 4.159.

[100] R. Osborne (2009) 15 is an exception, but he cites the Chronicle after the edition of Jacoby (*FGrH* 532 F1.17) with no reference to Blinkenberg.

[101] Chamoux (1953) 125.   [102] Malkin (2011) 80.   [103] Cf. Giangiulio (2009) 89.

[104] Blinkenberg (1912) 412–413; Badoud (2018a) 235; Badoud (2019e) 88; cf. Cioffi (2014) 239–240.

[105] Head (1891) 4; cf. Head (1887/1911) 867.

Fig. 2.10 Silver tetradrachm from Cyrene, c.525–480 BC (British Museum, GC29p4.13; scale 1.5:1). Obverse: silphium with lion's head. Reverse: Eagle's head holding writhing serpent.

argued, but 'with' Battos I, the oecist called to become the first king of Cyrene, as the *Lindian Chronicle* clearly affirms. In fact, the coinage activated a 'Rhodian' version of the foundation account, for reasons particular to the history of Cyrene, about which we know nothing. Herodotus (like Pindar)[106] would then pass down a version centred on the figure of Battos, whose aim was to legitimize the establishment of the monarchy. The decree of Cyrene, promulgated after the advent of democracy, conversely would insist on the role played collectively by the Therans during the process of colonization, while Menecles of Barca would explain the latter by an act of sedition.[107] Much later, Pausanias would recount that the Spartan athlete Chionis, Olympic victor in 664, 660, and 656 BC, was the partner of Battos in the foundation of Cyrene, yet another piece of information absent from the accounts transmitted by Herodotus.[108]

Let us now return to Xenagoras and the authors of the *Chronicle*, who were all convinced of the involvement of the Rhodians—or at least the Lindians—in the foundation of Cyrene. Several pieces of evidence show that their belief was justified.

The excavations conducted in the sanctuary of Demeter and Persephone at Cyrene have produced six terracotta figurines that may be attributed to the first half of the seventh century BC. According to Jaimee Uhlenbrock, three or four of these figurines (Fig. 2.11) would find their closest parallels at Rhodes and may have been brought over as sacred relics, or *aphidrúmata*,[109] by the colonists from this island, not c.570 BC but rather c.631 BC.[110]

---

[106] Pind. *Pyth.* 4 and 5.   [107] Menecles Barcaeus *FGrH* 270, F6.
[108] Paus. 3.14.3; cf. R. Osborne (2009) 15.   [109] On *aphidrúmata*, see Chapter 6, p. 161.
[110] Uhlenbrock (2015) 148–151. In a letter dated on 13 May 2020, Jaimee Uhlenbrock kindly confirmed to me that, in her view, the closest parallels to the terracotta figurines found in Cyrene still 'are the cited examples in the British Museum and the Louvre that come from Rhodes' but added this note of caution: 'I stumble over the fact that the Cyrene heads all wear a 'tiered' polos, which is absent from

Fig. 2.11 Fragment of a Rhodian (?) mould-made figurine found in Cyrene, c.700–650 BC. (Cyrene Archaeological Museum, inv. 76-492).

In the excavations of the sanctuary of the Dioscuri, which was probably established by Battos I himself,[111] a calyx from Chios datable to the end of the seventh century BC has been discovered (Fig. 2.12).[112] This vessel has a dedication in which the aspirated guttural is not indicated by a chi (X), as was ordinarily the case in Cyrene, but by the sign of the trident (Ψ). The first editor of this document, Silvia Marengo, has wisely considered 'the possibility that the letter was borrowed from the alphabet at Rhodes, where it had been used at an early date'.[113] As Catherine Dobias-Lalou has stressed, the alphabet—'red' according to the terminology of Adolf Kirchhoff—must be 'more precisely from Lindos or from Kamiros, since a "blue" alphabet was in use at Ialysos'.[114] In the absence of evidence that Kamiros was involved in the colonization of Cyrene (the tetradrachm

---

the other Rhodian figurines. The example in the Louvre Museum that is particularly close in all other respects seems to have more of a stephane-like headdress. This does not, of course, mean that the Cyrene heads are definitively *not* Rhodian.'

[111] Cf. *Scholia in Pind. Ol.* 5.10a and 124a, c (Drachmann).
[112] For parallels, see Lemos (1991) 242, nos. 236–237 (dating on p. 10).
[113] Marengo (2008) 30 = Marengo (2010a) 125.
[114] *BE* 2010, 631. On Rhodian alphabets, see Johnston (1975) 154. For the beginning of writing in Cyrenaica, see Dobias Lalou (2015) 59–80. For another attestation of the sign of the trident, dated to the first half of the fifth century but also attributable to a Rhodian (and highlighted by the latter author on pp. 67–68 of her article), see Boardman and Hayes (1966) 169, no. 976, with the commentary of Marengo (2010b) 20–23.

Fig. 2.12 Fragment of a calyx from Chios with dedication to the Dioscuri found in Cyrene, late seventh century BC (Cyrene Archaeological Museum, inv. CA06S3US3).

presented by Blinkenberg is telling), we should favour the attribution to Lindos. Although the calyx has been dated to the seventh century BC and comes from a sanctuary built by Battos I, the two epigraphists have revised the date of its dedication to c.570 BC, as the theory of Blinkenberg required.[115] It is worth keeping in mind once more the account of the *Chronicle*, which dates the arrival of the Lindians to c.631 BC in full agreement with the archaeological evidence.

In the archaeological level that separates the virgin soil from the architectural remains attributed to the reign of Battos I,[116] the excavations of the same sanctuary have uncovered a fragment of tile bearing a graffito particularly difficult to decipher (Fig. 2.13), on which, after an uncertain proper name (apart from its final letter, τô Ἀρχιλόχō, meaning 'of Archilochos', is convincing) and a possible lacuna, one may read the phrase *toû Rhodíou* (τô Φοδίō).[117] Might this refer to an ethnic, as suggested by Dobias-Lalou, the editor of the inscription? One of the graffiti from Abu Simbel, dated to 591 BC, names a mercenary of Psammetichus II who defined

---

[115] For the same point of view, see Dobias-Lalou (2013–2014) 185. Antonini (2016) 27–64 accepts the Rhodian origin of the graffito only with reservation, but her replacement hypothesis (Achaean) finds no support in the sources relating to the colonization of Cyrene (cf. *BE* 2017, 638, where Dobias-Lalou draws attention to other 'false-problems' in this article).

[116] See Luni, Mei, and Cardinali (2010) 576–580.

[117] *IGCyr* 118100. See Dobias-Lalou (2014) 31–37.

40 THE KOLOSSOÍ

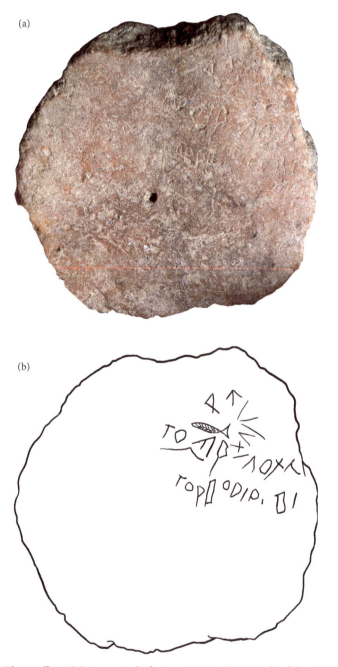

Fig. 2.13 The graffito *IGCyr* 118100, before 631 BC. a. Photograph of the inscription. b. Drawing of the inscription.

himself as 'Ialysian' and not as 'Rhodian'.[118] Before the synoecism of 408 BC, the latter adjective was used to designate not the citizens of a unified state but those living on the island of Rhodes.[119] It is true that, in the *Catalogue of Ships*, which forms Book II of the *Iliad*, Lindos, Ialysos, and Kamiros are presented as constituent parts of Rhodes,[120] but this description stems from the fact that the island had been peopled by the companions of Tlepolemos divided into three tribes,[121] and not from an early form of political unity.[122] If the graffito of Cyrene preserves an onomastic formula, *Rhódios* thus, in all likelihood, could not have been an ethnic (and the article that precedes would further confirm this impression); on the contrary, it would refer to a proper name (*Rhódios* is well attested as such)[123] and, perhaps more precisely, to a patronym. Be that as it may, it seems difficult to escape the conclusion that this word, inscribed even before the arrival of the colonists led by Battos (or at least before they constructed the Dioskoureion), has a close relationship with the island of Rhodes.

Finally, a fragmentary decree from Lindos established the monetary penalties for people breaking a now lost law concerning suppliants (Fig. 2.14).[124] As only

Fig. 2.14 Lindian decree concerning suppliants, third century BC (*AER* II, 1; Archaeological Museum of Rhodes).

---

[118] Bernand and Masson (1957) 10–14, no. 2. [119] Moggi (2009) 52–57.
[120] Hom. *Il.* 2.655–656. [121] Hom. *Il.* 2.668.
[122] Chapter 1, pp. 9–10. [123] *LGPN*, s.v. Ῥόδιος.
[124] *AER* II, 1; cf. Kontorini (1987) 579–580.

two laws about suppliants are attested (at Lindos and at Cyrene), with these texts closely connected in their terminology (as the decree makes clear),[125] there is no doubt that the law of Cyrene was introduced around 631 BC, at the moment of the colonization of the city by the Lindians. Therefore, the *kolossoí* mentioned in the law of Cyrene—and certainly in the lost law of Lindos—are the *kolossoí* of Rhodes.[126]

Rhodian Amphora Stamps

Let us now consider a series of Rhodian amphora stamps bearing an emblem that archaeologists, after calling it a 'mirror'[127] or a 'bust of Helios with schematic drawing,'[128] now identify as a 'symbol' of the god[129] (Fig. 2.15). The face of the Sun fixed on a shaft, however, would be a rather curious symbol; this image in fact is the depiction of a very crude statue, which seems planted in the earth as requested by the law concerning suppliants, namely a *kolossós* of Helios.[130] It differs notably from the herm of the Sun depicted on later stamps, an emblem which Roux interpreted as a schematic representation of the Colossus of Chares itself (Fig. 2.16).[131] The identification of the so-called symbol as a *kolossós* seems more certain, as no other name of a statue exists to designate this image. It served as an emblem for nearly forty years, between *c*.235 and *c*.198 BC,[132] and thus was introduced into the stamping system[133] of the city slightly before the destruction of the Colossus of Rhodes *c*.227 BC. In addition, according to Pseudo-Philo, who seems to follow a source written prior to this date,[134] the statue of Chares was no more than a '*kolossós* equipped as Helios' (κολοσσὸς [...] διεσκευασμένος εἰς Ἥλιον),[135] a definition that perfectly suits our emblem, only recognizable by its rays (as its earlier confusion with a mirror proves). Because ancient authors mention anatomical details that do not appear on amphora stamps, however, the *kolossós* depicted on these stamps is obviously not the Colossus of Chares.[136] Nevertheless, three texts posterior to the construction of the latter prove that it was not fundamentally different from its tiny counterpart.

---

[125] *IGCyr* 016700 (above, pp. 17–19), ll. 132, 138 and *AER* II, 1, l. 5 both use the verb *aphiketeúō* (meaning 'intercede for a suppliant'), which is not attested elsewhere. See Dobias-Lalou (2017) 160–162, who also points out the correspondence between *hupodékomai* in *IGCyr* 016700, l. 137 and *dékomai* in *AER* II, 1, l. 5 (both verbs mean 'to receive' a suppliant).
[126] Cf. Badoud (2020a) 340 and Badoud (2020b) 162–165, who focuses on *TC* 105—an inscription *not* directly related to the settlement of Cyrene by the Rhodians, despite Momigliano (1936) 49–51 and his followers—and corrects Badoud (2011a) 140, where the dating of this event to 570 BC, in accordance with Blinkenberg's theory, weakened the link between *kolossoí* and colonization.
[127] Hiller von Gaertringen, *IG* XII, 1, 1195 and 1303, 3.
[128] Nilsson (1909) 155; Grace (1963) 326 n. 17.
[129] Grace (1974) 197. [130] Cf. Badoud (2003) 586.
[131] Roux (1960) 17–18; cf. Grace (1965) 15; Langlotz (1976) 143; Hermary (1995) 59.
[132] Finkielsztejn (2001) 97–101 and 188–191.
[133] On this notion, see Badoud (2017a); Badoud (2019b) 195–209; Badoud (2019d) 375–401.
[134] Chapter 4, p. 82.   [135] [Philo Byzantius] p. 30, ll. 10–11 (Brodersen; below, pp. 80–82, §1).
[136] Badoud (2011a) 141, whose reasoning on this point is distorted by Moreno (2013) 52 and Queyrel (2020) 140, only to be refuted with his own arguments. Papini (2022) 186, n. 22, elaborates on the confusion of the latter authors.

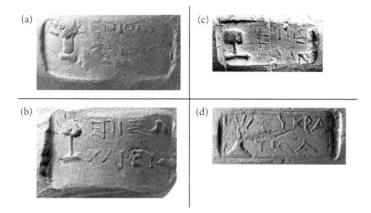

Fig. 2.15 Rhodian amphora stamps with the device of the *kolossós* of Helios (scale 1:1). a. Eponym Onasandros. *c*.220 BC. Athens, Agora (ASCSA, SS 11495). b. Eponym Sochares. *c*.218 BC. Athens, Agora (ASCSA, SS 6061). c. Eponym Simulinos. *c*.212 BC. Samaria (Istanbul Museum, inv. 4903). d. Eponym Eukratidas. *c*.201 BC. Athens, Agora (ASCSA, SS 1482).

Fig. 2.16 Rhodian amphora stamp of the manufacturer Menandros with the device of the herm of Helios, around 100 BC. Athens, Agora (ASCSA, SS 8602; scale 1:1).

Posidippus *On the Making of Statues*

The first text is a poem, *On the Making of Statues* (*Andriantopoiiká*), attributed to Posidippus and discovered in the so-called 'Milan Papyrus' published in 2001.[137] Composed in Dorian Greek by a non-Dorian author as a dialectical homage to the sculptors Polyclitus of Argos, Lysippus of Sicyon, and Chares of Lindos, the poem is a series of epigrams that recounts the progress made in bronze sculpture

---

[137] AB 68.1–4. For the *editio princeps* of *P. Mil. Vogl.* VIII 309, see Bastianini and Galazzi (2001). For a comment on the *Andriantopoiiká*, see Seidensticker (2015).

from its very origins to the middle of the third century BC. The poem actually is a history of art written in verse, but a prescriptive one. Indeed, Posidippus begins with an exhortation:

μιμ[ή]σασθε τάδ' ἔργα, πολυχρονίους δὲ κολοσσῶν,
ὦ ζ[ωι]ορπλάσται, ν[αί], παραθεῖτε νόμους.

Imitate these works, you sculptors who fashion lifelike figures, and, yes, outrun the rules of olden time to which the *kolossoí* have been subjected.[138]

The command of Posidippus to 'outrun' (παραθεῖτε) the earliest canons of Greek sculpture, embodied by the *kolossoí*, makes great sense according to the definition of Hesychius, namely that *kolossoí* are 'those who do not walk'.[139] Indeed, glossing in his own distinctive way the term *kolossoí*, Posidippus then defines the most ancient bronze statues as 'rough drafts' (σκληρ[οὶ τύ]ποι).[140] After exalting the genius of Lysippus, he once again uses the term *kolossós*, this time to indicate the statue constructed on Rhodes by Chares.[141] The monument thus is unquestionably linked to the ancient tradition of rigid and immobile *kolossoí*.[142]

A First Glance at the *Alexandra* of Lycophron

The epigrams by Posidippus allow us to better understand another poem, the *Alexandra* of Lycophron. From ancient times, this poem, which essentially consists of a series of prophecies given by Cassandra (= Alexandra), has posed two problems for its readers. The first concerns its arcane character, which transforms each prophecy into an enigma to decipher. The second centres on the fact that the final prophecy alludes twice to the Romans and their rule on land and sea (vv. 1226–1280 and 1435–1450). Three lines of interpretation have developed, each of which has its followers. For the 'Conservative Unitarians', the *Alexandra* would be, as tradition suggests, a work composed by the playwright and philologist Lycophron, who was active in the court of Ptolemy II[143] (or, at the very least, by a contemporary with the same name).[144] The 'Radical Unitarians' attribute it to another Lycophron or to a 'Pseudo-Lycophron' who would have lived at the

---

[138] AB 62.1–2. For a review of the bibliography, see Angiò (2013) 41–43; Angiò (2016) 96–105.
[139] Kosmetatou and Papalexandrou (2003) 53–58 wrongly gloss the term as 'any lifelike statue' or 'statue'. Stewart (2005) 186 and Männlein-Robert (2007) 175 rightly insist on the immobility of the *kolossoí*, without referring to Hesychius.
[140] AB 62.5.   [141] AB 68.1–4.
[142] This conclusion, expressed in Badoud (2011a) 143, is rejected by Moreno (2013) 52–53 and Papini (2022) 186, n. 22, who want *kolossós* to describe an oversized statue and the Colossus to be Lysippean: but see below, p. 47, n. 166, and Chapter 4, p. 92, with n. 214.
[143] e.g. Momigliano (1942) 57–62 and Hurst (2012) 15–22.   [144] Lambin (2005) 9–40.

beginning of the second century BC and would have left behind no other trace of his literary activity.[145] Finally, the 'Analysts' believe that most parts of the poem date to the period of Ptolemy II but that the 'Roman passages' derive from a late interpolation, whose date still needs to be agreed upon.[146] I shall argue in Chapter 5 that the most disputed verses of the *Alexandra* probably refer to the epigram inscribed on the base of the Colossus of Rhodes, and that they surely agree with the high chronology of the poem, despite the arguments developed by both the Radical Unitarians and the Analysts.[147] For now, let us concentrate on the passage of the *Alexandra* in which Diomedes, king of Argos, is described as *kolossobámōn*:

> κολοσσοβάμων δ' ἐν πτυχαῖσιν Αὐσόνων
> σταθεὶς ἐρείσει κῶλα χερμάδων ἔπι
> τοῦ τειχοποιοῦ γαπέδων Ἀμοιβέως,
> τὸν ἑρματίτην νηὸς ἐκβαλὼν πέτρον.[148]

In this passage (translated below), Diomedes has disembarked in Italy (Ausonia), where he stands on stones taken from the walls of Troy once built by Poseidon (Amoibeus). The hero has used these stones as ballast during his travel. His epithet *kolossobámōn* has been a point of confusion for generations of scholiasts[149] and translators.[150] The general consensus argues that it alludes to the size of the hero, who thus would have been compared to a large statue[151] or to the Colossus of Rhodes itself.[152] Both hypotheses are clearly incorrect. If used under the reign of Ptolemy II (283–246 BC), the term *kolossós* did not yet denote size.[153] Only later[154] would it have meant an oversized statue and alluded to the Colossus of Rhodes (how much later we shall discuss).[155] If, however, the *Alexandra* had been written in the second century, or even later, this interpretation would be at odds not only with the fact that the monument had fallen in *c.*227 BC, which would make a comparison with the glorious Diomedes irrelevant, but also with the context in which the word *kolossobámōn* appears.[156] Particularly common in the

---

[145] e.g. K. R. Jones (2014b) 41–55; Hornblower (2015) 36–39.
[146] e.g. West (1984) 127–151, from whom the classification used here is borrowed.
[147] Chapter 5, pp. 108–120. [148] Lycoph. *Alex.* 615–618.
[149] *Scholia in Lycoph.* 615 (Scheer): γλυφήσεται ὡς ἀνδριάς (ll. 19–20); ἐφ' ὑψηλοῦ τόπου (l. 28).
[150] Mair and Mair (1921) 373, Mooney (1921) 65, and Hornblower (2015) 265 translate it as 'like a Colossus'; Lambin (2005) 109 as 'campé comme un colosse'; and Hurst (2008) 37 as 'pied-de-colosse'. The translation of the *LSJ* ('with colossal stride') is better, even though the notion of size conveyed by the adjective is not correct.
[151] e.g. Cusset and Prioux (2009a) 11.
[152] e.g. Lambin (2005) 29. Hornblower (2015) 314–315 (v. 615) hesitates between the two interpretations.
[153] *Pace* Cusset and Prioux (2009a) 11, who follow the argumentation of Dickie (1996) 237–257, as discussed above, pp. 23–24, 26–27.
[154] *Pace* Lambin (2005) 29. [155] Below, pp. 50–51.
[156] *Pace* Hornblower (2015) 314–315 (v. 615).

works of Aeschylus,[157] one model for Lycophron, compounds ending in –*bámōn* are formed from the verb *baínō* ('to walk'). The neologism *kolossobámōn*, the first part of which most probably echoes Aeschylus' *Agamemnon*,[158] is therefore an oxymoron. Literally 'walking like a *kolossós*' (who precisely 'does not walk', as Hesychius tells us), Diomedes appears perfectly steady and immobile (*statheís*, as Lycophron writes). Furthermore, Lycophron uses the verb *ereídō* to explain how firmly the *kolossobámōn* hero fixes his legs on stones; as we have seen, the same verb is applied to the *kolossoí* mentioned in the sacred law of Cyrene and to the portions of meal which they receive.[159] This is hardly a coincidence, since both texts are concerned with the stability of the *kolossós*, and since the verb *ereídō* is not common. It remains to be stressed that Diomedes, as king of Argos, is a Dorian hero like Agamemnon, himself king of Mycenae by Homer but of Argos by most later authors, including Aeschylus. It is therefore beyond doubt that *kolossobámōn* refers to the tragedy of Aeschylus and that *kolossós*, in the latter compound, is to be understood in its original, Dorian sense. The verses of Lycophron can thus be translated as follows:

> Mobile like a *kolossós*, standing in the Ausonian glens, he will fix firmly his legs on blocks from the plots of Amoibeus, the builder of walls, throwing out of his ship the ballast-stone.

This admittedly limited piece of evidence suggests that the earlier chronology of the *Alexandra* is to be preferred to the later and that the author of the text therefore is indeed the poet who flourished at the court of Ptolemy II along with Posidippus. Both authors insist on the immobility of the *kolossós* and neither defines it as an oversized statue; this is also true for the Colossus of Chares, mentioned by Posidippus.

Polybius and His Rhodian Source

A third text suits this conclusion very well. I refer here to the long-known passage in which Polybius mentions the earthquake that destroyed the 'great *kolossós*' of Rhodes in *c.*227 BC:

Ῥόδιοι δὲ κατὰ τοὺς προειρημένους καιροὺς ἐπειλημμένοι τῆς ἀφορμῆς τῆς κατὰ τὸν σεισμὸν τὸν γενόμενον παρ' αὐτοῖς βραχεῖ χρόνῳ πρότερον, ἐν ᾧ συνέβη τόν τε κολοσσὸν τὸν μέγαν πεσεῖν καὶ τὰ πλεῖστα τῶν τειχῶν καὶ τῶν νεωρίων, οὕτως

---
[157] Björck (1950) 120–121 and 336–339. See especially Angiò (2012) 273–274, who agrees with Badoud (2011a) 143–144 but gives *kolossobámōn* the sense of 'standing like a *kolossós*'.
[158] Above, pp. 31–32.
[159] *IGCyr* 016700 (above, pp. 17–19), ll. 120–121.

ἐχείριζον νουνεχῶς καὶ πραγματικῶς τὸ γεγονὸς ὡς μὴ βλάβης, διορθώσεως δὲ μᾶλλον, αὐτοῖς αἴτιον γενέσθαι τὸ σύμπτωμα.

At about the time I have been speaking, the Rhodians, availing themselves of the pretext of the earthquake which had occurred a short time previously and which had cast down the great *kolossós* and most of the walls and arsenals, made such sound practical use of the incident that the disaster was a cause of improvement to them rather than of damage.[160]

Many scholars assume that Polybius wrote these words with emphatic intent, as when Stendhal evoked an 'enormous colossus' conceived of by Michelangelo.[161] The case of Polybius differs greatly, however, since his description immediately precedes the list of variegated gifts that foreign states sent to help Rhodes recover from the earthquake.[162] It is certain (and uncontested)[163] that Polybius or the author whom he follows draws this information from an official document, certainly preserved in the archives of the city.[164] Consequently, it would not have been Polybius, but an official of the Rhodian state, hardly inclined to effects of style, who created the expression 'great *kolossós*'. For him (as for Sopater a few decades before),[165] only size distinguished the sculpture of Chares from other *kolossoí*, such as that which appears on amphora stamps.[166] Although not represented on the latter,[167] it belonged to the same statue type.

A Base from Thespiae

The lone extant base for a *kolossós* was discovered in the *kástro* of Boeotian Thespiae (Fig. 2.17). At the moment of its publication in 1926, André Plassart explained its modest dimensions by referring to the preliminary remarks of Wilamowitz[168] regarding the *editio princeps* of the sacred law of Cyrene, namely that the word *kolossós* could designate a statue of normal proportions.[169] Nevertheless, the base played no role in the debate that appeared the following

---

[160] Polyb. 5.88.1–2, with the translation of W. R. Paton. The words 'their great Colossus' have been replaced here by 'the great *kolossós*'.
[161] Stendhal [Beyle] (1817) 269.   [162] Bresson (2021c) 189–227.   [163] Ullrich (1898) 28.
[164] *TRI* 16, ll. 2–3 and D.Chr. 31.86 refer to the archives of the city.
[165] Sopater frag. 1 (Kaibel).
[166] In his misleading discussion of Badoud (2011a) 111–152, Moreno (2013) 52 calls this conclusion a 'forzatura' only because it does not agree with his own opinion that *kolossós* has always meant an oversized statue. Yet this opinion is both groundless and proven false. The fact that Lysippus created a statue not designated as 'colossus' before the first century AD (Strabo 6.3.1) is useless for understanding what a *kolossós* was in Chares' day (cf. Chapter 4, p. 92). It is also untrue that the 'teorema Badoud' omits the anatomical details of the Colossus: see above, p. 42, n. 136. On the reconstructions of the statue by Dörig and Moreno, allegedly more in accordance with the sources, see Chapter 7, pp. 163–164, 195–196, 205–210. The same confusion appears in Papini (2022) 186, n. 22.
[167] Above, p. 42.   [168] Wilamowitz-Möllendorf (1925) 39.
[169] Plassart (1926) 460–461, no. 116.

48 THE KOLOSSOÍ

year, when Wilamowitz published his own commentary on the sacred law,[170] or in the new edition of the inscription from Thespiae provided by Joachim Ebert in 1967. Ebert merely observed that the term *kolossós* could refer to the massive appearance of the statue, which (in his opinion) honoured an athlete who was a specialist in combat sports:[171]

>   [- ⏑⏑ - ⏑⏑ -] ἀοίδιμος ὧι Βασίλεια
>   [- ⏑⏑ - ⏑⏑ - - Ν]εμέαι δὲ πατήρ
>   [- ⏑⏑ - ⏑⏑ - ⏑⏑ ἄ]νθετο τόνδε κολοσσὸν
>   [- ⏑⏑ - ⏑⏑ - μ]άρτυρα πιστότατον.
>
>   [---] worthy to be praised in song, to whom the *Basíleia*
>   [---] in Nemea, the father
>   [---] dedicated this *kolossós*
>   [---] most trustworthy witness.[172]

The monument was erected to celebrate victories at two games: the *Basíleia* of Lebadeia and the *Némea*. Does this monument, however, honour a specialist in combat sports? As the inscription is silent about the identity of the honorand, it could refer to another type of athlete, or even an artist, since both games included musical competitions. We should not cite here the comparison by Theocritus of a boxer to the Colossus of the Cypselids, for the poet refers to the striking of metal forming the skin of the statue, and not to its general shape.

The palaeography of the inscription (Fig. 2.17a) is enlightening. The slightly open sigma, the unequal vertical strokes of the pi, and the theta with a central point all suggest a date for the inscription in the second half of the third century BC. On the other hand, Denis Knoepfler has shown that the Boeotian games of the *Basíleia* were recognized as sacred or 'crowned'[173] from 230–220 BC.[174] Before this date, the author of the dedication probably would not have mentioned this festival on the same level as the Nemean Games, one of the most venerable contests in the Greek world. The inscription therefore should belong to the final third of the third century BC.

Written in metre and centred, with letters not exceeding 1.8 cm, the dedication gives us a fairly accurate idea of the base's original dimensions, of which only one corner remains (Fig. 2.17b–c). As the top side had no anathyrosis, we can exclude the placement of another block on it. As there is no trace of a cavity for a marble plinth or of dowel holes for a bronze sculpture on the fragment, we may admit a statue in the centre that suggests immobility (or simply a statue that was massive in appearance, as Ebert conjectured). The reconstruction of Fig. 2.17c, which

---

[170] Wilamowitz-Möllendorf (1927) 169.
[171] Ebert (1967) 411–412, no. 1.   [172] *I. Thespies* 333.
[173] On this concept, see Parker (2004) 9–22.   [174] Knoepfler (2008) 1460.

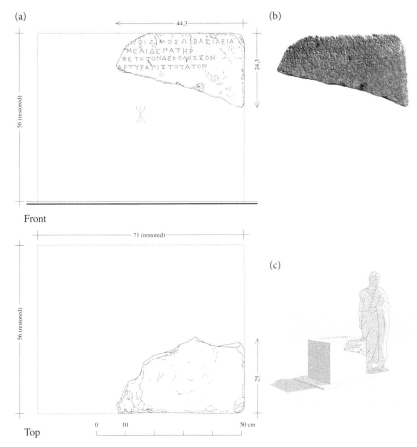

Fig. 2.17 Base of a *kolossós* found at Thespiae, c.230–200 BC (*I. Thespies* 333; Archaeological Museum of Thebes, Inv. 1526). a. Photograph of the inscription. b. Drawing of the stone. c. Reconstitution of the base.

proposes dimensions approaching the conceivable maximum for the sculpture, demonstrates that the base was not intended to hold a larger-than-life statue. At a moment close to—and perhaps slightly later than—the destruction of the Colossus of Rhodes, and even in the context of a comparison aiming at defining the appearance of a non-Dorian statue, the term *kolossós* did not yet apply, by definition, to an oversized statue.

A Short History of the *Kolossoí*

Of Indo-European origin and purely Greek in nature, the term *kolossós* first designated a type of statue whose use, attested from the seventh century BC, was limited to the Dorian world. This type of statue was defined neither by its size nor by its form; nor was it a 'double'. In contrast with lifelike and 'living' statues, whose creation was traditionally attributed to the sculptor Daedalus and to which the Greeks ascribed magical powers of venturing forth and committing murder,[175] the *kolossós* was an immobile figure, designed to enclose an external being, either a god whose protection one sought to attract or a person whom one wished to involve in a magic ritual. Thus, the *kolossós* differed from the kouros (or kore), which inscriptions clearly define as a 'sign' taking the place of an absent person.[176] It rather resembled the *hédos*, seat of the divinity in Greek sanctuaries, although it never seems to have served as a cult statue.[177] The only apparent exception to the rule is provided by a Delian account of 302 BC, which may use the word *kolossós* to describe a discarded *xóanon*.

From the fifth century BC, while the object itself remained exclusively Dorian, the word had indeed spread in the Greek world to describe either true *kolossoí* (thus by Aeschylus) or *kolossoí*-like statues, regardless of their origin and function (thus by Herodotus as well as in the inscriptions from Delos and Thespiae). Both categories of sculptures shared a motionless appearance; they were not defined by size.

The original meaning of the word *kolossós* is still preserved in Theocritus, Lycophron, Posidippus, and Sopater, contemporaries of the Colossus. It was also maintained (it seems) in the source that Pseudo-Philo relied upon to describe the monument. It eventually returned in the administrative record used by Polybius in his account of the earthquake that caused the fall of the 'great *kolossós*'. Attested from the fifth century BC in Herodotus[178] and also used by Sopater while speaking about the statue of Chares, the expression originally had nothing emphatic about it, but rather added meaningful information at a time when the statuary type was not defined by size.

Among ancient authors, Polybius is the first to use *kolossós* with the sense of 'large statue'[179] (but not in his narrative of the earthquake of *c.*227 BC, which—I must insist—certainly derives from an earlier text). This sense is continued both in later Greek[180] and Latin[181] authors; inscriptions testify to the same evolution.[182] It is significant, but hardly noted,[183] that the adjectives *kolossikós*, *kolossiaîos* ('colossal'), which describe any work of great size, also appear in the Greek

---

[175] Frontisi-Ducroux (1975) 95–120.
[176] Above, p. 26, n. 60.
[177] On the various kinds of cult statues, see Donohue (1997); Scheer (2000); and Bettinetti (2001).
[178] Hdt. 2.175.
[179] Polyb. 18.16.2 (ten-cubit statue of Attalus in the agora of Sicyon) and 31.4.4 (thirty-cubit statue of the Roman People in the sanctuary of Athena at Rhodes).
[180] Strabo 4.4.5, 6.3.1, 7.6.1, 12.5.2; Hero Mechanicus *Definitiones* 135.13; Joseph. *BJ* 1.413–414; Plut. *Vit. Fab.* 22.8; *Vit. Aem.* 32.4; *Vit. Luc.* 37.4; *Mor.* 498E (*An vitiositas ad infelicitatem sufficiat*); 779F (*Ad principem ineruditum* 2).
[181] Plin. *HN* 1.34a, 34.39, 42–43, 45.
[182] *SEG* XXVIII, 737, l. 3 (Gortyn, 170–164 BC?); *IDidyma* 217, l. 2 (Didyma, late Imperial period); *I. Milet* 735, l. 3 (Miletus, first century BC?); *TAM* V.2, 1308, l. 14 (Hyrkanis, 138–161 AD).
[183] Chantraine (1970) 558.

language after c.227.[184] These adjectives owe their meaning to the Colossus of Rhodes, and not to the original statuary type of the *kolossós*, which was condemned to oblivion by the enormous dimensions of its most famous representative.

Contrary to what has been commonly believed since Wilamowitz, the decisive event for this semantic shift is not the construction of the statue of Chares, but its inclusion in the list of the Seven Wonders of the World, shortly followed by its destruction.[185] As the list recognized no other quality to the Colossus than its size, the original sense of *kolossós* was destined to fade away. Robbed of its name, did the statuary type itself survive? Probably not: the old *kolossoí*, having disappeared from Rhodian amphora stamps at the beginning of the second century BC, fell into the shadow of colossal statues and remained immobile there until today, just as they were meant to be.

---

[184] The following inscriptions all refer to statues: *IK* 5-*Kyme* 13, l. 2 and *SEG* XXXIII, 1037, ll. 13–14 (Kyme, after 130 BC); Engelmann (2007) 157, no. 1, l. 6 (Patara, first half of the first century BC); *SEG* LV, 1503, l. 3 (Xanthos, *c*.85 BC); Drew-Bear and Fillon (2011) 277, l. 5 (text improved in Bresson (2012) 203–216, who dates this inscription from Apameia to 80–50 BC); *IGR* IV, 292, ll. 25–26 (Pergamon, 75–60 BC); *I. Sardis* I, 27, ll. 3–4 (Sardis *c*.75–50 BC); *IG* II², 1081/5 (Athens, AD 203). For literary sources, see Diod. Sic. 1.46.1 (*andriás*); 2.34.5 (*eikṓn*); 11.72.2 (*andriás*); Philo *De Opificio Mundi* 6; *De Josepho* 39 (*mégethē*); *Leg.* 118, 203, 306, 337 (*andriás*); Strabo 1.1.23, 14.1.14 (*érga*, in the sense of literary or artistic works).

[185] Chapter 4, pp. 64–66.

3
The Artist

The first two chapters have allowed us to consider the remote origins of the Colossus of Rhodes by exploring its subject (the god Helios) and the type of statue to which it belonged (the *kolossós*). We now may return to a more traditional point of view by looking at the sculptor who constructed the monument. Very little information on this matter has survived, and each piece of information is problematic, including his name: Chares of Lindos.

The Origin of Chares

In the Greek world, whenever a sculptor engraved his signature on the base of a statue, he often included an ethnic that indicated his city of origin. Accordingly, the creator of the Colossus[1] could only have signed his work as 'Chares of Rhodes' (Χάρης Ῥόδιος).[2] Nevertheless, he passed into history as 'Chares of Lindos' (Χάρης Λίνδιος), although Lindos was no longer a city but a mere community within the Rhodian state when the Colossus was built.[3] How can this be explained?

The expression 'Chares of Lindos' appears in the poem *On the Making of Statues* that Posidippus of Pella composed while the statue was still standing:[4]

> ἤθελον Ἥλιον Ῥόδιοι π[εριμάκε]α θεῖναι
> δὶς τόσον, ἀλλὰ Χάρης Λίνδιο[ς] ὡρίσατο
> μηθένα τεχνίταν ἔτι μείζονα [τ]οὐ̑δε κ[ο]λοσσὸν
> θήσειν· εἰ δὲ Μύρων εἰς τετράπ[ηχ]υν ὅ[ρον]
> σεμνὸς ἐκεῖνος ἀν̑ῆκε, Χάρης πρῶ[τος μ]ετὰ τέχνα[ς]
> ζῶιον ἐχαλκούργει γᾶς μεγ[έθει παρ]ισ[ῶ]ν.

> The Rhodians wanted to make the gigantic Sun
>   twice as big, but Chares of Lindos ensured
> that no artisan would build a kolossós higher than this one.

---

[1] Hebert (1989) 16–45 collects seventy-six ancient and medieval texts related to the Colossus and translates them into German (Q28–103). The texts about Chares, already gathered by Overbeck (1868) 291–924, nos. 1539–1556, have been translated into French by Muller-Dufeu (2004) 637–643, nos. 1886–1903, and into German, with some additions, by Kansteiner et al. (2014) 641–666 (*DNO* 2520–2547).

[2] On the signature, see Chapter 4, p. 87 (with a supplementary argument).

[3] Chapter 1, p. 7.   [4] Chapter 2, pp. 43–44.

> If Myron managed to reach the limit of four cubits
> —he, the venerable fellow—, Chares was the first with art
> to work in bronze a figure to match the magnitude of the earth.[5]

As Posidippus was especially well-informed, we may be confident that Chares (his elder by some years) was a native of one of the demes that formed the community of Lindos. Since it corresponded to a spondee and a dactyl (– – | – ᴗ ᴗ), the expression 'Chares of Lindos' (Χάρης Λίνδιος) quite certainly was inspired by the metrical requirements of the elegiac couplet in which the poet composed his verses.

It returns in a famous epigram, usually referred to as *Anth. Plan.* 82 (meaning the eighty-second epigram of the *Anthology of Planudes*), whose text is transmitted by various authors and has been reconstructed as follows:

τὸν ἐν Ῥόδῳ κολοσσὸν ἑπτάκις δέκα

Χάρης ἐποίει πήχεων ὁ Λίνδιος.

The Colossus in Rhodes, seven times ten cubits high, was made by Chares of Lindus.[6]

v. 1 Strabo omits the first three words; the *Chrestomathy* of his work has them replaced with κολοσσὸν Ἡλίου ποθ'; τὸν ἐν Ῥόδῳ κολοσσὸν Constantine Porphyrogenitus, Planudes, Kedrenos. ἑπτάκις Strabo; ὀκτάκις Constantine Porphyrogenitus, Planudes, Kedrenos. v. 2 Λάχης ἐποίει Constantine Porphyrogenitus; Λάχης ἐποίησε Kedrenos.

In his *Geography* (most of which was written under the reign of Augustus), Strabo is the first to mention these two trimeters, whose author was apparently unknown to him,[7] as he only mentions 'the writer of the iambic verses' (ὁ ποιήσας τὸ ἰαμβεῖον).[8] He omits the first words of the distich, which according to the *Chrestomathy* (an abbreviated version of the *Geography* composed around the end of the ninth century) were three in number: κολοσσὸν Ἡλίου ποθ' ('once the Colossus of Helios').[9] The name of the sculptor, Chares, and the height of the Colossus, 70 cubits, accord with the most trustworthy ancient sources.[10]

---

[5] AB 68, with the translation of C. Austin and G. Bastianini, slightly modified.
[6] *Anth. Plan.* 82; Gow-Page, *HE*, Anon. LXVIIIB; Campbell (1991) 570–571, LVII.
[7] It seems that Stark (1864) 384 was the first to suggest identifying this author with Callimachus, as Strabo 8.3.30 refers to the height of another Wonder of the World, the statue of Olympian Zeus. It has become clear, however, that Callimachus mentioned the statue of Pheidias in the sixth of his *Iambi*, which are not dedicated to the Wonders of the World and, as far as we can judge, do not refer to the Colossus of Rhodes; see Kerkhecker (1999) 147–181. Additionally, why would Strabo not have called Callimachus by his name?
[8] Strabo 14.2.5.   [9] Strabo 14 [*Chr.* 18].   [10] Chapter 4, pp. 73–74.

Maximus Planudes in his *Anthology*[11] (fourteenth century) adds that the author of the two verses is Simonides (of Keos), who died in 467 BC, nearly two centuries before the construction of the Colossus of Rhodes (numerous additional epigrams have been falsely attributed to this poet, who was thought to have invented the genre).[12] Like Constantine Porphyrogenitus[13] (tenth century) and his follower Georgios Kedrenos (eleventh century),[14] he cites the epigram in complete but erroneous form. In all three authors, the first trimeter starts with four words, τὸν ἐν Ῥόδῳ κολοσσὸν ('the Colossus in Rhodes'), and the height of the statue becomes 80 cubits. In Constantine Porphyrogenitus and Georgios Kedrenos, the sculptor additionally is named Laches (and the latter author has the imperfect replaced by the aorist).

Constantine Porphyrogenitus is the first to declare that the distich was 'engraved on the base that supported the feet of the Colossus'. He is not only discredited by his error about the sculptor ('Laches') but also contradicted by his own version of the epigram, whose *incipit* refers to a remote statue ('in Rhodes'). All of this did not deter scholars from trusting him,[15] which prompted them to arbitrarily correct the *incipit*.[16]

The historical value of the epigram *Anth. Plan.* 82 is thus limited to establishing that the expression 'Chares of Lindos', created or at least used by Posidippus in the early third century BC, was known to Strabo by the end of the first century BC or at the beginning of the first century AD. The account of Pliny the Elder, which also mentions the Colossus built by 'Chares of Lindos' (*Chares Lindius*),[17] demonstrates that this expression had already passed from Greek into Latin a few decades later.

The Pupil of Lysippus

Pliny states that Chares was a pupil of Lysippus (*Lysippi discipulus*); his general knowledge of Greek sculpture and the quality of information that he provides regarding the Colossus in particular encourage us to trust him as well as Posidippus. His testimony is incidentally confirmed by the *Rhetorica ad Herennium*, a work composed in the 80s BC and based on a Rhodian source usually placed in the

---

[11] *Anth. Plan.* 82.
[12] For other epigrams related to statues and wrongly attributed to Simonides, see Gow-Page, *HE*, vol. 2, 516–517.
[13] Constantine Porphyrogenitus, *De admin. imper.* 21, ll. 61–62 (*PG* CXIII, 205C).
[14] Georgios Kedrenos, *Compendium historiarum* I, p. 755, ll. 13–14 (Bekker; *PG* CXXI, 825B).
[15] Lüders (1865) 11; Bergk (1882) 512 (no. 185 B); Robert (1899) 2130; Amelung (1912b) 389; Gow-Page, *HE*, vol. 2, 588–589; Moreno (1973-1974) 455; Moreno (1994b) 136; Cameron (1993) 294–295; Wiemer (2011) 140 n. 42; K. R. Jones (2014a) 137–138; Kansteiner et al. (2014) 643 (*DNO* 2252).
[16] Bergk (1882) 512 (no. 185 B), who thought that the epigram had been composed after the destruction of the statue, proposed τὸν Ἡλίου κολοσσόν ('The Colossus of Helios'). Cameron (1993) 294–295, followed by Wiemer (2011) 140 n. 52, replaced the article τόν ('the' Colossus) by the demonstrative τόνδ' ('this' Colossus) to accommodate the idea of an authentic inscription. Robert (1899) 2130 suggested ὃν εἰσορᾷς κολοσσόν ('The Colossus upon which you look').
[17] Plin. *HN* 34.41 (below, pp. 64–65).

second century BC (but perhaps belonging to the third century or the start of the first century BC):[18]

> *Chares ab Lysippo statuas facere non isto modo didicit, ut Lysippus caput ostenderet Myronium, brachia Praxitelea, pectus Polycletium, sed omnia coram magistrum facientem videbat, ceterorum opera vel sua sponte poterat considerare.*
>
> Not thus did Chares learn from Lysippus how to make statues. Lysippus did not show him a head by Myron, arms by Praxiteles, a chest by Polycleitus. Rather with his own eyes would Chares see the master fashioning all the parts; the works of the other sculptors he could, if he wished, study on his own initiative.[19]

Although aiming to illustrate the need for an apprentice orator to choose his role models well (and being, in all likelihood, made up for the occasion), this anecdote is remarkable in two ways. It supposes that the link between Chares and Lysippus was held as true by the Rhodians themselves, and it insists on the fact that Chares had to observe Lysippus (and not only his sculptures) to be considered as his pupil.[20] Unfortunately, we do not know in what circumstances and for how long Lysippus trained Chares and his other pupils. Let us therefore formulate two hypotheses, which are not mutually exclusive.

Chares in Tarentum?

In the first hypothesis, Chares would have left his native island to join Lysippus.[21] There admittedly is no trace of activity by Chares beyond Rhodes,[22] but we should not formulate an argument from the silence of the sources on this matter, since the life of the artist is almost completely unknown to us. Thus, nothing would disprove the conjecture that Chares participated in the construction of the statues of Zeus and Heracles fashioned by Lysippus for the city of Tarentum, at least if we placed the works between 319 and 304 BC.[23] Nevertheless, this chronology is hardly convincing, since Lysippus is much more likely to have cast the bronzes before 331 BC.[24] Furthermore, even though the Zeus of Lysippus remained the tallest statue in the Greek world until the Helios of Chares was completed, the

---

[18] Calboli (1993) 494. [19] *Rhet. Her.* 4.9, with the translation of H. Caplan.
[20] On the other hand, there is no reason to conclude from this evidence that Chares was the favourite pupil of Lysippus, as has been repeated often after Sillig (1827) 146; cf. Brunn (1889) 292.
[21] Thus, for instance, Hoepfner (2003) 52. The same idea is implicitly admitted by the authors who suppose a direct link between the Zeus of Tarentum and the Colossus of Rhodes, among whom are Pollitt (1986) 55; Moreno (1994b) 136; Moreno (2013) 52.
[22] Below, pp. 61–63.
[23] A. Reinach (1913) 28, followed *inter alios* by Moreno (1977) 424 and 432; Moreno (2013) 52.
[24] Badoud (forthcoming 4).

56 THE ARTIST

link between the two monuments is much looser than previously assumed.[25] First, no ancient author evokes such a link in any way (even though Posidippus and Sextus Empiricus have been mentioned in this context).[26] Second, the testimony of Strabo, who calls the Zeus of Tarentum a *kolossós*,[27] is not relevant here, as the term designated an oversized statue in his time, irrespective of its form and function.[28] When the Colossus of Rhodes was built, however, the meaning of the term was entirely different, and nothing suggests that it could have applied to the statue cast by Lysippus, still less so as Posidippus praises this sculptor for breaking the ancient rules to which the rigid *kolossoí* were subjected.[29] Third, when a scholiast of Lucian says that the Colossus of Rhodes was built by Lysippus,[30] this is an obvious error, which does not imply that Lysippus rather than Chares planned the statue nor that it was based on a Tarentine model, of which there is no mention whatsoever. Finally, different techniques were most probably used to build the Zeus and the Helios.[31] To sum up, we would be wrong to rely on these statues to establish a relationship between their authors. While the possibility remains that Chares worked under the guidance of Lysippus in Tarentum, there is not the slightest clue to substantiate it.

Lysippus on Rhodes

In the second hypothesis, Chares would have benefited from the teaching of Lysippus while the latter was working on Rhodes.[32] This is very likely, as Lysippus has left several more or less certain traces of his passage through the island of Rhodes.

A Phantom Work
Colonel Rottiers, who visited the island in 1825 and 1826, states that he has seen a base signed by Lysippus within the Palace of the Hospitallers' Grand Master (Fig. 3.1); it would have supported 'a fine statue of white marble representing a gladiator', destroyed by the Turks.[33] His testimony is suspect for three reasons. First, Rottiers was an inveterate liar, who—among many other things—claimed to have discovered an inscription mentioning the Colossus, whose transport through the city of Rhodes would have required the intervention of six people, and which would

---

[25] Especially by Moreno (1973–1974) 461; Moreno (1977) 424; Moreno (1994a) 242; Moreno (1994b) 136 (followed by Musti and Pulcini (1996) 295); Moreno (2013) 52 (cf. Chapter 2, p. 47, n. 166). The idea had already been discussed by Wuilleumier (1939) 282.
[26] Chapter 4, pp. 76–77. [27] Strabo 6.3.1. [28] Chapter 2, pp. 49–51.
[29] AB 68. [30] *Scholia in Luc.* 24.12 (about *Icaromenippus* 12).
[31] Chapter 4, pp. 79–87.
[32] Thus, for instance, Moreno (1973–1974) 460–464; Moreno (1974) 72; Moreno (1977) 424–425, with biased arguments.
[33] Rottiers (1830) 150 (travel of 1826).

Fig. 3.1 View of the Palace of the Grand Master (1826).

have been stolen on behalf of the Turkish authorities.[34] Second, it is unlikely that Lysippus sculpted a statue of marble; he was known only as a worker in bronze, and nearly all of the statues from Rhodes were created in his favourite material, as the extant bases demonstrate. Finally, even if the statue mentioned by Rottiers recalls the 'Borghese Gladiator' signed by Agasias but now linked to a Lysippean model, we could hardly imagine that this bronze remained on its base until its destruction by the Turks.[35] Let us be content with the possibility that Lysippus had made a statue whose base was still visible in the town of Rhodes in 1826.

The Dedication *Lindos* 50

A fragment of a base discovered in the excavations on the acropolis of Lindos (Fig. 3.2) bears the signature of an artist that its editor, Christian Blinkenberg, restored as follows:

Λύσιπ[πος Σικυώνιος ἐπόησε].

Lysippus of Sicyon made (the statue).[36]

---

[34] Bastet (1987) 157–158 (travel of 1826, mentioned in the correspondence of Rottiers).
[35] Badoud (2019c) 45–47.   [36] *Lindos* 50.

Fig. 3.2 Base of a statue signed by Lysippus (?), c.330–320 BC (?) (*Lindos* 50; National Museum of Denmark, inv. 10 145).

The base has been dated 'around 325 BC' according to the palaeography,[37] but I have argued elsewhere that the stele to which it has been compared, being certainly related to the siege of Demetrius Poliorcetes, actually dates to c.304 BC.[38] We should be wary, however, of inferring from this dating that the signature of Lysippus (?) also dates to c.304 BC, as the palaeography alone does not permit such a precise conclusion.

The dates proposed by the successors of Blinkenberg are not convincing either. Charles Picard has suggested 333 BC, the year of the passage of Alexander through Anatolia.[39] Nevertheless, until 332 BC, the year of the siege at Tyre,[40] the Rhodians were under the hegemony of Persia, and it is difficult to imagine Lysippus taking advantage of the advance by Alexander's armies to build a statue in a city controlled by the enemies of his protector. Paolo Moreno preferred the year 331/0 BC, on the assumption that the statue presumably signed by Lysippus

---

[37] Blinkenberg (1941) 199 (*Lindos* 2), 243–244, and 257 (*Lindos* 51).
[38] Badoud (2015) 78–82 (*TRI* 15).   [39] Picard (1963) 520 n. 4.
[40] Diod. Sic. 18.8.1; Arr. *Anab.* 2.20.2; Curt. 4.5.9 and 4.8.12; Just. *Epit.* 11.11.1.

had arrived in the sanctuary of Athena Lindia with the *bucrania* and the weapons dedicated by Alexander after his victory at Gaugamela.[41] For him, the base of the statue, on which Blinkenberg had read the letters *ΙΠ* or *ΤΙ*, was actually dated by the eponym [Θευγένης] Πι[στοκράτευς] (Theugenes, son of Pistokrates), priest of Athena Lindia in 331/0 BC.[42] Nothing indicates, however, that the statue (or its creator) had been sent from Gaugamela with the *bucrania* and the weapons dedicated by Alexander. These offerings constituted a sign of gratitude addressed personally to the goddess, as the cloak worn by the king at Gaugamela had been taken from her sanctuary.[43] Moreover, the letters visible above the signature of Lysippus (?) cannot be read as *ΙΠ*, and the layout of the inscription excludes their attribution to the patronym of a priest whose mention as an eponym would additionally be out of place here. Blinkenberg rightly envisaged the 'name of the dedicator or of the man portrayed'.[44]

To sum up, while the palaeography of the inscription suits the identification of Lysippus as the author of the statue once carried by the base, there is no internal evidence allowing a more precise dating. Yet, it is likely that Lysippus cast the statue of Lindos (community of origin of his pupil Chares) on the same occasion as the Chariot of the Rhodians, which we shall now consider.

The Chariot of the Rhodians

Pliny attributes to Lysippus a 'quadriga with Helios of the Rhodians' (*quadriga cum Sole Rhodiorum*).[45] This work can be identified with the offering that was, according to two ancient authors, the only one to have been spared by Cassius Longinus when he pillaged the city of Rhodes in 42 BC.[46] Whereas Valerius Maximus limits himself to mentioning an 'effigy of Helios' (*effigies Solis*),[47] Cassius Dio more precisely speaks of the 'chariot of Helios' (τὸ ἅρμα τοῦ Ἡλίου).[48] Neither Valerius Maximus nor Cassius Dio, however, tells us who designed the statue.

That being said, two problems arise: (1) What relationship exists between the *quadriga cum Sole Rhodiorum* and the chariot erected by the Rhodians at Delphi, on a pillar in front of the temple and the altar of Pythian Apollo (Fig. 3.3)?[49] (2) What is the chronology, relative and absolute, of these two works? I have

---

[41] *Lindos* 2, C I, ll. 103–109 (chap. XXXVIII).
[42] Moreno (1974) 71–73 and Moreno (2004) 32; cf. Moreno (1977) 424, followed by Lippolis (2016) 159. Moreno attributes the date of 325 BC to Hiller von Gaertringen, but it was actually conjectured by Blinkenberg: see above, p. 57, n. 36. He also admits the existence of a dedication by Alexander at Lartos, but the testimony of William Gell on which he bases this hypothesis must be accepted with caution: see Badoud (2019c) 42.
[43] Plut. *Vit. Alex.* 32.6; cf. Ath. 2.30 (Hieronymus frag. 48 [Wehrli]). See also the commentary of Blinkenberg (1912) 70/386.
[44] Blinkenberg (1941) 241 (*Lindos* 50).   [45] Plin. *HN* 34.63.
[46] Delrieux and Ferriès (2010) 175–199.   [47] Val. Max. 1.5.8.
[48] Cass. Dio 47.33.6.
[49] Jaquemin and Laroche (1986) 285–307; Jaquemin and Laroche (2012); cf. Luce (2008).

Fig. 3.3 Reconstruction of the Rhodian pillar at Delphi.

attempted to answer these questions elsewhere.[50] In my opinion, the chariot of Rhodes was created slightly after Alexander the Great had put an end to Persian hegemony on the island by establishing a Macedonian garrison there. It therefore must be dated a bit after 332 BC and perhaps marks the *floruit* of Lysippus, which

---

[50] Badoud (forthcoming 4).

Pliny situates during the 113th Olympiad,[51] that is, during the years 328–325 BC. The chariot of Delphi may be dated independently to the years 330–323 BC. Fashioned in gilded marble, it was probably a copy or, at least, a derivative of the chariot of Rhodes. This idea finds support in a famous parallel, as at least one of the marble statues that decorated the votive monument of Daochos at Delphi (representing Agias, son of Daochos) copied a bronze original cast at Pharsalus by Lysippus.[52]

Since the quadriga cast in Rhodes was assuredly a large and complex work, it is quite possible that Chares earned his title as *Lysippi discipulus* by participating in its construction.[53] He would thus have been a young man in the 320s and was probably born in the 340s. If this holds true, he was around 50 years old when he started building the Colossus. As the political importance and the technical difficulty of the project required the talent of an experienced artist, the result seems convincing.

The Works Attributable to Chares

With his period of apprenticeship at an end, what was Chares' artistic activity? The *Rhetorica ad Herrenium* suggests that it was not limited to the Colossus,[54] though beyond this statue Pliny attributes to Chares only an oversized head set up in Rome on the Capitoline by the consul Publius Lentulus.[55] The magistrate may be identified as Publius Cornelius Lentulus, consul in 57 BC, about whom an inscription reveals that he visited the acropolis of Lindos and there offered a small statue to Athena as a *charistērion* (Fig. 3.4).[56] This 'thank-offering' may well have been motivated by the welcome prepared for him by the Rhodians; it seems likely that they offered to him the head sculpted by Chares ('of Lindos' precisely), the beauty of which Pliny praises.

The hypotheses formulated to augment the corpus of works attributed to the sculptor are not convincing. The first suggests that the 'Chaereas' who, according to Pliny, 'sculpted Alexander the Great and his father Philip',[57] was actually Chares.[58] If this were true, the sculptor would not have lived at the beginning of the third century, but in the middle of the fourth century, just as his models, since portraits of Philip are unlikely to have been sculpted after the demise of his

---

[51] Plin. *HN* 34.51.
[52] Marcadé and Croissant (1991) 91–98; cf. Bommelaer and Laroche (2015) 242–244, no. 511. Jacquemin (1995) 181 highlighted the importance of the parallel when the statue of Delphi was still considered as a bronze, which made it less relevant than it actually is.
[53] On the relationship between Lysippus and Chares, see also Chapter 4, p. 92, and Chapter 7, p. 211.
[54] Above, pp. 54–55.
[55] Plin. *HN* 34.44. Pliny says nothing about the dimensions of the statue, but the context makes clear that it was oversized.
[56] *Lindos* 323, with the commentary of C. Blinkenberg regarding the date of the visit (between 56 and 53, or in 47); cf. Badoud (2019e) 80–81.
[57] Plin. *HN* 34.75.
[58] Helbig (1896) 84–86; Schreiber (1903) 75, 268–272; S. Reinach (1905) 35; Laurenzi (1938) 15–16; Gebauer (1938–1939) 75; Stewart (1993) 106; H. P. Müller (2001) 130–131; Kansteiner et al. (2014) 664–665 (*DNO* 2545); Moreno (1973–1974) 461; Moreno (1977) 424.

Fig. 3.4 Base for a statue offered by Publius Cornelius Lentulus, c.56 BC (*Lindos* 323; Archaeological Museum of Rhodes).

dynasty in 309 BC.[59] If we must correct the text, for which I can see no compelling reason, we would do better by considering Leochares,[60] who created the gold and ivory statues of Philip II and his family at Olympia after 338 BC,[61] or Chairestratos, known as the sculptor of the Themis of Rhamnous, a statue now dated to 320–316 BC[62] (although this statue, like the other sculpture he signed,[63] was in marble, whereas Pliny's Chaereas worked in bronze). An identification of Chares with the engineer Charias, of whom Vitruvius says that 'he accompanied Alexander on his campaign',[64] was also suggested[65] but is no more acceptable. We may also rule out the possibility that the 'relief of Chares' ([τύ]πιον Χάρητος), mentioned in an inventory from the gymnasium of the Athenian Agora and dated to the middle of the second century BC, was the work of the sculptor.[66] As we are aware of no signed relief sculpture and as the creator of the Colossus is not known to have produced reliefs, the inscription presumably mentions the dedication by a Chares otherwise unknown.[67]

It is remarkable that Chares is not attested in epigraphical sources, especially since the excavations undertaken in Rhodian territory have produced some three hundred statue bases, signed by more than one hundred different artists[68]

---

[59] Cf. Amelung (1912a) 331. [60] As T. Reinach (1897) 120 already proposed.
[61] Paus. 5.17.4 and 5.20.10. [62] Themelis (1998) 55–56; see also Marcadé (1953) 12.
[63] *FD* III, 4, 229; see also Marcadé (1953) 11. [64] Vitr. *De arch.* 7, *praef.* 14.
[65] Moreno (1973–1974) 461; Moreno (1977) 424. [66] Clay (1977) 266.
[67] Ma (2008) 10. Kansteiner et al. (2014) 665 (*DNO* 2546) remain cautious.
[68] Badoud (2015) 278–287.

(among them probably his master Lysippus, as we have seen).[69] Chares remains for us the creator of one work: the Colossus.

The End of Chares

Sextus Empiricus relates that Chares killed himself after having made a crude error in estimating the cost of the construction of this statue.[70] Since the epigram *Anth. Plan.* 82 mentioned either Laches or Chares as the sculptor,[71] Johannes van Meurs (Meursius) supposed that the statue was finished by Laches after the suicide of Chares.[72] Although this hypothesis was frequently repeated between the seventeenth and twentieth centuries,[73] it does not withstand examination. The text of Constantine Porphyrogenitus, which mentions Laches, is merely the corruption of that transmitted by Strabo, which mentions Chares.[74] Additionally, if Sextus Empiricus agrees with Posidippus[75] in mentioning a resizing of the statue (by using like him the unusual verb *horízein*,[76] which supposes either a citation, direct or indirect, or a common source), he credits Chares with multiplying by two the initial expected height, while his predecessor suggested that the sculptor had divided it by two.[77] No other ancient author refers to the suicide of the artist. It is not unlikely that the story told by Sextus Empiricus was used by mathematics teachers to exemplify the law of proportion between linear measurements and volumes. Whatever the case may be, it is explicitly presented as hearsay (ὡς φασίν) by the author, who used it in a treatise meant to illustrate the limits of human reason. The theory of Meursius consequently amounts to an explanation of a copy error (Chares → Laches) through a presumably fictitious anecdote (the suicide of Chares).

---

[69] Above, pp. 57–59.   [70] Sext. Emp. *Math.* 7.107–108.
[71] Above, pp. 53–54.   [72] Van Meurs (1675) 42.
[73] Préchac (1919) 68–69 provides its extreme development. This author, known for having edited Seneca by rewriting his works, supposed that Strabo and Constantine cited two different parts of the same epigram.
[74] Cf. Brunn (1889) 292.   [75] AB 68 (above, pp. 52–53).
[76] Bastianini and Gallazzi (2001) 195 have already noticed this.   [77] Chapter 4, pp. 76–77.

4
The *Kolossós* of Rhodes

The time has now come to tackle the physical aspects of the Colossus of Rhodes. When was it created and destroyed? What was its height? What was the construction technique used? What did the statue look like? Answering these questions will allow us to verify if the statue corresponded, materially, to the definition of *kolossós* developed in Chapter 2.

Chronology

Construction, Completion, and Destruction

In 304 BC, the Rhodians emerged victorious from the siege that Demetrius Poliorcetes had inflicted upon them for a year, although his forces were vastly superior in number and were equipped with formidable war machines, including the helepolis,[1] a mobile assault tower weighing *c.*118 tonnes and wrapped in iron on all nine of its levels.[2] According to Pliny, they acquired the funding necessary for the construction of the Colossus by selling the material left in place by the invaders. The construction lasted no less than twelve years, yet the statue barely stood for fifty-six years before an earthquake toppled it. Pliny's description of the statue is almost certainly borrowed from his friend Gaius Licinus Mucianus, who visited the sanctuary of Athena at Lindos and the city of Rhodes shortly before the composition of the *Natural History*:[3]

> *LXX cubitorum altitudinis fuit hoc simulacrum, post LVI annum terrae motu prostratum, sed iacens quoque miraculo est. pauci pollicem eius amplectuntur, maiores sunt digiti quam pleraeque statuae. vasti specus hiant defractis membris; spectantur intus magnae molis saxa, quorum pondere stabiliverat eum constituens.*

---

[1] See Chapter 5, pp. 106–107, and Chapter 6, p. 133, for modern confusions involving the Colossus and the helepolis.
[2] Pimouguet-Pédarros (2011), with a description of the helepolis on pp. 160–168.
[3] See most recently Williamson (2005) 219–252. Although the description of the Colossus does not appear in the fragments assigned by Peter (1906) 101–107 to Mucianus, its origin was recognized by Brieger (1857) 60, followed *inter alios* by Sellers *apud* Jex-Blake and Sellers (1896) lxxxvii, whose list is considered incomplete by Münzer (1897) 392–395.

duodecim annis tradunt effectum CCC talentis, quae contigerant ex apparatu regis Demetrii relicto morae taedio obsessa Rhodo.

This statue was 70 cubits high; fifty-six years after its erection, it was overthrown by an earthquake, but even lying on the ground it is a Wonder. Few people can make their arms meet round the thumb of the figure, and the fingers are larger than most statues; and where the limbs have been broken off enormous cavities yawn, while inside are seen great masses of rock with the weight of which the artist steadied it when he erected it. It is recorded that it took twelve years to complete and cost 300 talents, money realized from the engines of war belonging to King Demetrius which he had abandoned when he got tired of the protracted siege of Rhodes.[4]

We know from Polybius[5] that the earthquake mentioned by Pliny is dated by the *Chronicle* of Eusebius (as translated by Jerome) to the first year of the 139th Olympiad, that is, 224 BC.[6] Maurice Holleaux has shown, however, that it must be dated between 229 and 226 BC.[7] The year 228, repeatedly advocated by Paolo Moreno,[8] is borrowed from an inscription found in Iasos,[9] whose chronology had already been proven wrong in 1971.[10] This inscription seemed to make sense when compared with the catalogue of the priests of Helios published by Luigi Morricone,[11] whose chronology is equally incorrect,[12] and with a reading of Pliny that also must be rejected, as we shall see. Nevertheless, the situation is not as desperate as it would seem. The *Chronicon Paschale*, whose authority seemed 'poor' to Holleaux,[13] places the destruction of the Colossus in the second year of the 138th Olympiad, 227 BC.[14] Polybius writes that, during this very year, a 'movement of the sea' occurred in the Euripus Strait.[15] Without mentioning the *Chronicon Paschale*, Édouard Will convincingly interpreted this movement, which would have been a tsunami, as a result of the earthquake that damaged the city of Rhodes.[16]

---

[4] Plin. *HN* 34.41, with the translation of H. Rackham, slightly modified: the correction of *LVI* to *LXVI* has been rejected for reasons explained below, and *miraculo* has been interpreted as alluding to the fact that the Colossus was one of the Seven Wonders (*miracula*).

[5] Polyb. 5.88.1 (above, pp. 46–47). Rieger (2004) 69–85, a study of the 'engineering aspects of the collapse of the Colossus', ignores the main testimony about the collapse (Polybius) and misunderstands the sole text about the engineering aspects of the Colossus (Pseudo-Philo). On the latter, see below, pp. 79–92.

[6] Euseb. *Chron.* II pp. 122–123 (Schoene). An incorrect date is provided by Hebert (1989) 23, followed by Kansteiner et al. (2014) 648 (*DNO* 2525).

[7] Holleaux (1923) 480–498 [(1938) 445–462], overlooked by Kansteiner et al. (2014) 648 (*DNO* 2525).

[8] Moreno (1973–1974) 453–463; Moreno (1994a) 240; Moreno (1994b) 131, 136, 140; Moreno (1999) 193.

[9] Pugliese Carratelli (1967–1968) 445–453, no. 2. See now *IK* 28-*Iasos* 2.

[10] Robert and Robert, *BE* 1971, 621.   [11] Morricone (1949–1951) 351–380.

[12] See now *TRI* 1.   [13] Holleaux (1923) 489 n. 3 [(1938) 454 n. 2].

[14] *Chronicon Paschale* I p. 331 (Dindorf). An incorrect page and date are provided by Hebert (1989) 23.

[15] Polyb. 20.5.7.   [16] Will (1979) 368.

Thus, 227 BC is now the most likely date for the destruction of the Colossus; the construction of the statue began *c*.295 BC (*c*.227 + 12 + 56) and was completed *c*.283 BC. This result agrees with the evidence from the *Suda*, which states that the statue was raised under the reign of Seleukos I Nikator (306–281 BC).[17]

In his commentary on Eusebius, published in 1606, Joseph Justus Scaliger nevertheless suggested correcting the manuscript tradition of Pliny to make the beginning of the construction of the Colossus coincide with the end of Demetrius' siege.[18] The earthquake therefore would not have occurred fifty-six (*LVI*) but sixty-six (*LXVI*) years after the completion of the works. Two and a half centuries later, Ludwig Urlichs realized that in the *Codex Bambergensis* (upon which all other manuscripts of Pliny depended) the number *LVI* resulted from a correction. The copyist seemed to have committed an error by first writing '*LLVI*'. Thus, nothing seemingly prevented the admission that the reading '*LXVI*' was the original, incorrectly restored by the author of the *Codex Bambergensis*.[19] Accepted afterwards by many editors of Pliny[20] and other scholars,[21] this hypothesis is in itself unlikely, since the dittography admitted by Urlichs does not make any sense and since one would not understand why the copyist would have committed a second error in correcting the first. The explanation proposed by Ursula Vedder is more convincing: the retouching of the manuscript was limited to rewriting in capital(s) the first letter(s) of '*LVI*' that the copyist had begun transcribing in small letters, without realizing that it referred to a number.[22] The erased '*L*' of which Urlichs noticed the trace before '*LVI*' is actually in lower case (Fig. 4.1).

Another argument may have dissuaded scholars from following the old, yet always tempting, conjecture of Scaliger. In a note presented by the numismatist Richard Ashton in 1988,[23] Peter Fraser drew attention to the description that Diodorus, following a local source, provides of the works undertaken by the Rhodians after the lifting of the siege by Demetrius.[24] It mentions the construction of a temple in honour of their ally Ptolemy I, the reconstruction of the theatre, and the repair of the fortifications, but the Colossus appears nowhere. This omission is no coincidence: in spite of what was commonly believed,[25] the statue

---

[17] *Suda, s.v. Κολοσσαεύς*. This testimony sufficiently excludes the hypothesis of Skaltsa (2021) 167 n. 10, according to which 'the date of the famous earthquake that hit Rhodos should be placed in 223/222', since 223 + 56 = 279, a year which does not fall in Seleukos I Nikator's reign.

[18] Scaliger (1606) 137.   [19] Urlichs (1857) 312.

[20] Thus Mayhoff (1897) 177; Rackham (1952) 158; Ferri (2011⁴) 86; *contra* Jex-Blake and Sellers (1896) 32.

[21] For some recent examples, see the publications of Moreno cited above, p. 65, n. 8; Berthold (1984) 80; Ntantalia (2001) 133; Hoepfner (2003) 51, 52; Anniboletti (2024) 12.

[22] Vedder (2010) 39–45, not followed by Kansteiner et al. (2014) 642 (*DNO* 2520).

[23] Ashton (1988) 87.   [24] Diod. Sic. 20.100.2–4.

[25] e.g. Dombart (1970) 69; Moreno (1973–1974) 454–455 (and the other publications of this author cited above, p. 65, n. 8); Adam and Blanc (1989) 218; Ekschmitt (1996) 176; Brodersen (2004) 87–88; Anniboletti (2024) 12. Romer and Romer (1995) 33–34 write that the Colossus was built in 280 BC and that it fell in 75 BC; in their view 'sixty-six years' separate those two dates, yet none of these figures is correct.

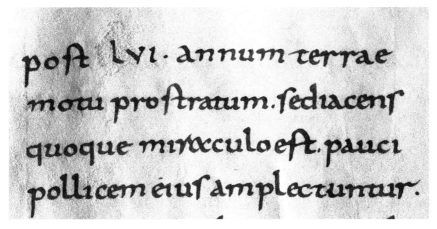

Fig. 4.1 Detail from ms. *Bambergensis class*. 42 (AD 820–840), f. 57r.

only began to be erected a decade later. Even though Ptolemy III offered them his assistance, the Rhodians refused to ever reconstruct the Colossus, following the commands of an oracle[26] that forbade them from doing so. Whether this explanation was sincere or whether it attempted to divert the aid granted by the king to other ends, the ruins of the statue, broken at the knees, were abandoned in place.[27]

In AD 141/2, another earthquake struck the city of Rhodes.[28] Addressing its survivors, Aelius Aristides enumerates the works that had not been affected by the catastrophe; several bronzes and 'the great statue' are part of this list.[29] If the Colossus is not designated by name, it is perhaps because the ruins of the statue could no longer bear the comparison with its fame. Be that as it may, we thus definitively lose track of it; its final remains were perhaps collected or melted down at the end of the fourth century, after the Edict of Thessalonica had made Christianity the sole religion of the Roman Empire.[30]

Alleged Reconstructions

Several authors, beginning with Eusebius, claim that Vespasian (AD 69–79) reconstructed the Colossus[31] and that Commodus (AD 161–192) replaced the

---

[26] Conrad (1996) 175 mentions without supporting evidence an oracle of Helios. The Rhodians probably consulted Apollo at Delphi. There was no oracle of Apollo on Rhodes: Badoud (2015) 113–115.
[27] Strabo 14.2.5; cf. Eustathius *in Dionysium Periegetem* 504 (*GGM* II, p. 312, l. 10).
[28] On this date, see Delrieux (2008) 220–221.
[29] Aristid. 25.53 (Behr). See Chapter 6, p. 132.   [30] *Cod. Theod.* 16.1.2.
[31] Euseb. *Chron.* II p. 158 (Schoene); cf. *Chronicon Paschale* I p. 464, ll. 13–14 (Dindorf); Georgius Syncellus p. 417, l. 11 (Mosshammer); Georgius Cedrenus *Compendium historiarum* I p. 377, ll. 15–16 (Bekker; *PG* CXXI, 416D).

original head with his own image.[32] On the other hand, according to the sixth-century historian John Malalas, who did not mention this latter episode, Hadrian (AD 117–138) also ordered a reconstruction of the statue.[33] Although these accounts have been viewed favourably to this day,[34] it has long been established that they result from a confusion between the Colossus of Rhodes and the Colossus that Nero had erected in Rome more than four centuries later.[35] Just like the fact that both statues were termed '*kolossós*' in Greek and '*colossus*' in Latin, their location could have been a source of error. The Colossus erected by Nero, finished under Vespasian[36] and moved by Hadrian,[37] with its head replaced by Commodus (among other changes),[38] was set up ἐν τῇ ἱερᾷ ὁδῷ[39] ('on the sacred way'), words that the manuscript tradition may have corrupted as ἐν Ῥόδῳ ('at Rhodes'). Yet the fame of the statue cast by Chares was enough to attract the history of its Roman counterpart.[40]

According to David Aune[41] and several New Testament scholars after him,[42] the Colossus of Rhodes allegedly reconstructed by Hadrian would have inspired the 'angel with the little scroll' about whom the *Book of Revelation*, usually dated to the reign of Domitian (AD 81–96), says that his 'face was like the sun and his legs like pillars of fire', and that he was 'standing on the sea and on the land'.[43] Even if this were the case, how could the *Book of Revelation*, whose definitive edition Aune places under the reign of Trajan (AD 98–117), refer to it? Probably aware of this paradox, Thomas Witulski argued that the *Book of Revelation* was actually composed under the reign of Hadrian (AD 117–138),[44] an argument no more acceptable, since it depends on Aune's first premise. A second argument developed by Aune is also marked by anachronism: 'the angel whom I saw standing on sea and land' would allude 'to a popular but erroneous view' according to which 'the Colossos stood astride the harbour of Rhodes permitting ships to pass through its legs'. As we shall see, this myth only appeared more than a millennium after the composition of the *Book of Revelation*.[45] Witulski defended the hypothesis according to which this work, written in Patmos, would have alluded to the epigram engraved on

---

[32] Euseb. *Chron.* II p. 174 (Schoene); cf. *Chronicon Paschale* I p. 492, ll. 1–2 (Dindorf); Georgius Syncellus p. 433, ll. 7–8 (Mosshammer).
[33] Joannes Malalas p. 279, ll. 14–15 (Dindorf); cf. *Chronicon Paschale* I p. 476, ll. 6–7 (Dindorf).
[34] Allazi [Allatius] (1640) 71; Lüders (1865) 15–20; Moreno (1994b) 140; Moreno (1999) 199; Conrad (1996) 177–178; Hoepfner (2000) 152–153; Hoepfner (2003) 101–102; Agusta-Boularot (2006) 120–121 (with reservations); Thurn et al. (2019) 286 n. 65 ('möglicherweise handelte es sich nur um den Plan einer Rekonstruktion'); Wujewski (2018) 295; Condello and Fioridi (2023) 60–61; M. D. Higgins (2023) 326.
[35] Chevreau (1691) 341–432; Chevreau (1697) 421–422; De Pestels [Caylus] (1759) 367; Van Gelder (1900) 390–391; cf. Robert (1899) 2131. On the Colossus of Nero, see Lega (1989–1990) 339–378; Bergmann (1993) 7–17; Smith (2000) 532–542; Albertson (2001) 95–108; Hijmans (2024) 930–937; below, pp. 77–79.
[36] Suet. *Vesp.* 18; Cass. Dio. 65.15.1.   [37] *Hist. Aug., Hadr.* 19.12.
[38] Cass. Dio 73.22.3; Hdn. 1.15.9; *Hist. Aug., Com.* 17.9–10.   [39] Cass. Dio 65.15.1.
[40] In the third century AD, Philostr. *VA* 5.21 writes as if the Colossus was still standing in the first century AD, but this is an anachronism within a literary cliché.
[41] Aune (1998) 556–557.
[42] e.g. G. R. Osborne (2002) 396 and Witulski (2011) 543–575. Brake (2019) 126 n. 6, confuses the description of the angel with that of the Colossus.
[43] Rev. 10:1–8.   [44] Witulski (2011) 572.   [45] Chapter 6, pp. 121–128.

the base of the Colossus,[46] but the two texts mention the land and the sea in different ways, and we would hardly expect a reference to Hellenistic poetry in biblical Scripture from the Imperial period. Nevertheless, the angel of Revelation was certainly inspired by the Colossus of Rhodes (if not by its dedication), as will become clear after examination of the myth of Muʿāwiya.

The Myth of Muʿāwiya

If specialists of classical antiquity have not all assumed that the Colossus had been reconstructed during the Imperial period, they have unanimously agreed that the statue (ruined or not) was still visible in AD 653/4.[47] In their opinion, the Arabs pillaged it during the attack that Muʿāwiya ibn ʾAbī Sufyān, governor of Syria and founder of the Umayyad Caliphate, launched that year against the city of Rhodes, which had become the seat of an important archbishopric.[48] A Jew from Emesa (Homs) then purchased the bronze from the statue and carried it away on a caravan made up of 900, or even 980, camels. Thus, the story goes, the masterpiece of Chares disappeared forever,[49] at least in part: for it has been supposed that the bronze of the statue, having arrived in Syria, served to mint the so-called Pseudo-Byzantine coins of the Caliph, some of which still survive.[50]

The medievalist Lawrence Conrad has shown that this narrative was a fictional story created by Theophilus of Edessa (Urfa),[51] chief astrologer at Baghdad during the reign of the caliph Al-Mahdi (AD 775–785), who wrote a *Chronicle* in Syriac. Although it is now lost, its contents may be reconstructed rather accurately, as several authors (Theophanes the Confessor, Agapius of Hierapolis, Michael the Syrian, and the Chronicler of 1234) made it their principal source, some of them through a Greek translation.[52] An adherent of Monophysitism (and therefore a

---

[46] Witulski (2011) 569–570.

[47] More recent works include Coutin (2001) 81; Jordan (2002) 149; Vedder (2003) 132; Brodersen (2004) 89; Hoepfner (2003) 102; Mariño Sánchez-Elvira (2008) 126; Maillot (2009) 57; Piel (2010). Badoud (2011a) 115–118 rejects the story as a forgery. Michalaki-Kollia (2013a) 21; Mattusch (2014) 16 and 160; Manoussou-Ntella (2017) 178; Wujewski (2018) 295; Anniboletti (2024) 22 still admit it; M. D. Higgins (2023) 326 suggests a rationalization.

[48] Bosworth (1996) 157–164.

[49] Theophanes Confessor *Chronographia* p. 345, ll. 8–11 (De Boor; *PG* CVIII, 764A); Anastasius Bibliothecarius *Historia tripertita* p. 216, ll. 24–27 (De Boor; *PG* CVIII, 1325B); Constantinus Porphyrogenitus *De admin. imper.* 20, ll. 3–10 (*PG* CXIII, 200B-C); Michael the Syrian *Chronicle* IV, p. 430a, ll. 25–31 and p. 526b, ll. 10–16 (Chabot: II, pp. 442–443 and III, p. 81, for the French translation); Landolfus Sagax *Historia miscella* 19.4; Georgius Cedrenus *Compendium historiarum* I, p. 755, ll. 8–16 (Bekker; *PG* CXXI, 825B-C); Zonar. *Annales* 14.19 (*PG* CXXXIV, 1289C-D); Agapius *Kitāb al-ʿunwān* [*Universal History*] p. 482, ll. 8–10 (Vassiliev = *PO* VIII). See also Hoyland (2011) 139–140.

[50] Moorhead (2007) 40–42.

[51] Conrad (1996) 165–187, whose argumentation is nevertheless not without fault: see above, p. 68, n. 34, about the alleged reconstruction of the Colossus and below, p. 90, n. 196, about the actual weight of the statue.

[52] Hoyland (2011) 9–19.

heretic according to the orthodoxy established in AD 451 by the Council of Chalcedon), Theophilus was inspired by the Bible when presenting the destruction of the Colossus of Rhodes as a warning sign for the end times. In the *Book of Daniel*, the king of Babylon, Nebuchadnezzar, dreams of an enormous statue whose head is golden, chest and arms are silver, belly and thighs are bronze, and lower part of the legs is iron; the feet are half-iron and half-clay. A rock breaks away from a mountain, strikes the feet of the statue, and causes the destruction of the monument. Under divine inspiration, the prophet Daniel understands that this destruction portends that of the Babylonian Empire.[53] In the *Chronicle* of Theophilus, the Arabs play the role of agents of the Apocalypse by destroying the Colossus. The archbishopric of Rhodes embodies the Orthodox clergy, which Theophilus implicitly accuses of provoking the fall of the Christian world by rejecting Monophysite doctrine. David Woods has challenged this reconstruction but has failed to present it accurately, as he wrongly attributes to Conrad the idea that Theophilus would have 'misunderstood some source containing an apocalyptic metaphor based on the biblical account of the dream of Nebuchadnezzar of Babylon'.[54] His alternative explanation, which would have Theophilus depend upon 'urban folklore', must be rejected, for the analogy between the Colossus of Theophilus and the statue dreamed of by Nebuchadnezzar goes much further than admitted by Woods and by Conrad himself.

In fact, although the events in the *Book of Daniel* take place in the sixth century BC, its composition is slightly earlier than the date of the death of Antiochus IV Epiphanes in 163 BC.[55] By a series of prophecies *post eventum*, the author of the book wished to encourage his people to revolt against the policy of Hellenization that the sovereign was forcing upon Judaea. The first part of the work, which includes the narrative of the statue, could have been noticeably older than the second. Nevertheless (as the followers of this hypothesis agree), when Daniel surmises from the composition of the feet of the statue that 'kings will ally themselves through marriage', he refers to the union of Antiochus II with Berenice in 252 BC, or rather to that of Cleopatra, daughter of Antiochus III, with Ptolemy V in 193/2 BC. At this point, there is already a significant chance that the allegory of the statue gave inspiration to its author by the collapse of the Colossus of Rhodes in 227 BC,[56] even more so as Helios played an important role in the Seleucid pantheon, with Antiochus IV being closely associated and even identified with the god.[57] However, Theophilus has greatly overestimated the age of the Colossus at 1,360 years, rather than approximately 936. Without questioning the authenticity of his account, Margarete Demus-Quatember is the first to have noted that his

---

[53] Daniel 2:31–45. [54] Woods (2016) 446.
[55] Collins (1993) 24–38 and 162–175. [56] Cf. Moreno (1994b) 127–128.
[57] Iossif and Lorber (2009a) 129–146; Iossif and Lorber (2009b) 19–42.

CHRONOLOGY 71

chronology reproduced that of John Malalas,[58] who places the construction of the statue just before the reign of Nebuchadnezzar.[59] Theophilus thus certainly got the idea for his 'Babylonian Colossus' while reading the *Chronicle* of John Malalas (which also led him to believe that the statue of Chares had been reconstructed by Hadrian)[60] and not from 'urban folklore', as argued by Woods. It also becomes clear that the author of the *Book of Daniel* dressed up the Colossus as a statue that Theophilus, in turn, dressed up as the Colossus. As in a Shakespearean play, where a male actor playing a female role could be required to dress as a man,[61] the first change of clothes (Colossus → statue with feet of clay) was undone by the second (statue with feet of clay → Colossus).

Nevertheless, Theophilus did not draw his inspiration entirely from the *Book of Daniel* and the *Chronicle* of Malalas. Although the raid that the Arabs launched against Rhodes in AD 653/4 is a proven fact,[62] there is no clue that it had any impact on the ancient remains which must still have been visible on the island. We know, however, that the soldiers of Muʿāwiya found at Syracuse the ancient bronzes that the emperor Constans II had seized in Rome in AD 663 in order to transfer them to Constantinople.[63] This episode was already considered contemporaneous with the alleged destruction of the Colossus by Cosmas of Jerusalem,[64] who dedicated (in the eleventh century?)[65] a commentary to the poems of Gregory of Nazianzus.[66] In addition to preserving a kernel of truth (the sack of Rhodes in AD 653/4), the myth created by Theophilus would owe part of its credibility to a slightly later event, in which the Orthodox proved to be incapable of protecting Classical heritage from the assaults of Muʿāwiya (the sack of Syracuse in the years AD 672–676). The historian ʾAḥmad ibn Yaḥyā al-Balādhurī, who lived in the ninth century, writes that some 'idols' brought from Sicily were dispatched to India to be resold there,[67] a narrative that evokes the figure of the Jewish merchant believed to have sold off the remains of the Colossus. The resemblance between the two episodes could be accidental, for although Theophilus mentioned the stay of Constans II at

---

[58] Demus-Quatember (1986) 147. [59] Joannes Malalas p. 149, ll. 9–11 (Dindorf).
[60] Above, p. 68.
[61] Such is the case with Julia in *The Two Gentlemen of Verona*, with Portia, Jessica, and Nerissa in *The Merchant of Venice*, with Rosalind in *As You Like It*, with Viola in *Twelfth Night, or What You Will*, and with Imogen in *The Tragedie of Cymbeline*.
[62] Bosworth (1996) 157–164.
[63] *Liber Pontificalis* 137.3 (Duchesne I, p. 346); Paulus Diaconus *Historia Langobardorum* 5.11 and 5.13. See also below, nn. 64 and 67.
[64] Cosmas Hierosolymitanus, *Commentarii in Greg. Naz. carmina*, p. 216 (Lozza; PG XXXVIII, 534). Discussing his account, Coates-Stephens (2017) 205 also takes as authentic the episode of the Colossus. Woods (2016) 448–449, who incorrectly reads this episode as a folk tale (above, p. 70), supposes that the objects which the Arabs had plundered at Syracuse and elsewhere were interpreted as scraps of the Colossus when they reached Emesa, from where the Jewish merchant invented by Theophilus was supposed to come.
[65] Kazhdan (1991) 396–412. [66] Cf. Chapter 7, p. 163.
[67] Amari (1880) 268–269; Amari (1881) 2. For later sources, see Amari (1880) 348 and Amari (1881) 1, 112, 273–274.

Syracuse,[68] he said nothing of the Roman spoils and the raid by the soldiers of Muʿāwiya. It is nevertheless more likely that Theophilus had access to the same information as al-Balādhurī, and that he chose to reassign it to his own account of the capture of Rhodes.

Be that as it may, the most fascinating part of the story is not the falsification itself, but rather the success that it has achieved even to the present day, despite its inconsistencies. The date attributed to the statue is completely incorrect, and the description of the monument—which would have contained no stone inside—is contradicted by ancient sources[69] (the alleged reconstructions of the statue obviously helped to circumvent the difficulty).[70] Furthermore, although many ancient statues were preserved and exhibited in the Byzantine world,[71] it is worth stressing that Theophilus, presumably aware that the Church would not have tolerated the presence of a gigantic statue of the Sun in the seat of an archbishop, used the Colossus to symbolize Rhodes rather than paganism. Finally, the use of 900 or even 980 camels to carry the remains of the statue[72] seems hard to believe when one considers that twenty-four elephants had reportedly been enough to transport the Colossus of Nero from the Domus Aurea to its final location.[73] As Conrad understood well, the explanation for the acceptance of Theophilus' narrative is partly found in the harmful role of the Arab invaders but also in the Jewish merchant, presented as the final agent in the destruction of civilization.[74] It was not, however, Edward Gibbon who established the 'dominant view' of this legendary episode in his *Decline and Fall of the Roman Empire*,[75] since it is already recorded in the *Historia Tripertita* of Anastasius and the *Historia Miscella* of Landolfus Sagax.[76] From 1454, Flavio Biondo, followed seven years later by Pope Pius II himself, made use of it—without mentioning the figure of the merchant—when lumping the Turks in with the Arabs and denouncing, within the perspective of a new crusade, the 'barbarity' of the Saracens who had just seized Constantinople and were damaging Venetian possessions in the Aegean.[77] In 1528, the theologian Johann Faber, sent to the court of King Henry VIII to obtain the aid of the English against the Turks, already provided the complete version of the myth.[78] It has hardly changed any further since then,[79] even if, apparently troubled by certain stereotypes that have become embarrassing, contemporary historiography tends

---

[68] Hoyland (2011) 150–151, 162–164.   [69] Below, pp. 82, 87–88.   [70] Above, pp. 67–69.

[71] For an overview, see Spieser (2017a) 123–144.

[72] De Choiseul Gouffier (1782) 108–109 questions if the episode of the caravan is authentic but does so with a faulty argument, namely that the remains of the Colossus were at the port, which would have made the use of camels unnecessary.

[73] *Hist. Aug., Hadr.* 19.12.   [74] Conrad (1996) 166 n. 5.

[75] Gibbon (1788), vol. 5, p. 331.   [76] See above, p. 69, n. 49.

[77] Biondo [Blondus] (1510) [first published in 1481 and written in 1454] 36 and Piccolomini [Pius II] (1534) [first published in 1477 and written in 1461] 237.

[78] Faber (1528), reproduced by von Grätz [Gratius] (1535) f. CCXXXVIIv.

[79] It returns most notably in Van Meurs [Meursius] (1675) chap. XV, pp. 40–46, which remained the most authoritative work on Rhodes until the end of the nineteenth century.

to pass over in silence the Jewish identity of the merchant, in order to retain merely the poetic image of a caravan of camels carrying away the final remains of the Colossus.[80]

We may now return to the *Book of Revelation*.[81] When John says of the angel that 'his face was like the sun and his legs like pillars of fire',[82] his vision reminds us of the gigantic and shining statue of which Nebuchadnezzar had dreamed.[83] As the *Book of Revelation* contains numerous allusions to the *Book of Daniel*, the angel of the Apocalypse can be considered as the transformation of the statue with feet of clay, which was inspired by the Colossus of Rhodes.[84] In other words, the angel of the Apocalypse actually derives from the Colossus of Rhodes, but via the statue with feet of clay.

The Height of the Statue

Seventy Cubits

Pliny attributes to the Colossus of Rhodes a height of 70 cubits.[85] We have seen that his testimony depended on information that Mucianus had gathered *in situ*,[86] which would suggest that the number transmitted by him is correct and that the unit of measure used is not Roman but Rhodian. The epigram cited by Strabo confirms this reasoning,[87] since it attributes the same height to the statue and since its Greek origin is not in doubt.[88] Several later authors, including Pseudo-Philo of Byzantium in his detailed account of the casting technique used by Chares, likewise mention a *kolossós* of 70 cubits.[89] Alternative figures, spread among non-authoritative sources,[90] are better explained by confusion with the Colossus of

---

[80] Among the authors cited above, p. 69, n. 47, such is the case in Vedder, Brodersen, Piel, and Mattusch.
[81] Above, pp. 68–69.   [82] Rev. 10:1.   [83] Daniel 2:31–45.   [84] Above, pp. 69–71.
[85] The speculations of T. Thieme (1988) 164–167 on 'the canon of Pliny for the Colossus of Rhodes' are pointless.
[86] Above, p. 64.   [87] *Anth. Plan.* 82 (above, p. 53).
[88] Cf. Albertson (2001) 105.
[89] [Philo Byzantius] p. 30, l. 10 (Brodersen; below, pp. 80–82, §1); Strabo 14 [*Chr.* 18]; Isid. *Etym.* 14.6.22; Eust. *Commentarii in Dionysium Periegetem* 504 (*GGM* II, p. 312, ll. 8–9); *Excerpta Vaticana* p. 89 (Festa) = *Codex Vaticanus Graecus* 305, f. 197v (Brodersen 23). The so-called *Appendix* to Vibius Sequester = *Codex Vaticanus Latinus* 4929, f. 149v (Brodersen 18) gives 105 ft, which stands for 70 cubits (1 cubit = 1.5 ft) and does not imply that the Colossus was actually 105 *Roman* feet in height, *pace* Moreno (1994b) 138.
[90] 19/60 or 600/1600 cubits: *Scholia Alexandrina in orationes Greg. Naz.* (Brodersen 13 and 14). 60 cubits: *Scholia in Luc.* 24.12 (about *Icar.* 12). 80 cubits: Constantinus Porphyrogenitus *De admin. imper.* 21, l. 61 (*PG* CXIII, 205C); Georgius Cedrenus, *Compendium historiarum* I, p. 755, l. 13 (Bekker; *PG* CXXI, 825B); *Anth. Plan.* 82 (see above, p. 53). More than 100 cubits: Ampelius *Liber memorialis* 8.19 (interpolation). 600 cubits: Nicetas Heracleensis *Commentarii in XVI orationes Greg. Naz.* 67, ll. 17–19 (Constantinescu; Brodersen 20; above, p. 22). 90 ft: [Hyg.] *Fab.* 223 (Brodersen 6). 107 ft: Michael the Syrian *Chronicle* IV, p. 430a, ll. 25–31 (Chabot: II, pp. 442–443, for the French translation). 125 ft: [Beda Venerabilis] *De septem miraculis huius mundi* (Brodersen 16). 127 ft: Georgius Cedrenus *Compendium historiarum* I p. 377, ll. 15–16 (Bekker; *PG* CXXI, 416D).

Nero,[91] copyists' errors, and authors' mere imagination, rather than by the optional inclusion of the base[92] or conversion of one local cubit to another.[93] Unfortunately, the exact length of the Rhodian cubit is unknown.[94] If we base our calculation on an average 'Doric' measure of 49 cm,[95] we may estimate the height of the Colossus at $c.70 \times 0.49 = c.34.3$ m.[96]

The Base

The base that accommodated the statue of Chares poses two additional problems: its height and its inclusion in the total height of the monument. Some parallels will help to address these problems. The gigantic Colossus that Zenodorus built for Nero originally stood in the vestibule of the Domus Aurea.[97] Under the reign of Hadrian, it was moved in front of the Meta Sudans, in close proximity to the Colosseum (Fig. 4.2).[98] A new base needed to be built for the statue: discovered in 1828 and destroyed in 1933, it measured 17.6 × 14.75 m, with a preserved height of 2.25 m[99] (Fig. 4.3). Even if these numbers do not account for the marble facing,

Fig. 4.2 Medallion of Gordian III (reverse) depicting the Flavian Amphitheatre; on the left, the Meta Sudans and, behind, the Colossus of Nero; on the right, a porch with a smaller statue. Legend: MVNIFICENTIA GORDIANI IMP (British Museum, inv. R.5048; scale 1:1).

---

[91] Below, pp. 77–79.   [92] Dombart (1970) 71; R. Higgins (1989) 130.
[93] Dickie (1996) 252 n. 42, wrongly attributes this hypothesis to R. Higgins (1989) 130.
[94] Moreno (1994b) 138 wrongly gives a value of 0.525 m to the Rhodian cubit (as if it were identical to the royal Egyptian cubit) and a height of 60 cubits to the statue (while citing the epigram that states the statue was 70 cubits tall). His error returns in Albertson (2001) 105 and later in Marlowe (2006) 226 and Mason (2013) 24.
[95] Büsing (1982) 9: 48.979 cm; M. W. Jones (2000) 73–93: 1.5 × 32.7 = 49.05 cm.
[96] According to Livadiotti (1996) 21, the Rhodian stadium would be based on a foot of 33.46 cm, which would suppose a cubit measurement of 33.46 × 1.5 = 50.19 cm. The height of the Colossus would thus be $c.70 \times 0.5019 = 35.133$ m. A foot noticeably smaller could have been used at Lindos; Dyggve (1960) 89 mentions the number 29.5 cm, but Lindos was not Rhodes, and the number remains problematic.
[97] Suet. *Nero* 31.   [98] *Hist. Aug., Hadr.* 19.12.   [99] Lega (1989–1990) 342.

Fig. 4.3 Base of the Colossus of Nero next to the Flavian Amphitheatre, photographed in 1890 (Gabinetto Fotografico Nazionale, D-2041).

which was removed before 1828, the height of the base, compared to that of the statue, clearly was modest (it is incidentally not visible on the medallion illustrated in Fig. 4.2). We should also consider the 30-cubit Apollo cast by Calamis,[100] as depicted on coins from Apollonia Pontica (Fig. 4.4),[101] whose base seems to be approximately ten times shorter than the statue and thus around 3 cubits (less than 1.5 m) in height. The solution adopted by Chares certainly was not different. Pseudo-Philo of Byzantium states that the footprint (*íchnos*) of the Rhodian base 'exceeded the other statues'.[102] Whatever the exact sense of this expression, it would not have been used if the height of this base had been noticeably greater than 2 m, as is the case with modern giant statues, including the statue of Saint Charles Borromeo or *Sancarlone* at Arona (total height: 32.1 m; base: 10.7 m),[103] the *Bavaria* of Munich (total height: 27.44 m; base: 8.92 m),[104] or the *Liberty Enlightening the World* in New York (total height: 93 m; base: 47 m).[105] The hypothesis of a base 15 m high, developed by Albert Gabriel[106] and accepted (with some variation) by Maria Dawid[107] and Wolfram Hoepfner,[108] is clearly anachronistic. The compressive

---

[100] Plin. *HN* 34.40. Cf. below, pp. 90–91. [101] See Lacroix (1949) 248.
[102] [Philo Byzantius] p. 32, ll. 5–6 (Brodersen; below, pp. 80–82, §3); cf. Chapter 6, p. 132.
[103] Rejna (1823) 30.   [104] Kretzschmar (1990) 75.   [105] Lemoine (1986) 218.
[106] Gabriel (1932) 337.   [107] Dawid (1968) 42: 8–13 m.
[108] Hoepfner (2000) 145: 18 m. Hoepfner (2003) 80: 9 m. Cf. Anniboletti (2024) 16.

Fig. 4.4 Silver tetradrachm from Apollonia Pontica (obverse), depicting a statue sculpted by Calamis, accompanied by the legend 'Apollo the Doctor' (Ἀπόλλωνος Ἰατρός) and the letters AΘ-H on the reverse, second century BC (Triton XII, lot 128, ex Sternberg XXV, lot 82; scale 1:1).

strength of Greek marbles ranging from $c.357$ to $c.843$ kg/cm^2,[109] a statue as heavy as the Colossus of Rhodes could have been built on a base with dimensions comparable to that of the Colossus of Nero.

Pliny shows no interest in the bases of the *colossi*. As we shall see,[110] there are even positive reasons to admit that, when discussing the height of the Colossus of Nero, he deliberately ignored the base of the statue. We thus may accept that the Colossus of Rhodes was a statue of 70 cubits = $c.34$ m resting on a base of at least $c.2$ m, with the total height of the monument slightly more than 36 m.

The Original Project

We may recall that, according to Posidippus, Chares would have divided the initial height planned for the statue by two, while, according to Sextus Empiricus, he would have multiplied it by as much.[111] This disagreement[112] places us in a bind, as the most trustworthy source relates the least believable information. It seems impossible that the Rhodians considered raising a statue of 2×70 cubits, or $c.68$ m. If the version related by Sextus Empiricus is at first glance more credible, it is hardly correct. The Rhodians would not have planned to erect a statue of $70 \div 2 = 35$ cubits, which would have conceded 5 cubits to the Zeus of 40 cubits that Lysippus had constructed at Tarentum (unless we admit that the Rhodian cubit was longer than the Tarentine and that the Rhodians took this fact into account, which is not only unlikely[113] but also contrary to the ancient way of measuring oversized statues).[114]

---

[109] Papantonopoulos (2006) 262.   [110] Below, p. 89.   [111] Above, p. 63.
[112] Unnoticed by Moreno (2013) 52.
[113] *Pace* Moreno (1994b) 56, 58 and Moreno (1995a) 278 who argues that the height of the Zeus of Tarentum would have been $c.15.72$–17.76 m (1994a) or $c.15$–16 m (1995a), without providing a reference for the length he attributes to the local cubit (see above p. 73, n. 89 and p. 74, n. 94 for his confusion about the Rhodian cubit and the height of the Colossus).
[114] Below, p. 79.

On the other hand, it would be tempting to suppose, after Posidippus, that the initial intention of the Rhodians was to build a statue 'twice as large' as the Zeus of Tarentum, consequently with a height of 80 cubits. After examining the technical possibilities at his disposal, Chares would have stopped at a height of 70 cubits, which he established as the unsurpassable maximum. It then would be necessary to assume that Posidippus evoked the Zeus of Tarentum in a lost epigram, which would have immediately preceded that dedicated to the Colossus. The coherency of the poem *On the Making of Statues* makes such a hypothesis unlikely[115] but is not sufficient to disprove it, since the tiny chariot sculpted by Theodoros (*Epigram* 67) could have been indifferently contrasted with the Colossus of Chares (*Epigram* 68)[116] or with the Zeus of Lysippus. In view of the extant documentation, however, I prefer to accept an exaggeration on the part of Posidippus and an error on the part of Sextus Empiricus.

The Highest Statue of the Ancient World

Let us return to Pliny, who dealt with the statues of Chares and Zenodorus within a chapter devoted to *colossi* (a term that, as the *kolossós* of Strabo, then applied to any oversized statue).[117] The list drawn up by Pliny allows us to follow the race towards gigantism in which the bronze artists participated. In the fifth century, Calamis had raised an Apollo of 30 cubits for Apollonia Pontica (after sacking the city in 72 BC, Marcus Terentius Varro Lucullus had it transported to Rome and set up as a trophy on the Capitoline).[118] In the fourth century, Lysippus had managed to construct a Zeus of 40 cubits for Tarentum (having taken the city in 209 BC, Quintus Fabius Verrucosus found it too large to be part of his spoils).[119] Several decades later, Chares had constructed a Helios of 70 cubits for the Rhodians[120] (having entered their walls in 42 BC, Cassius was probably not interested in its ruins).[121] It would take four centuries for Zenodorus to erect a statue of comparable height: the Colossus portraying the emperor Nero.[122] A short interval of time but a great difference in height separate the Zeus of Tarentum and the Colossus of Rhodes. Inversely, a long interval of time but no significative difference in height separates the Colossus of Rhodes from its Roman twin. The technical feat of Chares is obvious, but who eventually won the race? Writing around AD 85, Martial seems clear about it:

---

[115] On the organization of the epigrams contained in *P. Mil. Vogl.* VIII 309, see Seidensticker et al. (2015) 11–16 and Gutzwiller (2019) 357–361; on the section about statues more specifically, see Gutzwiller (2002) 41–59 and Seidensticker (2015) 247–250.
[116] Prioux (2007) 122–123.   [117] Above, pp. 50–51.   [118] Plin. *HN* 34.39.
[119] Plin. *HN* 34.40.   [120] Plin. *HN* 34.41 (above, pp. 64–65).
[121] Val. Max. 1.5.8; Cass. Dio 47.33.6.   [122] Plin. *HN* 34.45–47.

78   THE *KOLOSSÓS* OF RHODES

nec te detineat miri radiata colossi
   quae Rhodium moles vincere gaudet opus.

Do not be delayed by the rayed mass of the marvellous colossus that joys to outdo the work of Rhodes.[123]

According to Suetonius, the height of the Colossus of Nero was 120 ft,[124] but an official document from the reign of Diocletian (known from later sources) indicated that the statue, which had seven rays of 22.5 ft, was 106.5 ft in height.[125] In all likelihood, Pliny the Elder also attributed a height of 106.5 ft to the statue.[126] The most simple solution is to assume that the statue measured 106.5 ft = 71 cubits, and that the total height of the monument, base included, was 120 ft = 80 cubits[127] (unless this number was an expression of Neronian propaganda or the *opinio communis*, which for us would make little difference). We should note that these numbers correspond to the heights that several late authors have erroneously attributed to the Colossus of Rhodes, frequently confused, as we recall, with its Roman twin.[128] The clearest case is provided by the *Chronicle* of Michael the Syrian, which gives to the Colossus of Rhodes the height, rounded to 107 ft,[129] attributed by Eusebius to the Colossus of Nero.[130] We may wonder if the height of 80 cubits = 120 ft, given by Constantinus Porphyrogenitus,[131] Georgios Kedrenos,[132] and Maximus Planudes[133] to the Colossus of Rhodes in their altered versions of the epigram cited by Strabo,[134] does not echo (through an intermediary Greek source) the 120 ft that Suetonius attributes to the Colossus of Nero. The same question arises concerning the 125 ft from Pseudo-Bede,[135] who could refer back to the number cited by Suetonius (which would have been altered by the manuscript tradition).

---

[123] Mart. 1.70.7–8, with the translation of D. R. Shackleton Bailey.   [124] Suet. *Nero* 31.
[125] Valentini and Zucchetti (1940) 100, 169, 192, and 212.
[126] See the complete *apparatus criticus* in Le Bonniec and Gallet de Santerre (1953) 123. The best manuscript (*Bambergensis*) has *qui nonaginta*. Urlichs (1857) 314, followed by most editors of Pliny, supposed *CXIXS* → *CVIXC* → *qui nonaginta*. Detlefsen (1873) 78 rightly preferred *CVIS*→ *CVIXC*, since *CVIS* rather than *CXIXS* appears in other sources. It is true that Suet. *Nero* 31 refers to the *colossus CXX pedum* sponsored by the emperor, but *CXX pedum* stands here for *LXXX cubitorum* and thus cannot be regarded as a rounding of *CXIXS*.
[127] These two ratios escaped Albertson (2001) 105, who supposes that the Colossus of Nero had a height of 60.04 'Rhodian cubits', which was certainly not the case. As this was a Roman statue, it would have been measured according to Roman standards; the value attributed to the 'Rhodian cubit' is also unproven (see above, p. 74, n. 94).
[128] Above, p. 68.
[129] Michael the Syrian *Chronicle* IV p. 430a, ll. 25–31 (Chabot: II pp. 442–443, for the French translation).
[130] Euseb. *Chron.* II p. 159 (Schoene). Cf. Conrad (1996) 184.
[131] Constantinus Porphyrogenitus *De admin. imper.* 21, ll. 61–62 (*PG* CXIII, 205C).
[132] Georgius Cedrenus, *Compendium historiarum* I, p. 755, ll. 13–14 (Bekker; *PG* CXXI, 825B).
[133] *Anth. Plan.* 82.   [134] Strabo 14.2.5. See Chapter 3, p. 53.
[135] [Beda Venerabilis] *De septem miraculis huius mundi* (Brodersen 16).

By contrast with the height attributed to the Colossus of Nero, the Greek records mentioned in the *Natural History* of Pliny are all whole numbers, expressed in multiples of 10 cubits. On the other hand, the epigram cited by Strabo attributed to the statue of Chares a height of 'seven times ten cubits'.[136] It is thus clear that, in the Greek tradition, colossal statues were measured in tens of cubits, which was a way of compensating for aberrations in measurement due to the fact that the length of the cubit varied from city to city.

The strange measurements of the statue commissioned by Nero can now be explained. A Greek sculptor working for a philhellene emperor remembered for his 'aggressive competitiveness' (which was only one facet of his megalomania),[137] Zenodorus ensured that the *nominal* height of the Colossus of Rome was, in all respects, greater than that of the Colossus of Rhodes. Excluding the base, his sculpture would have surpassed that of Chares only by a single cubit, since 106.5 ft = 71 cubits; including the base, it would have surpassed it by 10 cubits, since 120 ft = 80 cubits.

Nevertheless, the Colossus of Rhodes measured 70 cubits without its base, and, although we do not know its exact value, the Rhodian cubit must have been significantly longer than the Roman cubit ($c.$490 mm vs 444 mm). While the Colossus of Rome measured 71 Roman cubits = 71 × 0.444 = 31.524 m without its base and 80 × 0.444 = 35.52 m with its base (if the explanation of the different numbers transmitted by the manuscript tradition is correct), the Colossus of Rhodes measured $c.$34.3 m without its base, and more than 36 m with its base.[138] In other terms, no ancient sculptor succeeded in equalling the record in height achieved by Chares. In bronze statuary, this record would only be surpassed in 1886, at the moment of the unveiling of the *Liberty Enlightening the World.* How did Chares accomplish such a feat?

Building the Statue

The Casting Process and the Signature of Chares

An author who may have lived between the fourth and the sixth century AD, wrongly identified with the engineer Philo of Byzantium (active in the third century BC),[139] provides a description of the Colossus all the more remarkable, in spite of the clichés scattered throughout,[140] as its specifications

---

[136] *Anth. Plan.* 82, v. 1 (above, p. 53).   [137] Champlin (2003) 58–59.
[138] Above, p. 76.
[139] Fabricius (1716) 590; Kroll (1941) 54; Łanowski (1985) 31–47; Adam and Blanc (1989) 21–45; Condello and Fioridi (2023) 14–36, 55–83; cf. De Choiseul-Gouffier (1782) 363.
[140] Adam and Blanc (1989) 44–45; Dickie (1996) 254–256.

appear in no other chapters of his treatise on the *Seven Wonders*, which lack any technical details:[141]

§1 Ῥόδος ἐστὶ πελαγία νῆσος, ἣν τὸ παλαιὸν ἐν βυθῷ κρυπτομένην Ἥλιος ἀνέδειξεν αἰτησάμενος παρὰ θεῶν ἰδίαν γενέσθαι τὴν ἀναφανεῖσαν. ἐν ταύτῃ κολοσσὸς ἔστη πήχεων ἑβδομήκοντα διεσκευασμένος εἰς Ἥλιον· ἡ γὰρ εἰκὼν τοῦ θεοῦ συμβόλοις ἐγινώσκετο τοῖς ἐξ ἐκείνου. τοσοῦτον δ' ὁ τεχνίτης ἐδαπάνησεν χαλκόν, ὅσος σπανίζειν ἤμελλεν τὰ μέταλλα· τὸ γὰρ χώνευμα τοῦ κατασκευάσματος ἐγένετο χαλκούργημα τοῦ κόσμου.

§2 μήποτε δὲ διὰ τοῦτο ὁ Ζεὺς Ῥοδίοις θεσπέσιον κατέχευε πλοῦτον, ἵνα τοῦτον εἰς τὴν Ἡλίου δαπανήσω ἔχευε πλοῦτον, ἵνα τοῦτον εἰς τὴν Ἡλίου δαπανήσωσι τιμήν, τὴν εἰκόνα τοῦ θεοῦ ταῖς ἐπιβολαῖς ἀπὸ γῆς εἰς τὸν οὐρανὸν ἀναβιβάζοντες· τοῦτον ὁ τεχνίτης ἔσωθεν μὲν σχεδίαις σιδηραῖς καὶ τετραπέδοις διησφαλίσατο λίθοις, ὧν οἱ διάπηγες μοχλοὶ κυκλώπιον ἐμφαίνουσι ῥαιστηροκοπίαν, καὶ τὸ κεκρυμμένον τοῦ πόνου τῶν βλεπομένων μεῖζόν ἐστιν· ἐπαπορεῖ γὰρ ὁ θαυμαστὴς τῶν θεωρούντων ποίαις πυράγραις ἢ πηλίκαις ὑποστάσεσιν ἀκμόνων ἢ ποταπαῖς ὑπηρετῶν ῥώμαις τὰ τηλικαῦτα βάρη τῶν ὀβελίσκων ἐχαλκεύθη.

§3 ὑποθεὶς δὲ βάσιν ἐκ λευκῆς καὶ μαρμαρίτιδος πέτρας ἐπ' αὐτῆς μέχρι τῶν ἀστραγάλων πρώτους ἤρεισε τοὺς πόδας τοῦ κολοσσοῦ, νοῶν τὴν συμμετρίαν ἐφ' ὧν ἤμελλε θεὸς ἑβδομηκοντάπηχυς ἐγείρεσθαι· τὸ γὰρ ἴχνος τῆς βάσεως ἤδη τοὺς ἄλλους ἀνδριάντας ὑπερέκυπτεν. τοιγαροῦν οὐκ ἐνῆν ἐπιθεῖναι βαστάσαντα τὸ λοιπόν· ἐπιχωνεύειν δ' ἔδει τὰ σφυρά, καὶ καθάπερ ἐπὶ τῶν οἰκοδομουμένων ἀναβῆναι τὸ πᾶν ἔργον ἐπ' αὐτοῦ.

§4 καὶ διὰ τοῦτο τοὺς μὲν ἄλλους ἀνδριάντας οἱ τεχνῖται πλάσσουσι πρῶτον, εἶτα κατὰ μέλη διελόντες χωνεύουσιν καὶ τέλος ὅλους συνθέντες ἔστησαν· οὗτος δὲ τῷ πρώτῳ χωνεύματι τὸ δεύτερον μέρος ἐπιπέπλαστῷ πρώτῳ χωνεύματι τὸ δεύτερον μέρος ἐπιπέπλασται, καὶ τούτῳ χαλκουργηθέντι τὸ τρίτον ἐπιδεδώμηται.καὶ τὸ μετὰ τοῦτο πάλιν τὴν αὐτὴν τῆς ἐργασίας ἔσχηκεν ἐπίνοιαν· οὐ γὰρ ἐνῆν τὰ μέλη τῶν μετάλλων κινῆσαι.

§5 τῆς χωνείας δὲ γενομένης ἐπὶ τῶν προτετελεσμένων ἔργων αἵ τε διαιρέσεις τῶν μοχλῶν καὶ τὸ πῆγμα τῆς σχεδίας ἐτηρεῖτο καὶ τῶν ἐντιθεμένων πετρῶν ἠσφαλίζετο τὸ σήκωμα, ἵνα διὰ τῆς ἐργασίας τηρήσῃ τὴν ἐπίνοιαν ἀσάλευτον, ἀεὶ τοῖς οὔπω συντελεσθεῖσιν μέλεσι τοῦ κολοσσοῦ χοῦν γῆς ἄπλατον περιχέων, κρύπτων τὸ πεπονημένον ἤδη κατάγειον τὴν τῶν ἐχομένων ἐπίπεδον ἐποιεῖτο χωνείαν.

---

[141] Romer and Romer (1995) wrongly claim that the entire treatise has the quality of the chapter dedicated to the Colossus, in order to be able to attribute it to Philo Mechanicus, which does not prevent them from arguing (p. 37) that this chapter is not technically credible, against archaeological evidence provided by the Nara Buddha (see below, pp. 82–83), not mentioned by the authors.

§6 ἐκ δὲ τοῦ κατ' ὀλίγον ἀναβὰς ἐπὶ τὸ τέρμα τῆς ἐλπίδος καὶ πεντακόσια μὲν χαλκοῦ τάλαντα δαπανήσας, τριακόσια δὲ σιδήρου τῷ θεῷ τὸν θεὸν ἴσον ἐποίησεν, μέγα τῇ τόλμῃ βαστάσας ἔργον· Ἥλιον γὰρ δεύτερον ἀντέθηκεν τῷ κόσμῳ.

§1 Rhodes is a sea island, which Helios once pointed out was hidden in the seabed. When he discovered it, he sought from the other gods to make it his own. There stood a *kolossós*, which was seventy cubits high and equipped as Helios; for the image of the god is recognizable from his salient attributes. The artist used up so much bronze on it that the mines were in danger of being exhausted; for the casting of the work was an operation which eventually involved the bronze industry of the entire world.

§2 Was it not to this end that Zeus showered divine wealth on the Rhodians, that they might spend it to the honour of Helios, raising up the image course upon course from earth to heaven? The maker ensured the stability of the statue from within by means of iron frameworks and squared stone blocks, the former connected to the latter by crossbars that looked as if they had been forged by the Cyclopes; and more labour was expended on the hidden parts of the statue than on the visible. For the astonished spectator is at a loss to imagine with what tongs, or on what mighty anvils, bars of such weight were wrought, or whence came the workforce.

§3 Having constructed a base of white marble, [the artist] first raised upon it the feet of the Colossus below the ankles, bearing in mind the proportions appropriate to a divine image which was to be seventy cubits high; for the sole of the base exceeded [the height of] the other statues. For this reason, it was not possible to hoist up the rest [of the statue] and set it on [the feet], but the ankles had to be cast on them; and, just as in building a house, the whole work had to rise on itself.

§4 And so it was that while other statues are first modelled by the artist, then dismembered and cast in section, and finally re-assembled and erected, in this case, after the first section had been cast, the second was modelled upon it, and when this had been cast in bronze, the third was raised upon it; and the same procedure was repeated throughout the rest of the work, for the bronze sections could not be moved.

§5 As each new course was cast on top of that which had already been completed, the cantilevers taken individually as well as the framework as a whole were attended to, and the counterpoise made of stone blocks put within the statue was checked, lest there should be any deviation from the original design during its execution. As each course of the Colossus was finished, a huge mound of earth was heaped up round it, hiding underground all the work already done and creating a level platform for the casting of the next course.

§6 Thus, gradually ascending towards the goal of his ambition and using up 500 talents of bronze and 300 of iron, [the artist] made the god the equal of the god, erecting by his audacity a great work; for he set up a second Helios in the world.[142]

Several details provided by Pseudo-Philo, including the size of the Colossus and the fact that heavy stones were used in its armature, are confirmed by the account of Pliny the Elder;[143] those that he does not give, beginning with the name of Chares, demonstrate that he followed a reliable source independent of the *Natural History*. This source is likely to have been written on Rhodes while the statue was being constructed or, at least, still standing,[144] perhaps by Chares himself, who is only designated as 'the artist' (*ho technítēs*): this would be a perfectly appropriate way for an ancient author to speak about himself.[145] With the notable exception of Albert Gabriel,[146] several scholars have ignored the text,[147] expressed their disbelief,[148] or failed to understand the technique as described.[149] The sculptor Herbert Maryon, for example, argued that the Colossus, like the Statue of Liberty, had been made of thin sheets of metal riveted to internal supports.[150] Correcting this error in 1957, Denys Haynes stressed that Chares had not worked like Auguste Bartholdi, nor had he assembled large bronze sections cast in a distant pit as ancient sculptors normally would have; as Pseudo-Philo made clear, he had over-laid horizontal courses cast *in situ*.[151] Returning to the subject in 1992, Haynes observed that the latter author was 'strikingly vindicated in this particular—and illuminated in general—by the contemporary record of the casting in AD 747–749 of the Daibutsu or Great Buddha of Nara' in Japan'. With an original height of 16.21 m and a weight of *c.*250 tonnes, this statue had been cast in eight courses. On the base intended to accommodate the statue was constructed a wooden frame, surrounded by an interlacing of bamboo and rope. On this core was applied a thick layer of clay, in which the Buddha was fashioned. From this figure was created a mould in eight sections, after which each section was removed to be fired separately. The figure was then abraded to a thickness of *c.*5 cm (measured

---

[142] [Philo Byzantius] pp. 30–32 (Brodersen); translation from Haynes (1992) 121–122 (overlooked by Condello and Floridi [2023]), modified; cf. Haynes (1957) 311–312.
[143] Cf. Condello and Floridi (2023) 153. De Pestels [Caylus] (1759) 362, 365 supposed that Plut. *Mor.* 780A [*Ad principem ineruditum* 2] was relevant to understand the internal structure of the Colossus. This passage, however, refers to statues cast in parts and to their core; cf. Chapter 6, p. 127, n. 28.
[144] Cf. Lüders (1865) 13; Hebert (1989) 20, followed by Kansteiner et al. (2014) 647 (*DNO* 2524).
[145] Condello and Floridi (2023) 155–156 stress, however, that the author of the Temple of Artemis at Ephesus is not identified either.
[146] Gabriel (1932) 332–342.   [147] Rice (1993) 239.
[148] Brunn (1889) 293; Robert (1899) 2131; Amelung (1912b) 389; Dickie (1996) 249–257; Ekschmitt (1996) 176; Mariño Sánchez-Elvira (2008) 116–118. Lüders (1865) 13 remains cautious. On Vedder (2015) 40–56 and Vedder (2017) 21–27, see below, pp. 83–86.
[149] Queyrel (2020) 140 and the authors cited in the following note.
[150] Maryon (1956) 68–86, followed in various ways by Dawid (1968) 44; Romer and Romer (1995) 37–39; Musti and Pulcini (1996) 293; Rieger (2004) 69–85; Wujewski (2018) 306–316.
[151] Haynes (1957) 311–312.

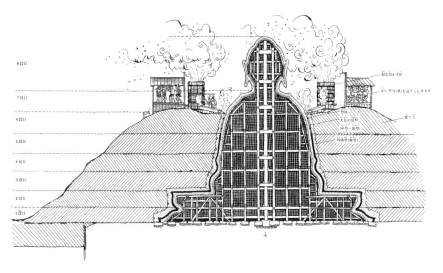

Fig. 4.5 Reconstruction of the casting by stages of the Buddha of Nara, AD 747–749.

thanks to nails placed in the clay) to become the core of the future statue. Once the lower section of the mould was set in place, it was surrounded by a mound of earth, on top of which was arranged a series of kilns, from which some 60 tonnes of bronze were simultaneously poured. The process was repeated up to the top course, as the mound surrounding the statue was progressively raised (Fig. 4.5).[152] The parallel with the testimony of Pseudo-Philo, which culminates in a reference to the 'huge mound of earth' created by Chares, is indeed remarkable. Furthermore, the statue of Nara is not the only one of its kind, since the Great Buddha at Kamakura was cast by the same technique in the thirteenth century; 11.3 m high, it weighs 120 tonnes, and the thickness of its wall varies between 1 and 12 cm (Fig. 4.6).[153]

Ursula Vedder nevertheless has tried to deny the significance of the parallel with the Nara's Buddha using the following arguments. First, while Pseudo-Philo states that 'the individual metal sections could not be moved', Greek architecture attests that extremely heavy pieces of marble could be manoeuvred and set into place.[154] Second, the largest foundry discovered on the acropolis of Rhodes, which was in use when the Colossus was being built, contains a ditch whose depth reaches 3.6 m; once assembled, the bronze pieces that were cast there allowed for the construction of statues able to attain a height of 15 m, according to Vedder, and of at least 10 m, according to the excavators (Figs 4.7 and 4.8).[155] Third, 'in important details, such as the master model and the use of wax, the description [of Pseudo-Philo] is incomplete and unreliable'. Instead of mentioning 'the making of a core',

---

[152] Katori (1981); Haynes (1992) 121–128.
[153] Maruyasu and Oshima (1965) 53–63; Sekino (1965) 39–46; Toishi (1965) 47–52; Fujisawa and Hemuki (2019) 16–24.
[154] Dawid (1968) 43 already had developed a similar argument against Pseudo-Philo's credibility.
[155] Kantzia and Zimmer (1989) 522 n. 81; Zimmer and Bairami (2008) 51 n. 132.

Fig. 4.6 Buddha of Kamakura, thirteenth century AD.

Fig. 4.7 Foundry no. 1 from the Mylonas plot at Rhodes, active around 300–275 BC.

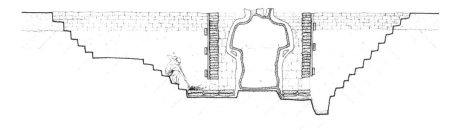

Fig. 4.8 Statue being cast 'in parts'.

Pseudo-Philo also would have incorrectly described 'a framework within the statue, growing higher with every cast course'. The method thus would be not only useless, but also unrealistic: 'it is not a factual account but rather a reconstruction of the casting of the Colossus'.[156]

---

[156] Vedder (2017) 21–27, by a slip of the pen, places the workshops of Rhodes 'in the city of Athens' (p. 22); cf. Vedder (2015) 40–56.

None of these arguments are acceptable. Blocks of marble are neither manoeuvred nor assembled as pieces of bronze are cast and welded. If the excavations at Rhodes have proved one thing, it is that the largest foundry discovered in the city, which has no rival in the whole ancient world, was *not* capable of producing statues comparable to the Colossus, even if one takes into account the figures of Vedder, which exceed the estimate of the excavators but are compatible with the testimony of Polybius, who mentions the thirty-cubit statue of the People of Rome that the Rhodians erected in the sanctuary of Athena; the height of this statue (produced in an unidentified foundry) would have been *c*.14 m, close to the 15 m admitted by Vedder (for the largest foundry excavated on the acropolis) but still far from the *c*.34 m of the Colossus.[157] It is true that the description of Pseudo-Philo is incomplete, but how can we blame a paradoxographer for not mentioning a 'master model', which, if it existed, was certainly of no interest to him? As for 'the use of wax', its mention is out of place, since it was not involved in the casting in courses. It is true that, according to Pseudo-Philo, the statue was cast around a structure which itself was raised level by level.[158] This would be a notable difference from the Buddha of Nara, whose internal structure was completed before the casting started. This difference could be justified, however, by the fact that the Colossus' structure was not made of bamboo but of blocks whose towing and set-up may have been facilitated by the mound used for the casting of each level. To return to the hypothesis of Vedder, I cannot see why Pseudo-Philo or his source would have propagated the falsehood that the Colossus was not built in the manner of other statues. Nor am I ready to accept that a writer invented a casting technique rediscovered by Japanese artists several centuries later, as even the largest bronze statues of his time (the late Imperial period) were still cast in pieces.[159] The error of Vedder stems from the fact that she based her reasoning on the premise that the traces of the Colossus '*must be* discoverable in the city of Rhodes' (my italics); in her hypothesis, an enclosure dug on the acropolis of Rhodes in the pre-war period by Italian archaeologists would be the pit where the statue would have been assembled.[160] Nevertheless, there is no reason why the workshop of Chares should have left its traces in a city whose ground has been turned over quite frequently since antiquity; the construction sites in which Zenodorus built his giant statues, in Gaul and then in Rome, have left no trace either.[161] As for the enclosure on the Rhodian acropolis, it cannot have functioned as a workshop but was used for the cult of Artemis.[162]

---

[157] Polyb. 31.4.4.
[158] Misunderstanding Pseudo-Philo, De Pestels [Caylus] (1759) 365 supposed that the stones were added after the bronze had been cast.
[159] e.g. Darblade-Audoin and Mille (2008) 31–68 and Mille and Darblade-Audoin (2012).
[160] Vedder (2017) 26; the hypothesis is fully developed in Vedder (2015) 57–69.
[161] Cf. Darblade-Audoin and Mille (2008) 50; Mille and Darblade-Audoin (2012) §18.
[162] Chapter 6, pp. 148–150.

It is thus pointless to reject the testimony of Pseudo-Philo, which is reinforced by two clues. On one hand, according to Strabo,[163] the Colossus did not break at the height of its ankles, which normally constituted the weakest part of a statue,[164] but at its knees. It may well be that these joints corresponded to the boundary between two courses of the statue, dismantled by the earthquake of *c*.227 BC (the Buddha of Kamakura also suffered from earthquakes but had its various courses firmly interlocked by means of a process called '*ikarakuri*', which made up for their lack of fusion).[165] On the other hand, to designate the 'casting' of the statue, Posidippus uses the verb *chalkourgéō*,[166] not attested before the first century BC,[167] except in the signatures of Rhodian sculptors.[168] This verb almost certainly appeared in the signature of Chares,[169] who may have preferred it to the traditional *poiéō* for the precise reason that the Colossus had not been fashioned by a traditional method, but by means of a revolutionary casting process. On the other hand, the authentic name of the sculptor was 'Chares of Rhodes';[170] purely literary, the formula 'Chares of Lindos' was even less appropriate for the base of the Colossus, since the statue was an offering raised by the entire city of Rhodes, and not by one of its constituent communities (Ialysos, Kamiros, or Lindos).[171] Thus, the signature may have read:

Χάρης Ῥόδιος ἐχαλκούργησε [or ἐχαλκούργει, as in Posidippus].

Chares of Rhodes worked (this statue) in bronze.

Pseudo-Philo incidentally uses the same verb to explain how the Colossus was built. As it was still rare in his time, it could have been borrowed from the source on which his description of the statue depended (as we have seen, this source was probably written at Rhodes in the third century BC, perhaps by Chares himself).[172]

The Internal Structure

Pseudo-Philo's text remains insufficiently precise to satisfy our curiosity. Whereas the concept of casting in courses is clearly described (although the process by which these courses were united is not even mentioned), the two paragraphs

---

[163] Strabo 14.18.   [164] As already noticed by Roux (1960) 13, 15–16.
[165] Sekino (1965) 30; Toishi (1965) 50. Technical objections by Romer and Romer (1995) 37 are thus pointless.
[166] AB 68.6.   [167] Diod. Sic. 9.19.1.
[168] Badoud (2015) 278–287. For the third century alone, see nos. 24 (*TC* 92, *c*.280–270 BC), 30 (*Lindos* 84, *c*.264 BC?), 31 (*SER* 51a, *c*.266–257 BC), 57 (*IK 41-Knidos* I, 111, *c*.220 BC), 61 (*Lindos* 137, *c*.215 BC), 62 (*TC* 41, 214 BC), 63 (*Lindos* 119, *c*.214 BC), and 65 (*NESM* 31, *c*.210 BC).
[169] The epigraphic evidence is entirely omitted by Papini (2022) 186, which allows him to states that the hypothesis already developed in Badoud (2011a) 121 is 'not necessary'. Cf. Sens and Keesling (2004) 75–76.
[170] Chapter 3, p. 52.   [171] Chapter 1, p. 7.   [172] Above, p. 82.

dealing with the internal structure of the statue (2 and 5) are obscure. They agree on the facts that the statue had a core built of blocks of stone and that '*obeliskoí*' ('bars of metal') were used both to join these blocks together and to connect them to the bronze walls of the statue. In the first paragraph, Pseudo-Philo terms as '*mochloí*' ('cross-bars') the elements used to join the blocks, and as '*schedíai*' ('parts of a frame'?)[173] the elements connecting the walls to the core; he says that the '*schedíai*' are made of iron. In the second paragraph, the meanings of '*mochloí*' and '*schedía*' (no longer used in the plural but in the singular) are reversed. Pseudo-Philo thus uses '*mochloí*' in a way which reminds us of Lucian in his *Gallus*,[174] where they probably designate the bars used to maintain the core of *kolossoí* (i.e. 'oversized statues') cast with the indirect lost-wax process.[175] It seems that Pseudo-Philo uses '*schedía*' to designate the joining of the stones as a whole.

Gabriel believed that upon horizontal *mochloí* were assembled *schedíai*, which he defined as 'rods of iron fashioned in the forge and hugging approximately the form of the statue.'[176] Nevertheless, this interpretation (later developed by Hoepfner)[177] does not agree with the text of Pseudo-Philo. It additionally supposes a system of bonding whose nature Gabriel himself was not in a position to define; the tubes and clamps visible on his sketch[178] are anachronistic and were most probably inspired by the iron framework that Gustave Eiffel designed for the Statue of Liberty.[179] Whenever iron bars were used in Greek architecture, they reinforced or lightened structures, or acted as cantilevers.[180] The *mochloí* of the Colossus of Rhodes could correspond to the latter use, if we suppose that their internal end was embedded in the stone, while the external end was held in the bronze that formed the wall of the statue. This hypothesis has two pieces of evidence in support. The first is philological: *mochlós* itself has the general meaning of 'lever', and Pseudo-Philo calls the stones arranged in the interior of the statue the *sḗkōma* ('weight' or 'counterpoise'). The second is technical: as the point when iron melts (1538° C) was much higher than that of bronze (+/− 890° C, depending on the alloy), the *mochloí* could withstand the casting of the statue wall.

A Huge Mound of Earth

According to Pseudo-Philo, the casting technique implemented by Chares resulted in the formation of a 'huge mound of earth'.[181] Gabriel calculated that the Colossus,

---

[173] *LSJ*, s.v. σχεδία (II), translates the word as 'cramp, holdfast' but provides no attestation other than the text of Pseudo-Philo for this meaning.
[174] Lucianus *Gallus* 24.   [175] On this process, see Haynes (1992) 42–74.
[176] Gabriel (1932) 334, followed by Laurenzi (1959) 773–774.
[177] Hoepfner (2000) 146–150; Hoepfner (2003) 94–97.   [178] Gabriel (1932) 339.
[179] Talansier (1883) 464–465; cf. Trachtenberg (1976) 125–143; Lemoine (1986) 121–141; Provoyeur (1986b) 126–130; Belot and Bermont (2004) 333–338.
[180] Dinsmoor (1922) 148–158; Coulton (1977) 149–151.
[181] [Philo Byzantius] p. 32, l. 23 (Brodersen; above, pp. 80–82, §5).

to which he ascribed an exaggerated height of more than 40 m,[182] would have required the construction of a mound of earth exceeding 100 m in diameter. To avoid this impediment, Chares would have progressively raised a wooden fence around the statue, with the embankment poured and the metal cast in the interior of this casing. This solution is clever but was inspired by the cramped space that Gabriel, fooled by the medieval myth locating the Colossus in the harbour of Rhodes, wrongly attributed to the statue.[183] Furthermore, it contradicts the text of Pseudo-Philo, which does not refer to any scaffolding but insists on the amount of earth spread around the statue. Figure 4.5, which illustrates the casting of the Daibutsu, provides some idea. At Rhodes, as at Nara, a perimeter wall and earthworks could have reduced the footprint of the embankment. It is worth stressing that the technique described by Pseudo-Philo and embodied by the Japanese Buddhas is fully at odds with the existence of a base *c*.15 m in height, which Gabriel and his followers conjectured against ancient evidence, with the Statue of Liberty in mind;[184] such a base would have increased enormously but unnecessarily the volume of earth required for a casting in courses.

The Materials and the Cost of the Statue

The quantities of metal necessary for the construction remain difficult to calculate. As it passed down to us, the treatise on the *Seven Wonders* mentions 500 talents of bronze and 300 talents of iron, but these numbers, perhaps invented by Pseudo-Philo, are clearly too low. In the first place, they are too low in the light of the technique employed. By calculating 25 kg per talent, and by attributing to the Colossus a height of 120 ft (*c*.36.5 m), Maryon has estimated that the riveted bronze sheets which he wrongly[185] attributed to the statue would have been even thinner than those of the Statue of Liberty (1.5 vs 2.37 mm).[186] The numbers are also too low in view of the cost of 300 silver talents that Pliny attributes to the works,[187] when he notes that this sum was gathered from the sale of the siege machines of Demetrius.[188] At a conversion rate of 125:1, which may have been in effect during the first half of the third century BC,[189] 500 talents of bronze were

---

[182] Above, p. 75.   [183] Chapter 6, pp. 129–131.
[184] Above, p. 75, and Chapter 7, p. 201.   [185] Above, p. 82.   [186] Maryon (1956) 74.
[187] According to Lucianus *Iupp. Trag.* 11, the construction costs of the Colossus would have equalled 'sixteen golden gods', but this estimate is probably fanciful. In any case, it is rendered useless in view of our ignorance of the price of a 'golden god'.
[188] Plin. *HN* 34.41 (above, pp. 64–65). On the origin of the funds used by the Rhodians, see Chapter 6, pp. 133–134; cf. Chapter 7, pp. 212–213.
[189] Doyen (2012) 51.

only worth four silver talents; at the minimal rate of conversion of 1200:1,[190] 300 talents of iron cannot have represented more than one-quarter of a silver talent. Byzantine tradition has equally been cited to demonstrate the error of Pseudo-Philo. After the attack of Mu'awiyah against Rhodes, 900 or even 980 camels would have been necessary to carry away the remains of the Colossus.[191] As the standard load of each animal was $c.$300 kg,[192] the caravan could have transported between 270 and 294 tonnes, or more than 10,000 talents of metal. Yet, we have seen that the Byzantine tradition was derived from a forgery of the chronicler Theophilus of Edessa.[193] Thus, we cannot invoke it to reject the number of 500 talents expressed by Pseudo-Philo,[194] but neither can we discredit Theophilus by citing this number, which is obviously erroneous.[195]

If we abandon the numbers given by Pseudo-Philo by starting from the assumption that the surface of the statue had a thickness of 5 cm, a value greater than all previous estimates,[196] but matching the parallels provided by the Japanese Buddhas, as well as the requirement to fit the *mochloí* into the walls of the statue (to say nothing about the fact that, according to Pseudo-Philo, 'the mines were in danger of being exhausted',[197] which sounds like a rhetorical exaggeration), the amount of bronze used for its construction could have been in the order of 400 tonnes. These 19,608 talents of bronze would have been worth $c.$150 silver talents,[198] or half of the price expressed by Pliny. The remaining half could have served to pay for the other materials (iron and stone, but also lead, wood, and charcoal), to finance the specialized workforce employed for twelve years at the construction site and to provide the salary of Chares, which—considering the duration of work and the importance of the monument, but also the high rates ordinarily received by bronze artists—[199] certainly rose to several talents.

The cost attributed by Pliny to the construction of the Colossus thus seems possible and dissuades us from subscribing to the correction of Ludwig Urlichs, who proposed increasing it to 1,300 talents by conjecturing the disappearance of a letter by haplography: *effectum <M>CCC talentis.*[200] It is true that, according to Polybius,[201]

---

[190] Van Driessche (2009) 92.   [191] Conrad (1996) 166–170.
[192] Bulliet (1990²) 20. Scaliger (1606) 138 suggested 800 pounds ($c.$400 kg) but committed an error of multiplication when he converted the weight carried by the whole caravan (900 × 800 = 720,000 pounds = $c.$360 tonnes → 144 quintals = 7.2 tonnes). See Bayle (1697) 811.
[193] Above, pp. 69–72.   [194] *Pace* Haynes (1957) 312; Hoepfner (2000) 146 n. 33.
[195] *Pace* Conrad (1996) 174–175.
[196] Maryon (1956) 74 calculates that, if the thickness of the walls had been 1 inch (2.54 cm), the statue would have weighed 204 tonnes. Hoepfner (2003) 99 suggests a weight between 75 and 150 tonnes, according to which the thickness of the surface would have been closer to 1 or 2 cm. Zimmer (1990) 172 ascribes a thickness of 2 cm and a weight of 2,896 kg to the statue of Athena Promachos on the Athenian Acropolis.
[197] [Philo Byzantius] p. 30, l. 13 (Brodersen; above, pp. 80–82, §1).
[198] Calculation based on the Rhodian standard introduced in the late 340s BC: Ashton (2001) 79. 1 talent = 6,000 drachmas = 6,000 × 3.4 g = 20.4 kg. 400,000 ÷ 20.4 = 19,607.84. 19,607.84 ÷ 125 (above, p. 89, n. 189) = 156.86 (a rough estimation reduced to 150 for the sake of simplicity).
[199] Stewart (1990) 66–67.   [200] Urlichs (1857) 313 n. 42.   [201] Polyb. 5.88.3.

Ptolemy III offered the Rhodians 3000 talents to allow them to reconstruct the statue but this figure is doubtul, if it refers to a monetary value (and not to a weight of raw materials). On the other hand, Pliny relates that the Apollo of Calamis would have cost 500 talents,[202] but this price may be abnormally high. I shall refrain from citing here the Athena Promachos constructed by Pheidias on the acropolis of Athens, since the accounts on which archaeologists have relied to reconstruct the cost and the duration of the construction probably bear no relationship to the statue.[203] As for the Mercury that Zenodorus created for the Arverni (before building the Colossus of Nero), Pliny indicates that the artist worked there for ten years for a price that would have been 400 sesterces: *HS. CCCC*. The number provided by the manuscript tradition is certainly too low to be accepted. The correction $HS.|\overline{cccc}|$, accepted by many editors,[204] would give a total of 40,000,000 sesterces, which seems too high. The correction $HS.\ \overline{cccc}$[205] is more economical from every point of view: it implies the omission of one sign instead of three and gives a total of 400,000 sesterces, which does not seem too far from the 180,000 drachmae that the Colossus of Rhodes would have cost. Indeed, 400,000 sesterces represent 100,000 denarii, coins whose weight, which was *c.*3.9 g from the rule of Augustus, decreased to *c.*3.4 g under Nero, owing to a reform dated to AD 63/64.[206] At the beginning of the third century BC, the Rhodian drachma had a silver weight of *c.*3.4 g.[207] Not allowing for inflation, the difference in cost between the Colossus of Rhodes and the Mercury of the Arverni thus would have been from 48 percent to 55 percent, depending on whether we place the construction of the latter statue before or after the reform of 63/64 AD. The shorter or longer duration of time for the works (twelve vs ten years), but also the use of different techniques (casting in courses vs in pieces) would explain this disparity well enough. Contrary to previous arguments,[208] Zenodorus employed a traditional casting procedure to create the 'Colossus' of Rome. The evidence from Pliny, who mentions the rods of wax used to make channels where the metal was poured,[209] the double *contrapposto* of the statue, and its external support (Figs 4.2 and 4.3) leave no doubt about this. Furthermore, if the statue had been cast in stages around a framework of stone, like that of Chares, it would not have been possible to move it during the reign of Hadrian. It is then reasonable to deduce that the Mercury of the Arverni had itself been cast in large parts and not in courses.

Generally speaking, the alteration of numbers in the manuscript tradition does not permit us to establish with certainty the cost of the largest statues of the ancient world nor the amount of raw material required. The twelve years that

---

[202] Plin. *HN* 34.39.
[203] *IG* I³, 435, with the comment of Foley and Stroud (2019) 87–153. While following the traditional interpretation of this inscription, Holtzmann (2003) 98–99 already cautioned against the uncertain identification of other evidence related to the Athena Promachos.
[204] Thus Ferri (2011⁴) 88; Jahn (1860) 41; Jex-Blake and Sellers (1896) 34; Mayhoff (1897) 178; Rackham (1952) 160.
[205] Ulrichs (1857) 314.   [206] Sydenham (1916) 17–18; Butcher and Ponting (2014) 170.
[207] Ashton (2001) 84.   [208] Albertson (2001) 99–102.   [209] Plin. *HN* 34.46.

the construction of the Colossus lasted at least do not seem abnormal when compared to the amount of time necessary to raise two smaller statues: eight years for the Buddha of Nara (with a similar technique) and ten years for the Mercury of the Arverni (with a different technique).

The Appearance of the Colossus

The Evidence

We may now gather the evidence concerning the appearance of the Colossus. Several ancient authors note its height as 70 cubits (*c.*34 m)[210] and its depiction of Helios, the patron god of the Rhodians.[211] They also provide some anatomical details (including feet, ankles, knees, and fingers) that define the statue as anthropomorphic.[212] As a *kolossós*, the statue built by Chares represented a fixed and immobile being.[213] This is confirmed by the testimony of Pseudo-Philo, who indicates that a single *sēkōma* ('weight' or 'counterpoise') of stone ensured the sturdiness of the Colossus. It follows that the two legs of the statue were joined, in a way that they could be cast in the same moulds and attached to the same internal structure by means of *mochloí* or *schedíai* ('cross-bars' or 'parts of a frame', namely cantilevers). For the same technical reasons, the arms of the statue had to be pressed against the body.

From the 'fact that Chares was a pupil of Lysippus', it would be wrong to infer 'that torsion, a dramatic turn of the neck, and an expression of pathos (all stylistic devices commonly ascribed to the works of Lysippus, especially his portraits of Alexander) were features of the statue',[214] as this assumption is contradicted not only by the nature of the *kolossós* but also by the technique used by the sculptor. Yet, it is illustrated by several reconstitutions or alleged 'replicas' of the Colossus scattered in archaeological literature (Figs 6.23, 7.42, 7.44, 7.46, 7.48).[215] The affinity that Luciano Laurenzi conjectured between the head of Helios by Lysippus and the head of Helios by Chares[216] is unsupported and made unlikely by the contrasting characters of the monuments to which they belonged; whereas the

---

[210] Above, pp. 73–74.
[211] Strabo 14.2.5; Plin. *HN* 34.41 (above, pp. 64–65); [Philo Byzantius] p. 30, ll. 10–11 and p. 34, l. 1 (Brodersen; above, pp. 80–82, §§1 and 6); *Suda, s.v.* Κολοσσαεύς. Many less authoritative testimonies can be added to the list; cf. *Anth. Pal.* 6.171, v. 2.
[212] Strabo 14.2.5; Plin. *HN* 34.41 (above, pp. 64–65); [Philo Byzantius] p. 32, ll. 2–3 (Brodersen; above, pp. 80–82, §3).
[213] Chapter 2, pp. 33, 44.
[214] Pollitt (2000) 95; cf. e.g. Jordan (2002) 29–30; Moreno (2013) 52; Papini (2022) 186, n. 22; M. D. Higgins (2023) 315; Anniboletti (2024) 16.
[215] Chapter 7, p. 211; see also Chapter 3, pp. 54–61.   [216] Laurenzi (1959) 774.

quadriga celebrated the inclusion of Rhodes in the empire of Alexander, the Colossus exalted the resistance of the city to one of his successors.

The indication of Pseudo-Philo that Helios was identifiable only by 'his salient attributes' (συμβόλοις τοῖς ἐξ ἐκείνου)[217] is much in keeping with the rest of his description and with the definition of the statue-type. These 'salient attributes' most probably are the rays comprising the crown of the god (especially in the sculpture of the island).[218] It is thus worth mentioning a verse from Simias of Rhodes, a poet and grammarian whose *floruit* in all likelihood was contemporaneous with the construction of the Colossus of Rhodes:[219]

χρυσῷ τοι φαέθοντι πολύλλιστος φλέγεται κράς.
By means of shining gold the most revered head gleams for you.[220]

John Powell, the editor of the fragment, attempted to attribute it to a poem dedicated to Apollo,[221] while Ulrich von Wilamowitz-Möllendorf had already suggested identifying in it an allusion to Helios, the patron deity of the Rhodians (and thus of Simias himself).[222] Preferring this hypothesis without excluding the former, Marco Perale attributed the fragment to an epigram that the Rhodians would have ordered to be engraved on the base of a statue of Helios.[223] Although the adjective *polúllistos* ('very revered') would be most appropriate to a cult statue, we cannot exclude the idea that Simias evoked the Colossus, whose merits other poets had celebrated without their verses destined to be inscribed on its base.[224] This very tentative hypothesis would lead to the conjecture that the rays of the Colossus were gilded.

There is no certain mention of gold being used for the Colossus before the sixth century AD. Gregory of Tours in his treaty *On the Course of the Stars* states the statue was gilded (*deaurata est*). This is certainly pure invention, since Gregory states that 'according to numerous authors' (*ferunt autem multi*) it was possible to enter into the tibia of the Colossus and to climb up to its head, information that is not found elsewhere; the other Wonders of the World are described with no less fantasy.[225] Writing in the eighth century AD, Theophilus also claimed that the Colossus of Rhodes had been made of gold, an idea which reappears in two authors who depend on his account. Constantine Porphyrogenitus mentions a 'bronze statue of Helios, gilded from head to foot',[226] while Michael the Syrian

---

[217] [Philo Byzantius] p. 30, ll. 11–12 (Brodersen; above, pp. 80–82, §1).
[218] Chapter 7, p. 208; cf. Gabriel (1932) 346; Laurenzi (1959) 774; Hebert (1989) 22.
[219] H. Fraenkel (1915) 10–11.
[220] Simias of Rhodes, frag. 4 (Powell, *Collectanea Alexandrina*).
[221] Powell (1925) 111, commentary on frag. 4.
[222] Wilamowitz-Möllendorff (1883) 422 n. 1.   [223] Perale (2011) 199.
[224] AB 68 (above, pp. 52–53); *Anth. Plan.* 82 (above, p. 53).
[225] Gregorius Turonesis *De cursu stellarum ratio* p. 859 (Arndt and Krusch; Brodersen 15).
[226] Constantinus Porphyrogenitus *De admin. imper.* 21, l. 58 (*PG* CXIII, 205B).

states that the sculpture allegedly destroyed by the Arabs 'was made of Corinthian bronze',[227] an alloy of copper, gold, and silver.[228] There is once again nothing to support such claims. We should remember that the Colossus of Theophilus is a pastiche of the statue described by the prophet Daniel, itself made of gold, silver, and bronze.[229]

Becoming a Wonder

According to the *Suda*, 'the Colossus of the Rhodians, albeit astonishing due to its size, [was] not pleasant.'[230] This statement may gloss a passage of Pseudo-Longinus' treaty *On the Sublime* discussing the unauthored opinion that 'the faulty *kolossós* is not better than Polyclitus' Doryphorus',[231] although it is not certain that the Colossus of Rhodes is meant here.[232] Doubts have long been expressed and are to some extent confirmed by the fact that earlier authors, including Posidippus, do not criticize the monument for its lack of beauty (Phidias' Zeus at Olympia may actually be the 'the faulty *kolossós*').[233] Whatever the case may be, size—and not beauty—made the Colossus worthy of being ranked among the Seven Wonders of the World, as the list of these monuments aimed only to collect structures elevated to the rank of technical masterpieces due to their extraordinary dimensions.[234] The most ancient attestations of this list are provided by a very fragmentary papyrus from the second century BC[235] and by a poem that would be approximately contemporaneous[236] if attributed to Antipater of Sidon but Augustan if attributed to Antipater of Thessalonica.[237] The monuments mentioned in this poem—which return, each time in a slightly different order, in Gregory of Nazianzus[238] and Pseudo-Philo of Byzantium—[239] are the Walls of Babylon, the Statue of Zeus at Olympia, the Hanging Gardens of Babylon, the Colossus of Rhodes, the Pyramids of Egypt (Memphis), the Mausoleum at Halicarnassus, and the Temple of Artemis at Ephesus. The construction of the Lighthouse of Alexandria seems to have lasted from 297 to 283/2 BC[240] and should have prompted the Rhodians to

---

[227] Michael the Syrian *Chronicle* IV, p. 430a, ll. 25–31 (Chabot: II, pp. 442–443 and III, p. 81, for the French translation).
[228] On this alloy, which was black and not gilded, see Descamps-Lequime (2010) 115–128.
[229] Daniel 2:32. See above, p. 70.   [230] *Suda, s.v. Σεβαστιανός*.   [231] [Longin.] 36.3.
[232] As admitted by Moreno (1994b) 130 and Badoud (2012) 5.
[233] For a review of the various interpretations of [Longin.] 36.3, see De Jonge (2013) 318–340.
[234] For other—hypothetical and secondary—criteria, see Łanowski (1965) 1027.
[235] *P. Berol.* 13044v, cols 8.22–9.6.
[236] *Anth. Pal.* 9.58 (Gow-Page, *GP*, XCI).   [237] Review of arguments in Neger (2014) 333.
[238] Greg. Naz. *Epigrammata* 50 = *Anth. Pal.* 8.177 (*PG* XXXVIII, 109–110; Brodersen 8); *Orationes* 43 (Bernardi; *PG* XXXVI, 577C–579B; Brodersen 9).
[239] [Philo Byzantius] pp. 20–36 (Bordersen).
[240] *Suda, s.v. Φάρος*, places the construction of the Lighthouse 'under King Ptolemy' (I) and makes it coincide with the moment when Pyrrhus succeeded to the throne of Epirus (297 BC); Euseb. *Chron.* II p. 118 (Schoene), on the other hand, situates it during the rule of Ptolemy II, in 283/2 BC. Both

emulate their ally Ptolemy I by building the Colossus from 295 to 283 BC.[241] Yet, although the list of the Seven Wonders has always been flexible,[242] no version of it includes the Lighthouse of Alexandria before the fifth century AD.[243] The Lighthouse thus seems to have been deliberately excluded from the original version, which would not have been composed in Alexandria, as has been argued,[244] but somewhere else, probably in the Greek East.[245]

The inclusion of the Colossus in the list of the Seven Wonders of the World, soon followed by the destruction of the statue, had two epistemic consequences: the first was to suggest that the statuary type of the *kolossós* was defined by size;[246] the second was to obliterate the other characteristics of the bronze cast by Chares.

---

authors use the verb *anéstēsen* ('he set up'), and it has generally been thought that the first indicated the beginning of the works and the second their end.

[241] Above, p. 66.

[242] Schott (1891), written before publication of *P. Berol.* 13 044; Łanowski (1965) 1020–1024, 1028–1030; Łanowski (1983) 182–186; Brodersen (1992); Condello and Floridi (2023) 3–14; see also Omont (1882) 40–59.

[243] *Anth. Pal.* 9.656 (Brodersen 10).

[244] Stark (1864) 384; Schott (1891) 15; Romer and Romer (1995) x–xi; Clayton and Price (1989) 11–12; cf. Brodersen (2004) 11. On Callimachus, Chapter 3, p. 53, n. 7.

[245] Łanowski (1965) 1025–1026, followed by Dawid (1968) 4 and Ekschmitt (1996) 9–10; cf. Adam and Blanc (1989) 34–37.

[246] Chapter 2, p. 51.

5
Over the Seas and on the Land

The previous chapter has established that the Colossus of Rhodes matched the criterium for appearance included in the definition of the original *kolossós*. The two other criteria of this definition, which are the origin and the function of the statue, will now be discussed. One question indeed has been deliberately left aside: why did the Rhodians decide to erect a *kolossós*? Pliny mentions their victorious resistance to the armies of Demetrius, and scholars have been satisfied with this explanation, which has, I am afraid, obscured the true significance of the statue.

The Dedicatory Epigram of the Colossus

The Text

The *Palatine Anthology* (6.171) and the *Anthology of Planudes* (6.1) both preserve an epigram, whose two first distichs the *Suda* (*s.v. Κολοσσαεῖς*) also cites:

> αὐτῷ σοὶ πρὸς Ὄλυμπον ἐμακύναντο κολοσσὸν
>   τόνδε Ῥόδου ναέται Δωρίδος, Ἀέλιε,
> χάλκεον, ἁνίκα κῦμα κατευνάσαντες Ἐννοῦς
>   ἔστεψαν πάτραν δυσμενέων ἐνάροις.
> 5 οὐ γὰρ ὑπὲρ πελάγους μόνον ἄνθεσαν, ἀλλὰ καὶ ἐν γᾷ
>   ἁβρὸν ἀδουλώτου φέγγος ἐλευθερίας·
> τοῖς γὰρ ἀφ' Ἡρακλῆος ἀεξηθεῖσι γενέθλας
>   πάτριος ἐν πόντῳ κἠν χθονὶ κοιρανία.

l. 3 ἡνίκα *Suda*; κατευνάσαντες *Plan.* l. 5 ἄνθεσαν *Plan.* (ἀν in rasura); κάτθεσαν *Pal.*; ἔκτισαν Stadmüller. l. 6 ἐλευθερίας Brunck; –ίης *Pal.*, *Plan.* l. 7 γενέθλας codicis *Pal.* corrector; –ης *Pal.*, *Plan.* l. 8 κοιρανία Brunck; –ίη *Plan.*; –ίαι *Pal.*

To thy very self, Halios, did the people of Dorian Rhodes raise high towards Olympus this brazen colossus, when having laid to rest the waves of Enyo [the War], they crowned their fatherland with the spoils of their foes. Not only over the seas, but on the land, too, did they establish the lovely light of a freedom that

---

The Colossus of Rhodes: Archaeology of a Lost Wonder. Nathan Badoud, Oxford University Press.
© Nathan Badoud 2024. DOI: 10.1093/oso/9780198903734.003.0006

is not to be enslaved. For those who spring from the race of Heracles sovereignty is a paternal heritage both upon sea and land.[1]

Historiographical Analysis

In an article published in 1876, Otto Benndorf was the first to argue that this text referred to the dedicatory epigram inscribed on the base of the Colossus of Rhodes.[2] Nevertheless, it was only in the 1930s and 1940s that the poem attracted a renewed interest closely related to the concerns of the times. Charles Edson noted the importance of the final distich, from which he drew the two strands of interpretation that have guided research to the present day; after having repelled the assaults of Demetrius and desiring to humiliate the Macedonians, the Rhodians would have presented themselves as 'true Heraclids' on the one hand and as masters 'of the land and sea' on the other. His argument is worth citing:

> At first sight this distich is an extraordinary example of tasteless hyperbole, for at no time, certainly not in 283 [the date he rightly attributed to the dedication of the Colossus],[3] could it be said that Rhodes exercised *koiranía* (a very strong word [meaning 'sovereignty']) on land and sea. But if this final distich is taken as a taunt aimed at Demetrius, the point becomes clear. 'You, Demetrius, pretend to be a Heraclid (as an Argead), but we Dorian Rhodians are the true Heraclids, as we have decisively shown by defeating you in battle; for only to those who are truly descended from Heracles does lordship on land and sea belong.'[4]

The year 1942 was marked by two key connections, proposed by Frank Walbank and Arnaldo Momigliano, who had previously exchanged views concerning the Rhodian epigram. To begin with, Walbank drew attention to another epigram, composed by Alcaeus of Messene when the poet numbered among the followers of Philip V of Macedonia (whom he would later sharply oppose):[5]

---

[1] *Anth. Pal.* 6.171 / *Anth. Plan.* 6.1 (Gow-Page, *HE*, Anon. LXVIIIA) with the translation of W. R. Paton, modified on several points.
[2] Benndorf (1876) 45–48; *contra* Bergk (1882) 513 ('*Alcaeai Messenii esse arbitror*'; '*manifesto est ἐπιδεικτικόν*').
[3] Chapter 4, p. 66.   [4] Edson (1934) 221.
[5] On the political trajectory of Alcaeus, see Gow-Page, *HE*, vol. 2, 7–8.

μακύνου τείχη, Ζεῦ Ὀλύμπιε· πάντα Φιλίππῳ
  ἀμβατά· χαλκείας κλεῖε πύλας μακάρων.
χθὼν μὲν δὴ καὶ πόντος ὑπὸ σκήπτροισι Φιλίππου
  δέδμηται, λοιπὰ δ' ἁ πρὸς Ὄλυμπον ὁδός.

> Raise high thy walls, Olympian Zeus; all is accessible to Philip: shut the brazen gates of the gods. Earth and sea lie vanquished under Philip's sceptre: there remains the road towards Olympus.[6]

In 1923, Gaetano De Sanctis had dated this second epigram to 200 BC,[7] thus placing it in the pivotal year during which the Cretan War ended and the Second Macedonian War began. After defeating the fleet of the Rhodians at Lade, Philip V had overwhelmed their Peraea, the part of the Asian continent attached to their territory. The merit of Walbank lies in his remark that the two epigrams (the second of which was later paraphrased by Alpheus of Mytilene)[8] were closely connected. Both mentioned domination on land and sea (with different words), both used the rare verb *makunâsthai* ('to raise high'), of which no other occurrence in the middle voice remains in all of Greek literature, and both contained the phrase *pròs Ólumpon* ('towards Olympus'). For Walbank, Alcaeus had responded to Rhodian ambition by re-establishing Philip V in his position of conquering Heraclid, master of the earth and sea;[9] in his eyes, the monarch had erased the insult of 304 BC, just as Hitler had erased that of the Armistice Treaty of 1918 at Compiègne.[10]

While following most of the conclusions of his colleague, Momigliano argued on his side that 'the attribution of rule over land and sea was, indeed, a compliment often used of respectable States and sovereigns of the Hellenistic age', so that its importance should not be overestimated, whether in the epigram of the Colossus (where it seemed disconnected from reality) or in that of Alcaeus (where it seemed only exaggerated). In his *Alexandra*, Lycophron had described the Romans as 'taking sceptres and monarchy over land and sea' (γῆς καὶ θαλάσσης σκῆπτρα καὶ μοναρχίαν λαβόντες).[11] After centuries of effort to decipher the prophecies of this 'obscure poem', several scholars argued that the author of these words could not be the famous poet Lycophron of Calchis, a member of the Alexandrian Pleiad who lived at the court of Ptolemy II Philadelphus (king from 283 to 246 BC). For them, the verses could only belong to an author living in the

---

[6] *Anth. Pal.* 9.518 (Gow-Page, *HE*, Alcaeus I), with the translation of W. R. Paton, slightly modified.
[7] De Sanctis (1923) 9–10.   [8] *Anth. Pal.* 9.526.
[9] Cf. *IG* XI, 4, 1100 and 1101, which mention the offerings that Philip V made to Apollo of Delos after his victories on land and sea (if we restore ἀπ[ὸ τῶν κατὰ θάλασσαν ἀγώνων] in l. 3 of the second inscription).
[10] Walbank (1942) 134–137. The remainder of his article (pp. 137–145) is dedicated to *Anth. Pal.* 16.6 / *Anth. Plan.* 1.6 (Gow-Page, *HE*, Anon. LIX), where Philip V is called *koíranos Eurṓpas* ('sovereign of Europe').
[11] Lycoph. *Alex.* 1229–1230.

second century BC, when the Romans had triumphed over the Greeks on land as well as on sea (such is now the dominant point of view today in the English-speaking world, where the hypothesis of a reworking of the poem in the Augustan Age has also been advanced).[12] Nevertheless, the final event to which the *Alexandra* clearly alluded was 'the murder of Heracles, the authentic or supposed son of Alexander and Barsine, by Polyperchon in 309 BC' and there was apparently no trace of the Punic Wars in the poem, nor of a second Lycophron to whom it could be attributed. For Momigliano, all difficulties vanished as soon as the claim to a 'monarchy' on land and sea was put into perspective. There was indeed no need to consider domination as large as that which the wars against Macedonia and Antiochos had achieved for the Romans: 'After all the Romans had been recognized as a naval power by Carthage in their first treaty, had *duoviri navales* since 311 BC, struck coins—the *aes grave*—with a prow on the reverse, and had an agreement with Tarentum about navigation, which they did not respect.'[13] It was as a maritime power that the Romans had entered into war against the Tarentines, before the latter called upon Pyrrhus I. In 272 BC, the Romans had defeated both adversaries on land and sea, one year after receiving from Ptolemy II the embassy that would initiate diplomatic relations with Egypt. For Momigliano, the *Alexandra* had been written slightly after this date but prior to the start of the First Punic War in 264 BC; its author was the only poet known by the name of Lycophron, active at the court of Ptolemy II.[14]

After the Second World War, Silvio Accame returned to the link created between the Rhodian epigram and that of Alcaeus, to reverse their chronological order. For him, the first was later than the second, as shown by its 'servile' style and its absence of historical consistency. The construction of the Colossus thus would have had 'no relationship at all' with Rhodian domination on land and sea; nor would this domination have had any relation to the siege of Demetrius. In fact, the Rhodian epigram would have been composed at the beginning of the second century,[15] at the height of Rhodian power.

Kenneth Jones reaffirmed the same point of view in 2014, with new arguments. The first relates to the fact that neither Pliny nor (Pseudo-)Philo mention a dedication inscribed on the basis of the statue inscription. If such a dedication existed, however, it would have been the epigram cited by Strabo (*Anth. Plan.* 82), which, according to Constantine Porphyrogenitus, was inscribed on the base of the Colossus,[16] rather than the text we are discussing (*Anth. Pal.* 6.171). Several clues would incidentally speak against the authenticity of the latter. First, the use of the verb *makunâsthai* ('to raise high') would seem 'odd', since, in referring to a statue,

---

[12] See the chart of Schade (1999) 220–228, who goes back until the twelfth century. For more recent hypotheses, see below, pp. 108–116.

[13] For an additional argument, see below, pp. 116–119 (regarding the alliance between Rome and Rhodes).

[14] Momigliano (1942) 53–64.   [15] Accame (1947) 95–97.

[16] Constantine Porphyrogenitus *De admin. imper.* 21, ll. 59–62 (*PG* CXIII, 205B–C).

one would rather expect the 'more common words' *hidrúō* ('to set up') or *títhēmi* and its various forms, especially *anatíthēmi* ('to dedicate'). The structure of the epigram would betray its dependence towards a model, since, according to Jones, 'the placement of the two verbal parallels that exist between the poems (*makúnou/emakúnanto* and *pròs Ólumpon*) makes more sense in the Rhodian dedication as an advertisement of its dependence of Alcaeus' epigram'. Moreover (as Momigliano has observed),[17] Alcaeus makes no reference to the ancestral figure of Heracles, from which we should conclude that his intention was not to respond to the Rhodian epigram. Finally, as noted by Accame, the claim to 'dominion over land and sea' would have been 'anachronistic' in the 280s, but it would fit perfectly into the aftermath of the Second Macedonian War, as the latter ended with the defeat of Philip V, who had presented himself as a descendant of Heracles (unlike his Antigonid predecessors). In their response to Alcaeus, the Rhodians would thus not only have asserted their military superiority but would also have appropriated the symbolic heritage of the Macedonian by presenting themselves as Heraclids at the very moment when they 'issued a series of tetradrachmas featuring the head of Alexander as Heracles on the obverse'. They would also have chosen to convey this response as 'the dedicatory inscription of the Colossus', a statue that 'was an expression of Rhodian confidence in its position'.[18] According to Momigliano, the epigram of the Colossus constituted the most flagrant example of the fact that the claim to exercise sovereignty on land and sea did not necessarily have a close link to reality, an argument justifying the early date that he attributed to the *Alexandra*, where the prophetess promised this sovereignty to the Romans. Having rendered considerably later the chronology of the epigram by placing it in the aftermath of the Second Macedonian War (200–197 BC), Jones did the same with the *Alexandra* by placing its composition after the War of Antiochos (192–188 BC). The land and sea supremacy of the Romans was then real—much greater in any case than it had been after the victory over Pyrrhus and the seizing of Tarentum in 272 BC. In short (according to Jones), Momigliano not only put into incorrect perspective Roman rule over land and sea but also overestimated the reality of Roman naval power in the first third of the third century.[19]

An identical point of view appears in the last edition of the *Alexandra*, published by Simon Hornblower, except that the 'Roman section' of the prophecy is more traditionally brought back to the Second Macedonian War, while the Rhodian epigram is not taken into consideration.[20] Returning to this text in 2018, however, Hornblower argued that it may have been even more recent than Jones

---

[17] *Apud* Walbank (1942) 136 n. 4.   [18] K. R. Jones (2014a) 136–151.
[19] Jones (2014b) 41–55.   [20] Hornblower (2015) 114.

believed it to be, in which case it would be 'much less excitingly derivative and much less significant'.[21]

In Defence of *Anth. Pal.* 6.171

None of the arguments advanced against the authenticity of the dedication of the Colossus withstand examination (for the moment, I will leave aside those regarding the epigram of Alcaeus, which, as we shall see,[22] also point in the direction of authenticity). First, neither Pliny nor Pseudo-Philo, who both were concerned not with literature but with art, had reason to be interested in this text in their descriptions of the statue, or at least to mention it. Nothing indeed prevents us from asking whether Mucianus, Pliny's source, did not gloss *dusmenéōn enárois* ('with the spoils of their foes') with *ex apparatu regis Demetrii relicto* ('from the engines of war belonging to King Demetrius').[23] The silence of Pliny and Pseudo-Philo thus does not mean that the base did not carry a dedication (the less so as the comment which Pliny dedicated to another sculpture, the Laocoon, largely consists in a Latin translation of the Greek inscription that was cut on its base but that he does not mention either).[24] Second, we cannot reject the authenticity of the epigram *Anth. Pal.* 6.171 by considering that the distich *Anth. Plan.* 82 was perhaps engraved in its place on the base of the statue, since the former poem is a dedication, while the latter cannot be interpreted as such and is certainly not a true inscription.[25]

Downdating *Anth. Pal.* 6.171 would also imply its falsity but is no more possible. On one hand, the hypothesis of a post-227 BC forgery cannot make sense: an epigram thought of as the dedicatory inscription of the Colossus certainly would not have been written after the collapse of the statue, whose ruins would have been a very strange 'expression of Rhodian confidence'.[26] On the other hand, the coins do not attest the existence of a sudden enthusiasm by the Rhodians for the figure of Heracles in the late third/early second centuries. While a fair number of states in southern and western Asia Minor did strike silver coinage representing the head of Alexander as Heracles during the same period, it was not used as a tool of propaganda to claim any kind of heritage, but rather as an internationally recognized currency to finance the wars against Philip V (and then Antiochos III). Hence there is no reason to assume that the epigram of the Colossus, where the Rhodians present themselves as Heraclids, is contemporary with these wars.

---

[21] Hornblower (2018) 81–82 n. 2.   [22] Below, p. 102.
[23] The two passages had already been brought together by Scaliger (1606) 137 and Gow-Page, *HE*, vol. 2, 589. See also Plut. *Vit. Demetr.* 20.9 and Vitr. *De arch.* 10.16.8.3–5 (below, p. 133).
[24] Badoud (2019e) 77–79.   [25] Chapter 3, pp. 53–54.   [26] K. R. Jones (2014a) 151.

Let us now examine the relationship between the epigram of the Colossus and that of Alcaeus. Under no circumstances could the first have replied to the second by posing as a more ancient text. In any event, Alcaeus' response to the Rhodians agrees with the fact that their epigram was taken as authentic. Let us evaluate the reasons that have led to the presentation of the style of this epigram as 'servile'. Accame provided none, but Jones considered that the verb *makunâsthai* was used in an 'odd' manner, which for him was a sign of borrowing from Alcaeus. Nevertheless, if the Rhodians did not use the banal *hidrúō* ('to set up') or *anatíthēmi* ('to dedicate'), this choice is due to the fact that the Colossus was not just any statue, but a monument unique in the world because of its *mâkos* ('great height'), substantive from which derives the verb *makunâsthai*.[27] The argument according to which 'the placement of the two verbal parallels that exist between the poems (*makúnou/emakúnanto* and *pròs Ólumpon*)' would make 'more sense in the Rhodian dedication as an advertisement of its dependence of Alcaeus' epigram' is a mere *petitio principii*. Moreover, the analysis of the sources on which it is based cannot be accepted. First, there is no reason to dismiss the correspondence *pelágous...gâi* ('sea...land') / *khthṑn...póntos* ('land...sea') from the discussion by arguing that it is thematic rather than lexical. Second, the 'verbal parallels' between the poems are not two in number, as has been accepted since Walbank, but three, since the correspondence is evident between the 'brazen gates' of Alcaeus (*khalkeías...púlas* in v. 2) and the 'brazen Colossus' of the Rhodians (*kolossón...khálkeon* in vv. 1–3). A reference to the epigram of the Colossus is thus to be found in every verse of Alcaeus' poem (v. 1: *makúnou*; v. 2: *khalkeías*; v. 3: *khthṑn...póntos*; v. 4: *pròs Ólumpon*), which proves that the former text, whose flawless style has nothing servile about it, has been influential, and that the latter is derivative.

On the other hand, as Hans-Ulrich Wiemer stressed, three arguments speak for the authenticity of our document. In the *Palatine Anthology*, the latter appears among several dedicatory epigrams whose authenticity is not in doubt (and which may have already been collected in the first century BC by Meleager of Gadara). Furthermore, no author's name is attached to the poem, which would easily be explained if the text, coming from the city and not from a particular individual, had been copied on the base of the monument. Finally, because he was a politically engaged author, Alcaeus is much less likely to have responded to a fictional epigram than to a dedication that the Colossus had made famous.[28] Thus, the arguments for the authenticity of *Anth. Pal.* 6.171 are strong, and there is absolutely no argument against it.

---

[27] For this meaning of the word, see Hom. *Od.* 11.312 and 20.71.
[28] Wiemer (2011) 131, overlooked by K. R. Jones (2014a) 136–151.

The Aim of the Colossus

If one agrees with the above, the epigram of the Colossus was composed in 283 BC, when the statue was dedicated to Helios, as Edson accepted. This brings us back to his interpretation of the final distich, which, as I have said, has guided debate until the present day.[29] The first assumption of Edson was that the Rhodians presented themselves as the 'true Heraclids' in a 'taunt' addressed to Demetrius, who, in their opinion, would have usurped this identity. Nevertheless, if Alexander the Great and the Argeads considered themselves as descendants of Heracles, this was not the case with Demetrius and the first Antigonids, contrary to that which Edson has suggested. On the other hand, the epigram of Alcaeus (which had not yet been identified as a reply to that of the Colossus when Edson wrote his article) makes no allusion to Heracles, which presumably indicates that the figure of the hero was not perceived as at stake in the rivalry between Rhodes and the Antigonids. The silence of the poet is even more suggestive given that his epigram celebrates the victories of Philip V, who may have been the first Antigonid to present himself as a descendant of the hero.[30] A follower of the idea of a 'taunt' directed against the Antigonids, Jones sought here a confirmation of the hypothesis that the epigram of the Colossus would have been composed not after the siege of Demetrius, but after the wars against Philip V, in response to that of Alcaeus. Yet, we have seen that his arguments for downdating the latter epigram and regarding it as a second century BC forgery cannot be accepted. One must therefore reject the idea of a 'taunt', or at least should strongly modify it. The *kolossós* was a type of statue closely linked to Dorian colonization; it had arrived at Rhodes with the colonists from Argos[31] whom legend placed under the command of the Heraclid Tlepolemos.[32] Such a link sufficiently explains why the Rhodians justified their choice to erect a *kolossós* to Helios by depicting themselves as Dorians and as Heraclids in the epigram that they engraved on the base of the statue. As the final distich makes clear, they derived a sense of superiority from their origins, but this feeling was not connected to a claim of descent with which the Antigonids would have competed.

Let us now address the second assumption of Edson: the ambition of the Rhodians to exercise 'lordship on land and sea' would be a 'tasteless hyperbole', which Edson himself explained by the supposed 'taunt' analysed above. Momigliano then conjectured that the association of land and sea had been 'invented not on behalf of the Dorians of Rhodes, who usually were satisfied with claiming thalassocracy alone, but for the benefit of some Hellenistic king,

---

[29] Above, p. 97.   [30] K. R. Jones (2014a) 144.
[31] Chapter 1, p. 6.
[32] Pind. *Ol.* 7.78; cf. Gow-Page, *HE*, vol. 2, 589; Wiemer (2011) 132; Hornblower (2018) 81–82 n. 2.

probably Demetrius Poliorcetes or Antigonus Gonatas',[33] as a way of remaining faithful to the idea of a 'taunt' developed by Edson (although Thucydides had already attributed a similar claim to Pericles).[34] Judging the explanation of his predecessor unsatisfactory, Accame altered the composition date of the epigram to the beginning of the second century BC, in order to place it at the height— maritime and terrestrial—of Rhodian power. Following the same path, Jones argued that the poem referred more precisely to the reconquest of the Rhodian Peraea, which the armies of Philip V had occupied during the Second Macedonian War (200–197 BC). In summary: for Edson and Momigliano, the epigram would be authentic, but its territorial claims would not be legitimate; for Accame and Jones, on the contrary, its claims would be legitimate, but the epigram would not be authentic. Historiography offers us the choice between two dead ends.

In reality, the epigram is authentic (as we have seen) and its territorial claims legitimate. However, they do not refer to regions taken (Accame) or retaken (Jones) in the second century BC, since the epigram dates prior to this period.[35] According to the *opinio communis*, the Peraea was integrated—or reintegrated— into the city of Rhodes soon after the synoecism of 408 BC, or at the latest in 386 BC, during the Peace of Antalcidas.[36] However, the Peraea became Rhodian much later: in 304 BC, at the exact moment when the siege of Demetrius Poliorcetes ended.[37] I shall recall the main arguments supporting this conclusion. First, no source proves that the Rhodians held a part of the continent of Asia before 304 BC.[38] Second, Diodorus Siculus recounts that Demetrius launched his attack from the site of Loryma:[39] at no moment does the historian present this site as a possession of Rhodes, while he himself follows a Rhodian source that was extremely well informed.[40] Third, the archaeological and epigraphic finds agree in showing that the Rhodians did not build the fortress of Loryma before the beginning of the third century BC.[41] The inscriptions additionally inform us that the '*strategós* of the Peraea' (a sort of military governor) was not instituted at the moment of the synoecism of 407 BC, as were the nine *strategoí* charged with defending the island of Rhodes, but at a date between 323[42] and *c*.210 BC.[43] Finally, the citizens of the Peraea are absent from Rhodian inscriptions in the fourth century, where they appear in massive numbers from the beginning of the third century.[44]

---

[33] Momigliano (1942) 55.
[34] Thuc. 2.14.4 and 2.62.2, with the commentary of Hornblower (2015) 437–438 (v. 1229).
[35] Above, pp. 101–102.
[36] Van Gelder (1900) 191–194; Meyer (1925) 49; Meyer (1937) 577–578; Fraser and Bean (1954) 94–98; Berthold (1984) 42; Papachristodoulou (1989) 49–50; Bresson (1994) 143; Debord (1999) 270–272; Bresson (2001) 147; Bresson (2003) 172; Constantakopoulou (2007) 244; Van Bremen (2009); Wiemer (2010) 418–419.
[37] Badoud (2011b) 533–566, overlooked by K. R. Jones (2014a) 136–151.
[38] For [Scylax] 99 and [Aeschines] *Epistulae* 10, see Badoud (2011b) 545–546.
[39] Diod. Sic. 20.83.4.   [40] Wiemer (2001) 222–250.
[41] Held (2003) 58–61; Nöth (2019) 292.   [42] Badoud (2011b) 563–565, appendix 2.
[43] *NESM* 31, with the date of Badoud (2015) 211, no. 154.
[44] Badoud (2015) 75–82; Badoud (2015–2016) 239–246.

The integration of the Peraea is thus the actual event (*pace* Momigliano), closely connected to the siege of Demetrius (*pace* Accame and Jones) but distinct from the latter (*pace* Edson), celebrated in the final distich. The inscription is clear on this matter. While Edson and his successors (with the exception of Accame) commented on the rule over 'land and sea', the text evokes domination 'not only over the seas, but also on the land'. The order of words is crucial: Rhodes is not depicted as a power on 'land and sea', but as a maritime power that had become a continental power, which occurred in 304 BC. These two aspects of the *koiranía* (which seem to have been already advertised in an Argive decree for the Rhodians probably dating to 303 BC)[45] were closely related to each other. Unlike the army, which was essentially a mercenary force, the Rhodian navy excluded foreigners; its abilities were thus proportional to the size of the civic body. In 304 BC, the territory of Rhodes, limited up to that point to the island itself, was more than doubled by the incorporation of the Peraea and several islands (such as Kalche and Karpathos) that were divided into new demes (Fig. 5.1). The inhabitants of these territories, having become Rhodian citizens, immediately reinforced the crews of the fleet, which could be equipped with ships not only more numerous but also larger than in the past.[46] As the epigram emphasizes, the liberty of the Rhodians was dependent on their role as holders of the *koiranía* ('sovereignty').[47] Consequently, the date attributed to the epigram (283 BC), *earlier* than that agreed upon today, and the date attributed to the integration of the Peraea (304 BC), *later* than that admitted to this point, are confirmed by the fact that the epigram explicitly alludes to the latter event.

Our analysis of the text also matches that of the statue type. Closely linked to the Dorian world, the *kolossós* was characterized by its ability to encapsulate the presence of an external being and thus, for instance, to install a god somewhere.[48] The Colossus constructed by 'the people of Dorian Rhodes' aimed at ensuring the stability of the maritime and terrestrial empire born in 304 BC by definitively placing Helios at its centre. Functionally and ethnically, it was a perfect *kolossós*.

Rhodes and Macedonia

The reason for which the epigram of the Colossus of Rhodes resounds so strongly in the corresponding epigram of Alcaeus also now becomes clear. While the first text celebrated the conquest of the Peraea by the Rhodians in 304 BC (a fact not recognized until now), the second marked its brief re-conquest by the Macedonians in 200 BC (as De Sanctis was the first to realize). Let us use these texts to explore two other aspects of the rivalry between Rhodians and Antigonids.

---

[45] See the new edition of this document in Badoud (2019a) 77–96, where ll. 7–8, which mention the Rhodians helping the Argives and the other Greeks on sea and land, are discussed on pp. 87–88.
[46] Badoud (forthcoming 3).   [47] Cf. Wiemer (2011) 132.   [48] Chapter 2, p. 33.

Fig. 5.1 Map of the Rhodian territory.

The Shadow of the Helepolis

The epigram engraved on the base of the Colossus tells us that, by erecting the statue, the Rhodians 'crowned their fatherland with the spoils of their foes'.[49] Perhaps glossing this epigram,[50] Pliny explains that the construction of the monument was financed by the sale of the siege machines abandoned by Demetrius.[51] Modern authors have wished to be more specific: the helepolis would have

---

[49] *Anth. Pal.* 6.171 (above, pp. 96–97), v. 4. [50] Above, p. 101.
[51] Plin. *HN* 34.41 (above, pp. 64–65).

provided the metal for the statue,[52] the wood necessary for its scaffolding,[53] or even for its master model;[54] its height would have dictated that of the statue,[55] which would have been constructed where the Rhodians dismantled the siege machine.[56] All of these hypotheses are groundless; the first is only an extrapolation of the text of Pliny (and ignores the fact that, according to Diodorus, the plating of the helepolis was not bronze, but iron);[57] the second is contradicted by the description that Pseudo-Philo gives of the worksite of Chares (where it is not a matter of scaffolding but of a 'huge mound of earth');[58] the third faces the problem of the numbers provided by ancient authors (the height of the tower is said to be 66 cubits in Plutarch,[59] 90 cubits in Athenaeus Mechanicus,[60] 100 cubits in Diodorus,[61] 125 ft in Vitruvius,[62] but is nowhere 70 cubits);[63] the fourth is a distortion of the evidence from Vitruvius (who makes no reference to the Colossus).[64] The rationale of Chares was that of an artist competing with his peers;[65] the Colossus was intended to be the tallest statue in the world and not to surpass the helepolis which, dismantled after the siege of 305–304, no longer formed a benchmark. The idea that the 'helepolis' ('taker of cities'), once converted into a statue of Helios, made Rhodes a victorious 'Heliopolis' ('city of the Sun')[66] is thus also pointless, the more so as the orthography of the two words was different, the first beginning with an epsilon pronounced /e/, the second with an eta pronounced /ɛː/ or /i/ in Koine Greek but with an alpha pronounced /aː/ in the Rhodian dialect.

The Nike of Samothrace Revisited

The response that Alcaeus wrote to the epigram testifies to its lasting impact and indicates that, more than a century after the siege of Demetrius, the resistance of the Rhodians was still perceived as a humiliation at the court of Macedonia. If it is correct to believe that the text was composed in 200 BC, when Philip V had overtaken the Peraea, I should note that, one year earlier, the Macedonian fleet, once victorious at Lade, had been crushed off the coast of Chios by the Rhodians allied to Attalos I. Polybius relates that, in spite of the extent of the disaster, Philip V refused to admit defeat,[67] which would explain why Alcaeus, acting as a propagandist,[68] wished to present him as master of land and sea.[69] In 197 BC,

---

[52] K. O. Müller (1848) 159 n. 1: bronze; Pimouguet-Pédarros (2011) 346: bronze and iron.
[53] Gabriel (1932) 338; Haynes (1957) 312 n. 2; Laurenzi (1959) 774; Jordan (2002) 26; Rieger (2004) 78; Pimouguet-Pédarros (2011) 346; Rowland (2016) 448; Anniboletti (2024) 16.
[54] Vedder (2017) 23; cf. Vedder (2015) 45.
[55] Piel (2010) 138; Pimouguet-Pédarros (2011) 345; Anniboletti (2024) 16.
[56] Piel (2010) 138.   [57] Diod. Sic. 20.91.5.
[58] [Philo Byzantius] p. 32, l. 23 (Brodersen; above, pp. 80–82, §5).
[59] Plut. *Vit. Demetr.* 21.1.4.   [60] Athenaeus Mechanicus 27.   [61] Diod. Sic. 20.91.4.
[62] Vitr. *De arch.* 10.16.4 (below, p. 133).   [63] Despite Piel (2010) 137.
[64] Chapter 6, p. 133.   [65] Chapter 4, p. 77.   [66] Moreno (1994b) 137.
[67] Polyb. 16.8.   [68] On other pieces of propaganda, see below, p. 120.
[69] *Anth. Pal.* 9.518 (above, p. 98).

however, it was no longer possible to conceal the extent of the disaster: the Rhodians had expelled the armies of Philip V from the Peraea; allied to the Romans and the kingdom of Pergamon, they had won the Second Macedonian War. Two interesting events occurred in this context. First, the Rhodians presented themselves as the depositaries of the will of Alexander the Great, a document that they forged to assert, among other things, their rule over the Peraea.[70] Second, they decided to raise their famous Nike in the Sanctuary of the Great Gods at Samothrace (Fig. 5.2). From the time of the Argeads, this sanctuary had been filled with Macedonian offerings, the last of which was the 6.2-metre column that held the statue of Philip V himself (Fig. 5.3). The Nike of the Rhodians faced this monument (Fig. 5.4) and its aim was, I believe, to make clear that they had won the war against the king.[71] If this theory is correct,[72] the Nike of Samothrace should be interpreted as a counterpoint to the Colossus, as it came to settle, in a definitive manner (contrary to the slightly earlier epigram of Alcaeus, which itself referred to the Colossus), the century of hostilities begun by the siege of 305/4 BC.

Rhodes and Rome

Illuminating the *Alexandra*

We cannot fully address the historical value of the epigram of the Colossus without returning to its relationship with the *Alexandra*. In the first poem, the Rhodians claim to exercise a form of hegemony on sea and land. In the second, it is the Romans who are seen as destined for 'monarchy over land and sea' (v. 1229).[73] We recall that the 'Conservative Unitarians' believe that it was composed by Lycophron of Chalcis (or, as a last resort, by a contemporary with the same name) during the reign of Ptolemy II, the 'Radical Unitarians' attribute it to an author from the beginning of the second century BC, and the 'Analysts' maintain an intermediary position, in which the 'Roman passages' (vv. 1226–1280 and 1435–1450) would result from an interpolation noticeably later than the

---

[70] *Epitoma rerum gestarum Alexandri magni cum Libro de morte testamentoque Alexandri* 107–108 (Thomas) with the comment of Badoud (forthcoming 2).

[71] Badoud (2018b) 279–305, whose chronology is now supported by a numismatic argument: Meadows (forthcoming).

[72] Clinton et al. (2020) 551–573 repeat the arguments developed in Stewart (2016) 399–410 but refuted in Badoud (2018b) 279–305; they distort the arguments of the latter and ignore the bibliography regarding Rhodian epigraphy while dealing with the topic; plain repetition of already refuted arguments in Palagia (2021) 148–167; La Rocca (2018) 63 makes the effort of a discussion but is no more convincing: see Badoud (forthcoming 5).

[73] Above, p. 98.

Fig. 5.2 Winged Victory of Samothrace (*c*.197 BC) in the Louvre.

remainder of the poem.[74] Let us briefly examine the arguments of each, without entering into the debates on the identification of the 'lion' (v. 1441), the 'wolf' (v. 1444), and the 'unique wrestler' (v. 1446) evoked at the end of the prophecy of

[74] Cf. Chapter 2, pp. 44–46.

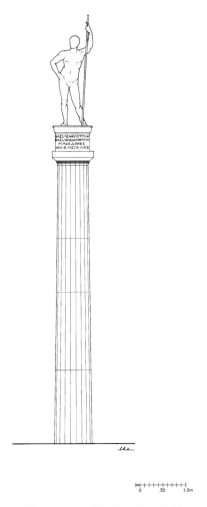

Fig. 5.3 Reconstruction of the column of Philip V (probably erected before 197 BC) at Samothrace.

Cassandra, which have given rise to numerous hypotheses, none of which is solid enough to support a particular chronology for the poem.

It must be emphasized that we know of only one author with the name of Lycophron, to whom the *Suda* explicitly attributes the *Alexandra*.[75] Thus, it is not the identification of the poet that one must prove, but rather the fallacy or the inaccuracy of this identification (if one attributes the composition of the work to an author of the same name or pseudonym, or if one accepts an interpolation). Doubts arose from the 'Roman passages' and were expressed for the first time by a scholiast whose commentary depends on a statement of a commentator who

---

[75] *Suda, s.v. Λυκόφρων.*

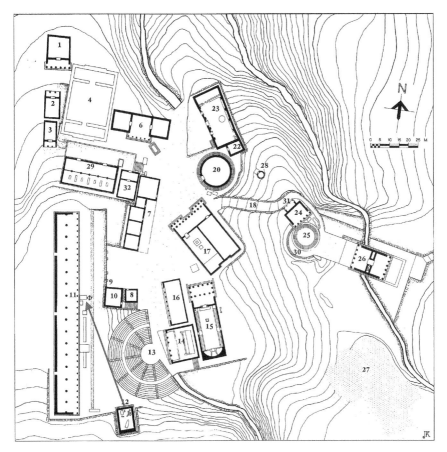

Fig. 5.4 Map of the Sanctuary of the Great Gods at Samothrace (with the arrow indicating the visual relationship between the building housing the Winged Victory of Samothrace and the column of Philip V).

could (or not) be the grammarian Theon of Alexandria, active in Rome at the beginning of the first century AD.[76] Since the nineteenth century, two arguments based on history have been used to justify these doubts: the first concerns the actual power of Rome during the time of Ptolemy II, which has been considered much weaker than implied by the prophecy of Cassandra; the second regards the fact that an author active at the court of Ptolemy II would not have exalted the Romans in his poem, but rather the sovereign. A 'Radical Unitarian', Hornblower has adduced two additional arguments to demonstrate that the *Alexandra* could not have been written before the start of the second century BC. First, the work would be based on sources too late to agree with the traditional chronology.

---

[76] *Scholia in Lycoph.* v. 1226 (Scheer) with the commentary of Ceccarelli and Steinrück (1995) 77–89.

Sprinkled with quotes from other Hellenistic poets (the latest of whom would be Euphorion of Chalcis, born between 275 and 268 BC), it also would show influence from Eratosthenes and Philostephanos, two scholars who had their family origins in Cyrene and were active in the second half of the third century BC. Second, contrary to Momigliano's assumption,[77] the *Alexandra* would contain an allusion to the Punic Wars, or at least to the second of them. It would be hidden in the passage where Cassandra vows that the curse cast against the lands of Daunia desecrated by Diomedes (who had wounded Aphrodite in Troy)[78] will be lifted when they have been ploughed by Aetolian descendants of the hero:[79] 'This must allude to a particular family, the Dasii, who were prominent at inland Arpi (Greek Argyrippa, a foundation of Diomedes) in the Hannibalic war, as Livy and coins demonstrate.'[80] Defining herself as an 'Analyst', Stephanie West identified a certain number of abrupt transitions and redundancies establishing, in her opinion, that not only the 'Roman passages' but a total of approximately 200 verses of the *Alexandra* would have been interpolated.[81] Nevertheless, the verses in question are distinguishable from the remainder of the poem neither by their metrics nor by their style, and the aesthetic arguments used to isolate them are debatable.[82] The 'Radical Unitarian' thesis defended by Hornblower is no more convincing. First, the difficulties and the risks associated with the chronological use of intertextuality must be stressed. The composition date of the works compared with the *Alexandra* is not always well known, dependence on a common source is impossible to exclude, and authors developing in the same intellectual milieu more generally are likely to cultivate similar themes, sometimes in identical terms.[83] Above all, it is circular reasoning to understand the *Alexandra* as a derivative rather than an influential work. If its author is truly the authoritative Lycophron of Chalcis, the poem was certainly read by his colleagues of the Pleiad and other librarians, such as Apollonios at Alexandria or Euphronios at Antioch. The case of Eratosthenes and Philostephanos, examined by Peter Fraser,[84] raises problems of the same kind. To begin with, we cannot exclude the possibility that the two Cyrenaean scholars and the author of the *Alexandra* depend on a common source (which could be the Androcles studied by Hornblower).[85] Nor can we forget that Eratosthenes surely used the voluminous treatise that Lycophron of Chalcis had dedicated to comedy,[86] which does not recommend the hypothesis of a 'pseudo-Lycophron' dependent on this same Eratosthenes. Finally, it is true that Appian wrote about a certain Dasios who 'being considered a descendant of

---

[77] Above, p. 99.   [78] Hom. *Il.* 5.336.
[79] Lycoph. *Alex.* 592–631.   [80] Hornblower (2015) 38.
[81] West (1984) 127–151.   [82] See especially Schade (1999) 8–11.
[83] Cf. Żybert (2016) 381–382.
[84] Fraser (1979) 328–343, whose interpretation of the scholia of Lycophron is rejected by Parson, *apud* Hornblower (2015) 219 n. 1.
[85] Hornblower (2015) 219–221 (v. 447).   [86] Meliadò (2019).

Diomedes' and thus an Aetolian, encouraged the support of Arpi/Argyrippa for Hannibal during the year 216/15 BC.[87] Nevertheless, nothing indicates that the Dasii, also mentioned by Livy[88] and whose importance is further made clear by coins issued during the years 325-275 BC,[89] had begun to present Diomedes as their ancestor at the precise moment of the Carthaginian invasion; this hypothesis is even less credible, since the hero had already been honoured in Daunia and Italy for centuries, as Hornblower himself underlines.[90] The verses in which Cassandra announces that Daunia will be delivered from the curse when Aetolians will plough its land thus have little chance of referring to the Second Punic War, which cannot provide a *terminus post quem* for the composition of the *Alexandra*.

Let us move on to the arguments cited in support of the early chronology of the poem, by considering them rather as arguments against the 'radical unitarian' and 'analyst' theses (since we have seen that, strictly speaking, the 'conservative unitarian' position does not have to be proven true). All are not of equal value. In his 1942 article, Momigliano mentioned the absence of any trace of the reception of the *Alexandra* in Latin literature, yet today it is accepted that the poem influenced Roman authors during the Augustan Age.[91] In a famous article published three years later, Momigliano attempted to confirm his chronology by using as support the tribute of two maidens that the Locrians were required to send to Troy as expiation for the rape of Cassandra by Ajax, son of Oileus;[92] Hornblower has shown that he was on the wrong track.[93] As for the reference to the murder of the young Heracles, committed in 309 BC, it only provides us with a *terminus post quem*. A century or more later, this event would have seemed completely insignificant, as Pierre Lévêque has stressed;[94] this could have been the very reason why, if living in the second century BC, the author mentioned it in a less obscure way than that to which he was accustomed. Providing more reliable evidence is the fact that Aristophanes of Byzantium, cited by Eustathius, describes as a 'Chalcidism' the form *escházosan*, which 'Lycophron' uses in verse 21 in place of the common form *éschazon* ('they let off').[95] While the explanation is probably incorrect, it is all the more valuable,[96] as the error of Aristophanes (who died 190-180 BC) itself proves that he held Lycophron *of Chalcis* to be the author of the

---

[87] App. *Hann.* 31, with the commentary of Hornblower (2015) 266 (v. 623).
[88] Livius 21.48.9, 24.45.1, 26.38.6.
[89] Rutter (2001) 76 (no. 633), 77 (no. 642), and 91 (no. 809).
[90] Hornblower (2015) 259-260 (v. 599) and 266-267 (v. 623), who gathers all of the evidence cited here.
[91] To the bibliography cited by Durbec (2014) 7 n. 23 add Hornblower (2015) 96-100.
[92] Momigliano (1945) 49-53. The tribute was halted in 346 and restored in an attenuated form by a 'king Antigonus'. Momigliano identified the latter with Antigonus II and thus placed the *Alexandra* before the inauguration of his reign in 277.
[93] Hornblower (2015) 411-412 (vv. 1141-1173).   [94] Lévêque (1955) 38.
[95] Ar. Byz. frag. 19 (Slater) = Eustathius *in Od.* 12.350.
[96] *Pace* Hornblower (2015) 124 (v. 21).

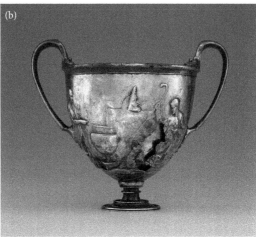

Fig. 5.5 Silver skyphos belonging to the Berthouville Treasure, probably Augustan (Bibliothèque nationale de France, inv. 56.13). a. Aratos of Soloi and Urania. b. Lycophron of Chalcis and Cassandra/Alexandra.

Alexandra. For those still not convinced, Charles Picard has drawn attention to a pair of skyphoi from the Berthouville Treasure: skyphos A represents Aratos and Urania on one side, a dramatist and Cassandra on the other side (Fig. 5.5a–b); skyphos B represents Menedemus and a Muse on one side, Theocritus and a different Muse on the other side. The dramatist associated with Cassandra on skyphos A can only be Lycophron of Chalcis, contemporary of Aratos, Theocritus, and Menedemus, to whom he dedicated a satyrical drama.[97] It is striking that the 'Radical Unitarians' present the Berthouville Treasure as a mere example of

[97] Picard (1950) 53–82; cf. Lapatin (2014) 142–145.

'Kassandra in art'[98] without noticing the true importance of the deposit. Buried in the second or third century AD, the two skyphoi have little chance of being Hellenistic (as Picard assumed), yet they are likely to have been modelled on Hellenistic originals. In any case, they show that, during the Imperial period, Lycophron of Chalcis was believed to be the author of the *Alexandra*, in spite of the doubts formulated by Theon of Alexandria (?).[99]

We now can return to the 'Roman passages' that 'Radical Unitarians' and 'Analysts' agree could not have been written before the second century BC, even though, as we have seen, the entire *Alexandra* does not seem attributable to any other author than Lycophron of Chalcis, active at the court of Ptolemy II. Momigliano had already stressed that this monarch dispatched his first embassy to Rome in 273 BC, which was matched by the sending of a delegation to Alexandria.[100] In 252 BC, a mercenary by the name of Dinnus is attested in the Ptolemaic army,[101] yet well before this date Callimachus reports from Alexandria the story of the soldier Gaius wounded by the Peucetians (neighbours of the Daunians of whom we have just spoken)[102] during an assault against the city of Rome.[103] As there was thus some knowledge of (and interest in) Roman affairs at Alexandria in the first half of the third century BC, it becomes easier to agree that Lycophron alluded to the war against Pyrrhus and the Roman conquest of southern Italy in one of his poems. The verses dedicated to Diomedes and the 'Roman passages', however, leave no doubt that the author of the *Alexandra* had a special relationship with Italy. The *Suda* states that Lycophron of Chalcis, son of a certain Socles, had been adopted by the historian Lycos of Rhegium (now Reggio Calabria).[104] The accuracy of this testimony has been challenged. Describing adoption as 'a Roman custom rather than Greek' and recalling the hesitation of John Tzetzes regarding the question of whether Socles or Lycos was the actual father of the writer,[105] Gérard Lambin has suggested distinguishing two contemporaneous Lycophrons: the first, from Chalcis, would be the philologist and dramatist who entered the court of Ptolemy II, while the second, from Rhegium, would be the author of the *Alexandra*.[106] This hypothesis is hardly convincing, since adoption was a widespread practice in the Greek world,[107] and since Tzetzes probably relied on the same source as the *Suda*, namely the *Onomatologus* of

---

[98] Hornblower (2015) 5 n. 11.
[99] For other evidence likely to support the attribution of the *Alexandra* to Lycophron of Chalcis, see Linant de Bellefonds, Pouzadoux, and Prioux (2017) 199–246; cf. Pouzadoux and Prioux (2009) 481–485 and Massa-Pairault (2009) 487–505.
[100] Livius *Per.* 14 and Cass. Dio frag. 41 (Zonar. *Annales* 8.6; *PG* CXXXIV, 652C-D) mention both embassies. Eutr. 2.15 mentions the Ptolemaic embassy. Dion. Hal. *Ant. Rom.* 20.14, Val. Max. 4.3.9, and Just. *Epit.* 18.2.9 mention the Roman embassy. Cf. below, p. 119.
[101] *P. Lond.* VII 1986, l. 12.   [102] Above, pp. 112–113.
[103] Callim. *Aet.* frag. 106–107 (Pfeiffer) / 209–210 (Massimilia).   [104] *Suda, s.v.* Λύκος.
[105] Tzetz. *Chil.*, 8.474; *ad Lycoph.* p. 4 (Scheer, *Lycophronis Alexandra*, II).
[106] Lambin (2005) 16.
[107] For an overview, see Huebner (2013) 513–521.

Hesychius. The *Suda* adds that Lycos was 'a contemporary of the successors of Alexander and a victim of a plot by Demetrios of Phaleron'.[108] The latter, driven from power by Demetrius Poliorcetes, found refuge at Alexandria, where he established the Musaeum and the Library. It is reasonable to deduce that Lycos of Rhegium was living in Alexandria during the reign of Ptolemy I, but also to accept that Lycophron of Chalcis (the metropolis of Rhegium), fellow of the Library and author of at least one poem dedicated in part to Italy (for the *Alexandra* may be joined to the tragedy *Telegonos*, named after the hero born in Latium from the love affair between Odysseus and Circe), could have been his adopted son.[109] It is hardly believable that the *Suda* arrived at a such a coherent result from historical, geographical, and literary points of view by confusing two authors, one of whom is not attested in any way. Hence we can overturn the traditional question of whether the *Alexandra* 'was possible at the court of Alexandria'[110] by asking ourselves if such a work could have been composed elsewhere.[111] The fact that Clement of Alexandria could compare 'the *Alexandra* of Lycophron' to works of Callimachus and Euphorion[112] owes nothing to chance, since the three authors held senior positions in two of the greatest libraries of the Hellenistic world, outside which they would not have been able to gather the literature necessary to compose their works (this is incidentally the reason why one wonders whether the 'super-literate' Hyssaldomos, son of Eirenaios, who had engraved at Mylasa a poem of 121 lines in the style of the *Alexandra*,[113] was educated on the neighbouring island of Rhodes,[114] which certainly had an excellent library, of which a part of the catalogue has survived).[115] If the *Alexandra* dates to the first half of the third century, a period when the libraries of Antioch and Pergamon did not yet exist (a hypothesis which is supported by several clues and undermined by none), it was very probably composed in Alexandria. The cryptic character of the poem and its original perspective may well explain the absence (?) of reference to Ptolemy II. There only remains the 'sceptres and monarchy over land and sea' promised to the Romans that make suspect the attribution of the *Alexandra* to Lycophron of Chalcis. This leads us back to the Colossus and its epigram.

A Common Struggle against Piracy

As we saw in Chapter 2, the epithet *kolossobámōn* ('mobile like a *kolossós*'), used by Lycophron, agrees particularly well with the early chronology of his *Alexandra*,

---

[108] *Suda*, s.v. Λύκος.
[109] Cf. Jacoby (1955) 597–598 with n. 1 (*FGrH* 570), who does not consider the relation between Chalcis and Rhegium nor the existence of the *Telegonos*.
[110] Lévêque (1955) 56.   [111] Cf. Żybert (2016) 382.   [112] Clem. Al. *Strom.* 5.50.2.
[113] Marek and Zingg (2018) 1–139.   [114] Hornblower (2019).
[115] Segre (1935) 214–222; cf. Rosamilia (2014) 355–360.

since it preserves the original sense of *kolossós*, which vanished shortly after 227 BC.[116] On the other hand, the analysis of the epigram engraved on the base of this statue has established that, in 283 BC, the Rhodians could proclaim themselves masters of sea and land while claiming hegemony over limited territory.[117] We are thus nearly ready to admit that Cassandra could promise 'sceptres and monarchy over land and sea' to the Romans by having in mind their conquests of the 270s. No one indeed would deny that Rome had reached the rank of a land power at this point. Yet were its naval capabilities enough to justify the expression used by Lycophron?

From Rhodes comes the fragment of an inscription published by Vassa Kontorini in 1983 (Fig. 5.6).[118] This alludes to diplomatic relations with Rome and makes the effort to explain that the sanctuary of Capitoline Jupiter was the most sacred of this distant city, a clarification suggesting that these relations had been recently established. It also refers to a third state, with which the Romans (?) sought to enter into relations through the mediation of the Rhodians (?). On the other hand, Polybius ascribes these words to the Rhodian ambassador who came to plead the cause of his city before the Senate in 167 BC:

οὕτως γὰρ ἦν πραγματικὸν τὸ πολίτευμα τῶν Ῥοδίων ὡς σχεδὸν ἔτη τετταράκοντα πρὸς τοῖς ἑκατὸν κεκοινωνηκὼς ὁ δῆμος Ῥωμαίοις τῶν ἐπιφανεστάτων καὶ καλλίστων ἔργων οὐκ ἐπεποίητο πρὸς αὐτοὺς συμμαχίαν.

The policy of Rhodes had been so little dictated by sentiment, that although that state had for nearly a hundred and forty years taken part in the most glorious and finest achievements of the Romans, they had never made alliance with Rome.[119]

Fig. 5.6 Inscription alluding to diplomatic relations between Rhodes and Rome (Kontorini [1983] 24–32; Archaeological Museum of Rhodes).

---

[116] Chapter 2, p. 51.   [117] Above, pp. 103–105.
[118] Kontorini (1983) 24–32.   [119] Polyb. 30.5.6, with the translation of W. R. Paton.

In an article published in 1903,[120] then in his famous work *Rome, la Grèce et les monarchies hellénistiques au IIIe s. av. J.-C.*, published in 1921,[121] Holleaux corrected this text to establish the near total absence of relations between Rome and the East until the First Illyrian War (229–228 BC). The words meaning 'hundred' (πρὸς τοῖς ἑκατόν) would thus be an interpolation, and the agreement with the Rhodians would have commenced only in 200 BC, or 'nearly 40 years' before 167 BC. Following this theory, Kontorini thus dated the above-mentioned inscription to the end of the third century. Nevertheless, the correction of Polybius' text by Holleaux can no longer be accepted. As its author himself admitted, it supposes an interpolation which is impossible to explain and is not supported by the manuscript tradition. Moreover, it is particularly radical and leads to a most unsatisfactory result, since the number of years separating 200 and 167 is closer to thirty than to forty. As for the inscription published by Kontorini, it is most probably a decree, whose dating is clearly too late, as the palaeography points towards the beginning of the third century, perhaps the 270s.[122] In fact, relations between Rome and Rhodes had already commenced at the end of the fourth century, just as Polybius writes, and the inscription discovered at Rhodes, cut slightly after the establishment of these relations, is proof of this.[123] If the document refers to the sanctuary of Capitoline Jupiter, this mention certainly is not 'one of the banal formulae used for official religious ceremonies',[124] as the editor would wish, but occurs because the treaty of friendship concluded between Rome and Rhodes was preserved there, in the same way, for example, as the famous Carthaginian treaties that Polybius read *in situ*.[125]

Another inscription, also attributable to the turn of the fourth and third centuries, mentions three brothers killed at sea while they were fighting against unidentified pirates (most probably from Phalasarna)[126] and against the 'Tyrrhenians', that is, the Etruscans (Fig. 5.7).[127] As Rome itself was engaged in the battle against piracy, especially Etruscan, during the same period,[128] the nature of the 'most glorious and finest achievements' evoked by Polybius is hardly in doubt. Since the end of the fourth century, the Romans and Rhodians strove to secure the seas, if not together, at least in parallel.[129]

Like Rhodes, Rome was thus a maritime power at the end of the fourth century BC. The evidence gathered by Arnaldo Momigliano and then by William Harris points in the same direction.[130] The decade 314–305 BC is marked by a series of aggressions and colonial foundations suggesting significant activity at sea. Livy's account seems to imply that the *duoviri navales* instituted in 311 BC were not an

---

[120] Holleaux (1903) 183–190. [121] Holleaux (1921) 30–46.
[122] Badoud (2015) 215 (no. 245).
[123] Badoud (2015–2016) 243–244. [124] Kontorini (1983) 25.
[125] Polyb. 3.21–27 (see especially 22.3 and 26.1). [126] Sekunda (2004–2009) 595–600.
[127] Bresson (2007) 162–163 (no. 2). [128] Strabo 5.2.5.
[129] Badoud (2015–2016) 239–243; cf. Schmitt (1957) 1–49; Bresson (2007) 145–164.
[130] Harris (2017) 14–26.

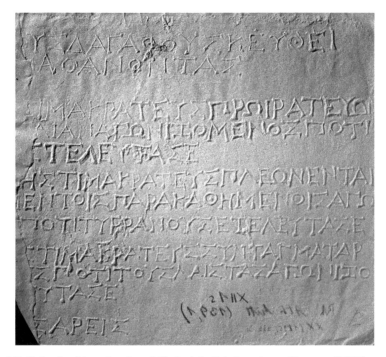

Fig. 5.7 Epitaph of three brothers killed while fighting pirates (Bresson [2007] 162–163 [no. 2]; squeeze of W. Peek, kept at the Berlin-Brandenburgische Akademie der Wissenschaften).

occasional office.[131] The fleet of the Romans and their *socii navales* perhaps was that which dissuaded Pyrrhus from attacking them on the sea after 280 BC. The acquisition of half of a forest of Bruttium during the 270s BC[132] was motivated by the need to construct ships, while Rome also undertook intense diplomatic activity during the war against Pyrrhus and the Tarentines. Its ambassadors are found in Carthage,[133] in Sagunto (?),[134] in Alexandria,[135] and in Rhodes, whose support they sought in order to establish relations with another state.[136] Contrary to the thesis developed by Holleaux, the early Hellenistic Mediterranean was not a partitioned but an integrated space, in which Rome interacted with the Punic, Iberian, and Greek worlds.

---

[131] Livius 9.30.3–4. [132] Dion. Hal. *Ant. Rom.* 20.15.
[133] Polyb. 3.25.
[134] Polyb. 3.30.1 with the commentary of Coarelli (2001) 325.
[135] Above, p. 115, n. 100.
[136] I have wondered whether this state could be Carthage, but this is unlikely.

Imperialism and Propaganda in the Mediterranean

In 283 BC, the Rhodians proclaimed themselves masters of sea and land in the epigram inscribed on the base of the Colossus. Supported by the renown of the statue, the news must have quickly reached the allies of the city (and its enemies, as the poem of Alcaeus several decades later attests). Around 270 BC, a poet established in Alexandria, but intimately linked to Italy, Lycophron of Chalcis, attributes to the Romans the 'sceptres and monarchy over land and sea'. It is thus likely that the most famous verse of the *Alexandra* echoes the epigram inscribed a few years earlier on the base of the most famous statue of the ancient world. The question remains whether Lycophron is responsible for the borrowing, or if he only continued in his own way a formula that already constituted an element of Roman propaganda addressed to the Greeks.

The epigram of the Colossus and the *Alexandra*, in any case, have both suffered from the same interpretive bias, as the claim they express has been exaggerated. This has wrongly led not only to the later dating of the two poems but also to the supposition of a forgery in the first and an interpolation in the second. If, at the beginning of the third century BC, the Rhodians and the Romans asserted sovereignty over different lands (the Peraea for the former, Italy for the latter), their claim to rule the seas was based on a common fight against piracy, the object of the 'most glorious and finest achievements' mentioned by Polybius in a text which has also been wrongly believed to be an interpolation, leading to the incorrect, late dating of the decree (?) referring to the relations between Rhodes and Rome. In one sense, the similar way in which the epigram of the Colossus, the *Alexandra* of Lycophron, the testimony of Polybius, and the decree (?) have been treated by scholars constitutes the best proof of their affinity.

6
The Location of the Colossus

Since the Middle Ages, the location of the Colossus of Rhodes has given rise to a large number of hypotheses, none of which has been able to prevail until the present day. Let us therefore examine each of these to arrive, by elimination, at the most likely. We shall then gather all of the evidence that can support it and shall eventually return to the dedicatory epigram of the statue, whose importance has been stressed in the previous chapter: it will allow us not only to discover the location of the Colossus but also to understand what motivated the Rhodians to give the statue such an extraordinary size.

The Port

The Medieval Myth

From the time when Rhodes was under the control of the Knights of Saint John (1309–1522), the location of the statue was already an object of curiosity for pilgrims along the route to Jerusalem. The journal of Nicola de Martoni, a solicitor from Campania, echoes a tale recorded in 1394 or 1395:

> *De ecclesia Sancti Nicolai et de quodam ydolo.—In capite moli est quedam ecclesia vocabuli Sancti Nicolai, et dictum ac certificatum fuit michi quoddam magnum mirabile quod, antiquo tempore, fuit quidam magnus ydolus, sic mirabiliter formatus quod unum pedem tenebat in capite dicti moli ubi est ecclesia Sancti Nicolai et alium tenebat in capite alterius moli ubi sunt molendina, que mola distant unum ab alio per medium mileare, super quibus stabat squarratus et rectus, et est corpus dicti ydoli tante altitudinis quod naves et alia navilia, in quantumcumque fuissent magne altitudinis, cum volebant intrare portum Rodi, transiebant cum arboribus et belis subtus inter tibias et crura dictiy ydoli, et quisquis ascendebat ad capud dicti ydoli videbat centum milearia longe, tante erat altitudinis. Deinde destructus fuit.*

On the Church of Saint Nicholas and on an idol.—At the end of the mole, there is a church by the name of Saint Nicholas. I have been told and assured of a quite extraordinary fact. In ancient times, there was a great idol, so amazingly constructed that it had one of its feet at the end of the aforementioned mole, where the Church of Saint Nicholas is located, and the other at the end of another mole, where there are found some mills. The distance between these two moles is one thousand feet, above which it stood square and straight; the body of this idol was of such a height that the ships and other boats, whatever their size was, when they wished to enter the harbour of Rhodes, passed with their masts and their sails between the legs of the aforesaid idol. When someone climbed up to the head of this idol, he saw one hundred miles, so great was its height. Afterwards, it was destroyed.[1]

The 'great idol'—which De Martoni later calls *Coliseus*—would thus have spanned the two main harbours of Rhodes, with one foot on the pier occupied during that period by the Church of Saint Nicholas and the other foot on the 'mole of the mills', 400 m away. Reporting the same story to the Dominicans of Ulm in 1483, Felix Fabri stresses that he did not read about it but merely heard it.[2] Seven years later, the Milanese Santo Brasca takes this account at face value.[3]

The location endorsed by De Martoni gave the statue a height significantly greater than 1 km and opposed both logic and aesthetics by involving two different harbours (Fig. 6.1a). André Thevet remedied the aesthetic problem in 1575 by placing the monument at the entrance to the great harbour (Fig. 6.1b),[4] the drawing of which was borrowed from Bernhard von Breydenbach (Fig. 7.16). A century later, Cornelis de Bruijn adopted the same solution.[5]

In 1731, Charles Marie de la Condamine placed the Colossus at the entrance to the small harbour, known as the *mandraki* (Fig. 6.1c) and rejected the hypothesis, obviously inspired by Chares' community of origin, according to which the statue would have been erected at Lindos, whose port to him seemed too large[6] (in 1545, Sebastian Münster had already placed the Colossus in Lindos but on a hill, with no consideration for the myth first mentioned by Nicola de Martoni).[7] In 1800, the diplomat and orientalist Josef von Hammer-Purgstall, who was spending time on Rhodes as the interpreter for the British admiral Sidney Smith (after whom the ancient acropolis would be named)[8] during the period of the Napoleonic Wars, took advantage of his stay to make some observations on the topography of the city. He also wished to place the statue on the moles of the *mandraki*, which,

---

[1] Le Grand (1895) 585.   [2] Hassler (1849) 252.
[3] Momigliano Lepschy (1966) 121; De Vaivre and Vissière (2014) 739 (and p. 777 for the account of Grünenberg, who locates the Colossus vaguely in the harbour).
[4] Thevet (1575) f. 205r–v.   [5] De Bruijn (1698) 173, 174.
[6] De la Condamine, C. M., *Journal de mon voyage du Levant (21 mai – 6 octobre 1731)*, BnF, ms. Français 11333, f. 297.
[7] Münster (1545) DCCX, contradicted by Thevet (1575) 206r–v. See Chapter 7, 166–167.
[8] The house of Sidney Smith, which occupied the top of the acropolis, can be seen on Figs 6.1 and 6.19.

THE PORT 123

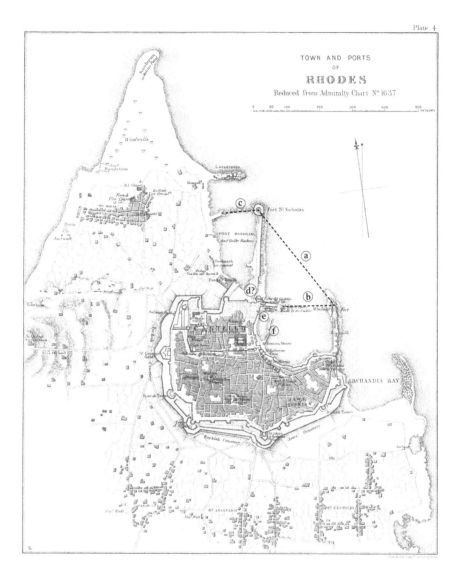

Fig. 6.1 Proposed locations for the Colossus of Rhodes, from 1394 to 1856, reported on the British Admiralty chart no. 1667 (1862). a. Nicola de Martoni (1394–1395). b. André Thevet (1575) and Cornelis de Bruijn (1698). c. Charles Marie de la Condamine (1732) and Josef von Hammer-Purgstall (1811). d. William Turner (1820). e. Bernard Rottiers (1830) and Victor Guérin (1856). f. William Hamilton (1842) and Ludwig Ross (1845).

contrary to those of the great harbour, appeared close enough to allow for his hypothesis.[9]

While visiting Rhodes in 1815, the painter William Turner alluded to another possibility:

> At the extremity of the Mandraici [sic], towards the land, is a small causeway, on the southern (land) side of which is still a small pool of water. The distance which this causeway crosses is just sixty feet, and some (among them the Ἀρχιμανδρίτης [archimandrite]) suppose this to have been the site of the Colossus.[10]

This solution seemed convincing, since it ascribed to the Colossus a height which was 'neither immoderately great nor contemptibly little' and since it could 'be reconciled with the authenticated fact of the Jew who bought the brass of the statue from the Arabs'.[11] Yet this 'authenticated fact' is a historical forgery.[12] The sketch that illustrates the description of Turner is at odds with the actual topography of Rhodes, so that the description itself was perhaps written from memory and is thus likely to be misleading. The 'small pool' mentioned by the painter is absent from the slightly later British Admiralty Chart No. 1637 (Fig. 6.1) but is reminiscent of the duck pond seen in an illumination of the manuscript of Guillaume Caoursin's *Gestorum Rhodiae obsidionis commentarii* (Fig. 6.2). In this case, it would have been an ephemeral shallow lagoon located in the marshy zone created by the partial filling-in of the ancient military harbour, which had become the *mandraki* (Fig. 6.1d).

Several years later, a French consular agent by the name of Simian claimed to have identified the base of the Colossus at the site of the gate known as *Eghrì-limàn* (Fig. 6.1e), which local tradition regarded—and still regards—[13] as the southern tip of a canal that would have connected the two harbours before it was allegedly backfilled by the Grand Master d'Aubusson, who died in 1503.[14] Such a tradition is certainly groundless, as it is not verified by any pre-sixteenth century map or description and as the safety of Rhodes always required the separation of the port that was completely fortified from the port that was not (the great harbour in Antiquity, the small harbour in the Middle Ages). The illumination from the *Gestorum Rhodiae obsidionis commentarii* incidentally shows that, around 1480, the gate of *Eghrì-limàn* led to the arsenal, which included three warehouses (Fig. 6.2): I cannot see how a canal could have traversed this location at any time. Colonel Rottiers[15] nevertheless followed the hypothesis of Simian, by

---

[9] Von Hammer-Prugstall (1811) 65.   [10] Turner (1820) III, 15.
[11] Ibid.   [12] Chapter 4, pp. 69–73.
[13] See, for instance, Hoepfner (2003) 22; Manoussou-Ntella (2017) 176.
[14] Gabriel (1923) 69–70.   [15] Rottiers (1830) 80–87.

THE PORT 125

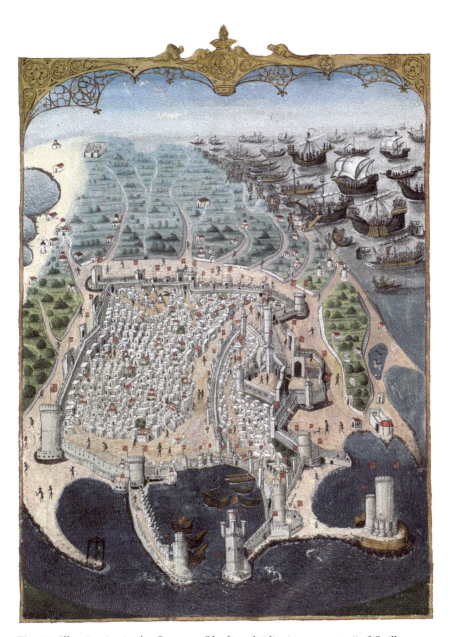

Fig. 6.2 Illumination in the *Gestorum Rhodiae obsidionis commentarii* of Guillaume Caoursin, manuscript from 1483/1484 (Paris, Bibliothèque Nationale de France, ms. Latin 6067, f. 18r).

passing him off as a Greek guide by the name of 'Dimitri', whom he would cite repeatedly in his misleading *Monumens de Rhodes*.[16]

Among the first archaeologists to explore the city, William Hamilton[17] and Ludwig Ross[18] suggested locating the statue on the 'double embankment' that had long divided the grand basin (Fig. 6.1f), by again arguing for the suitability of its dimensions. Victor Guérin, however, preferred to follow the hypothesis popularized by Rottiers.[19]

Writing as late as 1900, Hendrik van Gelder was the last scholar to accept the existence of a Colossus whose legs stood on distinct bases. He situated the statue over the canal which, in his opinion, connected the military harbour with a third harbour[20] (the Western harbour, whose remains had been discovered by Charles Newton).[21] This canal existed no more than the canal mentioned by Rottiers and his followers.

The Origin of the Myth

The myth of the Colossus straddling the port of Rhodes was recognized as such by the Count of Caylus in 1753:

> Il est assez étonnant que dans ces derniers temps on ait imaginé le colosse placé à l'entrée du port, avec les jambes écartées; on ne le trouve décrit dans cette position dans aucun auteur, ni représenté dans aucun monument ancien.
>
> It is quite striking that, in recent times, one would believe that the Colossus was located at the entrance of the port, with its legs apart; we neither find it described this way within any author nor represented in any ancient monument.[22]

This myth was wrongly ascribed to Blaise de la Vigenère[23] by Caylus and his followers.[24] Despite many conjectures, it can be explained neither by the original configuration of the statue,[25] nor the misunderstanding of an ancient text, be it the *True Histories* of Lucian,[26] the epigram of the statue,[27] or the treatise in which

---

[16] Badoud (2019c) 44–45.   [17] Hamilton (1842) 66.   [18] Ross (1845) 86.
[19] Guérin (1856) 106, with reservations derived from De Pestels [Caylus] (1759) 364.
[20] Van Gelder (1900) 387.   [21] Newton (1865) 174–175.
[22] De Pestels [Caylus] (1759) 364, followed, among the early travellers, only by De Choiseul-Gouffier (1782) 108.
[23] De la Vigenère (1578) 137.
[24] De Pestels [Caylus] (1759) 364, followed by Lesbazeilles (1876) 124; Augé de Lassus (1878) 16.
[25] *Pace* Moreno (1994a) 241; Moreno (1994b) 141; Moreno (1999) 195 (see Chapter 7, pp. 205–210, on the Apollo of Santa Marinella); Michalaki-Kollia (2007) 71–72; Michalaki-Kollia (2013a) 27; Michalaki-Kollia (2017) 142.
[26] Lucianus *Verae historiae* 1.18, mentioned by De Pestels [Caylus] (1759) 362; Bursian (1863) 92 n. 3.
[27] *Anth. Pal.* 6.171 (above, pp. 96–97), vv. 5–6, mentioned by Benndorf (1876) 45–48; Robert (1899) 2131; Dombart (1970) 72; R. Higgins (1989) 134; Ntantalia (2001) 133. See also below, pp. 127, 151, 153–155.

Plutarch compares certain 'kings and rulers' to 'unskilful sculptors, who think their colossal figures look large and imposing if they are modelled with their feet far apart, their muscles tense, and their mouths wide open'.[28] None of these texts connects the harbour of Rhodes with the Colossus or states that the latter had separated legs, nor does the epigram of the Colossus say that the statue stood 'high above the sea'.[29]

The myth of the statue spanning the harbour of Rhodes has, in fact, a purely archaeological origin. A few years after 1464, the Church of Saint Nicholas, where De Martoni had situated one of the bases of the Colossus, had given way to a fort, which would play a crucial role in 1480 and 1522, during the two Ottoman sieges of the town (Fig. 6.3).[30] In their accounts of the events, Guillaume Caoursin,[31]

Fig. 6.3 Fort Saint Nicholas.

---

[28] Plut. *Mor.* 779F–780A [*Ad principem ineruditum* 2] (with the translation of H. N. Fowler), mentioned by Lüders (1865) 23; Dombart (1970) 72; Vedder (2006a) 151–153; Vedder (2015) 14–15, 80–82. Ironically, De Pestels [Caylus] (1759) 363 used this passage *against* the myth of the Colossus bestriding the harbour of Rhodes by arguing that Chares was too skilled to have produced the kind of statue described by Plutarch. Cf. Chapter 4, p. 82, n. 143.

[29] *Pace* Hoepfner (2007) 74 (in German) and 109 (in Greek), using the German translation of Beckby (1965) 543, which is here misleading.

[30] Gabriel (1921) 80.

[31] G. Caoursin [Caorsin], *Gestorum Rhodie obsidionis commentarii* (1483/1484). BnF, ms. Latin 6067 (twelve editions from 1480 to 1502, among which the best is Caoursin [1496]), f. 23r = De Vaivre and Vissière (2014) 401.

Fig. 6.4 Ancient block reused in the entrance of Fort Saint Nicholas. a. Photograph of the block. b. Drawing by Albert Gabriel (1932).

the anonymous author of the *Histoire journalière*,[32] and Jacques Fontaine[33] place the statue at this location, but on a single base. Their descriptions, like that of De Martoni and the later pilgrims, aim to make sense of ancient architectural remains, some of which are still visible today. Such is the case with a curved block measuring 190 cm that belonged to a circular building with a diameter of *c.*17 m (Fig. 6.4). This building can only be the tower which was needed to protect the entrance of the military harbour.[34]

It is certainly no coincidence that Nicola de Martoni was the first to mention the myth of the Colossus spanning the harbour of Rhodes, while discussing the Church of Saint Nicholas: both were built, so to speak, on the same remains.

The Perpetuation of the Myth

While summarizing his stay on the island in 1853, Charles Newton proposed that the ancient remains visible at Fort Saint Nicholas be considered as those of a single base belonging to the Colossus; like a seamark if not a lighthouse, the statue would have been erected on the mole that extended the pier of the ancient

---

[32] *Histoire journalière de ce qui se passa soubs la conduite de fr. Pierre d'Aubusson, Grand Maistre de Roddes, au siège de la ville de Roddes, faict par Mahomet II empereur des Turcs, en l'année 1480* (1495). BnF, ms. Dupuy 255, f. 17r = De Vaivre and Vissière (2014) 174.

[33] Fontaine [Fontanus] (1524) 37.

[34] Although the presence of such a building is beyond doubt, Filimonos-Tsopotou (2004) 49–54 and her predecessors place no ancient tower at the Fort of Saint Nicholas.

military harbour,[35] the location once adopted by Caoursin.[36] This argument was made even more appealing from 1864, when Fort Saint Nicholas started to be exploited as a lighthouse by the French company Collas & Michel,[37] and nearly irresistible from 1886, when the Statue of Liberty, the modern sister of the Colossus, was unveiled in New York harbour.[38] Taking up Newton's hypothesis in 1932,[39] Albert Gabriel attributed the curved block once included in the tower which guarded the military harbour of Rhodes to the base of the Colossus; he added that it was 'of white marble', which agreed with the description of the monument given by (Pseudo-)Philo of Byzantium.[40] In the opinion of Wolfram Hoepfner, the last archaeologist (if not the last scholar)[41] who—as late as 2007— subscribed to this hypothesis, the pedestal identified by Gabriel was included in a mole of rough stones with a diameter of *c.*50 m (Fig. 7.34); statue bases discovered at Kamiros, allegedly contemporaries of the Colossus, would have been inspired by this arrangement (Fig. 6.5).[42]

While he did not take at face value the legend of the Colossus spanning the harbour of Rhodes (endorsed by his predecessors), Newton believed that it contained a kernel of truth, namely the location of the statue in the port complex, mentioned by Caoursin. The Statue of Liberty then provided a parallel that both Gabriel and Hoepfner used. However, the account of Caoursin carries no weight here, for it is itself part of an aetiological narrative meant to explain the presence of ancient blocks at the site of Fort Saint Nicholas. The hypothesis of Newton thus perpetuates the myth that it wished to debunk.

By citing the example of the Statue of Liberty, Gabriel and Hoepfner have only added another loop to a circular argument, since the monument in New York was conceived in the light of the common beliefs about the Colossus.[43] A mole of the sort conjectured by these scholars, stripped of all defensive value, would have allowed any attacker—Demetrius in 305 BC (if it already existed), Mithridates in 88 BC, and Cassius in 42 BC—to reach the interior of the Rhodian harbour and to

---

[35] Newton (1865) 176–177, followed by Biliotti and Cottret (1881) 32. Cf. already K. O. Müller (1848) 159, n. 1: 'der Koloss [...] stand beim Hafen, aber nicht über dem Eingang'.
[36] Above, p. 127, n. 31.
[37] Thobie (2004) 272, no. 72. Cf. Manoussou-Ntella (2008) 206–207 (the year of inauguration and the name of the company being incorrect here).
[38] Chapter 7, pp. 198–202.
[39] Gabriel (1932) 358, with n. 1, whose hypothesis is accepted or not ruled out by Laurenzi (1959) 774; R. Higgins (1989) 137; Romer and Romer (1995) 32–33; Musti and Pulcini (1996) 293; Jordan (2002) 27; Anniboletti (2024) 20. Hoepfner (2003) 62 and (2007) 76 (in German) and 111 (in Greek) mentions a discovery by 'Isaac Newton' (*sic*) allegedly neglected by Gabriel. Cf. Badoud (2017c) 41 n. 55, and Chapter 7, pp. 195–198.
[40] [Philo Byzantius] p. 32, ll. 1–2 (Brodersen; above, pp. 80–82, §3).
[41] Kansteiner et al. (2014) 662 still agree with Hoepfner, whose hypothesis is not excluded by M. D. Higgins (2023) 321–322, in spite of the arguments developed in Badoud (2012) 10.
[42] Hoepfner (2000) 136–145, 150; Hoepfner (2003) 53–64; Hoepfner (2007) 75–77 (in German) and 110–113 (in Greek).
[43] Chapter 7, pp. 198–200.

Fig. 6.5 Naturalistic base *TC* 31 (Kamiros).

annihilate all naval forces of the city in one fell swoop.[44] From a strictly military point of view, the statue of Chares had no reason to be there. It is worth adding that the curved block mentioned by Gabriel is not 'of white marble' but of bluish limestone (Fig. 6.4a) and thus not in accordance with the description that Pseudo-Philo of Byzantium gives of the base of the Colossus. As for the 'naturalistic' bases which, according to Hoepfner, would reproduce or, at least, be inspired by the arrangement of the pier, they are not specific to Rhodes;[45] the only inscribed example from Kamiros can be dated to 219 BC and is therefore later than the destruction of the Colossus.[46] Furthermore, if the statue had occupied a pier, it would have crashed down into the sea, a fact that ancient authors certainly would have mentioned. Not only did they say nothing about this, but the testimony of Pliny (which evokes the gaping caverns created by the breakage of the statue) excludes

---

[44] Compare the treatment of two other buildings by the same author: below, pp. 134–139 and pp. 140–142.

[45] Marcadé (1969) mentions five 'rock bases' (86–87), which he connects with 'Alexandrian taste' (456–457). The material of the first four, described as 'bluish marble', could actually be Rhodian (stone from Lartos?), but this hypothesis seems to be excluded by the fifth, which is unique in being of white marble. Either way, the rock bases were quite common in Rhodes. See Merker (1973); Gualandi (1976) [1979] 7–260; Machaira (2011).

[46] *TC* 40. Its editor saw here a calf, which is incorrect. For the chronology, see Badoud (2015) 221, no. 390.

such a hypothesis.[47] All in all, numerous pieces of evidence argue against the placement of the statue in the port of Rhodes, and there remains not the slightest evidence for it.

Nevertheless, the medieval myth is so strongly anchored in the Western imagination that it will always find supporters,[48] one of whom was Ann Dankbaar. In April 1985, while spending her vacation on Rhodes, this Dutch-born tourist and clairvoyant had a revelation: the Colossus was lying 800 m from the lighthouse of Saint Nicholas, at a depth of 120 to 200 ft. Two years later, on the basis of this information, the Greek Merchant Marine Minister, Stathis Alexandris, launched an underwater research campaign to discover the remains of the statue. He dismissed the archaeologists from the Ministry of Culture then directed by Melina Mercouri, who herself protested vigorously—but in vain—against the schemes of her colleague. After three weeks of dives, the announcement that one of the statue's hands had been brought to the surface piqued the interest of journalists from around the world. Archaeologists were finally able to examine the precious relic, placed under strict surveillance. 'The fist-shaped stone', they said, 'was an ordinary piece of rock, and what appeared to be fingers probably had been scraped out by a dredging bucket'. The so-called 'hand' (Fig. 6.6) was eventually dated to *c.* 1984.[49] It is worth noting that, from 1980, a group of American clairvoyants had made headlines by claiming to identify the location of several ancient monuments of Alexandria, including the Lighthouse. The results of their 'survey' had been published in 1983,[50] two years before the alleged discovery of Ann Dankbaar, which they may have suggested.

The *Deîgma* and the Agora

In 1703, Olfert Dapper had already rejected the location of the Colossus in the harbour of Rhodes, by arguing that it would have been created later than the statue[51] (an obviously indefensible theory). More recently, Thomas Dombart has relied on the 'Greek manuscript' cited by Guillaume du Choul[52] to imagine that the Colossus would have been 'in the middle of the city'[53] (although Guillaume du Choul says no such thing). Are there better arguments for a location of the Colossus in an urban context?

---

[47] On these two last points, already mentioned by De Pestels [Caylus] (1759) 362 (who misunderstands Lucianus *Verae historiae* 1.8) and many authors after him, cf. Rolley (2004) 297–298.
[48] Above, p. 129, n. 41.
[49] *Associated Press* 7 July 1987; *New York Times* 8 July 1987. [50] Schwartz (1983).
[51] Dapper (1703) 97.   [52] Du Choul (1556a) 194–195.   [53] Dombart (1970) 75.

Fig. 6.6 So-called 'hand of the Colossus' (Ephorate of Antiquities of Dodecanese, Rhodes).

We may recall that, according to Pseudo-Philo, the single base of the Colossus, due to its dimensions, towered over all other statues.[54] Cecil Torr explained this comparison by supposing that all of these works were displayed in some public place, 'such as the Deigma'.[55] Sergey Selivanov arrived at the same conclusion by a different path: since two churches of Rhodes, according to him, bore the epithet of *Colossensis*, the statue must have been roughly equidistant from both, that is, in the location indicated by Torr.[56] Finally, François Préchac argued that, according to Aelius Aristides,[57] the Colossus apparently stood in or close to the *deîgma*.[58]

It goes without saying that the comparison of Pseudo-Philo has only rhetorical value, just like all other comparisons scattered throughout his text. Since the *deîgma* was a place where the samples of merchandize to be sold in the (so far not surely located) agora were examined,[59] the statues it accommodated were probably related to the commercial sphere. This at least seems true for the group depicting the People of Rhodes being crowned by the People of Syracuse, which Polybius mentions among the gifts offered to the Rhodians after the earthquake of *c*.227,[60] since other gifts made on the same occasion—such as the tax exemption granted

---

[54] [Philo Byzantius] p. 32, ll. 5–6 (Brodersen; above, pp. 80–82, §3); see also Chapter 4, p. 75.
[55] Torr (1885) 97. [56] Selivanov (1892) 157. [57] Aristid. 25.53 (Behr).
[58] Préchac (1919) 74 n. 1.
[59] For the function of the *deîgma*, see Bresson (2016) 309–313; for its location, see below, p. 145, n. 152. Hoepfner (2003) 22 locates the agora between roads P10 and P15, P30, and P32.
[60] Polyb. 5.88.8.

by Hieron II and Gelon II of Syracuse—were inspired by trade relations. Incidentally, would the king and his son have dedicated their statuary group on the *deîgma* (as reported by Polybius) if the Colossus had just fallen at this place? The argument drawn from the epithet *Colossensis* has no more weight.[61] There only ever existed one church (of Saint John) with this epithet in Rhodes. Rottiers[62] was the first to mention a chapel that shared the same name in the lower part of the town.[63] As this was just one of his countless mistakes, there is no need to linger over the conclusions drawn from it. Nor can anything be drawn from the testimony of Aelius Aristides, who mentions the *deîgma* and the 'great statue' (but also other bronzes and paintings) in one and the same sentence, since it does not tell the reader about their topographical relation.

On the other hand, Vitruvius reports that Diognetos, an engineer working for the Rhodians, having managed to ensnare one of the mobile assault towers of Demetrius, the helepolis, was authorized to take possession of it once victory was won:

Diognetus eam helepolim reduxit in urbem et in publico collocavit et inscripsit: 'Diognetus e manubiis id populo dedit munus.'

Diognetos brought this helepolis into the city, placed it in a public place, and inscribed on it: 'Diognetos, from the spoils, has offered this present to the People.'[64]

From this testimony, Thierry Piel concluded that the Rhodians had installed the Colossus itself, constructed thanks to the plunder of the helepolis, 'in the agora of the city'.[65] Nothing confirms this hypothesis, since Vitruvius mentions neither the agora nor the Colossus. If the anecdote is authentic (which I believe),[66] Diognetos was required, according to custom, to dedicate his offering in a sanctuary; it is impossible not to think of the so-called 'Pantheon' uncovered on the eastern slope of the acropolis or Monte Smith (Fig. 6.7, 5), where stone projectiles dating most probably to the period of the siege of Demetrius have been found.[67] The tower immobilized by the stratagem of the engineer was certainly carried on site in separate parts; Demetrius had transported his siege machines in the same way.[68]

On the other hand, Pliny informs us that the Colossus cost 300 talents, a sum financed 'from the engines of war belonging to King Demetrius'.[69] This material was not limited to the helepolis but presumably included it. The large quantity of wood and raw metal used to build the tower was especially suitable for sale at auction. We may safely assume that the spoils taken from the army of Demetrius

---

[61] Cf. below, p. 156.
[62] Rottiers (1830) 81.   [63] Gabriel (1932) 348.
[64] Vitr. *De arch.* 10.16.8.3–5, with the translation of F. Granger. Cf. Plut. *Vit. Demetr.* 20.9.
[65] Piel (2010) 137–138.   [66] Cf. Chapter 7, p. 176.
[67] Kantzia (1999) 75–82; Badoud (2017b) 111; Bairami (2023) 93–104.
[68] Pimouguet-Pédarros (2011) 168–173 and 345–346.
[69] Plin. *HN* 34.41 (above, pp. 64–65). See Chapter 5, pp. 106–107.

134 THE LOCATION OF THE COLOSSUS

had been used as (or for) offerings to several gods. Thus the religious sentiment of the Rhodians would not have prevented them from having these same offerings absorbed, once sold, into the construction of a *kolossós* dedicated to Helios alone. Be that as it may, the reuse of offerings, valuable or not, was normal practice.

The Soichan-Minetou Plot

Let us now examine a site that has rarely been imagined as the location of the Colossus, but has, quite inconspicuously, guided the most recent discussions about it. In 1954, to the north and below the sanctuary of Apollo Pythios (briefly

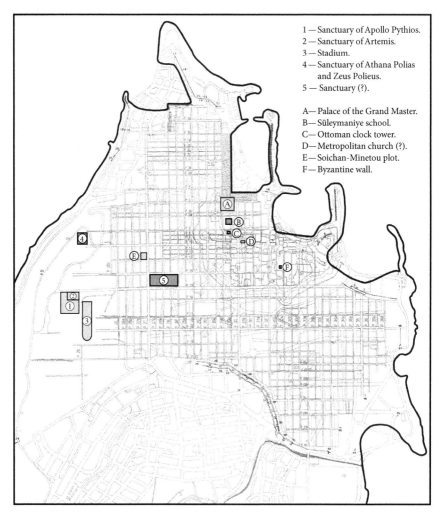

Fig. 6.7 Street map of Rhodes illustrating several proposed locations for the Colossus.

the Pythion),[70] more precisely in the plot (Ali Riza) Soichan-Minetou, located at the corner of the ancient road *P* 27 and the ancient street *P* 13,[71] corresponding to the modern streets Cheimarras and Sofouli (Fig. 6.7, E), a building with a peristyle was discovered (Figs 6.8–6.10), whose excavation—suspended in 1975 and so far incomplete—[72] has brought to light forty inscriptions.[73] Since ten of them were identified as dedications erected by the priests of Helios at the end of their term[74] (Fig. 6.11), the building was recognized as a sanctuary of the divinity, at first hesitantly by the director of the excavation, Grigoris Konstantinopoulos,[75] and then more firmly by the editor of the epigraphic collection, Vassa Kontorini, who, like Ellen Rice after her, also suggested that the Colossus stood there (although there is no space for it).[76] Konstantinopoulos then reproached his colleague for not having properly taken into account the evidence

Fig. 6.8 Peristyle structure discovered in the Soichan-Minetou plot (1975).

---

[70] Below, pp. 139–151.
[71] Kontis (1954) remains the fundamental reference. For an updated map of the city, see Filimonos-Tsopotou (2004) Ἀναδ. Σχέδ. I.
[72] Konstantinopoulos (1973) 136; Konstantinopoulos (1975) 239–248.
[73] Konstantinopoulos (1963) 1–8, nos. 1–12; *AER* II, 53–84.
[74] To *AER* II, 53–62 may be added *AER* II, 73 (*TRI* 34) and, perhaps, Konstantinopoulos (1963) 1–2, no. 1 (*TRI* 38), if this inscription, like the previous one, began with [τὸν ἱερῆ τοῦ Ἁλίου]. The reference to Rhodes' two sacred crews (ἀνφ[οτέροις] τοῖς πληρώμασ[ι], l. 15), must also be restored in Konstantinopoulos (1963) 7, no. 11, l. 6.
[75] Konstantinopoulos (1986) 243 and pl. XIII.
[76] Kontorini (1989) 178–184; Rice (1993) 239.

136 THE LOCATION OF THE COLOSSUS

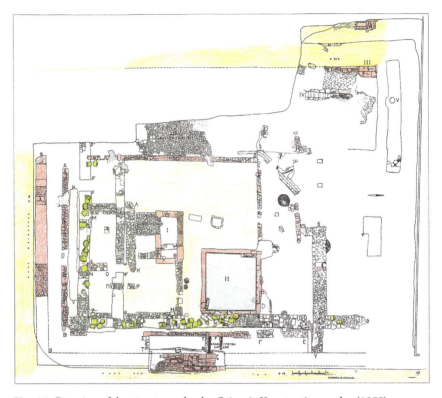

Fig. 6.9 Drawing of the structure plan by Grigoris Konstantinopoulos (1975).

pointing towards a location of the sanctuary of Helios in the area of the Palace of the Hospitallers' Grand Master.[77] Yet Konstantinopoulos himself did not provide any alternative identification for the building he had dug.[78] Maria Michalaki-Kollia attempted to solve the problem by suggesting, from 1999, that this building was 'the house of the priests of Helios' or the seat of their 'association'.[79] In 2003, Wolfram Hoepfner went a step further by identifying the building as the seat of an association of *Haliastaí*, or devotees of Helios,[80] which meant that the sanctuary of the god had to be sought elsewhere; followed (with some differences) by Ursula Vedder and Enzo Lippolis, he opted for the Pythion,[81] while Maria Michalaki-Kollia preferred the Palace of the Grand Master.[82]

From an architectural point of view, however, one must be aware that the banquet rooms on which Hoepfner relied to establish the building's use as a meeting

[77] Below, p. 153.   [78] Konstantinopoulos (1997) 71–82.
[79] Michalaki-Kollia (1999) 73; Michalaki-Kollia (2013b) 89; cf. Skaltsa (2022) 55–71; Michalaki-Kollia (2023) 163–164.
[80] Hoepfner (2003) 43–49, followed by Mariño Sánchez-Elvira (2008) 124 and Vedder (2015) 30, 130; not rejected by Lippolis (2016) 163.
[81] Below, pp. 140–144.   [82] Below, p. 153.

Fig. 6.10 Interpretation of the structure plan by Wolfram Hoepfner (2003).

space have been entirely restored (Fig. 6.10).[83] Furthermore, the inscriptions discovered *in situ* or in the immediate vicinity[84] consist largely of dedications erected by the priests of Helios,[85] victors at the *Halíeia*,[86] or notable locals and foreigners[87] honoured by the People[88] or the Council of Rhodes,[89] or closely associated with the latter body.[90] The homogeneity of this ensemble is even more remarkable when one considers that a small number of inscriptions not mentioning Helios have perhaps been wrongly associated with it. Such may be the case with two inscriptions regarding the cult of the Dioscuri, which come from a parcel of land bordering the plot where nearly all the dedications erected by the priests of Helios were discovered.[91] From this plot may on the other hand originate three documents discovered elsewhere on the acropolis. Writing about his visit to Rhodes in 1853, Newton had already noted: 'A little to the east of the stadium (Fig. 6.7, 3) is a great platform, where, perhaps, stood a temple of the Sun, as several inscriptions mentioning priests of this deity have been found near this spot.'[92]

---

[83] Compare the treatment of two other buildings by the same author: above, pp. 129–131, and below, pp. 140–142.
[84] *AER* II, 53–84. [85] *AER* II, 53–62 and *TRI* 34 (new edition of *AER* II, 73).
[86] *AER* II, 74 and 76. [87] *AER* II, 63–69. [88] *AER* II, 66–69.
[89] *AER* II, 64, 65 (?). [90] *AER* II, 63.
[91] *AER* II, 71 and 75. The first inscription also mentions Rhodos, the wife of Helios. Cf. Lippolis (2016) 166.
[92] Newton (1865) 169.

Fig. 6.11 Base of a statue offered by the priest of Helios Archokrates in c.189 BC, discovered in the Soichan-Minetou plot (*AER* II, 55; Archaeological Museum of Rhodes).

He actually mentioned only one such inscription, which he read on the base of the statue of the priest of Helios Antisthenes.[93] Yet he also described a dedication recording victories 'in the Pythian, Isthmian, and Nemean Games, and in the games called Halieia, celebrated at Rhodes in honour of the Sun-god',[94] which reminds us of similar inscriptions unearthed on the Soichan-Minetou plot. The third document mentioned above, discovered much later, is the catalogue of the Rhodian prophets, who—in my opinion—were not seers in the service of Apollo, as previously thought, but auxiliary magistrates attached to the sanctuary of Helios.[95] Thus, forty-one inscriptions can be attributed to the Soichan-Minetou plot. In none of them do the *Haliastaí* appear, which is no surprise since they

---

[93] Newton (1865) 171, referring to *TRI* 28; see below, p. 160, and Habicht (2003) 566.
[94] Newton (1865) 170, referring to *IG* XII, 1, 73. The inscription mentioned on p. 167, found on the way leading to the acropolis from the north, is *IG* XII, 1, 23.
[95] *TRI* 2.

were not a 'club' of ancient priests (or victors of the *Halíeia*, we should add), but a private association that included non-citizens and women (*Haliádai*),[96] as many people excluded from the magistracies of the city[97] and especially the priesthood of Helios. The original hypothesis that would make the Soichan-Minetou building the headquarters of an association of priests (who would not be the *Haliastaí*)[98] is not admissible either, since there is no trace of any association of this sort.

With its cistern and its rooms spread around a peristyle courtyard, the building excavated on the Soichan-Minetou plot is reminiscent of domestic architecture.[99] It differs, however, in the presence of a central *naḯskos* (?) and the inscriptions that it has produced. The inscriptions mentioning the Council do not seem numerous and specific enough to allow for its identification as a *bouleutḗrion*, and this identification, for a time envisaged by Michalaki-Kollia,[100] is at odds with the architectural evidence. We could rather think of the *prutaneîon* mentioned by Polybius and inscriptions, but those from the Soichan-Minetou plot mention neither this building[101] nor the board of magistrates that it housed[102] (although one prytanis is honoured as such).[103] The hypothesis of a *hierothuteîon*, also proposed by Michalaki-Kollia,[104] is no more convincing, if it refers to the building attested in the inscriptions from Lindos,[105] Kamiros,[106] and Ialysos,[107] which was the local equivalent of the *prutaneîon* (where honorands were entertained). The dedications of the priests of Helios (like any other dedications of the same kind) and the catalogue of the prophets of Helios (like any other catalogue of the same kind) were to be set up in the sanctuary of the god, or at least in a building associated with his cult, where other officers, like the *hierothútai* in charge of the sacrifices or the secretary whom they shared with the priest,[108] could also meet. From that point of view (and if its identification is correct), the naiskos noted by the excavators would make complete sense, an argument to which I shall return later.[109]

The Pythion

Above the stadium built on the eastern slope of the acropolis (Fig. 6.7, 1–3) extends a vast peribolos or square precinct (Fig. 6.12) that surrounds two buildings:

---

[96] See especially *IG* XII, 1, 155–156 and *NS* 46. [97] Badoud (2019b) 195.
[98] Michalaki-Kollia (1999) 73; Michalaki-Kollia (2013b) 89.
[99] Patsiada (2013) 63–65; Lippolis (2016) 163.
[100] Michalaki-Kollia (1999) 73.
[101] See Polyb. 15.23.3, 16.15.8, and the inscriptions Scrinzi (1898–1899) 259–260, no. 2; *NS* 3, l. [1]; *Lindos* 117, l. 7; cf. Polyb. 29.11.6 and Badoud et al. (2015–2016) 400.
[102] On the Rhodian prytaneis, see Van Gelder (1900) 242–244; Badoud (2015) 17–26; Badoud (2019a) 89 with n. 63.
[103] *AER* II, 63, ll. 1–2. [104] Michalaki-Kollia (1999) 73.
[105] e.g. *Lindos* 281a, l. 8 and *Lindos* 281b, l. 9. [106] e.g. *TC* 86, l. 10.
[107] Papachristodoulou (1989) 171, no. 7*. [108] *TRI* 35, ll. 7–17. [109] Below, p. 161.

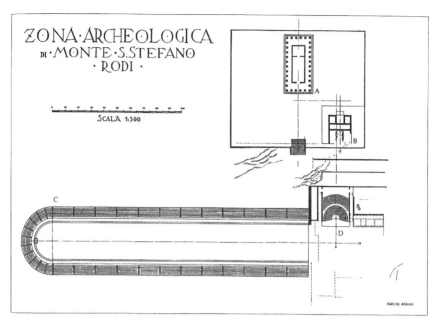

Fig. 6.12 Plan of the sanctuary of Pythian Apollo drawn by Mario Paolini in 1938.

the first (A) is the peripteral hexastyle temple traditionally attributed to Apollo Pythios; the second (B), in poor condition, is itself an enclosure—smaller and deeper than the former, with which it shares two sides—in the middle of which rises a foundation, oriented east-west and long attributed to a temple of Artemis.[110]

A Sanctuary of Apollo-Helios?

According to Hoepfner, who first attempted to overturn the established consensus, this foundation would be, in reality, the base of Helios' chariot, a statuary group mentioned by the literary sources;[111] the small enclosure, when flooded, would have provided marine scenery for it (Fig. 6.13). As for the larger peribolos, it would have enclosed the *témenos* (sacred area) of Helios mentioned in an inscription.[112] Apollo and Helios would thus have been the object of a common cult on the acropolis.[113] The pillar raised by the Rhodians across from the temple of Apollo at

---

[110] Rocco (1996b) 17–20.   [111] Chapter 3, pp. 59–61; Badoud (forthcoming 4).
[112] *IG* XII, 1, 2, l. 7.
[113] Caliò (2012) 265 and Wujewski (2018) 305 accept this part of Hoepfner's theory. As for Lippolis (2016) 170–176, see below, p. 144.

Fig. 6.13 The sanctuary of Apollo-Helios, as imagined by Wolfram Hoepfner (2003).

Delphi[114] would confirm this theory, since it was topped by a quadriga of Helios spurting sculpted streams on its base (Fig. 3.3).[115]

There is more than one archaeological difficulty with this theory. First, the Sun of the Rhodians would move from North to South and would be installed several metres above the water from where he should spring. The incongruity of such a solution would be made even more obvious by a comparison with the Delphian monument, where the Sun headed West, or with the Fountain of Apollo designed by Charles Le Brun for the Palace of Versailles, where the quadriga of the god, sculpted by Jean-Baptiste Tuby, rises from the pond, not from a pillar. Second, the entirety of the Rhodian scenery is inspired by the 'fountain' in which Karl Lehmann placed the Nike of Samothrace,[116] a fountain that never existed.[117] The pool imagined by Hoepfner does not account for the influx of water, its walls are not covered with hydraulic coating but with simple stucco, and they are decorated with pilasters that would have had no reason for existence if they had been submerged.[118]

Historical errors also occur. Flavius Josephus states that the Pythion was destroyed by a fire, most probably during the sack of Rhodes by C. Cassius Longinus in 42 BC. According to Dio Cassius, the chariot of the Sun was the only statue respected by the conqueror.[119] It is therefore difficult to assume that this chariot was in the Pythion. On the other hand, Helios became the patron deity of the Rhodians for the precise reason that, unlike Apollo, he was not part of the pantheon in the three cities united through the synoecism, a fact aimed at guaranteeing

---

[114] Jacquemin and Laroche (1986) 285–307; cf. Jacquemin and Laroche (2012).
[115] Hoepfner (2003) 33–42; Hoepfner (2007) 69–73 (in German) and 104–108 (in Greek). His theory is entirely endorsed by Partida (2017) 211–212.
[116] Lehmann (1973) 181–259.
[117] Sismondo Ridgway (2004); Hamiaux (2006) 58–60; cf. Badoud (2018b) 286 with n. 39.
[118] Compare the treatment of two other buildings by the same author: above, pp. 129–131 and pp. 134–139. Cf. also Lippolis (2016) 139.
[119] Cass. Dio. 47.33.6.

his (ethnical, if not political) neutrality.[120] Helios and Apollo could not be mistaken for one another, nor were they ever, as inscriptions attest.[121] The situation was different abroad, where the cult of Helios was hardly practised; at Delphi, for instance, Apollo could be assimilated to the guardian deity of the Rhodians,[122] although its identification as sun-god was still limited to the Orphic milieu in the fifth century BC.[123] I suppose that the current confusion between the two Rhodian gods owes much to the fact that, from the sixteenth century, artists and archaeologists have represented the Colossus of Helios as a statue of Apollo.[124]

A Sanctuary of Helios Only?

According to Ursula Vedder, the large *témenos* would have been the exclusive territory of Helios, and the base visible in the small enclosure that of his Colossus.[125] This hypothesis differs from the preceding one in that it also challenges the traditional identification of the principal sanctuary, which relies on a dedication of the Athenian statesman Glaucon, son of Eteocles, to Pythian Apollo.[126] According to the *Inscriptiones Graecae*, in 1881, Édouard Biliotti first referred to this document, found 'on the doorstep of a house' close to the structure.[127] Nevertheless, in his *Geschichte der Insel Rhodos*, finished in 1854 but remaining mostly unpublished, the medical doctor and explorer Johan Hedenborg states that he discovered this inscription while it was still among the ruins of the building (Fig. 6.14).[128] Vedder did well to cite this evidence, but the conclusion that she drew from it is incorrect. The mention by Hedenborg of 'a large cinerary urn' shows that the base had not yet been removed in his time and had apparently not been moved, or had moved only little, since antiquity. Hedenborg then reflects upon the respective identities of Helios and Apollo. In Vedder's opinion, 'if he had not followed the usual scientific convention of his time, according to which even an isolated inscription gave the name of a sanctuary, he could today be considered the first author to have glimpsed the sanctuary of Helios in the great sanctuary overlooking the terrace of the stadium'.[129] Significantly, as early as 2006, Vedder had rejected the testimony of our inscription by arguing that its find-spot was not the sanctuary.[130] When it became clear that Hedenborg's testimony contradicted this conclusion, she rejected the identification of the sanctuary because—I suppose—it disagreed with

---

[120] Chapter 1, pp. 13–14.
[121] The priests were never confused in any inscription. *Lindos* 134 distinguishes them explicitly.
[122] Chapter 3, pp. 59–61.   [123] Larson (2007) 123.   [124] Chapter 7, pp. 175–182.
[125] Vedder (2015) 57–68, followed by Lund (2017a) 141–142 and Lund (2017b). M. D. Higgins (2023) 322 is also ready to admit her hypothesis.
[126] IG XII, 1, 25. For a new dating of this inscription, see Rosamilia (2018) 263–300.
[127] Biliotti and Cottret (1881) 480.
[128] J. Hedenborg, *Geschichte der Insel Rhodos von der Urzeit bis auf die heutigen Tage* III (1854), Rhodes, Ephorate of Antiquities, ms. KK. 5093, ff. 216–218. The inscriptions and the stamps are published in Badoud (2017c); see pp. 40–42, no. 59, for the dedication of Glaucon.
[129] Vedder (2015) 32.   [130] Vedder (2006b) 365.

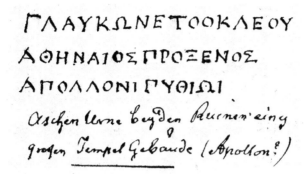

Fig. 6.14 Rhodian inscription mentioning Apollo Pythios (*IG* XII, 1, 25: third century BC), as copied by Johan Hedenborg (before 1854).

her own theory.[131] With the 'scientific convention' according to which archaeological argument must be founded on the sources still relevant, there is no reason to assume that the inscription seen by Hedenborg did not come from the sanctuary of Pythian Apollo. The city of Rhodes has not provided any other dedication to the divinity.[132]

The proximity of the sanctuary and the stadium, also suggested by Vedder, does not constitute proof either, insofar as the stadium hosted other games than the *Halíeia*, and as the *Halíeia* themselves culminated in chariot races[133] organized in a hippodrome distinct from the stadium. An inscription on a statue-base shows that an association honouring not only Helios but also Athena and Hermes 'jointly operated' (rather than 'built'?) the hippodrome when the text was carved, most probably during the late Hellenistic or early Imperial period (Fig. 6.15).[134] While it is true that, during the final (Imperial) phase of its history, the stadium could have been used as a hippodrome by means of a removable *spina*, this hypothesis is not without technical difficulties, as stressed by its own author, Panos Valavanis. More importantly, the latter was mistaken when he dated the inscription to the second century AD and assumed its relationship to an

---

[131] Compare the treatment of Joseph. *BJ* 1.424 (below, p. 145) and of [Philo Byzantius] p. 32, ll. 10–17 (Brodersen; above, pp. 80–82, §4) (below, p. 147) by the same author.

[132] For another inscription found in the sanctuary, unfortunately incomplete and currently lost, see *TRI* 37.

[133] Badoud (forthcoming 4).

[134] *NSER* 3 (second or first century BC). Commenting on this inscription, Maillot (2015) 139 n. 13 remarks that 'some doubt remains about the sense of *synergaxámenoi*: one thinks of the Delian expression *hoi tēn tetrágōnon* [*agoràn*] *ergazómenoi*, where *ergazómenoi* means "traders" (Roussel, *I. Délos* 1709), or more precisely, "those who make business there"'. She eventually translates this phrase as 'those who built the hippodrome'. As a verb such as *kataskeuázō* would have been more appropriate to render the idea of 'building', the Delian parallel suggests that the usual meaning of *sunergázomai* ('co-operating') is preferable. The Rhodian association, which is also mentioned in *IG* XII, 1, 162, l. 1, would thus have been involved in the organization of festivals, like the *Erethimiázontes* in the Ialysian sanctuary of Apollo, but on a temporary basis.

Fig. 6.15 Rhodian inscription mentioning the hippodrome (*NSER* 3).

association responsible for the final building phase of the stadium.[135] The inscription, which would then have mentioned the stadium and not the hippodrome, proves instead that both structures were long (if not always) distinct. The hippodrome was probably not built before the first century BC, the date that can be attributed to the earliest mentions of chariot races at Rhodes.[136] Its exact location is unknown but may correspond to the *Halíeion pedíon* (the 'plain of Helios'), if this is the authentic name of the *Ēlúsion pedíon* (the 'Elysian fields') which the *Etymologicum Magnum* mentions on Rhodes.[137]

A Sanctuary of Apollo and Helios?

The author of the last study dedicated to the acropolis of Rhodes, Enzo Lippolis, also engaged in the debate regarding the identification of the history of Temple A and Temple B. For him, if the former actually belonged to Apollo, the latter was dedicated to Helios. This hypothesis would make Helios a god subordinate to Apollo.[138] Previous discussion about Hoepfner's theory[139] is therefore worth recalling: despite misconceptions rooted in collective imagination since the Renaissance, the Rhodians never assimilated Helios and Apollo and always gave precedence to the former over the latter. The theory of Lippolis can therefore not be accepted.

A Sanctuary of Apollo and Artemis

Temple A
In reality, the efforts to overturn the traditional identification of Temple A rest only on the idea (taken from Hoepfner)[140] that the largest temple in the city must

---

[135] Valavanis (1999a) 108; Valavanis (1999b) 91–93.   [136] Badoud (forthcoming 4).
[137] *Etym. Magn.*, s.v. Ἡλύσιον πεδίον, with the commentary of Van Gelder (1900) 295–296.
[138] Lippolis (2016) 116–142, 170–176; cf. Monaco (2023) 132.   [139] Above, pp. 140–142.
[140] Hoepfner (2003) 33; Hoepfner (2007) 70 (in German) and 105 (in Greek).

belong to its patron deity. This argument is unsatisfactory, as it would make, for instance, Olympian Zeus and not Athena the patron deity of Athens, since his temple is much bigger than the one which his daughter possessed on the acropolis. Furthermore, it is now clear, thanks to Lippolis' study, that Temple A acquired its imposing proportions only at a later date; when the Colossus was built, it was still a notably smaller building.[141] The date of the addition of the peristyle is uncertain. While the damage caused by the earthquake of *c*.227 BC may have been the reason for the reorganization of the acropolis, as has been supposed for the reconstruction of the stadium,[142] Polybius does not mention the temples or the stadium among the damaged buildings[143] (unlike the ramparts, for which an inscription[144] confirms the accuracy of his account, which was based on a Rhodian source).[145] On the other hand, Flavius Josephus states that, probably after the sack of 42 BC, the Pythion was reconstructed through a grant given 'to Rhodes' by Herod the Great.[146] His testimony reinforces the traditional identification of Temple A, whose importance justified an act of evergetism, and which shows capitals independently datable to the first century BC.[147] I must insist that the historian explicitly refers to a building that belonged to all Rhodians, and not, as Vedder claimed (to discard his testimony),[148] to a sanctuary of a secondary centre (e.g. Ialysos, Kamiros, or Lindos) that neither Cassius would have destroyed nor Herod rebuilt. We should therefore consider whether 42 BC is a more satisfying *terminus* than *c*.227 BC for the addition of the peristyle. Be that as it may, other Rhodian temples could have been larger than that of Apollo Pythios at some point in their history, such as the temple of Athena Polias and Zeus Polieus on the acropolis and an edifice whose column drums have been reused in a Byzantine wall (Fig. 6.7, F).[149] The latter, for a time attributed to Helios,[150] may have been the Dionysion, which itself has long been identified with as building now recognized as a tetrapylon.[151] The Dionysion stood in the lower part of the city near the *deîgma*[152] and was surrounded by porticoes sheltering valuable offerings.[153]

A major figure in the Rhodian pantheon, Pythian Apollo was in any case entirely worthy of his sanctuary, whose importance is better reflected in the size

---

[141] Lippolis (2016) 124–125.
[142] Valavanis (1999a) 101; Valavanis (1999b) 79; cf. Kontis (1958) 156–157.
[143] Polyb. 5.88.1 (above, pp. 46–47).
[144] Konstantinopoulos (1967) 124–128; on this inscription, see Badoud (2015) 88 with n. 43.
[145] Chapter 2, p. 47.   [146] Joseph. *BJ* 1.424.
[147] Rocco (1996b) 14; cf. Lippolis (2016) 124.
[148] Vedder (2006b) 367. Vedder (2017) ignores Josephus. Compare the treatment of *IG* XII, 1, 25 (above, p. 143) and of [Philo Byzantius] p. 32, ll. 10–17 (Brodersen; above, pp. 80–82, §4) (below, p. 147) by the same author.
[149] Kontis (1951) 224–234.   [150] Hoepfner and Schwandner (1986¹) 24.
[151] Cante (1986–1987) 175–266, correcting Jacopi (1926) 326 and Maiuri (1928) 46.
[152] Diod. Sic. 19.45.4.
[153] Lucianus *Amores* 8. Konstantinopoulos (1994–1995) 75–82 suggests that the Berlin Adorant, found in Rhodes in the fifteenth century, could have been dedicated to Dionysos.

and position of its precinct. In regard to its position, a dedication from the end of the third century BC[154] provides an interesting hierarchy: the priest of Helios, eponymous magistrate of the city, begins the list as expected and is followed by the priests of Athena Polias and Zeus Polieus, Poseidon Hippios, Apollo, and a dozen other gods or heroes. The top of the acropolis was occupied by the temple of Athena and of Zeus;[155] Apollo had his location down in the lower sanctuary. In other words, the topography of the acropolis, if correctly understood here, reflects the hierarchy of the gods, as expressed by the epigraphy;[156] we recall that Zeus joined Athena on the top of the Rhodian acropoleis precisely when Helios became the major divinity of the island,[157] which makes it very likely that the latter's sanctuary was situated elsewhere.

Temple B

One can therefore not assume, in opposition to all available documentation and through an additional conjecture, that the substructure of the Temple B (Fig. 6.16) was actually the base of the Colossus, erected in the sanctuary of Helios. The hypothesis of Vedder is supported only by the size of the foundation (23.4 × 17.7 m), comparable with that of the Colossus of Nero (14.75 × 17.6 m: Fig. 4.3) but also of many aediculae.[158] It is contradicted not only by the fact that a statue intended

Fig. 6.16 The sanctuary of Artemis, viewed from the south-west.

---

[154] *Lindos* 134, ll. 9–10.   [155] Chapter 1, p. 15, n. 80.
[156] Cf. Michalaki-Kollia (2023) 181.   [157] Chapter 1, p. 15.   [158] Below, pp. 155–156.

to be the highest in the world would not have been installed under ground level but also by the complete absence of metalworking activity in the immediate area, itself hardly compatible with the text of Pseudo-Philo of Byzantium stating that the statue was cast in place and not in some distant pit.[159] Hence the need to reject once more the available evidence, by arguing that the statue was not cast in place but assembled in the precinct,[160] which Vedder eventually presented as a (subterranean) 'workshop'.[161] This hypothesis is certainly no more satisfying than the pool imagined by Hoepfner.[162]

In fact, elevation fragments still visible on site, which include Corinthian capitals attributable to the late Hellenistic period, confirm the presence of a temple of secondary importance within the peribolos of Apollo (Fig. 6.17). If it is correct to assume that the temple was characterized by an internal colonnade in the shape of a Π, the building plan may find parallels at both Rhodes and Ialysos.[163] In 1938, Italian archaeologists discovered nearby a 'very huge number of terracottas'[164] depicting female mortals, dressed with the elegance of Hellenistic fashions, a standing divinity with a kalathos on the head or seated on a throne, like the

Fig. 6.17 Fragments of the elevation of temple B (epistyle in the first plan, drums in the second plan).

---

[159] [Philo Byzantius] p. 32, ll. 10–17 (Brodersen; above, pp. 80–82, §4). See Chapter 4, pp. 79–83.
[160] Vedder (2015) 40–56; Vedder (2017) 21–25. Compare the treatment of *IG* XII, 1, 25 (above, p. 143) and Joseph. *BJ* 1.424 (above, p. 145) by the same author; see also Chapter 4, pp. 83–87.
[161] Vedder (2017) 25–26. [162] Above, pp. 140–142.
[163] Rocco (1996b) 17–20; Lippolis (2016) 127–140; cf. Livadiotti and Rocco (1999) 109–118.
[164] Rocco (1996b) 19 mentions 'three hundred small terracotta heads of Hellenistic coroplastic'.

Fig. 6.18 Hellenistic terracotta discovered in a votive deposit near temple B.

Hecate of the frieze of Lagina, and numerous *baskania*[165] and apotropaic symbols, among which also the phallus'.[166] This material would clearly be out of place in the sanctuary of Helios. As Vedder noted, Lili Kahil had some doubts regarding the identification of certain figurines,[167] but these doubts, if justified, would concern the identification of Artemis with Hecate in Rhodian sculpture (Fig. 6.18). As a whole, the deposit would suit a divinity closely linked to the female sphere, with both protective and punitive powers, such as Artemis.[168]

The Deer of Artemis

Following a suggestion I made in 2011,[169] Lippolis identified the surrounding structure of temple B with an enclosure that allowed for the entrance of animals to be sacrificed to the divinity.[170] We have seen that, for historical reasons, his attribution of Temple B to Helios cannot be accepted.[171] If, however, my identification of the precinct as an enclosure holds true, which animals were brought into it? The lower level can only be accessed by a doorway and a staircase that are certainly too narrow for the cattle sacrificed to Helios[172] or for the horses cast into the sea in his honour.[173] At any rate, these domesticated animals did not need to be kept in an enclosure before being led to the altar and sacrificed, which is yet another reason to exclude the attribution of Temple B to Helios.

The enclosure, however, was perfectly appropriate for wild animals, such as the deer that were frequently sacrificed to Artemis in the Greek world, as established by osteological remains, texts, and images,[174] among which are the skulls sculpted on altars from Rhodes (Fig. 6.19).[175] Victor Guérin in the middle of the nineteenth

---

[165] A *baskánion* (plural *baskánia*) is an amulet used against *baskanía*, i.e. 'malign influence'.
[166] Laurenzi (1939) 56.   [167] Kahil (1984) 686–687; cf. Lippolis (2016) 140 and n. 48.
[168] Long considered as lost, the deposit may have been spotted in the archaeological museum of Rhodes: Michalaki-Kollia (2013b) 92. A comprehensive study would be in order.
[169] In a draft of the present chapter that I sent to and discussed with E. Lippolis.
[170] Lippolis (2016) 169–170.   [171] Above, p. 144.   [172] At least in Kamiros: *TRI* 67.
[173] Badoud (forthcoming 4).
[174] Part of the evidence has been collected by Chandezon (2011) 164–169 and Léger (2017) 64, 72–73.
[175] For an example from Pergamon, see Picón and Hemingway (2016) 159 (*Altertümer von Pergamon* VII, 419).

Fig. 6.19 Four Hellenistic funerary altars decorated with deer skulls, from Rhodes (Archaeological Museum of Rhodes). a. Jacopi (1932a) 9–14, no. 27. b. *NS* 152. c. Without inscription (Italian inv. 13599). d. Without inscription (inv. E6600).

Fig. 6.20 Fallow deer of Rhodes.

century[176] and Amedeo Maiuri in the early twentieth century[177] both mention the presence of deer in the southern part of the island, where they still live today; the Lindian sanctuary of Artemis Kekoia was set in the same wild, forested area.[178] Several studies by Marco Masseti and other biologists have showed that the local population of fallow deer (*Dama dama dama*, L. 1758: Fig. 6.20) dates back to Neolithic times and retains a very specific mitochondrial DNA. When compared to populations from central and northern Europe, its specimens appear rather small.[179] In the city of Rhodes, a male and a female deer are depicted by the statues set on the two columns erected by the Italians at the entrance of the *mandraki* (a clear reference to the columns at the entrance of the Piazzetta San Marco in Venice). While the male dates back to the Italian occupation, the female replaced the Roman wolf after 1945. The Italians are also responsible for the tradition, continued until the early 2000s, of keeping deer in the ditch below the bridge that leads to what has become the main entrance of the medieval city (the Liberty Gate, opened in 1923 and once called *Porta dei cervi*).[180] The depth of this ditch is comparable to that of the enclosure on the acropolis, which also could have hosted a few deer.

---

[176] Guérin (1856) 234: around the modern village of Apolakkia.
[177] Maiuri (1992) 31: at Agios Fokas.
[178] Badoud (2017c) 46.   [179] Masseti et al. (2006) 167–175; Masseti et al. (2008) 835–844.
[180] Masseti (2002) 157.

The Relationship of Temples A and B

From an ancient perspective, the inclusion of a *témenos* of Artemis in a *témenos* of Apollo would not be unusual, since religious architecture brought together the two divinities (and occasionally their mother Leto) in many ways and allocated to them separate spaces as required.[181] At Rhodes, since Artemis was a divinity clearly less important than Apollo, it would not be surprising to find her *témenos* included within that of her brother, as in many other sanctuaries.[182] Finally, the enclosure dug into the rock of the acropolis, like the terracottas discovered in the area, matches perfectly a cult with a strong chthonian element, such as that of Artemis (but certainly not that of Helios). It is therefore safe to conclude that the traditional attribution of Temple A to Apollo and of Temple B to Artemis is correct, and to assume that the Colossus was not built there.

The Top of the Acropolis

The examination of the Python has given us the occasion to recall that the summit of the acropolis was dedicated to Athena Polias and Zeus Polieus, a fact that discredits any attempt to place the Colossus of Helios in this location.[183] Unaware of this difficulty, Paolo Moreno and Tomasz Wujewski have nevertheless suggested this very site, with the argument that the myth of the statue as a lighthouse originated from this location, which is proven to be false.[184] Paolo Moreno rightly argued that, according to the epigram carved on its base,[185] the statue must have been on an eminence,[186] but this is not sufficient ground to exclude any other location, as he himself acknowledged.[187] Tomasz Wujewski used different arguments. On the one hand, the Asianic etymology of *kolossós* would suit the location of the Colossus on a rocky eminence, comparable to those of Kolossai and Kolophon in present-day Turkey. On the other hand, the fact that the ruins of the Colossus remained untouched until the raid of Muʿāwiya in AD 653/4 could be explained not only by the cost but also by the uselessness of a removal (according to Wujewski, the situation would have been different if the statue had fallen in the centre of the city).[188] Nevertheless, *kolossós* is not an Asianic word, and its etymology does not refer to the geographical position of the statue but to its appearance.[189] The reasons provided for the ruins of the Colossus being abandoned and not removed are anachronistic; the final destruction of the statue by the Arabs is a forgery.[190] The top of the acropolis did not accommodate the Colossus.

---

[181] Sassu (2013) 13 n. 82.   [182] Aurigny and Durvye (2021).   [183] Above, p. 146.
[184] Above, pp. 128–129; cf. Chapter 7, pp. 168, 201.
[185] *Anth. Pal.* 6.171 (above, pp. 96–97), vv. 4–5.
[186] Moreno (1994a) 241; Moreno (1994b) 141; Moreno (1999) 194.
[187] Moreno (1994b) 141 and Moreno (1999) 194, contradicting Moreno (1994a) 241. See below, p. 157.
[188] Wujewski (2018) 296–306.   [189] Chapter 2, pp. 16–17, 33.   [190] Chapter 4, pp. 69–73.

Fig. 6.21 The so-called 'lower acropolis' and the Monte Smith.

The Palace of the Grand Master and Its Environs

Prior Arguments

The Italian Theory and a Byzantine Dungeon
There remains a final hypothesis to analyse. In his *Geschichte der alten Rhodier*, published in 1900, Hendrik van Gelder was the first[191] to suppose that 'the temple of Helios stood presumably in the place of today's Turkish fortress', which he confused with the ancient acropolis.[192] It was not until the Italian occupation of the Dodecanese that the sanctuary of Helios was hypothetically located at the top of the Street of the Knights (Fig. 6.7, A), on the small hill (Fig. 6.21) where the Church of Saint John and the Palace of the Grand Master were built in the fourteenth century (Fig. 6.22).[193] Occasionally called the 'lower acropolis' (I shall use this convenient term, although Ioannis Kontis rightly stressed that it was born from a misinterpretation of some archaeological remains and had nothing ancient about it),[194] the area had produced the aforementioned decree that ordered its own display 'in the *témenos* of Helios' (ἐν τῷ τεμένει τοῦ Ἁλίου),[195] three inscriptions involving the priests of Helios,[196] as well as a Hellenistic marble head of the divinity (Fig. 6.23).[197]

The hypothesis of the Italian archaeologists nevertheless was generally considered obsolete after the excavations of the Soichan-Minetou plot on Monte Smith had revealed the existence of a building that was considered from 1986 as the *témenos* of Helios and from 1999 as the seat of an association of priests

---

[191] Konstantinopoulos (1997) 71–72, followed by Michalaki-Kollia (2017) 141 n. 34, wrongly mentions Dittenberger (1886–1887).

[192] Van Gelder (1900) 8; cf. Hiller von Gaertringen (1931) 818, who said about the book: 'fleissig und gewissenhaft, nur fehlt die Autopsie'.

[193] Maiuri (1918) 42 and Maiuri (1922) 31; cf. Hiller von Gaertringen (1931) 765 and Gualandi (1976) 52. Morricone (1965) 750 inaccurately mentions 'il santuario di Halios […] non lontano dal sito della moschea di Solimano'.

[194] Kontis (1973) 124.   [195] *IG* XII, 1, 2. See above, p. 140.

[196] *IG* XII, 1, 64 (honorific statue of a priest of Helios); *NS* 14 (dedication erected by a priest of Helios, perhaps independently from his service); *NESM* 59 (commemorative inscription for a priest of Helios).

[197] Badoud (forthcoming 4); cf. Chapter 7, p. 208, n. 180.

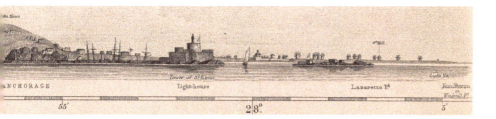

(which led to challenge the identification of the Pythion with the aim of connecting this sanctuary with Helios).[198] According to Vassa Kontorini[199] and Enzo Lippolis,[200] the Helios-related inscriptions found in the area of the Palace of the Grand Master actually originated from the (remote) Soichan-Minetou plot.

When Grigoris Konstantinopoulos returned to the Italian theory in 1997, he described these regular inscriptions as 'gigantic' and 'enormous' to give credence to the idea that they could not have been brought from another place; yet he also recalled that the marble head of the god and a catalogue of the priests of Helios[201] had been found nearby.[202] Two years later, Maria Michalaki-Kollia in turn affirmed her preference for a location of the sanctuary on the 'lower acropolis', with supplementary arguments. From the epigram once inscribed on the base of the Colossus,[203] it would indeed be possible to determine that the statue dominated the military harbour, located at the foot of this hill. Furthermore, the testimony of Polybius would establish that 'the Colossus fell during the great earthquake of 227–226 BC, destroying the greatest part of the walls and arsenals';[204] a scholium to the *Philebus* of Plato,[205] according to which 'the Colossus, as it fell, knocked over (κατέσεισεν) many houses', would confirm this fact.[206]

In line with this reasoning, Katerina Manoussou-Ntella has proposed that the core of a dungeon erected in the seventh century AD, in the north-western quarter of the *kástro* that preceded the Palace of the Grand Master, may be identified as the base of the Colossus. The principal arguments cited in support of this hypothesis are the size of this 'base' (12.5 × 15.5 m), once again comparable with that of the Colossus of Nero (14.75 × 17.6 m), and the fact that the feet of the statue would have been set on a higher level than the masts of the ships in the military harbour of Rhodes, to which the epigram cited by Michalaki-Kollia would have alluded.[207]

---

[198] Above, pp. 134–139.   [199] Kontorini (1989) 181 n. 479 and 184.
[200] Lippolis (2016) 155 with n. 93.
[201] Below, pp. 158–160.   [202] Konstantinopoulos (1997) 71–82 (citation p. 79).
[203] *Anth. Pal.* 6.171 (above, pp. 96–97), vv. 5–6.
[204] Polyb. 5.88.1 (above, pp. 46–47).   [205] *Scholia in Plat. Phlb.* 15 (Bekker).
[206] Michalaki-Kollia (1999) 73–74; Michalaki-Kollia (2013a) 22 and 27; Michalaki-Kollia (2017) 131, 138; Michalaki-Kollia (2023) 181.
[207] Manoussou-Ntella (2010a) 65–67; Manoussou-Ntella (2010b) 588–592; Manoussou-Ntella (2017) 179, whose hypothesis is favoured by M. D. Higgins (2023) 322. Cf. Jordan (2002) 28.

154 THE LOCATION OF THE COLOSSUS

Fig. 6.22 Palace of the Grand Master, as reconstructed by the Italians in the years 1937–1940.

Fig. 6.23 Hellenistic head of Helios, found in a mediaeval wall of the 'Inn of Provence' (Museum of Rhodes, inv. E49).

If this epigram had mentioned the location of the Colossus, it would probably have said that the statue dominated 'not only the land, but also the sea'. The epigram, however, does not speak about the Colossus but about the Rhodians, and it says that the latter dominated 'not only the sea, but also the land'. The reason for this has become clear: since its victory over the armies of Demetrius, the city was no longer a merely maritime power, but also a land power.[208] The evidence of Polybius has also been misunderstood, since he attributes the destruction of the ramparts and the arsenals to the earthquake itself, and not to the fall of the Colossus:

τὸν σεισμὸν [...] ἐν ᾧ συνέβη τόν τε κολοσσὸν τὸν μέγαν πεσεῖν καὶ τὰ πλεῖστα τῶν τειχῶν καὶ τῶν νεωρίων.

the earthquake [...] during which it happened that the great Colossus, as well as most of the walls and arsenals, fell.[209]

As for the scholiast to the *Philebus*, he reports that the Rhodians, invited by a king to reconstruct the Colossus, refused to do so by citing the Greek version of the proverb 'let sleeping dogs lie' or more literally 'do not move inconveniently what is conveniently lying' (μὴ κινεῖν κακὸν εὖ κείμενον). Presented in this way, the anecdote makes sense, as it echoes the religious prohibition of which the Rhodians availed themselves to divert the materials that Ptolemy III had offered for the reconstruction of the statue.[210] According to the scholiast, however, the decision of the Rhodians resulted from the fact that the Colossus had 'overturned many houses' when collapsing. This explanation, used more than once,[211] renders the anecdote incomprehensible: why would the Rhodians have quoted the proverb if the statue was not 'conveniently lying' (for instance within a sanctuary)? On this specific point, we must follow the verdict of the editor of the scholia: 'these are mere trifles' (*hae nugae sunt*).[212]

The identification of the base of the Colossus deriving from the reasoning discussed above must also be rejected. It depends on an argument already familiar to us: the 'base' would have been suitable for the Colossus. The same has been said about a tower,[213] a causeway,[214] a gate,[215] a double embankment,[216] and the

---

[208] Chapter 5, pp. 104–105.
[209] Polyb. 5.88.1 (above, pp. 46–47, for the complete text and translation).   [210] Strabo 14.2.5.
[211] Préchac (1919) 73 n. 9; R. Higgins (1989) 136; Moreno (1994a) 241 (with wrong attribution to Strabo); Moreno (1994b) 129–130; Mariño Sánchez-Elvira (2008) 125; Wujewski (2018) 294; Anniboletti (2024) 24; cf. Konstantinopoulos (1986) 114–115.
[212] Bekker (1826) 434.   [213] Above, pp. 121–124, 128–129.
[214] Above, p. 124.   [215] Above, pp. 125–126.   [216] Above, p. 126.

foundations of a temple.[217] Moreover, the location of the 'base' is not supported by ancient sources but was determined by the medieval myth that made the ships pass under the legs of the statue.[218] While no reason exists to subscribe to the identification of the 'base', reasons exist for rejecting it. For instance, how could we explain that this 'base' was built on a slope and on weak clay soil, or that it was limited to some rubble, with the sturdy ancient blocks of marble on which the Byzantine dungeon could have been erected being absent? In fact, the structure in question does not seem to belong to a statue base; even its antiquity is not assured (and cannot be in the absence of study).

Saint John *Colossensis*
Another argument for a location of the Colossus somewhere on the 'lower acropolis' has been drawn from the epithet of *Colossensis*[219] that Jacques Fontaine gave to the Church of Saint John.[220] Yet this epithet does not seem to appear elsewhere, and Fontaine himself located the Colossus under Fort Saint Nicholas, in keeping with the tradition of the historians of the Order.[221] In fact, the adjective *Colossensis* has the value of an ethnic used to refer to the Latin archbishopric and to distinguish it from its Greek counterpart.[222] Its origin is dual. According to John Malalas and many other Byzantine authors, the inhabitants of Rhodes owed their nickname to the Colossus,[223] and Fontaine still uses the adjective in this sense. They subsequently were—as Fontaine notes—confused with the Colossians of Phrygia, addressees of the *Epistle* of Paul and Timothy; Gabriel himself committed this error.[224] One would only add to the confusion by conjecturing that the Knights (who arrived on the island in the fourteenth century) 'acquired their name *Colossensis* from the state of Colossi on Cyprus' (where they were established since the thirteenth century).[225] It would not be less misleading to state that 'from κολοσσός, through Late Latin, comes also the term *Collachium*, which indicates the fortified town of the Early Middle Ages',[226] as *collachium* derives in fact from *collocare* and means a building where things or persons were 'placed'.[227]

---

[217] Above, p. 146. [218] Above, pp. 126–128.
[219] *Pace* Maryon (1956) 81; Dombart (1970) 76; Ekschmitt (1996) 180–181; and Moreno (1999) 194. See also above, pp. 132–133.
[220] Fontaine [Fontanus] (1524) 39. [221] Ibid. 37. Above, pp. 127–128.
[222] Torr (1887) 70; Luttrell (1987) 363.
[223] Joannes Malalas p. 149, ll. 10–11 (Dindorf); Georgius Monachus *Chron.* p. 285, ll. 20–22 (De Boor; *PG* CX, 340B); *Suda*, s.v. Ῥόδος; Eustathius *in Dionysium Periegetem* 504 (*GGM* II, p. 312, ll. 18–20); Manuel Philes *Carmina* p. 23, XLIV (Miller).
[224] Gabriel (1932) 349.
[225] Meinardus (1973) 35. For the fortress of Cyprus, which probably owes its name to an ancient toponym, see De Vaivre (2010) 73–155.
[226] Moreno (1994b) 777 n. 237; Moreno (1999) 194, followed by Hoepfner (2007) 73 (in German) and 108 (in Greek).
[227] Du Cange, *Glossarium mediae et infimae Latinitatis* II, s.v. *colacium*.

The Süleymaniye School and the Ottoman Clock Tower

Sites close to the Castle, such as the Süleymaniye school[228] and the Ottoman clock tower (Fig. 6.7, B–C),[229] have also been suggested. Both were built after the explosion that destroyed the Church of Saint John in 1856.[230] The school partly overlaps the ruins of the church,[231] while the clock reuses the lower courses of a watchtower, which was part of the Byzantine wall.[232] Investigations in and around the school did not bring to light any remains attributable to the Colossus; nor does the base of the statue seem to have been merged in the Byzantine tower. Traces of a sanctuary of Helios could have been but are not visible at either location.

New Arguments

Arguments for the Colossus

Do these difficulties require us to give up on locating the sanctuary of Helios and the Colossus on the 'lower acropolis'? Certainly not, since the top of this hill recommends itself for several reasons. The first is the presence of the Palace of the Grand Master, the successor to the Byzantine *kástro* (Fig. 6.22), which sufficiently explains why Nicephorus Gregoras could not identify any remains of the Colossus despite his efforts in 1342.[233]

On the other hand, the epigram of the Colossus presented the statue as a crown for the city and alluded to the Peraea,[234] which the Rhodians seized after the departure of Demetrius' troops in 304.[235] The Peraea could be seen from the summit of the acropolis but the latter was occupied by the sanctuary of Athena Polias and Zeus Polieus.[236] We must therefore look for another place, which could—or should—be the 'lower acropolis'. The Byzantine *kástro* and the Palace of the Grand Master would both benefit from its centrality and its panoramic view. But while these buildings were designed to watch the Asian continent, the Colossus was to be seen from there, as it symbolized Rhodian domination over the Peraea. There is no doubt that such was the case. Today, if one looks eastwards from the fortress of Loryma,[237] which was built after the departure of Demetrius Poliorcetes' army in 304, at the very moment when the Rhodians took control of the Peraea, one can easily distinguish the houses of Rhodes, 13 km away (Fig. 6.24). In antiquity,

---

[228] Dawid (1968) 44; Ekschmitt (1996) 180–181.
[229] R. Higgins (1989) 136, followed by Mariño Sánchez-Elvira (2008) 125.
[230] De Vaivre (2020) 25–46.   [231] Ntellas (2007) 378–379.
[232] Manoussou-Ntella (2001) 116.
[233] Nicephorus Gregoras *Historia Romana* 22.6 (Bekker III, p. 16, ll. 13–18). Cf. Moreno (1994b) 141; Manoussou-Ntella (2010a) 68; Manoussou-Ntella (2010b) 591–592.
[234] *Anth. Pal.* 6.171 (above, pp. 96–97), vv. 4–5.
[235] Cf. Moreno (1994a) 241; Moreno (1994b) 141; Moreno (1999) 194.
[236] Above, p. 146.   [237] Nöth (2019) 177–295.

Fig. 6.24 The island of Rhodes, as seen from the fortress of Loryma (on the left, the tip of the island and the city of Rhodes; on the right, the acropolis of Ialysos).

the Colossus would have been taller than any other building of the city, and thus clearly visible from the Peraea: Rhodian power appeared at its dawn.

Arguments for the Sanctuary of Helios

While the 'upper acropolis' was devoted to the deities of the city conceived as urban entity—just as at Ialysos, Kamiros, and Lindos—, the 'lower acropolis' would have been reserved for the *théos propátôr* of the city conceived as political entity. In this respect, epigraphy may provide a clue. The catalogue of the priests of Helios, of which only the upper part remains (Fig. 6.25), was discovered in 1943, after the bombing that destroyed the probable Metropolitan church (dating to the fourteenth century and converted into the 'Iron Mosque' by the Ottomans) that occupied the site of a Byzantine church, itself built on an early Christian basilica (Fig. 6.7, D).[238] The editor of the inscription, Luigi Morricone, underlined the proximity of this building (or succession of buildings) to the 'lower acropolis', without going as far as to make the sanctuary of Helios—which was then located on the 'lower acropolis'—the place where the inscription was set up. For him, the stone, which had served as a step of a staircase before being somehow reused in the Metropolitan (?) church, could have been carried far from its original location; if copies of the catalogue had been erected in various places in the

---

[238] On this building, see Luttrell (2003) 128–129.

Fig. 6.25 Catalogue of the priests of Helios, engraved in Rhodes from c.382/1 BC (*TRI* 1; Archaeological Museum of Rhodes). a. Side A. b. Side B.

town, no proof would exist that the fragment found in 1943 came from the sanctuary itself.[239]

Among the numerous Rhodian catalogues—more than a dozen[240]—that we possess, none is known to have several copies, and all have been (or could have been) set up in the space where the officials whom they listed served. There is no reason to think that the catalogue of priests of Helios was an exception to the rule. Inscribed on a stele of Parian marble, an exceptional material that signalled its importance, but which also recalls both the 'white foliage' of which the crowns given to the victors of the *Halíeia* were made[241] and the 'white marble' from which the base of the Colossus was allegedly constructed,[242] it was dedicated by a holder of the office, following a custom also attested in the sanctuary of Athena at Kamiros.[243] We additionally know that, from the Byzantine period, the buildings of ancient Rhodes were transformed into quarries, whose exploitation likely intensified during the two centuries (1309–1522), when the Knights of Saint John

---

[239] Morricone (1949–51) 359.   [240] Badoud (2015) 7; Badoud (2019c) 20.
[241] *Scholia in Pind. Ol.* 7.147c (Drachmann).
[242] [Philo Byzantius] p. 32, ll. 1–2 (Brodersen; above, pp. 80–82, §3).
[243] *TRI* 9.

fortified the town. The written sources show that such quarries existed beyond, but also inside, the urban perimeter.[244] Hence it is unlikely (but certainly not impossible) that the catalogue comes from the Soichan-Minetou building on the acropolis, located more than 1 km from the church where the inscription was found in 1943. The preserved fragment measures 132 × 78 × 12.5 cm, while the original height of the stele of which it was a part can be estimated at 240 cm. The dimensions of the catalogue, intact or already broken, would thus have complicated its transport without justifying it, since they hardly would have been tailored to the stair in which the stone was at first (?) reused. Consequently, the possibility exists that the stele was erected on the 'lower acropolis' and that this was the location for the *témenos* of Helios.

Bringing the Arguments Together

Among the pieces of evidence collected so far, a first group points towards a location of the Colossus on the 'lower acropolis', and a second group towards a location of the sanctuary of Helios at the same place. This convergence is satisfying, for it seems likely, or at least possible, that the statue of the god was erected in his sanctuary. Can we find arguments in support of the latter hypothesis and explain, in a broader perspective, the role that the building discovered on the Soichan-Minetou plot played in the cult of Helios, to which it was certainly related?

Among the dedications discovered on Monte Smith, none predates the third century BC. The earliest seems to be that of the priest Antisthenes, which had been inscribed twice, the first probably before *c.*270 (Fig. 6.26).[245] Could the reason for this oddity be the removal of the base from its original location? On the other hand, the catalogue discovered by Morricone, which starts in 407 BC (first eponymous year of Rhodes), also presents an oddity: its second side was not inscribed, although it had been divided into two columns by a double line (Fig. 6.25b), as its first side had (Fig. 6.25a). When the stele was made in 380 BC,[246]

Fig. 6.26 Base of a statue dedicated by the priest of Helios Antisthenes, *c.*298–270 BC (?) (*TRI* 28, squeeze of F. Hiller von Gaertringen).

---

[244] Manoussou-Ntella (2001) 21–22.
[245] *TRI* 128. Cf. Badoud, *REG* 132 (2019), 120.
[246] Badoud (2015) 157: year of Πολυκράτης Κητίδα.

use on both sides was intended; yet, after 298 BC, the date of the last priest mentioned on the preserved part of the stele, an unforeseen event occurred that caused the abandonment of the catalogue and perhaps disrupted the organization of the sanctuary. Was this event the construction of the Colossus, begun in 295 BC and completed in 283 BC?[247]

The building unearthed on the Soichan-Minetou plot, modest in its dimensions and ordinary in its position, would thus have served only as a subsidiary sanctuary since the work started by Chares would have taken over most of the available space in the principal sanctuary. In this regard, it is worth recalling that Pseudo-Philo mentions the 'huge mound of earth' (χοῦν γῆς ἄπλατον) necessary for the building of the bronze statue, cast in courses.[248] This would explain why no dedication predating the third century was discovered on the acropolis, why the catalogue of the priests of Helios remained incomplete, and why it was found reused near the 'lower acropolis'. The distribution of inscriptions between the two sites agrees with this hypothesis, insofar as the dedications to Helios discovered on Monte Smith were made by priests upon leaving office,[249] whereas those on the 'lower acropolis', while small in number, were never made.[250] After the initiation of the project for the Colossus, most cultic activities would have been moved to Monte Smith; the sanctuary of the 'lower acropolis' would have continued to accept a certain number of offerings and public documents, but the priests no longer would have set up their dedications there.

The epigraphic clues gathered here are obviously tenuous. Yet, if the Colossus was erected in the sanctuary of Helios, the oracular ban on moving the remains of the statue implies that the place was not deconsecrated after the earthquake of 227 BC. A proper 'relocation' of the sanctuary, which sometimes occurred within a city, would therefore have been impossible.[251] It may have been convenient instead to use an auxiliary sanctuary, created several decades before through a procedure normally used for spreading a cult overseas: the *aphídruma*.[252] If its identification is correct, the naiskos reported in the centre of the building that has come to light on the Soichan-Minetou plot may be evidence of a such a procedure.

The proper sanctuary of Helios, housing his altar and perhaps a temple (for which there is however no certain evidence),[253] would have required a large space, which would have been set aside at the exact moment of Rhodes' foundation in 408 BC, or even before, if one supposes that the Eratids already used it as a

---

[247] Chapter 4, p. 66.
[248] [Philo Byzantius] p. 32, l. 23 (Brodersen; above, pp. 80–82, §5).
[249] Above, p. 137.
[250] Above, p. 152. Cf. Xenophon Ephesius 1.12.2 and 5.10–11 (imaginary dedications by foreigners).
[251] Quantin and Quantin (2007) 175–196.
[252] Malkin (1991) 77–96; Icard-Gianoloi and Lochin (2004) 471–476.
[253] *IG* XII, 1, 2, l. 7, mentions the *témenos* (precinct) of Helios, while Xenophon Ephesius 1.12.2, 5.10.6, 5.11.2–5.12.2; *Suda, s.v. Διονύσιος Μουσωνίου* (*FGrHist* 511 T1); and Eustathius *in Od.* 6.266 mention his *hierón* (sanctuary).

cult place for the god.²⁵⁴ If it is correct to assume that the Rhodians had to provide a new space for their patron deity when the construction of the Colossus began in 295 BC, the choices were certainly more limited than one century before. Nevertheless, the account of Diodorus proves that, in 304 BC, it was still possible to find place for a sanctuary as large as the Ptolemaion.²⁵⁵ The years following the siege of Demetrius were indeed marked by a large extension of the perimeter of the city, as witnessed by its walls.²⁵⁶ Thus, the small size of the building discovered in the Soichan-Minetou plot should not be explained by a lack of space on the acropolis but rather by the fact that Helios, being merely a political god, was never the object of important popular devotion²⁵⁷ (and we recall that the dedications found in the Soichan-Minetou are closely linked to the People and Council of Rhodes),²⁵⁸ as opposed, for instance, to Dionysus, whose sanctuary was overflowing with offerings.²⁵⁹ Some aspects of the cult could be accommodated by a relatively modest building on the slopes of Monte Smith, while the sanctuary that Helios had on the 'lower acropolis' continued to indicate his political pre-eminence. When ascending to the facilities where the festivals were organized, the procession of the *Halieia*²⁶⁰ perhaps connected the two sites.

A Final Assessment
If one considers the topography of Rhodes as a whole, prudence will remain the watchword: no source confirms that the Colossus was erected in the sanctuary of Helios (but this is likely), the position of this sanctuary remains uncertain (although the site occupied from the fourteenth century by the magisterial Palace supports this location in many respects), and the function of the building that the god had on Monte Smith is difficult to determine (yet it was surely linked to a public cult).

If, however, we focus on the Colossus, concluding this chapter in a more straightforward and affirmative manner becomes possible. The epigram engraved on the base of the statue proves that it was erected on an eminence and that it symbolized Rhodian domination over the Peraea. Since the 'upper' acropolis was the domain of Athena Polias and Zeus Polieus, the 'lower' acropolis remains the only location for the statue, which would thus have been perfectly visible from the Asian mainland. The reason why the Rhodians decided to make their *kolossós* the biggest statue of the world is clear: it had to connect visually the two parts of their empire, the 'sea' and the 'land', Rhodes and the Peraea.

---

[254] Chapter 1, p. 14.
[255] Diod. Sic. 20.100.3-4, with the commentary of Filimonos and Kontorini (1989) 128–177 and the correction of Badoud (2015) 121 regarding the inscriptions published by the latter author.
[256] Cf. Filimonos-Tsopotou (2004) 35, Σχέδ. 9 and Ἀναδ. Σχέδ. I.
[257] Xenophon Ephesius 5.11.4 makes his hero pray to Helios, but this is more likely a cliché than proof of popular devotion. Cf. Chapter 4, p. 68, n. 40, on Philostr. *VA* 5.21.
[258] Above, p. 137.   [259] Above, p. 145.
[260] Xenophon Ephesius 5.11.2–5.12.2.

7
The Image of the Statue

Although more informative than expected,[1] the sources do not allow us to precisely know the appearance of the Colossus. It is therefore valuable to explore how our image of the statue was formed and how archaeologists have come to identify 'copies' of the bronze cast by Chares, the more so as these 'copies' are at odds with the available evidence.

The Most Ancient Representations

Byzantine Iconography

In his eulogy for Basil the Great, composed between AD 379 and 390, Gregory of Nazianzus declares that the hospital founded by the Bishop of Caesarea was beyond comparison with the Seven Wonders of the World.[2] Commenting on this speech at the beginning of the sixth century AD, an anonymous author, conventionally designated as Pseudo-Nonnus, explains that the Colossus was the 'statue of a man' (*andriás*).[3] Dated to the second half of the eleventh century AD, the *Codex Taphou* 14 of the Greek Patriarchal Library in Jerusalem is one of many manuscripts that preserve his work. Its illumination depicts the Colossus as a man standing on a column, armed with a spear and a sword (Fig. 7.1). This is the first known image of the monument, thirteen centuries after its destruction. Kurt Weitzmann has stressed that it reflected absolutely no reality in antiquity but followed conventions of Byzantine iconography; it most probably recreated a model developed during the so-called 'Macedonian Renaissance' (867–1056),[4] as did other illustrations in the *Codex Taphou*.[5] One would therefore err in recognizing this standard representation as the true form of the Colossus and then using it to identify other figures as 'copies' of the Rhodian monument. According to José Dörig, these copies would have included statuettes of Sol (belonging to the late Roman Empire), a sculpture of the Sun (likely symbolizing the Christ) depicted in a sixth-century AD mosaic from Qasr in Libya that places it on the

---

[1] Chapter 4, pp. 92–94.
[2] Greg. Naz. *Orationes* 43 (Bernardi; *PG* XXXVI, 577C–579B; Brodersen 9).
[3] [Nonnus] *Scholia mythologica in orationes Greg. Naz.* 18, ll. 19–20 (Nimmo Smith; Brodersen 12).
[4] For a history and a critique of this concept, see Spieser (2017b) 43–52.
[5] Weitzmann (1984²) 9, 35–37, and 87–92.

Fig. 7.1 Detail from the illumination in the *Scholia mythologica* of Pseudo-Nonnus; manuscript from the eleventh century (Greek Patriarchal Library in Jerusalem, *Codex Taphou* 14, f. 311v).

Lighthouse of Alexandria,[6] and the figure of a warrior engraved on a Byzantine ivory from the twelfth century AD kept in the Victoria and Albert Museum (entirely unrelated to Helios).[7] The whip of the statue and the ship rudder of the mosaic additionally have been confused with the spear from the ivory, which belongs to the same (Byzantine) iconographic conventions as the Colossus of the *Codex Taphou*.

Western Colossi

In the West, the earliest representation of the monument appears in a manuscript of the *Miroir Historial* of Jean de Vignay, a French translation of Vincent de Beauvais' *Speculum historiae*, dated to 1396 and illuminated by Perrin Remiet; the statue tumbles from its base, overturned by the earthquake of *c.*227 BC (Fig. 7.2). Written in French by Jean Wauquelin between 1446 and 1448, the *Chroniques de Hainaut* also originates from the *Speculum historiae*, through the intermediary of Jacques de Guyse's *Annales historiae illustrium principum Hannoniae*, which it essentially translates. We find here another illustration of the statue falling from its base (Fig. 7.3), which, in breaking, reveals the bones that were hidden inside. Jean Wauquelin strayed from De Guyse's *Annales*[8] by referring to a lexicographer of the twelfth century (Osbern of Gloucester or his follower Huguccio of Pisa), according to whom the Colossus was named '*a Colens ossa*', 'because it concealed bones'.[9] The page layout shows that the image representing the Colossus was not originally planned but presumably added at the request of the work's sponsor, Philip the Good, Duke of Burgundy from 1419 to 1467. This image therefore reveals a new interest in ancient sculpture and may be considered as one of the first appearances of Renaissance ideals at the court of Burgundy.[10] It also shows, however, that Renaissance was still in its infancy. In the absence of

---

[6] For this statue, see Giorgetti (1977) 256.

[7] Dörig (1999) 188–191. For the links between the Colossus of Rhodes and the Lighthouse of Alexandria, see below pp. 171–172.

[8] De Fortia d'Urban (1826) 440–441 (edition of the *Annales historiae illustrium principum Hannoniae*).

[9] Busdraghi et al. (1996) 114.   [10] Van Buren (1972) 257–260; Piérard (2000) 171.

THE COLOSSUS AS A COLUMN   165

Fig. 7.2 Illumination in the *Miroir historial* of Jean de Vignay, by Perrin Remiet, manuscript from 1396 (Bibliothèque nationale de France, ms. Français 312, f. 204r).

information on the Colossus' appearance, the illustrator represented it like a warrior of his times. He thus felt the need to clarify the subject of his miniature by adding a caption, which incidentally reveals that, for him, 'Colossus' was the name of the man depicted by the statue.[11] Some twenty years later, the *Hypnerotomachia Poliphili* transposes the remains described by Pliny[12] into the dream world where the hero's quest for his beloved Polia is set, but provides no illustration of the monument.[13]

Fig. 7.3 Illumination in the *Chroniques de Hainaut* of Jean Wauquelin, by the anonymous 'maître de l'Alexandre de Wauquelin', manuscript completed in 1448 (Bibliothèque royale de Belgique, ms. 9242, f. 175v).

The Colossus as a Column

The *Nuremberg Chronicle*

Published at Nuremberg in 1493 (in Latin on 12 July and in German on 23 December), the *Nuremberg Chronicle* of Hartmann Schedel recounts the history

---

[11] For the inscription hidden on the thigh of the Colossus, see Wittek (2000) 57–60.
[12] Plin. *HN* 34.41 (above, pp. 64–65).
[13] [Colonna (?)] (1499) [35–36]. The text was written in 1467.

166   THE IMAGE OF THE STATUE

Fig. 7.4 Hand-coloured woodcut printed in the *Buch der Croniken* [*Liber chronicarum*] of Hartmann Schedel, Nuremberg, 1493, f. LXXXIIv (Bayerische Staatsbibliothek, Rar. 287).

of mankind with the help of 1,165 wood engravings created in the workshop of Michael Wolgemut, the master of Albrecht Dürer. One of these engravings, which represents the fall of the Colossus, gives it the appearance of a column[14] (Fig. 7.4). This depiction has no precedent, and no descendant other than an illustration inserted into the *Cosmographia* of Sebastian Münster, printed at Basel in 1545 (Fig. 7.5). Although José Dörig has suggested that the latter image related to the illumination of the *Codex Taphou*, this idea can be disregarded, for a statue-column clearly differs from a statue set upon a column.[15] Ursula Vedder has argued that the explanation for this motif lies in the ambiguity of the terms that the *Nuremberg Chronicle* applies to the Colossus.[16] It is true that, when summarizing Pliny, the Latin edition of the work uses the word *simulacrum*, meaning 'image', while the German version provides the more specific word *sawl*, meaning either a 'column' or a 'statue'.[17] Yet, between these two meanings, why would the illustrators working for Schedel have chosen that of 'column', which contradicted the common representation of the Colossus as a 'statue'? As the Latin edition already depicted the Colossus in the form of a column, the explanation for this motif certainly cannot be based on an incorrect interpretation of the German version, which was written later. In fact, far from having required the engravers to correct their interpretation during the months separating the two versions of the *Chronicle*, Schedel confirmed this interpretation by glossing *simulacrum* with *sawl* ('column'), rather than translating it as *bild* ('image').[18] He thus drew on a source other than Pliny, as proven by the final words of his description of the Colossus, which have no equivalent in the *Natural History*: 'One says that it was the largest of the Seven Wonders of the World'. From where do these words derive?

[14] Schedel (1493a–b) f. LXXXIIv.   [15] Dörig (1999) 189.
[16] Vedder (2003) 141.   [17] *Mittelhochdeutsches Wörterbuch*, s.v. sûl.
[18] *Glossarium Latino-germanicum mediae et infimae aetatis*, s.v. simulacrum.

Nicetas of Heraclea and Cyriac of Ancona

To answer this question, we should return to the commentary that Nicetas of Heraclea wrote on Gregory of Nazianzus, the exegete of Basil the Great, during the 1080s: 'Certain people state that [the Colossus] was a bronze *kíōn* of great height, 600 cubits according to Aristotle.'[19] As we have seen in Chapter 2[20] while discussing its interpretation by Georges Roux in 1960,[21] the first part of this sentence derives from the dedication of one of the obelisks that adorned the Hippodrome of Constantinople (Fig. 2.3); the second part is borrowed from the scholia for the eulogy of Basil the Great, which include a list of Wonders presenting the Colossus as a statue with a height of 19, 600, or even 1,600 cubits 'according to Aristotle'[22] (the authority of the philosopher, who died thirty years before the construction of the monument, obviously would not excuse the fantastical character of such dimensions). Since the term *kíōn*, used in the first part of the sentence, generally described a column or a pillar, Cyriac of Ancona rendered it as *columna* in his Latin translation of Nicetas' commentary, before adding that the height of the statue was '600 cubits according to Aristotle' (*aliqui enim dicunt id columpnam* [sic] *esse aeneam maximam altitudinis cubitorum, secundum Aristotelem, DC*).[23] Cyriac dedicated his translation to Pietro Donato, the Bishop of Padua, between 1428 and 1447. As he had studied medicine in Padua from 1463 to 1466 and had copied (or had copies made of) some manuscripts of Cyriac during his stay in Italy,[24] Schedel certainly availed himself of this translation both to infer that the Colossus was a column and to state that 'it was the largest of the Seven Wonders of the World'.

With five centuries of distance between them, Cyriac and Roux followed the same reasoning. To begin, both relied on the text of Nicetas to argue that the Colossus of Rhodes was a column, a *kíōn*. This term, however, referred to the obelisk in

Fig. 7.5 Engraving from the *Cosmographia. Beschreibung aller Länder* [...] of Sebastian Münster, Basel, 1545, p. DCCX (Bayerische Staatsbibliothek, Res/2 Geo.u.45).

---

[19] Nicetas Heracleensis *Commentarii in XVI orationes Greg. Naz.* 67, ll. 17–19 (Constantinescu; Brodersen 20; above, p. 22). See also Madonna (1976) 45, fig. 30, who notes already that the statue reproduced by Münster seems 'in agreement with the definition of Nicetas (Colossus as "column" or "pilaster")'.
[20] Chapter 2, pp. 25–26.   [21] Roux (1960) 14–15.
[22] *Scholia Alexandrina in orationes Greg. Naz.* (sixth century): *Codex Taurinensis* B I 4, f. 35v; *Codex Laurentianus* VII 8, f. 265r (Brodersen 13; tenth century): *Codex Laurentianus* IV 13, f. 54v; *Codex Monacensis Graecus* 204, f. 50v (Brodersen 14).
[23] Cyriac of Ancona, *Ex Gregorio Nazanzeno theologo de VII mundi spectaculis* [...] *brevis in latinum expositio ad R.P.D. P(etrum) Donatum episcopum Patavinae Urbis* (Brodersen 25).
[24] On Cyriac and Schedel, see Bodnar (1998).

Constantinople that Constantine Porphyrogenitus had only *compared* to the Colossus; hence the mistaken conclusion by Nicetas that the Colossus *itself* was an obelisk. Cyriac and Roux then committed a second error by admitting that the Colossus described as a *kíōn* by Nicetas was a column rather than an obelisk. This second error gave birth to the statue-column depicted in Schedel's *Nuremberg Chronicle*.

The Colossus Spanning the Port of Rhodes

A Landscape by Heemskerck

In the so-called *Panorama with the Abduction of Helen Amidst the Wonders of the Ancient World*, which Maerten van Heemskerck painted at Rome in 1535–1536,[25] a statue straddles the entrance to a port thus designated as Rhodes (Fig. 7.6). How should this dramatic change in the iconography of the Colossus be explained? The myth illustrated by Heemskerck had been mentioned from the fourteenth century in the accounts of pilgrims crossing the Aegean, without attracting the interest of any artist.[26] It returns in the commentary that Giovanni Britannico devoted in 1512 to the *Satires* of Juvenal,[27] but one would certainly be wrong to suppose that a remark buried in this erudite work inspired Heemskerck. As late as 1527, for instance, the chapter of the *Antiquitates Urbis* dedicated by Andrea Fulvio to colossal statues remained faithful to ancient sources.[28] A misunderstanding of the dedicatory epigram of the Colossus[29] may also be excluded for many reasons: such a difficult text could be read by skilled philologists only; a skilled philologist like Britannico does not mention it when referring to the myth of the Colossus; this myth is not philological but archaeological in nature, as it is born from the misinterpretation of the remains of a tower that protected the military harbour of Rhodes in antiquity.[30] It must have been widely spread by oral tradition from 1522, when the Westerners whom Suleiman the Magnificent had expelled from Rhodes returned home.

Heemkerck's Colossus, which would be imitated a few years later by Gualtiero Padovano at the Villa Godi Malinverni in Lugo di Vicenza,[31] copies the Capitoline Hercules. The designer of several sketches for this gilded bronze (Fig. 7.7),[32] Heemskerck replaced the apples of the Hesperides with a lantern in the left hand and cleverly allowed the right hand, which held a club, to disappear as if it had broken off—the beauty of statues, like that of Helen, being ephemeral.

---

[25] King (1944–1945) 60–73; Stritt (2004). On Heemskerck and his followers, cf. Beschi (1986) 308–313.
[26] Chapter 6, pp. 121–122.
[27] Britannico [Britannicus] (1512) f. 78v (concerning Juv. 8.230).
[28] Fulvio [Fulvius] (1527) f. 64r.
[29] As suggested by Fischer (2014) 153–154, citing the editions of *Anth. Plan.* 6.1 by Aldus Manutius, the first of which dates in fact to 1503 (the version of the epigram known as *Anth. Pal.* 6.171 was not published until 1776). For other misinterpretations of the poem, studied in Chapter 5, see Chapter 6, pp. 126, 151, 153–155, and below, pp. 200–202.
[30] Chapter 6, pp. 126–128.   [31] Fischer (2014) 149–154.
[32] Bober and Rubinstein (2010) 129–130, no. 129.

THE COLOSSUS SPANNING THE PORT OF RHODES 169

Fig. 7.6 Detail from the *Panorama with the Abduction of Helen Amidst the Wonders of the Ancient World*, oil on canvas by Maerten van Heemskerck, 1535 (Baltimore, The Walters Art Museum, inv. 37656).

Fig. 7.7 Drawing of the Capitoline Hercules, surrounded by an altar and fragments of the statue of Constantine, by Maerten van Heemskerck, 1532–1536 (Kupferstichkabinett der Staatlichen Museen zu Berlin, Römische Skizzenbücher I–II, inv. 79 D 2, f. 53v).

A Lost Manuscript and an Alexandrine Legend

In his work of 1547, *Des antiquités romaines (premier livre)*, which has remained unpublished, Guillaume du Choul, an antiquarian from Lyon, cites 'an ancient Greek author who spoke rather at length about the antiquities of Rhodes' when describing the Colossus:

> La base qui soubstenoit la statue estoit de forme triangulaire & chacune de ses extremitez se soubstenoit par soixante colonnes de marbre & par le dedans estoient degrez a la facon dune coclee par lesquelz lon montoit iusques a la machine a la cyme de laquelle estoient bons & variables instrumens dung chant suave & tresdoulce musique. le chanter & la symphonie estoit de vers iambiques [.] dudit colosse estoient veues toute [sic] les parties de la syrie & les nauires qui alloient en egipte par le moien dung grant mirouer qui estoit pendu au col de la statue qui auoit le visaige tourne droit a legipte [.] la statue se monstroit droitte & nue tenant de lune de ses mains vne espee & de lautre vne haste.

> The base that held up the statue had a triangular form; each of its ends was held up by sixty marble columns; inside were stairs in the manner of a snail, which rose up until a device at the top, of which were good and variable instruments that played soft and sweet music. The song and the symphony were written in iambic verse. From the aforementioned Colossus were seen all parts of Syria and the ships that were bound for Egypt by means of a great mirror hung from the neck of the statue, whose face turned right towards Egypt. The statue appeared standing upright and naked; it held a sword in one hand and a spear in the other.[33]

Reusing this passage in his *Discours de la religion des anciens Romains*, which appeared in 1556, Du Choul more precisely describes his source as 'a very ancient Greek book, although anonymous, which Georges de Vauzelles, knight of Rhodes, Commander of La Tourette, lent to me, and which he formerly had brought from Greece.'[34]

This manuscript has a long history. While staying on Rhodes, Cristoforo Buondelmonti consulted it no later than 1420,[35] as the author of the *Histoire*

---

[33] Du Choul, G., *Des antiquités romaines, premier livre* (1547), Turin, Biblioteca Reale, ms. Varia 212, f. 43v.

[34] Du Choul (1556a) 194.

[35] For the Latin version of the *Liber insularum Archipelagi*, see Sinner (1824) 72; for the Greek version, see E. Legrand (1897) 26, with a French translation on p. 182, where the mention of the 'banner' allegedly worn by the Colossus must be removed. The words *cubitorum LXXXta supereminebat, ubi velum a longe LXXX. mi. manifestabat* are a corruption of the Latin original (now lost) that seems to have been correctly rendered by πηχῶν ἦν γὰρ ἑβδομήκοντα, ἐν ᾧ σημαία ἦν, ἥτις ὀγδοήκοντα μιλίοις πόρρωθεν ὁρᾶτο: the statue was so large that it was used as a navigation mark by the ships.

journalière, who used it without acknowledging the fact, did in the following century.[36] After the 1522 siege, Fontaine noted that the manuscript was 'with him' in Italy.[37] We do not know at what moment and under what circumstances he entrusted it to Vauzelles. We do know, however, that the latter took up command of La Tourette on 15 February 1528[38] and exchanged this position for command of the Temple of Ayen on 20 September 1540.[39] He thus lent the document to Du Choul (described as 'Commander of La Tourette' by Thevet) during this period.

The sword and the spear placed by the author in the hands of the Colossus of Rhodes evoke the miniature in the *Codex Taphou* too strongly not to have been borrowed from Byzantine iconography.[40] On the other hand, the mirror, whose reflection carried all the way to Egypt, and the musical instruments hidden in the interior of the statue refer to the descriptions of the Lighthouse of Alexandria that appeared in Islamic literature during the ninth century AD,[41] as a result of the reception of Greek treatises on mechanics[42] and mathematics.[43] Al-Mas'ūdī recounts that one of the statues situated on top of the tower 'indicated the hours of the day and the night by a harmonious sound that chimed each hour'. He then mentions the magical mirror used by the Alexandrians to watch for the arrival of enemy ships.[44] Even if its sixty columns compare unfavourably with the glass crab placed by the historian at the base of the Lighthouse, the prismatic base of the Colossus also presents a wondrous character, unrelated to the ancient sources.[45] It follows that the Alexandrine legends, one version of which Buondelmonti and his successors found reproduced in the Greek manuscript, did not reach Rhodes before the ninth century AD. This timeline is confirmed by the fact that the author of the manuscript continued these legends with the myth of the destruction of the Colossus by the Arabs, which appeared during the eighth century AD.[46] Furthermore, it is significant that the same legends did not interfere with the myth of the Colossus spanning the harbour(s) of Rhodes, mentioned for the first time in 1394–1395, and that they were recorded in Greek rather than in Latin, the use of which the Hospitallers spread when they settled on Rhodes in 1309. The source cited by Du Choul thus was probably created between the ninth and

---

[36] De Vaivre and Vissière (2014) 174.   [37] Fontaine [Fontanus] (1524) 37.
[38] AOM 411, f. 71r and AOM 412, f. 82r.
[39] AOM 417, f. 48r.   [40] Above, pp. 163–164.
[41] Baltrušaitis (1978) 145–160; De Polignac (1984) 425–439.
[42] See the various contributions gathered by Zielinski and Weibel (2015).
[43] Ng (2019) 89–91.
[44] Al-Mas'ūdī *Murūj aḏ-Ḏahab wa-Ma'ādin al-Jawhar* [*Meadows of Gold and Mines of Gems*] II, pp. 433 and 435 (De Meynard and De Courteille).
[45] Préchac (1919) 69 'corrects' the sources and interprets them in his own way to demonstrate the opposite.
[46] Chapter 4, pp. 69–72.

thirteenth centuries: it is no coincidence that the *Codex Taphou* and its warrior-like Colossus belong to this period.

The iconographic fate of Du Choul's Colossus is limited to an image that appears on an engraving titled *Li sette miracoli del' mondo*, of which the humanist Orazio Tigrini had several copies printed in Rome between 1574 and 1578—a particularly accurate image, as the reflection of a ship is visible within the mirror on the statue (Fig. 7.8).[47] The triangular base noted by Du Choul is also faithfully represented; convinced that it symbolized the island of Rhodes, (wrongly?) called *Trinacria* by Pliny the Elder,[48] the Count of Caylus considered it as the only credible element of the Greek manuscript. He identified it with the single base mentioned by (Pseudo-)Philo of Byzantium[49] and stated that it contradicted the myth of the Colossus spanning the harbour of Rhodes.[50]

Fig. 7.8 Detail from an engraving by Franz van Aelst, printed in *Li sette miracoli del' mondo* by Orazio Tigrini, 1574–1578 (Bibliothèque nationale de France, Rés. Ge DD 95).

---

[47] On the engraving, see Demus-Quatember (1981) 213–225. Vedder (2003) 135–136 is the first to have connected this document with the description of Du Choul.
[48] Plin. *HN* 5.31.   [49] [Philo Byzantius] p. 32, ll. 1–2, 5 (Brodersen; above, pp. 80–82, §3).
[50] De Pestels [Caylus] (1759) 363.

The First Numismatic Colossi

According to a letter dated 12 August 1445, Cyriac of Ancona is the first to have described the head of Helios depicted on Rhodian coins as that of the Colossus of Rhodes,[51] although he elsewhere assumes that the statue was a column.[52]

In his *Cosmographie de Levant* of 1554, André Thevet describes and illustrates a Colossus 'with his legs over the two arches of the harbour, [...] raised so high that the ships entering the port passed between his two legs. He held in his right hand a sword, and in his left hand a pike, and on his chest was a burning mirror'[53] (Fig. 7.9). The aetiological account (Colossus < ruins in the harbour) mingles with the Alexandrian legend (Colossus ~ Lighthouse); if Thevet possibly collected the first at Rhodes, where he had sojourned for two months in 1551, he certainly found the second in the unpublished manuscript of the *Antiquités romaines*, to which he acknowledges his debt elsewhere.[54] He changed his source only by replacing the 'reflecting' mirror with a more dramatic 'burning' mirror. Du Choul had thus kindly allowed his friend to use the translation of the Greek manuscript that he himself would only publish two years later in his *Discours de la religion des anciens Romains*.

Du Choul would be paid back for his generosity. The Colossus depicted in Thevet's *Cosmographie de Levant* indeed has its head taken from a Rhodian coin on which Helios appeared with a mane of hair serving as his crown of rays.[55] This derivation is hardly surprising, since Thevet himself later would declare:

I'ay apporté de ceste isle [Rhodes] plusieurs medalles d'or & d'argent, entre autres vne espece de cuiure, où il y a effigié vne grosse teste de Colosse auec ses rayons solaires, imberbe, les cheueux fort longs: le renuers representant vne belle fleur en façon de rose, & tout autour certaines lettres Grecques abbregees: desquelles ie fey present à vn Gentilhomme Lyonnois, qui depuis les a fait imprimer auec plusieurs autres antiques, en son liure des Castrametations.

I have brought back from this island [Rhodes] several coins of gold and silver, including a bronze specie, upon which is portrayed a great head of Colossus with his solar rays, cleanshaven, the locks of hair very long. The reverse shows a beautiful flower in the shape of a rose and, all around, are certain abbreviated Greek letters. Of these, I have made a present to a gentleman from Lyon, who has since printed them with many other antiquities in his *Livre des Castrametations*.[56]

---

[51] Bodnar (2003) 194–195 (no. 25, 12 August 1445); Badoud (2019c) 38.
[52] Above, pp. 167–168.   [53] Thevet (1554) 106.
[54] Thevet (1554) 137. For the circulation of manuscripts in the milieu of antiquarians in Lyon, see Badoud (2002) 182–183.
[55] Vedder (2003) 142.
[56] Thevet (1575) f. 208v. The recto of the same folio mentions early excavations on Rhodes and antiquities collected by Thevet's Jewish Spanish-speaking guide, among which was a two-foot jasper statue of a child with frizzy hair reminiscent of other small red sculptures brought from Rhodes to Italy before 1530: see Badoud (2019c) 40.

Fig. 7.9 Engraving from the *Cosmographie de Levant* of André Thevet, Lyon, 1554, p. 104 (Bibliothèque de Genève, PFt 15).

Fig. 7.10 Rhodian coins reproduced by Guillaume du Choul, *Discours de la religion des anciens Romains*, Lyon, 1556, p. 192 (Bibliothèque nationale de France, Rés. J 557[1]).

The 'gentleman from Lyon' is none other than Du Choul, who did not reproduce the coins in his *Discours sur la castrametation et discipline militaire des Romains*[57] but in his *Discours de la religion des anciens Romains*,[58] published the same year (Fig. 7.10). As for the coin used to recreate the head of the Colossus, it is not the bronze coin struck during the first century BC[59] on which one recognizes the 'rays' and the 'very long locks of hair' of the god (the lower image of Fig. 7.10), but a silver coin (didrachm or tetradrachm) dated to the years 230–205 BC[60] (the upper image of Fig. 7.10).

The Hidden Gods

Apollo . . .
Dedicated to Catherine de' Medici by the apothecary, patron, and collector Nicolas Houel, *L'histoire de la Royne Arthemise* recounts the great deeds of a

---

[57] Du Choul (1556b).   [58] Du Choul (1556a) 192.
[59] Cf. *BMC Caria* 262, no. 358.   [60] Ashton (2001) 106, nos. 213 and 219.

sovereign of Halicarnassus who originates from the confusion of Artemisia I, a major figure in the Battle of Salamis in 480 BC mentioned by Herodotus,[61] with Artemisia II, an equally capable fighter who nevertheless was remembered more by Vitruvius for the tomb that she built for her husband Mausolus, whose death in 353 BC had left her inconsolable.[62] The intensity of the mourning of Catherine de' Medici and her decision to construct the Valois Mausoleum after the accidental death of Henry II of France in 1559 established the idea of a parallel between the two queens. Thus, the Rhodians defeated by Artemisia II (in an event whose authenticity seems beyond doubt)[63] are assimilated to the Protestants confronted by Catherine, just as the young Lygdamis, orphaned from his father Mausolus, foreshadows Charles IX, son of the late Henry II.

Houel recounts how Artemisia (II), having seized the Rhodian ships that had recklessly attacked Halicarnassus, adorned them with victory laurels and appeared onboard under the walls of Rhodes, accompanied by Lygdamis. Believing that they saw their own fleet returning, the Rhodians allowed them to enter the harbour and, in so doing, to conquer the city.[64] Houel enlivened this episode with a digression devoted to Rhodian antiquities, where the description of the Colossus copies word for word that of Thevet.[65]

In the month of February 1563, Houel had completed his historical novel, accompanied by a certain number of drawings intended to serve as models for tapestries. Three years later, encouraged by Catherine de' Medici, he ordered new illustrations from the 'best men as much from Italy as from France'[66] and had each of these drawings introduced by an explicatory sonnet. In 1571, an important series of single loose-leaf sheets had already appeared, yet Houel waited over a decade before submitting the entire work to the queen, probably because he had not received the recompense that she had promised to cover his costs.[67]

An unforeseen event rescued the work from probable oblivion. In 1601, Henry IV of France invited the Flemish tapestry-makers François de Comans and Marc de la Planche to establish themselves in Paris. When the Crown placed an order for a wall painting for Marie de' Medici, eight drawings from *L'histoire de la Royne Arthemise* were retained as models; a contract created in 1607 informs us that they were 'from the hand and the invention of Anthoine Carron [Antoine Caron], talented painter and artist'.[68] Henri Lerambert saw to their completion with seven supplementary pictures representing scenes from the education of Lygdamis and from the war against the Rhodians. The collection had thus transformed its

---

[61] Hdt. 7.99, 8.68–69, 8.87–88, 8.93, 8.101–103, and 8.107.   [62] Vitr. *De arch.* 2.8.14–15.
[63] Berthold (1978) 129–134 and Hornblower (1982) 129 agree that the story cannot be true; *contra* Jeppesen (1986) 86–96 and Bresson (1994) 145–154. For another piece of Rhodian history only mentioned by Vitruvius, see Chapter 6, p. 133.
[64] BnF, ms. Français 306, f. 56r.   [65] Ibid., f. 57r–v.
[66] BnF, ms. Réserve, AD-105 (dedicated to Catherine de' Medici).
[67] On the chronology of the work, see Auclair (2000) 155–188.
[68] Archives nationales, Minutier central, XIX, 358. See also Ehrmann (1968) 6.

Fig. 7.11 Drawing by Antoine Caron for the *L'Histoire de la Royne Arthemise* of Nicolas Houel, before 1571, introduced by the sonnet 'Estant donc en ce point la victoire obtenue' (Bibliothèque nationale de France, Rés. Ad 105).

meaning to evoke the birth of the future Louis XIII and to celebrate triumphant royalty.[69]

As the drawing depicting both the attack and the Colossus of Rhodes (Fig. 7.11)[70] was one subject retained for the tapestry (Fig. 7.12), we can attribute it to Caron, rather than to one of the other illustrators of *L'histoire de la Royne Arthemise*, whose participation in the project of Houel was only marginal.[71] In accordance with the contract of 1607, the tapestry recreated its model by magnifying it; the Colossus extends out of its frame, on which the emblems of mourning, the border half-France and half-Tuscany, and the motto recalling the memory of a deceased king[72] have yielded their place to decoration with flowers and *putti* that accompany the figures of the royal couple and the heraldry of France and Navarre. The scene would be chosen regularly to appear on the tapestries depicting the history of Artemisia during the course of the seventeenth century.[73]

---

[69] Auclair (2007) 19–26.
[70] The Colossus reappears in a drawing that depicts the departure of the queen for Halicarnassus, introduced by the sonnet 'Donc s'estant en cela brusquement acquité'.
[71] Auclair (2010) 163–177.   [72] De Conihout and Ract-Madoux (2002).
[73] Auclair (2007) 19 alludes to around one hundred. See also Fenaille (1903) 200–212.

Fig. 7.12 Tapestry belonging to the 'Tenture d'Artémise' by François de Comans and Marc de la Planche, around 1607 (collections of the Mobilier national/Les Gobelins, inv. GMTT 12/4).

The originality of the drawing by Caron is due first to its urban setting, a pure invention;[74] absent from previous representations of the statue, it also did not follow the famous image of Rhodes presented by Bernhard von Breydenbach in his *Peregrinatio in terram sanctam*[75] (compare Fig. 7.11 with Fig. 7.16). The image, however, was reworked to accommodate the tower from which the trumpeter, duped by the stratagem of Artemisia, announces their false victory to the inhabitants of Rhodes. This tower might have evoked one of the fortifications of La Rochelle; in this case, the modification would have been introduced to emphasize the parallelism developed by Houel, after the Huguenots of the town, having revolted in 1568, again submitted to the authority of Catherine de' Medici.[76]

By placing the Colossus at the entrance to the harbour of Rhodes (even though its construction had not begun during the rule of Artemisia II) and by providing it with a mirror and a spear, Caron followed the directions given by Thevet and Houel. He nevertheless distanced himself from the latter by replacing the sword with a bow, by arming the statue with a quiver, and by conferring upon the statue

---

[74] *Pace* Ffolliott (1993) 19.   [75] *Pace* Adelson (1994) 284–285.
[76] Ffolliott (1993) 19 mentions 'a replica of one [tower] that stood in the French port city of La Rochelle'. Nevertheless, the tower in question remains to be identified.

an Apollonian character not present in the *Cosmographie de Levant*. He was not inspired by the iconography of this book[77] but by the Apollo Belvedere, which had been acquired by Cardinal Giuliano Della Rovere (the future Pope Julius II) at the end of the fifteenth century.[78] As an intermediary work, we may think of the cast ordered by Francesco Primaticcio from Rome in 1540, which was then set up in the gardens of the Palace of Fontainebleau,[79] where Caron, his pupil, worked around 1560. Yet Caron more likely followed an engraving published in 1552 within the *Speculum Romanae Magnificentiae* of Antoine Lafrery, which had already inspired his *Massacres du Triumvirat*, a painting dated to 1566 (Fig. 7.13).[80]

... and Sol

The new Colossus[81] that Heemskerck drew in 1570 features in his series of the *Octo mundi miracula* (Fig. 7.14), a new version of the list of the Wonders of the World[82] based on verses by the Dutch doctor and humanist Adriaen de Jonghe (Hadrianus Junius).[83] It also holds a quiver and a bow over the shoulder. Its resemblance to the Colossus of Caron is evident but cannot be explained by influence, since *L'histoire de la Royne Arthemise* was finished before[84] but distributed after[85] the *Octo mundi miracula* were put into circulation. One must therefore suppose the existence of a common source, which is none other than the Apollo Belvedere that Heemskerck drew at Rome in the 1530s (Fig. 7.15),[86] along with the Capitoline Hercules, the model for his first Colossus.[87]

In its left hand, the statue no longer holds a lantern but a fire pot. In its right hand, a new accessory appears, closely tied to the rays that form a crown around its head. The artist himself possibly had difficulty identifying it, while his successors wavered between an arrow and a sceptre. In fact, this accessory is likely to have been the whip associated with the Roman figure of Sol, frequently represented in small bronze statuary (Figs 7.32 and 7.34) and on coins[88] (independently from the Colossus iconography, the whip was also chosen as the attribute of the Sun in the *Imagini delli dei de gl'antichi*, published in 1647).[89] The Colossus of Heemskerck would thus result from a combination of the Apollo Belvedere and an unidentified work or rather an iconographic type from the Imperial period. As in the drawing of Caron,

---

[77] *Pace* Adelson (1994) 284–285; Auclair (2010) 116–117.
[78] Haskell and Penny (1988) 148–151.
[79] Pressouyre (1969) 223–239.   [80] Ehrmann (1986) 19–20 and 30–31.
[81] On Heemskerck's first Colossus, see above, pp. 168–169.   [82] Chapter 4, pp. 94–95.
[83] The engravings are collected and commented in Kunze (2003); see also Brodersen (2004). The poem *In miracula orbis octo* was published posthumously in De Jonghe (1598) 177–178 (Brodersen 30).
[84] Auclair (2010) argued the opposite view as his starting point.
[85] Adelson (1994) 287 n. 12 offers the opposite hypothesis, but very tentatively.
[86] See Bober and Rubinstein (2010) 77, no. 28.   [87] Above pp. 168–169.
[88] For this type, see Matern (2002) 99–165; Hijmans (2024) 68–69.   [89] Cartari (1647) 25.

180 THE IMAGE OF THE STATUE

Fig. 7.13 Engraving of the Apollo Belvedere from the *Speculum Romanae magnificentiae* of A. Lafrery, Rome, 1552, f. 67 (Institut national d'histoire de l'art, NUM FOL EST 175).

Fig. 7.14 Drawing by Maerten van Heemskerck, from the collection of the *Octo mundi miracula*, 1570 (Courtauld Institute Gallery, inv. D.1952.RW.648).

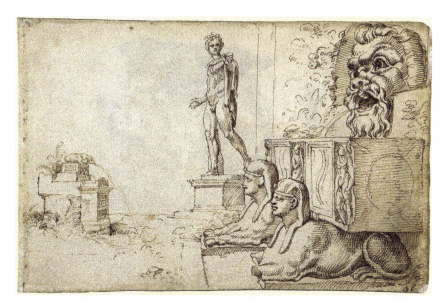

Fig. 7.15 Drawing of the Apollo Belvedere, with two fountains combining various antiquities, by Maerten van Heemskerck, 1532–1536 (Kupferstichkabinett der Staatlichen Museen zu Berlin, Römische Skizzenbücher I–II, inv. 79 D 2, f. 23r).

the setting is that of an imaginary city; through analepsis, the foreground depicts the construction of the statue, already completed in the background.

Heemskerck's Triumph

In his *Cosmographie universelle* of 1575,[90] Thevet proposed a new version of his Colossus, now without its spear and situated in the Rhodes of Bernhard von Breydenbach (Fig. 7.16),[91] but its success would be very limited.[92] Supported by the artistic and intellectual influence of the Low Countries during the sixteenth and seventeenth centuries, the new Colossus of Heemskerck would embody the archetype of the statue. It was engraved by Philippe Galle in 1572,[93] reworked

Fig. 7.16 Engraving from the *Cosmographie universelle* of André Thevet, Paris, 1575, f. 205v (Augsburg, Staats- und Stadtbibliothek, 2 HV 95-1).

[90] Above, p. 173.   [91] Breydenbach (1486) f. 24; cf. Vedder (2003) 136–137.
[92] e.g. Megiser (1606) 60–61.   [93] Galle (1572).

Fig. 7.17 Engraving by a Chinese artist for the *Explanation of the World Map* [*Kunyu tushuo*] of Ferdinand Verbiest, Beijing, 1674, ff. 75–76 (Biblioteca Apostolica Vaticana, Borg. Cin. 350, fasc. 30).

184   THE IMAGE OF THE STATUE

twice by Maarten de Vos to be engraved by Gerard de Jode[94] and by Crispin de Passe the Elder,[95] reproduced in a painting by Louis de Caullery,[96] reshaped in another painting by Abraham Storck,[97] and employed as a decorative feature by Flemish tapestry-makers,[98] an illustrator of books like Rubens,[99] or a cartographer like Willem Blaeu.[100] Inspired by this iconography, like Victor Hugo after him,[101] William Shakespeare made Julius Caesar 'bestride the narrow world like a Colossus', while Cassius and Brutus 'walked under his huge legs'.[102] In 1674,[103] Ferdinand Verbiest, a Jesuit missionary from the Low Countries operating in China, even transposed the Colossus of Heemskerck into the aesthetics of the Qing Dynasty to portray the statue 'taller than a pagoda' (Fig. 7.17), of which his predecessor Giulio Aleni had provided the first description in Mandarin.[104] From the beginning of the seventeenth century until the final decades of the nineteenth century, the statue was consistently accompanied by the fire pot imagined by Heemskerck.[105]

A Lonesome Colossus on a Lonely Base

Although his Colossus of 1608, equipped with a fire pot, participates in the Flemish tradition (as the verses by Josse de Rycke make clear)[106] Antonio Tempesta[107] is alone in placing the statue on a single base and in giving it the appearance of a Jupiter, as suggested by his source, the *Silva de varia lección* of Pedro Mexía, as translated in Italian by Mambrino Roseo.[108] (Fig. 7.18). As another original feature, the image appears as the inverse of the drawing by Heemskerck, since its construction acts as a prolepsis: the statue, still intact in the distance, has already been demolished in the foreground. The artist here refers to the episode during which the Arabs, led by Muʿāwiya, allegedly pillaged the ruins of the Colossus and then sold the bronze from the statue to a Jewish merchant, who carried it off on a caravan of 900 camels. As discussed in Chapter 4, this episode is a forgery created in the eighth century. After the fall of Constantinople in 1453, its meaning changed, since Westerners used it to symbolize the barbarity of the 'Saracens', who were no longer the Arabs of the

---

[94] The engraving by Gerard de Jode kept in the British Museum (inv. 1876,0510.552) is the inversed and slightly modified version of a drawing from the James and Marilynn Alsdorf collection, sold by Christie's on 28 January 2020 (lot 79), which bears the inscription '216: martin de voss' [Maarten de Vos].
[95] Van de Passe (1614).   [96] Louvre, MNR 727.
[97] Mâcon, Musée des Ursulines, A.699.   [98] Brett (1949) 347–353.
[99] e.g. de Aguilón [Aguilonius] (1613) 105 (vignette of P. P. Rubens).
[100] Blaeu (1606). This map was reprinted in the atlases published later by his family.
[101] *La Légende des siècles* X. *Les Sept merveilles du monde* VI. *Le Colosse de Rhodes*.
[102] *Julius Caesar* 234–236. Cf. *Troilus and Cressida* 5.5.9–10.   [103] From Blaeu (1606).
[104] Aleni [艾儒略] (1623). See also De Troia (2009) 80–81; cf. Menegon (1994) 94–97.
[105] On the influence of the Low Countries, see also below, p. 193.
[106] Beschi (1986) 312.
[107] Confused with André Thevet by Rowland (2016) 449–450.
[108] Mexía (1576) [*parte terza*] 298v, with Folin and Preti (2022) 40–43.

Fig. 7.18 Print from the series *Septem orbis miracula* […] *in aeneas tabulas ab Antonio Tempesta Florentino relata, a Iusto Rychio Gaudene versibus celebrata*, Rome, 1608 (British Museum, Prints & Drawings, inv. 1872,0511.1245).

seventh century but rather the Turks of their own times.[109] This reversal is apparent in the drawing of Tempesta, with its cavalry in Ottoman attire.[110]

The originality in the layout of the Colossus responds to that of the scene represented. In fact, the artist was forced to choose between two contradictory myths. If the statue destroyed in *c*.227 BC had spanned the harbour of Rhodes, as local legend had claimed since the fourteenth century, its ruins would have fallen into the sea and would not have been gathered up and carried away on the backs of camels, as the literary tradition had insisted since the eighth century. Although remarkable in all aspects, the engraving of Tempesta has remained without genuine descendants. Matthäus Merian managed only to distort it by introducing the soldiers of Muʿāwiya into his version of the Colossus of Heemskerck. While the various parts of the statue straddling the harbour were in the process of being gathered together in the drawing produced by his forerunner, he treated them as debris from the earthquake of *c*.227 that mysteriously ended up on solid ground (Fig. 7.19).[111]

---

[109] Chapter 4, p. 72.
[110] Roberts (2016) 256 notes that 'at least one of the men' depicted on Martin de Vos' drawing of the Colossus engraved by Crispijn de Passe already 'wears a central cone or Taj, associated specifically with Ottoman dress', which probably 'signalled, if obliquely, the island's state of affairs after 1522'.
[111] Vedder (2003) 137.

Fig. 7.19 Engraving by Matthäus Merian published in the *Historische Chronica, Oder Beschreibung der Fürnemsten Geschichten so sich von Anfang der Welt biß auff das Jahr Christi 1619. zugetragen of Johan Ludwig Gottfried*, Frankfurt am Main, 1674⁵ [1630¹], p. 211 (Bibliothèque publique et universitaire de Neuchâtel, NUM 53.1.1).

Theme and Variations

At the end of the 1630s, Gilles Vignon dedicated a group of drawings to the Wonders of the World by reducing them to small decorative elements. This idea guaranteed the notoriety of his work, as attested by the sixains dedicated to it by the poet Charles de Beys and by the numerous copies (claimed as such or not) of his now lost Colossus (Figs 7.20 and 7.21).[112] The statue appeared behind a certain Theagenes, presented by the poet as the sculptor of the monument[113] but perhaps understood by the illustrator as its sponsor.

---

[112] The entirety of this group was engraved by Gilles Rousselet and Abraham Bosse with the legend '*Vignon inventor*'; see Pacht Bassani (1993) 364–368. It also forms the subject of seven painted panels that decorated the alcove of a hotel located on Rue des Bernardins in Paris. Six have been preserved at the Musée Carnavalet. On one, the figure of Theagenes has been removed to make way for the Colossus: Bruson and Leribault (1999) 414. The same choice is found in Manesson Mallet (1683) 152, fig. 127. The pairs Theagenes/Colossus and Semiramis/walls of Babylon were accurately reproduced on the panels of a small Bohemian cabinet last published by Vedder (2003) 137 and 139, without the models being identified.

[113] De Beys (1651) 97–100.

THE COLOSSUS SPANNING THE PORT OF RHODES 187

Fig. 7.20 *Teagene*, engraving by Gilles Rousselet and Abraham Bosse, after Claude Vignon, around 1640 (British Museum, Prints & Drawings, inv. 1894,0611.36).

Indeed, falsely claiming one century later to take his information from Pliny,[114] Johann Bernhard Fischer von Erlach placed the construction of the monument 'under the government of Theagenes, prince of Caria, around the year after the creation of the world 3600'. Banal iconographically, his famous Colossus is distinguished from its contemporaries[115] by the numismatic parallels meant to justify the reconstruction of the head (Fig. 7.22);[116] the first is borrowed from Du Choul (the upper image of Fig. 7.10) and the second is a drachma with the name of Euphanes, dated to the years 88–84 BC.[117]

In the seventh volume of his *Histoire ancienne*, published in 1734, Charles Rollin had the virtue of remaining faithful to the ancient literary sources without repeating the legend of the Colossus spanning the harbour of Rhodes.[118] The illustrator of the Dutch version of this work, Simon Fokke, nevertheless returned to the medieval myth in an engraving that depicted the fall of the statue during

---

[114] Plin. *HN* 2.62 (defining features of the sky according to the location) and 36.26 (stone of Skyros).
[115] See especially Kircher (1679) 89 and Calmet (1728) 156–157.
[116] Fischer von Erlach (1721) pl. VIII.   [117] Jenkins (1989) 114, no. 240.
[118] Rollin (1734) 647, 649–650.

Fig. 7.21 Engraving from the *Description de l'univers* of Allain Manesson Mallet, Paris, 1683, p. 152, fig. 127, after Claude Vignon (Bibliothèque de Genève, A 2795).

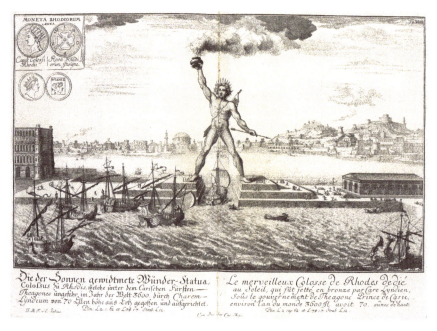

Fig. 7.22 Engraving from Johann Bernhard Fischer von Erlach, *Entwurf einer historischen Architectur*, Vienna, 1721, pl. VIII (Bibliothèque de Genève, Ia 283).

the earthquake of *c*.227 BC (Fig. 7.23).[119] Condemned as such by the Count of Caylus in 1753, the myth still persisted until 1900 in scientific literature under the cover of rationalization.[120] Colonel Rottiers, for instance, went so far as to position his Colossus on the 'canal' that allegedly connected the military harbour to the port of commerce during the Middle Ages (Fig. 7.24).[121]

Works of scientific popularization also perpetuated the legend. Published in Cincinnati in 1885, the historical encyclopaedia of John Clark Ridpath presents an Apollonian Colossus spanning the harbour opening of Rhodes (Fig. 7.25). The lantern brandished in his right hand evokes that of a lighthouse and was certainly inspired by the Statue of Liberty.[122] The monument was not unveiled before 1886 but the torch had been exhibited in Philadelphia in 1876 and in New York in 1877 (Fig. 7.26).[123] It is nevertheless to an Apollo Cytharoedus (itself a derivation from the Lycian Apollo erected at Athens around 330 BC) that the Colossus of Ridpath

Fig. 7.23 Engraving by Simon Fokke for the Dutch version of the *Histoire ancienne* of Charles Rollin (*De geschiedenis der waereld, vertoont in de lotgevallen der oude volke*, Amsterdam, 1774, p. 231, fig. LIX).

---

[119] Rollin (1774) 231, fig. LIX.   [120] Chapter 6, p. 126.
[121] von Hammer-Prugstall (1811) 64; Rottiers (1830) 80–87 (pl. IX–X); Hamilton (1842) 65–66; Ross (1845) 86–87; Guérin (1856) 105–108.
[122] On the Statue of Liberty, see below pp. 198–202.
[123] Hargrove (1986) 170–171; Lemoine (1986) 100–107.

Fig. 7.24 Engraving by Pierre-Joseph Witdoeck from the *Description des monuments de Rhodes* of Bernard-Eugène-Antoine Rottiers, Brussels, 1830, pl. X (Bayerische Staatsbibliothek, 4 H.gr.55).

owes the instrument that he carries on his back (Fig. 7.27). The fantastical panorama of the town of Rhodes painted by Antonio Muñoz Degraín in 1914 includes a Colossus that also copies the Apollo Cytharoedus (Fig. 7.28). The latter statue imposed itself as a model because its general design was close to that of Rottiers' Colossus (Fig. 7.24).

It is hardly necessary to add that, since the eighteenth century, numerous caricatures (frequently associated with allusions to Shakespeare's *Julius Caesar* in the English-speaking world)[124] have contributed to spreading the image of the Colossus spanning the port of Rhodes.[125] They have been transmitted since the twentieth century by innumerable tourist souvenirs, advertising material, stamps, and coins.

Japanese Imagery and Colossal Genitals

Nothing prevents us from assuming that Chares had represented Helios dressed only with his crown,[126] as

Fig. 7.25 Engraving from the *Cyclopaedia of Universal History: Being an Account of the Principal Events in the Career of the Human Race from the Beginnings of Civilization to the Present Time* I. *The Ancient World of John Clark Ridpath*, Cincinnati, 1885, p. 621 (New York Public Library, Digital Gallery, inv. 1625165).

the representation of nudity posed no problems in classical antiquity (it has been rightly stressed that the perfection of the bodies of gods and heroes acted as a sort of clothing).[127] At the beginning of the sixteenth century, the situation was radically different: not only was nudity associated with the idea of original sin, but the god was put in an obscene position by the myth that made him straddle the harbour of Rhodes. Hiding the sexual organs of the Colossus or rendering them as discrete as possible became mandatory, unless one wished to produce a

---

[124] Above, p. 184.   [125] Wriedt Sørensen (2019) 20–34; cf. Roberts (2016) 252.
[126] Chapter 4, pp. 92–93.   [127] Bonfante (1989) 543–570.

192 THE IMAGE OF THE STATUE

Fig. 7.26 Photograph of the right arm of the Statue of Liberty, exhibited at Philadelphia in 1876 (New York Public Library, MFY Dennis Coll 91-F380).

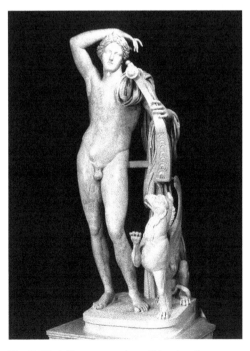

Fig. 7.27 A Roman version of the Apollo Citharoedus, found near Tivoli, AD 130–138 (Musei Capitolini, inv. Scu 736).

pornographic image. In Japan, during the years 1820s, such was the way chosen by the anonymous author of a flyer, which was meant to serve as an advertisement for an aphrodisiac called *chōmeigan* (Fig. 7.30). An ointment made of mussel secretions mixed with cloves, opium, a derivative of arsenic, camphor, and musk, it aimed at guaranteeing the 'long life' of the male erection and was distributed by the sex-shop Yotsumeya. The Colossus appears in the midst of five vignettes representing explicit scenes, each of which is associated with a 'foreign country' from popular mythology. By

Fig. 7.28 Antoni Muñoz Degraín, *El Coloso de Rodas*, 1914 (Real Academia de Bellas Artes de San Fernando, inv. 787).

straddling a harbour, the statue conforms to the scheme created by Heemskerck and transposed into the aesthetics of the Edo period by Utagawa Kunitora (Fig. 7.29). However, thanks to the *chōmeigan*, its erect penis escapes the clothing and thus breaks with tradition. In the right hand, the Colossus no longer holds the whip (?) chosen by Heemskerck but a packet containing the powerful ointment. In the left hand, a scent burner containing aphrodisiac incense has replaced the usual fire pot. The title of the flyer, *Horanda baninkoku no zu* (*Dutch World Map of Genitalia*), alludes to the Dutch cartographic tradition and the place that the Colossus of Rhodes held within it, but also to the alleged origin of the ointment and the incense. Indeed, during the Edo period, Japan was totally closed to strangers and held commercial relations only with the Netherlands and with China.[128]

---

[128] Little (1996) 90; Clark and Gerstle (2013) 31–33; cf. Winkel (2005) 199–201 (see p. 201 n. 1 for the transcription and translation of the Japanese title, which contains a pun).

Fig. 7.29 Utagawa Kunitora, *Dutch Ships Entering the Port of the Island of Rhodes* [*Rokosuto minato Oranda fune nyushin no zu*], c.1818–1830 (Art Institute Chicago, inv. 1926.1720).

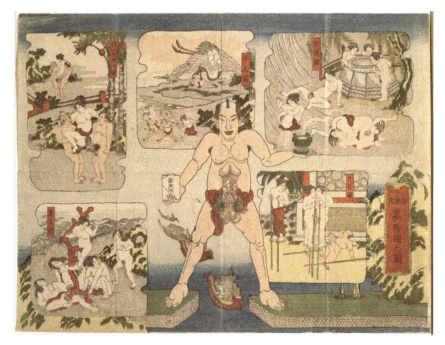

Fig. 7.30 Anonymous flyer depicting the *Dutch World Map of Genitalia* [*Horanda baninkoku no zu*], c.1823–1826 (Fine Arts Museums of San Francisco, inv. 1996.144).

Artists and Archaeologists

Two Statuettes

In 1878, Lucien Augé de Lassus and his architect Louis Bernier, who had just prepared a restoration project for the Mausoleum of Halicarnassus, were the first to revive the vision (made fashionable by the—then under construction—*Liberty Enlightening the World*) of a statue installed on a single base (Fig. 7.31).[129] Nevertheless, their Colossus remains very much in line with the model of Heemskerck: still overlooking the harbour of Rhodes, it was clearly inspired by a statuette of Sol kept in Paris at the Cabinet des Médailles (Fig. 7.32). As the other Wonders illustrated in the book of Augé de Lassus and Bernier, it served as a model for a series of paintings by František Kupka, who represented it in 1906 along with the quadriga of Helios cast by Lysippus[130] in a geographically realistic setting. The original tension of the right arm has been exaggerated, likely in homage to the Statue of Liberty but with an unsettling result; the god's Roman salute seems to foreshadows the Italian and then fascist domination over the Dodecanese (Fig. 7.33).

Fig. 7.31 Reconstitution of the Colossus of Rhodes by Louis Bernier (engraved by Sidney Barclay) for the *Voyage aux Sept merveilles du monde* of Augé de Lassus, Paris, 1878, p. 17 (Musée d'art et d'histoire de Genève, BAA CA 269).

The subject of a book published in 2003,[131] the Colossus of Wolfram Hoepfner (Fig. 7.34) is nothing more than the enlargement of another statuette of Sol,

---

[129] Augé de Lassus (1878) 17. See below, pp. 198–204.
[130] On this statue, see Chapter 3, pp. 59–61, and Badoud (forthcoming 4).
[131] Hoepfner (2003). The argument is also made in Hoepfner (2000) 129–153; Hoepfner (2007) 69–103 (in German) and 104–119 (in Greek).

Fig. 7.32 Bronze statuette of Sol (height 9.7 cm) discovered at Chalon-sur-Saône, first–second century AD (Bibliothèque nationale de France, Cabinet des Médailles, Bronze 114).

discovered at Montdidier (Fig. 7.35), which José Dörig already believed to be a copy of the Rhodian monument.[132] According to Hoepfner, this rough bronze statuette must be a faithful reproduction of the model that Chares used to construct his masterpiece; the modification of the natural proportions would have corrected the optical distortions caused by the gigantism of the Colossus. This hypothesis was used thereafter to explain the reference to several *kolossoí* in Posidippus' poem *On the Making of Statues*, as if they were copies of Chares' Colossus.[133] In reality, the substandard quality of the bronze at Montdidier, most probably a product of Egypt from the second or third century AD, is sufficient to explain its unattractive proportions. In addition, should we imagine that its creator would have travelled to Rhodes to copy a model whose existence and preservation are by no means attested? Would he have gone to the lengths of incorporating characteristics detrimental to his creation? Despite the measurements that attempt to give scientific weight to his argument, Hoepfner unconsciously reproduced the approach of Heemskerck in 1570 and Bernier in 1878. At least these artists—who did not claim to produce scientific work—should not be reproached for having committed a truly colossal anachronism by assimilating the statue of Chares to the figure of Sol that appeared several hundred years later, in a completely different context.[134]

---

[132] See Dörig (1999) 190 and above p. 163.   [133] Männlein-Robert (2007) 78, about AB 62.
[134] Without reconsidering the identification proposed by W. Hoepfner, Matern (2002) 260 notes that 'explaining the great gap of a good 500 years between the erection of the Colossus and the emergence of Sol Invictus remains difficult'.

Fig. 7.33 František Kupka, *The Colossus of Rhodes*, 1906. Oil on canvas (Národní Galerie, Prague, O 17456).

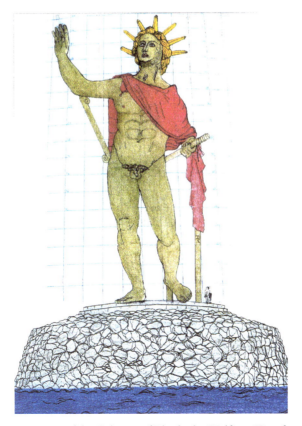

Fig. 7.34 Reconstitution of the Colossus of Rhodes by Wolfram Hoepfner (2003).

Fig. 7.35 Bronze statuette of Sol (height 35.5 cm) discovered at Montdidier, second–third century AD (Musée du Louvre, Br 1059).

The Liberty Enlightening the World

If the influence of Roman art on modern and contemporary representations of the Colossus remained little known until now, the model offered by the Statue of Liberty (Fig. 7.36) has already been emphasized. The two monuments nevertheless maintain relations more complex than they first appear. Although the Statue of Liberty was unveiled in 1886, Auguste Bartholdi had already produced rough sketch in 1870 by following the outlines of a statue planned to mark the entrance of the Suez Canal, *Egypt Carrying the Light to Asia*, which remained at the draft stage.[135] By their position in a harbour, their function as a lighthouse, and the torch held above their head, both statues reflect the traditional iconography of the Colossus of Rhodes; the Statue of Liberty additionally borrows its rays from the

---

[135] Trachtenberg (1976) 49–57; Lemoine (1986) 26–35; Provoyeur (1986c) 97–109.

ARTISTS AND ARCHAEOLOGISTS   199

Fig. 7.36 Auguste Bartholdi, *The Liberty Enlightening the World*, unveiled in New York on 28 October 1886.

Fig. 7.37 Project of Auguste Bartholdi for *The Liberty Enlightening the World* (Colmar, Musée Bartholdi).

Fig. 7.38 Bronze Rhodian coin depicting the nymph Rhodos, late first century–early second century AD (National Museum of Denmark, SNG Copenhagen Caria 905; scale 1.5:1).

same repertoire, without owing anything to the literary sources.[136] A comparison between the projects of Fischer von Erlach (Fig. 7.22) and Bartholdi (Fig. 7.37) makes this perfectly clear.[137]

In the work *Les Colosses anciens et modernes*, published in 1876, Eugène Lesbazeilles (acting as a spokesman of Bartholdi) rejected the idea that the 'Apollo of Rhodes' had been located 'at the entrance to the town harbour, one foot on each side of the channel'.[138] 'Nevertheless', he went on to say (plagiarizing a recent publication by François Lenormant),[139] 'there exist medals and coins originating from the island of Rhodes that contain a figure in which one may see a representation of the famous Colossus: it is an image of the Sun, protector-god of Rhodes, mythical founder of the race of its kings of old; he stands, his two feet together, wearing a long robe reaching to the ground and his head crowned with rays'.[140]

Described (if not understood) correctly, the issues to which Lenormant and Lesbazeilles refer may be identified without difficulty (Fig. 7.38).[141] The construction of the *Liberty Enlightening the World* had commenced one year before the publication of the book on the Colossi, which occurred when the promotional campaign to finance the statue was in full swing. The Rhodian coins therefore did not inspire the creator of the statue, but served to establish the idea that the monument embodied the *New Colossus*, as Emma Lazarus would call it in the poem that she wrote in 1883 to raise money for the construction of the pedestal, where it can be read on a bronze plaque since 1903.[142] Just as it had been the case with the obelisk of Constantinople eight centuries before,[143] Bartholdi's work, although at first only compared to the Colossus, quickly came to be regarded as a replica of it (although the poem of Lazarus perpetuated the medieval myth of 'the brazen giant of Greek fame, with conquering limbs astride from land to land').

With the Statue of Liberty in mind, Martin Nilsson indeed believed that he had discovered an image of the Colossus of Rhodes not only on coins of the same type as those spotted by Lenormant, but also on certain Rhodian amphora stamps produced by the manufacturer Nysios, which he incorrectly believed were

---

[136] *Pace* Moreno (1994a) 241, who writes that the Statue of Liberty was inspired by the epigram of the Colossus (*Anth. Pal.* 6.171), a groundless statement at odds with the history of the New York monument.
[137] Trachtenberg (1976) 113.
[138] Lesbazeilles (1876) 123–124; cf. Bartholdi (1885) 38. See also Provoyeur (1986a) 72–74.
[139] Lenormant (1867) 166–167.   [140] Lesbazeilles (1876) 125.
[141] See the examples collected by Boussac (1992) 122–123 and pl. 45.
[142] Lazarus (1889) 202–203. See also Belot and Bermond (2004) 406, and below, p. 218.
[143] Above, pp. 167–168.

contemporaneous with the statue (Fig. 7.39).¹⁴⁴ Zofia Sztetyłło then suggested the presence of the symbol of the Colossus on other Rhodian (and even Sinopean) stamps.¹⁴⁵ In fact, the coins mentioned by Lesbazeilles (in order to confer upon the *Liberty Enlightening the World* the status of 'New Colossus') and by Nilsson (as this status had become obvious to him) do not represent Helios but his spouse, the nymph Rhodos.¹⁴⁶ Remarkably, Nilsson himself is responsible for this identification;¹⁴⁷ yet, eager to rediscover traces of the statue of Chares on the amphora stamps that he was publishing, he artificially distinguished two series of coins, one of which would have represented Rhodos and the other the Colossus.

Fig. 7.39 Rhodian amphora stamp of the manufacturer Nysios depicting the nymph Rhodos, c. 158–138 BC (scale 1.5:1).

Published in 1932 and repeated by Jean-Claude Golvin until 2005,¹⁴⁸ the reconstruction designed by Albert Gabriel (Fig. 7.40) is another example of the influence exerted by the Statue of Liberty, to which it owes not only its base, its structure, its stance¹⁴⁹ and its location in a harbour¹⁵⁰ but also its general posture and its torch, eventually retained (as a hypothesis) by Antoine Hermary in 1995¹⁵¹ and by Michael Higgins in 2023.¹⁵² This new accessory replaced the fire pot suggested by Heemskerck in 1570, which only Augé de Lassus had omitted since then.¹⁵³ Gabriel justified its presence by recalling the epigram inscribed on the base of the Colossus, according to which the Rhodians, by raising their statue after the siege of Demetrius, 'did establish the lovely light (*phéggos*) of a freedom that is not to be enslaved'.¹⁵⁴ The text, however, does not refer to a torch but to the halo ignited by the epiphany of the gods, particularly Helios.¹⁵⁵ Gabriel's interpretation is only justified by 'the gesture repeated by the Statue of Liberty two millennia later at the entrance to the harbour of New York'.¹⁵⁶ The spear of his Colossus, on the other hand, is that attributed by Thevet to his statue in 1554, following a Byzantine author.¹⁵⁷

It is finally worth noting that, according to several scholars, the Colossus of Rhodes would have depicted 'Helios Eleutherios' ('Liberator').¹⁵⁸ While the god is

---

[144] Nilsson (1909) 174–180 and pl. II.
[145] Sztetyłło (1966a) 54–62; cf. Sztetyłło (1966b) 673–674; cf. Langlotz (1976) 149.
[146] Chapter 1, pp. 11, 13.   [147] Nilsson (1909) 178–179.
[148] Golvin and Coutin (2001) 73–84; Golvin et al. (2005²) 72.
[149] Chapter 4, pp. 88–89.   [150] Chapter 6, p. 129.
[151] Hermary (1995) 59.   [152] M. D. Higgins (2023) 315.
[153] For the specific case concerning the Colossus of Ridpath, see above, pp. 189–191.
[154] *Anth. Pal.* 6.171. Regarding this text, see Chapter 5.   [155] Cf. Dombart (1970) 72.
[156] Gabriel (1932) 345–346; cf. below, p. 210.   [157] Above, pp. 173–174.
[158] Jessen (1912) 72 ('Die Rhodier weihten ihre Kolossalstatue der H. nach *Anth. Pal.* VI 171 dem Gott als Befreier'); Dörig (1999) 185–192 (communication on 'der Helios Eleutherios des Chares von Lindos' presented in 1993); Moreno (1994b) 140 (probably from Dörig but with no reference to his communication); Musti and Pulcini (1996) 290, 293, 296, 300, 308 (from Moreno).

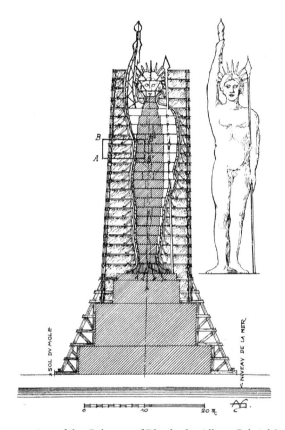

Fig. 7.40 Reconstruction of the Colossus of Rhodes by Albert Gabriel (1932).

associated with this epithet in Troezen,[159] and while the epigram of the Colossus mentions the word *eleuthería* ('liberty'),[160] 'Helios Eleutherios' is not attested on Rhodes. The confusion between the Colossus and the *Liberty Enlightening the World* clearly suggested the opposite.

A Relief from Rhodes and a Painting by Salvador Dali

In 1956, the sculptor Herbert Maryon, taking advantage of the model provided by the Statue of Liberty (but only concerning technical matters), attempted to argue that the outside of the Colossus consisted of fine bronze plaques riveted upon one another,[161] although Pseudo-Philo of Byzantium described a completely different technique of construction.[162] The form of his statue (Fig. 7.41) originates from a relief

---

[159] Paus. 2.31.5.
[160] *Anth. Pal.* 6.171 (above, pp. 96–97), v. 6.
[161] Maryon (1956) 68–86; Chapter 4, p. 82.
[162] [Philo Byzantius] p. 32, ll. 12–17 (Brodersen; above, pp. 80–82, §4).

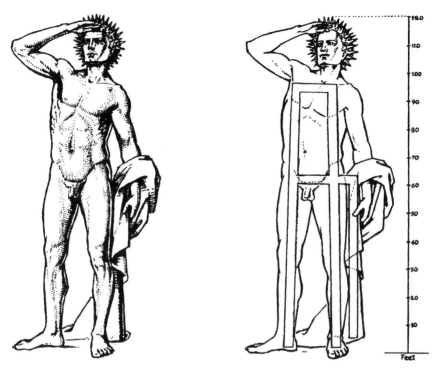

Fig. 7.41 Reconstruction of the Colossus of Rhodes by Herbert Maryon (1956).

Fig. 7.42 Hellenistic relief in the Archaeological Museum of Rhodes, as published by Giulio Jacopi (1932a).

in which Giulio Jacopi wished to see 'a figure of Helios, presumably a replica of the Colossus of Rhodes'[163] (Fig. 7.42). This relief, which represents either an athlete crowning himself[164] or the *aposkopeîn* gesture (expressing the approach of a god),[165] has no connection whatsoever with Helios. The Colossus of Rottiers, with its right arm raised (Fig. 7.24), had influenced the identification of Jacopi, as it had convinced Ridpath and Muñoz Degraín to take the Apollo Cytharoedus as a model (although the arm gesture meant here the epiphany of the god himself). The statue imagined by Maryon, in turn, is the basis for a famous painting by Salvador Dali, in which the bronze plaques whose existence the sculptor

Fig. 7.43 Salvador Dali, *The Colossus of Rhodes*, 1954 (Kunstmuseum Bern, inv. G 82.007).

---

[163] Jacopi (1932a) 25, fig. 15 and pl. II, followed by Stewart (1990) 299 and more hesitantly by Ekschmitt (1996) 178.
[164] Merker (1973) 30, no. 66.   [165] Zervoudaki (1975) 19; cf. Jucker (1956).

conjectured are clearly visible (Fig. 7.43);[166] it also became the object of a three-dimensional modelling in the United States.[167]

A Statue from Santa Marinella and a Painting by William Blake

The reconstruction of the Colossus developed by Paolo Moreno during the 1990s is the last to display the influence of the Statue of Liberty (Fig. 7.45). It is however based on an archer Apollo found at Santa Marinella and preserved in the museum of Civitavecchia (Fig. 7.44). In 1976, Ernst Langlotz had already identified this statue, which hypothetically brandished a torch discovered in the same area, as a 'derivation' of the Colossus, because 'the very wide striding out of the right leg' reminded him of the Renaissance iconography of the Seven Wonders of the World. In his opinion, this iconography originated from lost medieval manuscripts whose illuminations would have provided the readers with images more faithful to ancient monuments; the Colossus, in particular, would have been depicted not on the piers of the harbour but on its West side; yet it would already have had its characteristic stride.[168] According to Moreno, the statue found at Santa Marinella was sculpted during the reign of Hadrian; its head would resemble a head of Helios discovered on Rhodes, which would be barely later than the time of Chares (Fig. 7.46).[169] As John Malalas presented the emperor as the restorer of the Colossus,[170] the Apollo of Santa Marinella would then be a copy of the statue raised from its ruins at the beginning of the second century, and this copy would have been brought by a tourist of the Imperial era from Rhodes to Italy. The myth of the Colossus spanning the harbour of Rhodes could thus be born from its function as lighthouse and from the idea that a boat could pass between its feet. A 'visionary painter', William Blake then would have recreated 'the balance and the gesture of the original work in his *Angel of the Revelation*' (Fig. 7.47) before Bartholdi, by restoring its torch, allegedly revealed the authentic form of a statue whose replica would be discovered only in 1957. Hence it would be possible to 'imagine' that the torch of the Colossus was gilded 'like that of the Statue of Liberty in New York'.[171]

Fooled by an error established early in the manuscript tradition, Malalas confused the Colossus of Rhodes with the Colossus erected in Rome by Nero, the

---

[166] Dörig (1999) 189 is the first to note the relationship between this painting and the Rhodian relief. De Callataÿ (2006) 54 has shown that it can be explained very simply, with the article of Maryon already the object of a conference in 1953.
[167] Dawid (1968), fig. 141.
[168] Langlotz (1976) 141–150. [169] Archaeological Museum of Rhodes, inv. E337.
[170] Joannes Malalas, p. 279, ll. 14–15 (Dindorf).
[171] Moreno (1990) 343–344; Moreno (1994a) 24; Moreno (1994b) 127–146; Moreno (1999) 193–200. Cf. Musti and Pulcini (1996) 293–298; Prioux (2017) 50.

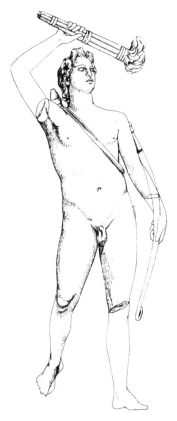

Fig. 7.44 Reconstruction of the Apollo of Santa Marinella by Paolo Mingazzini (1974), with hypothetical attribution of a torch found in the same area as the statue.

object of numerous modifications under his successors.[172] Moreover, a philhellene emperor like Hadrian would never have violated the oracle that forbade the reconstruction of the statue destroyed by the earthquake *c.*227 BC. Finally, the Apollo of Santa Marinella has been re-dated to the first century AD and its relationship with the torch called in question;[173] the original views of its editor, Paolino Mingazzini,[174] were maintained because they suited the hypothesis of a reconstruction of the Colossus under Hadrian.[175] On the other hand, Mingazzini had already stressed that this statue was an archer characterized by a strong *contrapposto*, like the Apollo Belvedere, and wondered whether both marbles

---

[172] Chapter 4, pp. 67–68. [173] Simon (1978) 223 n. 116; Simon (1984) 382, no. 59.
[174] Mingazzini (1974) 55–56, who already considered an attribution to the Antonine period.
[175] In her review of Moreno (1994b), Sismondo Ridgway (1996) 426 noticed: 'When there is total disagreement [between the views of the author and those of other scholars], this is so seldom acknowledged that the approach borders on hubris.'

Fig. 7.45 Reconstruction of the Colossus of Rhodes by Paolo Moreno (1994b).

depicted the god in his role of *Katharsios* ('purifying').[176] What is certain is that the Apollo Belvedere was a model for the Colossus imagined by Heemskerck, which explains why the Apollo of Santa Marinella reminded Langlotz of the latter. There is no reason to suppose instead that Heemskerck found his inspiration in non-extant medieval manuscripts nor that these non-extant manuscripts preserved an exact image of the Colossus, the less so as the Byzantine and medieval depictions of the statue, overlooked by Langlotz, represent only the conventions and misconceptions of their time.[177] As for the head of Helios discovered at Rhodes and discussed by Moreno, it does not belong to the period of Chares but, perhaps, to the second century BC;[178] its characteristics are not those of the Apollo of Santa Marinella,[179] and nothing suggests its association with the Colossus, in spite of conjectures based only on its rays, to which similar creations

---

[176] Mingazzini (1974) 53–55. Simon (1978) 220–227 preferred to identify the statue of Santa Marinella as an Apollo Caelispex; same point of view in Simon (1984) 382.
[177] Above, pp. 163–165.   [178] Zervoudaki (1975) 19.   [179] Dörig (1999) 189.

Fig. 7.46 Hellenistic terracotta head of Helios, found in Rhodes (Archaeological Museum of Rhodes, E337).

have been subjected more than once.[180] By contrast, regardless of the attribution of the torch, which remains hypothetical, it is striking that the Apollo of Santa Marinella does not have rays (Fig. 7.44), as opposed to the 'model' which Moreno imagined for this statue (Fig. 7.45). Under such conditions, the status of 'replica' attributed to the Apollo of Santa Marinella depends only on the heuristic value recognized in the painting of Blake and the statue of Bartholdi. The first is an illustration faithful to the text of the *Book of Revelation*,[181] while the second, which Gabriel already considered of prophetic nature (after having made it the model of his own reconstruction), was inspired by the traditional imagery of the

---

[180] Head from (the necropolis of?) Koskinou published by Graef (1900) 99–110 and heavily damaged in 1943 when the house of Hiller von Gaertringen, to whom it belonged, was bombed (Berlin, Altes Museum, Sk 1886): Kleiner (1957) 101–104, who compared the Rhodian head to the face of 'Helios' (an obvious Dionysus) depicted on a relief kept in the Louvre (Ma 1367) and made both sculptures depend on 'the shared model of the Colossus', *contra* Zervoudaki (1975) 19; Préchac (1919) 72 had already regarded the Louvre relief as a depiction of the Colossus (none of the authors mentioned in his n. 3 made such a suggestion). Head from the 'Inn of Provence' (Museum of Rhodes, inv. E49: fig. 7.46): Picard (1943) 229; Fuchs (1967) 514; Fuchs (1969) 571; Pollitt (1986) 55; Ekschmitt (1996) 178; Vedder (1999–2000) 30; cf. Chapter 4, p. 92, and below, p. 211.

[181] Rev. 10:1–8. On the relationship of this text with the actual Colossus, see Chapter 4, pp. 68–73.

ARTISTS AND ARCHAEOLOGISTS   209

Fig. 7.47 William Blake, *The Angel of Revelation*, 1803–1805 (The Metropolitan Museum of Art, inv. 14.81.1).

Seven Wonders of the World[182] and by the allegorical tradition of the time, itself rooted in antiquity.[183] These works are therefore of no heuristic value. It must be added that their right arm is emphatically raised, while that of the Apollo of Santa Marinella, as originally reconstituted by Mingazzini (Fig. 7.44), is not;[184] hence the need for another 'correction' of this Apollo by Moreno (Fig. 7.45). The influence of the supposed model of this statue on the reliefs of the Pergamon Altar is also illusory.[185]

We should rather compare the Colossus of Moreno with the purely fictional version published by Ridpath in 1885 (Fig. 7.25). Both stress the Apollonian character of the statue created by Heemskerck, both have movement similar to that of the *Angel of the Revelation* (painted c.1803–1805), and both adopt the gesture of the *Liberty Enlightening the World* (unveiled in 1886, ten years after the first display of its right hand, brandishing the torch). As Blake's and Bartholdi's works follow the iconographic and symbolic tradition of antiquity, it is not surprising to

---

[182] Above, pp. 198–200.   [183] Trachtenberg (1976) 63–83.
[184] The arm is lost, but the movement of the flames bursting from the torch attributed to the statue allows for a reconstitution of the gesture; see Mingazzini (1974) 51–53.
[185] *Pace* Moreno (1994b) 466.

find several of their characteristics—considered pertinent for this very reason—already amalgamated in the Apollo of Santa Marinella. Although this statue attests the classicism of the sources that have shaped the modern image of the Colossus, it is surely not an ancient replica of the Colossus. One can only be disappointed to have the Civitavecchia museum claiming the opposite.[186]

There is no evidence for the Colossus brandishing a torch; there is only Gabriel's misinterpretation of the epigram mentioning the 'light' (*phéggos*) of the god,[187] repeated by Moreno,[188] who argued, like his predecessor,[189] that it was confirmed by the 'decisive' testimony of Lucian. Yet, when Lucian states, in the second century AD, that the Lighthouse and the Colossus can be seen from the sky,[190] this certainly does not mean that the statue, destroyed four centuries before, had a torch, which is incidentally foreign to the Rhodian iconography of Helios. There is thus no need to 'imagine' that this torch was gilded.[191] One can compare, however, such a suggestion with a statement of Werner Ekschmitt, according to which the Colossus' 'hair and robe were certainly gilded'.[192] While it is safe to assume that the god had hair, there is no mention of his robe. Before the forgery of Theophilus,[193] there is no explicit reference to the colour(s) of the statue either. An epigram by Simias of Rhodes, however, possibly alluded to its rays, which would have been gilded.[194]

Additional Numismatic Colossi

As a last resort, can Rhodian coinage help us to discover a reproduction of the Colossus, or at least of its head? The suggestion, already formulated by Cyriac of Ancona,[195] Thevet (Fig. 7.9), and Fischer von Erlach (Fig. 7.22)[196] reappears from time to time,[197] with no other argument than Helios = Colossus. In his *Historia Numorum*, a manual for generations of numismatists, Barclay Head merely

---

[186] Anniboletti (2024) 8–51, who adds some mistakes to the theory of Langlotz and Moreno; cf. already Anniboletti (2023) 309–326.

[187] Above, p. 201.

[188] Moreno (1990) 344; Moreno (1994a) 241; Moreno (1994b) 140 and 143, followed by Musti and Pulcini (1996) 294; Moreno (1999) 196 (first reference to Lucian).

[189] Gabriel (1932) 354.

[190] Lucianus *Icaromenippus* 12.   [191] Above, n. 188.

[192] Ekschmitt (1996) 180; cf. Préchac (1919) 74.

[193] Constantine Porphyrogenitus *De admin. imper.* 21 ll. 14–15 (*PG* CXIII, 205B); Michael the Syrian *Chronicle* IV, p. 430a, ll. 25–31 (Chabot: II, p. 442, for the French translation). See Chapter 4, pp. 69–72.

[194] Simias of Rhodes, frag. 4 (Powell, *Collectanea Alexandrina*; above, p. 93).

[195] Above, p. 173.

[196] The Colossus illustrated by Vedder (1999–2000) 32, Vedder (2003) 131, Vedder (2015) 127, 137, and Vedder (2017) 22, owes its head to a tetradrachm dating to the end of the fourth century, its body to a pancratiast of the same period (the Agias of Lysippus), its sacrificial bowl to Apollo, and its base (although this is not said) to the Bavaria of Munich. The author underlines, however, that this hypothesis reflects less a reconstruction and more a comment upon the difficulty at arriving at one.

[197] Laurenzi (1959) 773; Dombart (1970) 77–78; Stewart (1990) 299; Moreno (1994b) 146; Ekschmitt (1996) 180; Moreno (1999) 198; cf. M. D. Higgins (2023) 315.

observed that 'the radiate head on the tetradrachms [of the period 304–168] may serve to give us some idea of the style and general aspect of the features of the colossal statue of Helios by Chares of Lindus, commonly called the Colossus of Rhodes'.[198] Yet, noting a certain resemblance between the head of Helios depicted on Rhodian coins and two idealized portraits of Alexander that he had himself identified, Wolfgang Helbig formulated three additional hypotheses. First, the portraits of Alexander derived from the cult-statue used to worship the sovereign at Alexandria. Second, this cult-statue was the work of the 'Chaereas' to whom Pliny attributes portraits of Philip and Alexander. Third, this 'Chaereas' was actually Chares of Lindos; hence the similarity between the portraits of Alexander and the head of the Colossus represented on Rhodian coins (the latter statement being itself a hypothesis of Helbig wrongly presented as a conjecture of Head).[199] In his *Studien über das Bildniss Alexanders des Grossen*, Theodor Schreiber went even further. For him, the 'Barracco head' (one of the portraits of Alexander identified by Helbig) reflected a Lysippean model, but the influence of Chares could actually be seen in a colossal head housed in the Capitoline Museum, very close to its predecessor but of a style supposedly more recent. The portrait of 'Helios-Alexander' at the origin of this copy was itself different from the 'Helios' by the same sculptor, two small bronze replicas of which Schreiber identified; this 'Helios' was none other than the Colossus of Rhodes.[200] The philological proof intended to justify all of these hypotheses must be rejected, since the 'Chaereas' of Pliny cannot be identified as Chares.[201] The other arguments developed by Helbig and Schreiber are gratuitous conjectures that have led to a conclusion which Johann Jacob Bernouilli rightly described as 'almost ridiculous', since the 'Colossus' of Schreiber (probably an 'Alexander with the lance': Fig. 7.48) shows no attributes of Helios.[202]

The Colossus was also sought on non-Rhodian coins actually depicting the emperor as Sol. Ernst Langlotz thought of bronzes from Nikopolis and Mopsos,[203] to which Giovanni Maria Staffieri, convinced that replicas of the Colossus were spread all around the ancient world, added twelve other cities (Fig. 7.49), with Alexandria allegedly having even two replicas, one on the Lighthouse,[204] the other on the 'column of Diocletian' (aka 'Pompey's pillar').[205] This is pure fantasy, but some remarks may be made. Staffieri based his identifications on two different 'Colossi', the first belonging to Schreiber ('Alexander with the lance'?) and the

---

[198] Head (1887[1]) 540; Head (1911[2]) 639.
[199] Helbig (1896) 84–86, with reference to Head (1887[1]) 540, quoted above.
[200] Schreiber (1903) 67–79, 124–138, 268–272.   [201] Chapter 3, pp. 61–62.
[202] Bernouilli (1905) 110; cf. Amelung (1912b) 390; Laurenzi (1938) 23.
[203] Langlotz (1976) 148.   [204] Above, pp. 163–164.
[205] Staffieri (1996) 262; Staffieri (1997) 612–620; cf. Moreno (1994b) 144–145 and Moreno (1999) 197.

Fig. 7.48 Late Hellenistic (?) bronze statuette of Alexander with a lance (height: 16.51 cm) discovered in Orange (British Museum, inv. 1877,0810.1).

second to Moreno (Apollo);[206] the latter scholar based his reasoning on an identification proposed by Langlotz, who had already mentioned some of the coins used by Staffieri to verify Moreno's (i.e. Langlotz's own) identification. Circularity is not the only flaw in the reasoning, for the small bronze portraits of Alexander (?), the marble statue of Apollo, and the numismatic depictions of Sol can hardly be compared. Their only common feature is a *contrapposto* certainly foreign to the actual Colossus of Rhodes, although Renaissance iconography has been influential enough to make scholars believe the contrary.

Richard Ashton eventually drew attention to a small series of didrachms dated to the beginning of the third century BC, whose obverse depicts a profile head of Helios (Fig. 7.50), while other didrachms struck concurrently show the god with a bare head from a three-quarter view, following the custom at the time. This

---

[206] Above, pp. 205–210.

small series would depict the Colossus and commemorate its construction.[207] The Rhodians, however, probably did not break a well-established tradition in Greek cities of representing the statue in its entirety, especially as it was celebrated precisely for its height.[208] Furthermore, the type presented by Ashton appears in various denominations struck from the fourth century BC until the Imperial period; its early introduction and prolonged use do not allow for its identification as the head of the Colossus.[209] Even if such identification were correct, one could not make an argument of it (as did Alan Cadwallader) to suggest that the profile head of Helios depicted on the obverse of some imperial coins from Kolossai[210] refers to the Colossus and was used to promote a 'pseudo-etymology' that 'civic authorities' would allegedly have 'crafted for the city's name',[211] as the profile head of Helios is quite common on the obverse of Roman provincial coins.[212] The possibility remains, however, that the didrachms studied by Ashton actually served to finance the construction of the Colossus.

Fig. 7.49 Large bronze coin from Epiphaneia (reverse) depicting a figure of nude Helios facing left, with a globe in his left hand and the right hand raised in a gesture of greeting. Legend: ΕΠΙΦΑΝΕΩΝ ΕΤ ΣΤ (AD 306) (Bibliothèque nationale de France, Département des Monnaies, médailles et antiques, Fonds général 545; scale 1:1).

Spaghetti Archaeology

'Casting' the Colossus

Released in 1961, *The Colossus of Rhodes* (*Il Colosso di Rodi*), the first full-length movie directed entirely by Sergio Leone, may be regarded as a prologue to his famous series of 'spaghetti westerns' (an appellation he vigorously rejected). The only film devoted to the statue, it provided its audience with a unique occasion to

---

[207] Ashton (1988) 75–90, followed by Musti and Pulcini (1996) 294 and Ashton (2001) 93. See also Ashton's comment on Badoud (2012) 39 in Ashton, Kinns, and Meadows (2014) 25 n. 104.

[208] For other famous statues whose heads were incorrectly said to have been identified on coins, see Lacroix (1949) 15, 257, 262, 285–286, and 313.

[209] Cf. already Laurenzi (1959) 774.

[210] RPC III, 2307A, 2307C, 2307E, 2313, 2313A, 2314, 2317; RPC IV.2 (temporary numbers), 1889, 1895, 1902, 10833.

[211] Cadwallader (2003) 476 (and pp. 71–128 for the whole argument).

[212] See for instance RPC I, 1186 (Corinth), 2640 (Tralles), 4393A (Laodicea ad Mare), 4478 (Aradus), 4796 (Damascus); RPC II, 1124 (Briula), 1260 (Cidrama), 1776 (Aegae); RPC III, 1210 (Amastris), 2282 (Apollonia Salbace), 2562 (Tripolis); RPC IV.2 (temporary numbers), 10669 (Nicaea Cilbianorum), etc.

214 THE IMAGE OF THE STATUE

Fig. 7.50 Silver didrachm from Rhodes (obverse) depicting a head of Helios in profile. First half of the third century BC (British Museum, Coins & Medals, inv. RPK, p144C.8.Rho; scale 1.5:1).

see Lysippus (Georges Rigaud) and Chares of Lindos (Mimmo Palmara) on the big screen. Except for the earthquake that marks its end, the plot owes very little to historical reality. Rhodes is presented as a kingdom whose despot wishes to ally himself to the Phoenicians in order to cut off the maritime trade routes of Greece (which is not a collection of cities but a unified state). The statue spans the entrance to the harbour: its interior houses a prison and a torture chamber, its head conceals catapults that allow for the flinging of Greek fire onto opponents of the tyrant, and the vessel held in its arms also provides for the pouring of fire onto any ship entering or leaving. Thus, the Colossus of Leone acts as the exact opposite of the Statue of Liberty, whose light guides the stranger to a haven of peace and the opportunity to begin a new life. It does not symbolize liberty, but tyranny. Although Sergio Leone wished to give the statue the face of Mussolini,[213] the idea was eventually rejected, perhaps because the film was being shot in Spain, whose dictator, Franco, had seized power after overthrowing the legitimate government of the Republic with the aid of fascist

Fig. 7.51 The bust of Sergio Leone's *Colossus* during construction at Laredo in 1960.

[213] Kinnard and Crnkovich (2017) 40. See also Burke (2011) 179–181.

Italy. When Ramiro Gómez sculpted the Colossus of Leone (Fig. 7.51), he therefore did not give it the face of Mussolini but rather the appearance of a kouros, in which we may recognize the Strangford Apollo, kept in the British Museum (Fig. 7.52). He constructed the statue as if it had a height of 110 m by building only the lower part of the legs, erected at the entrance to the harbour of Laredo; while the chest was installed on set, the full figure seen on screen was, in fact, a small model.[214]

The Colossus of Sergio Leone inspired the animated statue of the warrior Talos in the pioneering fantasy film *Jason and the Argonauts* (1963), which itself gave rise to the Titan of Braavos, created by George R. R. Martin in his novel *A Song of Ice and Fire* (2005)[215] and brought to the screen in the television series *Game of Thrones* (2014).[216] Not surprisingly, the warrior Talos also served as a model for the Colossus in video games, such as *Rise of Nations* (2003) and *God of War II* (2007). Other games, including *Civilization* (1991–2016) and *Cities XL* (2012), remained faithful to the traditional iconography of the Colossus; *Grepolis* (2009) offered an image of the statue based on that of Rottiers (Fig. 7.24).

Fig. 7.52 The Strangford Apollo, found in Anaphe (?), c.490 BC (British Museum, inv. 1864,0220.1).

Reconstructing the Colossus

By attributing to the Colossus the height necessary for spanning a small harbour and by partially reconstructing it, Sergio Leone and Ramiro Gómez had opened a new path: why not go further and make the myth a reality? Such a project has been mentioned more than once on Rhodes. As early as 1958, the construction of the Atomium in Brussels had inspired the first project to rebuild the Colossus on the island, which had become part of Greece only eleven years earlier.[217] Not until 1999, however, did the mayor of the town announce his intention to reconstruct the statue before the Olympic Games of 2004, by drawing inspiration from the

---

[214] Saiz Viadero (2010) *passim*.   [215] Martin (2011) 126.
[216] See 'The Laws of Gods and Men' (season 4, episode 6) and 'The Lion and the Rose' (season 5, episode 2).
[217] *To Vima*, 17 November 2008.

'original Colossus'.[218] In 2008, his successor mentioned a new project that would place the statue at the entrance of the harbour and would make it a symbol of peace 'like the original', in the hope of attracting new visitors to the island to overcome the economic crisis caused, among other factors, by the Olympic Games of 2004.[219] Gert Hof, the architect, planned to make a 'highly innovative light sculpture' with a height between 60 and 100 m.[220] In 2015, a team comprising architects, engineers, economists, and even a local archaeologist created worldwide buzz by proposing to construct a Colossus more than 150 m tall that not only would have housed an archaeological museum, a library, an exhibition hall, and a restaurant, but also would have served as a lighthouse (Fig. 7.53).[221] Costing around 250 million euros, it would have been financed, like its predecessors, by private investments and international crowd funding. Meant to restore 'historical value' to Rhodes, this Colossus exactly matches the statue in the video game

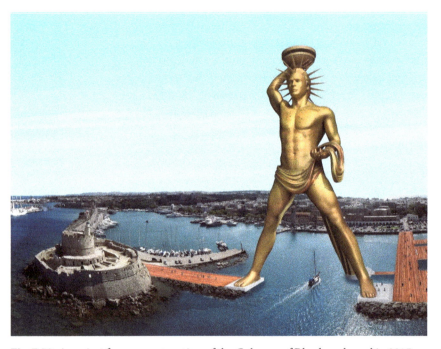

Fig. 7.53 A project for a reconstruction of the Colossus of Rhodes released in 2015.

---

[218] *The Associated Press*, 21 October 1999. See *Newsweek*, 17 July 2015, for the project of Nikolaos Kotziamanis.
[219] A specialist in marketing, George Barboutis developed similar ideas in a series of conferences and articles from 1999 to 2018.
[220] *The Guardian*, 17 November 2008.   [221] *The Guardian*, 27 December 2015.

Grepolis (itself derived from Rottiers, the most deceptive explorer of Rhodes)[222] except for one small detail: the restaurant placed in the torch. This addition would extend a long series of revolving restaurants, the most famous of which (apart from the Neronian *cenatio rotunda*) was built on the summit of Schilthorn, in the Swiss Alps, and appears in the James Bond film *On Her Majesty's Secret Service* (1969). Even if one might rejoice—or be concerned—that a museum and a library would replace the prison and the torture chamber of Leone's Colossus, the 2015 statue no less symbolizes the destructive tendencies of mankind. Its construction, passing off a mere decorative element within a video game as a Wonder of the World, would involve the definitive obliteration of the very past that it claims to glorify as a statue and to preserve as a museum. A monument of both ignorance and deculturization, it would substitute the political despotism embodied by the Colossus of Sergio Leone with the tyranny of consumerism and thus open wide the way to the most damaging forms of over-tourism. Not by coincidence,[223] the reconstruction of the Colossus was announced a few months after that of the Lighthouse of Alexandria, reportedly approved—but neither budgeted nor realized—by the political and archaeological authorities. This latter scheme was the last of a long series of projects involving once again 'light architecture'. It has been criticized not only for its dramatic consequences regarding the environmental and cultural heritage of the city but also for the commercialization of that heritage.[224] Ultimately, Michael Higgins designed a 'New Statue at Rhodes' which is nothing else than the Colossus of Gabriel set on a pedestal built to withstand the effects of earthquakes. Once again, 'the interior of the statue' would have to be 'accessible for maintenance and tourism, a bit like the Statue of Liberty in New York'.[225]

In fact, the meaning recently attributed to the Colossus is no more accurate than the various reconstructions of its image. The warlike origins of the statue and its ethnic (nationalist, by today's standards) value have been obliterated to make it a universal symbol of peace. Again, the *Liberty Enlightening the World* played a role. This statue also had its meaning quickly redefined:[226] while it had been constructed both as a symbol of friendship between France and the United States of America and as a monument commemorating (liberal) Revolutions, it

---

[222] Badoud (2019c) 42–47.
[223] Seers also successively 'discovered' the Lighthouse and the Colossus: see Chapter 6, p. 131.
[224] See the article of Amro Ali published on the website of *Mada Masr* (2 July 2015) and available on the website opendemocracy.net: 'A Frightening Vision: On Plans to Rebuild the Alexandria Lighthouse'. See also the advertisement of Bernand (1995) 52 for a project of reconstruction by Électricité de France (EDF), which was at the time financing the French excavations of the Ptolemaic Lighthouse.
[225] M. D. Higgins (2023) 434–435.
[226] Trachtenberg (1976) 186–187; Roger (1986) 282–289.

has become a 'welcome' addressed to immigrants, the famous verses of Lazarus being instrumental in the process:

> Give me your tired, your poor,
> Your huddled masses yearning to breathe free,
> The wretched refuse of your teeming shore.
> Send these, the homeless, the tempest-tossed to me,
> I lift my lamp beside the golden door![227]

Fully at odds with its alleged model, the 'new Colossus' of Rhodes would, in fact, be a 'new Statue of Liberty', with the immigrants replaced by tourists.

---

[227] Lazarus (1889) 203.

Conclusion

The Tradition

Even if no physical remains of the Colossus of Rhodes are extant, the statue has left numerous traces in ancient sources. To rediscover and understand these traces, it has been necessary to uncover them from the various layers of tradition that had settled throughout the centuries to eventually form the collective unconscious of contemporary scholars. This intellectual excavation now allows us to distinguish five layers, each of which corresponds to a different historical period. The absence of critique concerning the tradition explains why the ancient sources have been distorted to verify it, discredited to maintain it, or simply ignored.

The most recent layer of the tradition was created in the nineteenth century, when the Statue of Liberty became the 'new Colossus'; from that point, the way in which the Rhodian monument had been constructed became hardly comprehensible. As a result, the testimony of Philo of Byzantium has been translated and interpreted as if it described a technique like that used by Auguste Bartholdi. Moreover, from its function as a lighthouse and its position in a harbour, the Statue of Liberty has reinforced two older stereotypes concerning the Colossus.

The first of these stereotypes dates back to the sixteenth century, the period to which the lower layer of the tradition belongs. At this time, the painter Maarten van Heemskerck gave to the Colossus a lantern, then a fire pot, to convert it into a lighthouse located at the entrance to the harbour of Rhodes. He based his interpretation on two models—the Apollo Belvedere and (it seems) a figure of Sol—to fashion the image of the statue that has remained the most influential to this day. The ancient 'replicas' of the Colossus identified so far and the 'reconstructions' which rely on them result only from an unconscious analysis of this image by the archaeologists; hence the endless return, in scientific literature, of the gods hidden by Heemskerck, as seen in the two most recent 'reconstructions' of the Colossus. The first, from 1994, is based on an Apollo belonging to the Belvedere type, while the second, from 2003, replicates a statuette of Sol. The attempt of various archaeologists to install a statue or a temple of Helios in the sanctuary of Apollo is equally due to a confusion of the two divinities that the work of Heemskerck can only have facilitated.

The second stereotype reinforced by the construction of the Statue of Liberty (and earlier by the iconography of the Renaissance) finds its origin in the third layer of the tradition, which dates to the late medieval period. The myth of the statue spanning the harbour of Rhodes was developed at the end of the fourteenth century, when pilgrims discovered vestiges of fortifications that once protected the ancient military harbour and believed that they were the remains of the statue. Numerous scholars have tried to rationalize this myth by reducing it to a kernel of truth, namely that the statue would have been set in the harbour. To support their reasoning, some have offered a series of literary references, none of which place the Colossus in the harbour, while others have repeated the error of the Middle Age pilgrims by attributing to the base of the statue architectural elements that actually belonged to the fortifications of the ancient city. One of these elements, in blue limestone, has been presented as a block of white marble to match the testimony of Pseudo-Philo of Byzantium, according to whom the base of the statue had been constructed from this material.

The fourth layer of the tradition, dating from the early medieval period, is founded upon a deliberate forgery. The chronicler Theophilus of Edessa used a historical event—the capture of Rhodes by the armies of Muʿāwiya in AD 653/4—as an opportunity to spread the idea according to which the Colossus would have been destroyed by the Arabs and its ruins sold by a Jewish merchant. From the second century BC, the author of the *Book of Daniel* had used the Colossus as a model for his statue with feet of clay, whose destruction foreshadowed the fall of the Seleucid Empire. From this statue was born, in the last decades of the first century AD (?), the angel with the little scroll mentioned in the *Book of Revelation*, whose face was like the sun. Theophilus relied on these two narratives to create a Colossus whose alleged destruction by the invaders would announce the end of the orthodoxy that prevailed on Rhodes as well as in most of the Christian world. He drew the remainder of his inspiration from the work of John Malalas (according to whom the statue would have been reconstructed in the Imperial period, which would allow for the idea that it would still have been standing in AD 653/4) and, most probably, from an event in recent history (the pillage and the sale by Muʿāwiya of the statues moved by the emperor Constans II from Rome to Syracuse). Of all the accounts associated with the Colossus in the tradition, this is the most frequently cited in scientific literature, despite—or because of—its strong ideological content. It has overshadowed the undeniable proofs of the destruction of the Colossus during the Hellenistic Period, or has coexisted with them at the expense of a contradiction, which evidence concerning the reconstruction of the statue during the Imperial period was used to solve. In addition to the fact that it includes one of the sources surreptitiously used by Theophilus to make up his forgery, this evidence bears no weight, as it confuses the Colossus of Rhodes and the Colossus built at Rome for Nero.

The most ancient layer of the tradition dates back to antiquity itself, since the Greek term *kolossós*, from which derives the word 'colossus', only began to designate an oversized statue from the second century BC, at a moment when the Colossus of Rhodes had already been destroyed. Written in the first century AD, the testimony of Pliny the Elder thus carries a bias; yet, it is on his text that all archaeological and historical studies of the statue are founded. The inscriptions from the fourth century BC showing that the *kolossós* was not, by definition, an oversized statue have been interpreted in light of the opposite premise. The text of Polybius about the 'great *kolossós*', which implies the existence of 'small *kolossoí*' (in Rhodes and elsewhere), has similarly been discredited because of its alleged semantic redundancy. On the other hand, the testimony of Pliny has reduced the Colossus to a kind of trophy celebrating the resistance of the Rhodians against Demetrius. This is the second bias going back to antiquity: it has obscured the meaning and the function of the statue, and thus blured the discussion about its location.

The simple desire to discover a trace of the Colossus or to identify an image of it also has played an important role. From the fifteenth century, the head of Helios depicted on the coinage of Rhodes time and again has been represented as that of the Colossus, even though it had appeared before the construction of the statue and continued to appear after its destruction. From the nineteenth century, various heads of Helios sculpted in stone also were presented as copies of the head of the Colossus, whose appearance is however completely unknown to us. Several statues that do not even represent Helios have equally been interpreted as copies of the Colossus.

Lastly, epigraphic and literary sources validating the identification of the sanctuary of Apollo have been rejected in order to allow the attribution of this sanctuary to Helios. Then, archaeological and historical evidence supporting the identification of the sanctuary of Artemis likewise has been set aside to make it the site of construction for the Colossus. Finally, the testimony of Pseudo-Philo has been dismissed due to its incompatibility with this theory. As many other structures spread through the city of Rhodes before it, the podium visible within the sanctuary of Artemis has been presented as the base of the Colossus with no other argument than the suitability of its dimensions.

The historiography of the Colossus thus reveals the importance of the unconscious and of the desire in the thinking of archaeologists. It belongs to a broader tradition which finds its symbol, or rather its fetish, in the garment that covers the genitals of the Colossus straddling the harbour of Rhodes: for this garment hides ancient reality at its most specific (the nudity of Helios and his 'colossal' genitals), while drawing attention to the incongruity of the tradition which it represents (the position of the god being not only ridiculous but also obscene).

The Sources

Let us now summarize what the sources uncovered by our intellectual excavation tell about the Colossus. Formed from an Indo-European root denoting an object that was set up, the term *kolossós* began by describing a distinctively Dorian statue with a motionless appearance, meant to encapsulate an external being and used for this reason in magical or religious settings. Attested (indirectly) from the seventh century BC, the word and the object both spread from the Peloponnese into the Aegean and farther abroad within the context of Dorian colonization. Originally, the *kolossós* was not defined by its size, which was only one means among others to suggest immobility and permanence.

The *kolossós* could represent either a mortal or a god. Such was the case with the Colossus of the Cypselids; dedicated at Olympia by the dynasty that ruled over Corinth at the beginning of the sixth century, this statue of Zeus was the most famous *kolossós* until the construction of the Colossus of Rhodes, which itself was a gigantic bronze statue of Helios, the god who embodied the city founded in 408 BC.

The decision to construct the Colossus was taken after the Rhodians repulsed the attack of Demetrius Poliorcetes against their city, at the end of a nearly one-year-long siege (305–304 BC). Yet, the statue celebrated more than this victory. It also celebrated its cause, which was said to be found in the Dorian origin of the city. It eventually celebrated its consequence, namely the integration of a portion of the Asian continent (the Peraea) and of several islands into the territory of the city. All of this results from the analysis of the epigram engraved on the base of the Colossus, whose text is echoed by one of the most debated works in Greek literature, the *Alexandra* of Lycophron. Once connected to a decree (?) discovered at Rhodes and to the testimony of Polybius concerning the establishment of relations between Rome and this city, the epigram and the *Alexandra* invite us not only to reject all attempts to question their authenticity or to lower their date but also, more fundamentally, to rethink the beginnings of the Hellenistic world, marked by the early emergence of Rhodes and of Rome as powers on land and sea.

The victory of 304 BC and the subsequent construction of the Colossus of Rhodes did not mark the end of the rivalry between the city and the dynasty that soon would reign over Macedon. In fact, the Rhodians and the Antigonids would fight again at the turn of the third and second centuries BC. After Philip V of Macedon invaded the Peraea in 200 BC, Alcaeus would compose an epigram that responded point by point to the epigram of the Colossus (both poems being closely connected to the struggle for this territory). Following the defeat of the Macedonian king, the Rhodians would dedicate the Winged Victory to the Great Gods of Samothrace, whose sanctuary had been until then a repository for Macedonian offerings.

The place chosen to build the Colossus probably corresponds to the location of the Byzantine *kástro* and of its successor, the Palace of the Grand Master of the Order of St John. The statue would thus have crowned the city and would have cast its gaze towards the territories of the mainland whose annexation it celebrated, as required by the epigram inscribed on its base.

The height of the Colossus was 70 cubits (*c*.34 m) without its base, and a bit more than 36 m with its base. The height of the Colossus constructed by Zenodoros for Nero was nominally greater than that of the Colossus of Rhodes

(71 cubits without its base, 80 cubits including the base). Because of the difference in length between the Rhodian and Roman cubits, the Colossus of Rhodes nevertheless remained the tallest bronze statue in the world until the unveiling of the *Liberty Enlightening the World* in 1886. The intention of the Rhodians was to create a statue big enough to be seen from the Asian continent, 13 km away.

The work commenced in 295 BC and was completed only twelve years later, in 283 BC. It was entrusted to the sculptor Chares of Rhodes, whose name poets passed down to posterity as Chares of Lindos. He was a student of Lysippus, under whose direction he perhaps participated between 332 and 323 BC (more precisely between 328 and 325 BC?) in the creation of a statuary group that represented Helios in his quadriga. In addition to the Colossus, only one other work, taken by the Romans to be exhibited on the Capitoline, can be attributed to him.

Chares developed a revolutionary casting technique, whose description by Pseudo-Philo of Byzantium seemingly dates back to an author (the sculptor himself?) contemporary with the construction of the Colossus. This technique is attested nowhere else in antiquity, nor in Western history, but was used in Japan one thousand years later to construct the Great Buddha of Nara and, even later, the Buddha of Kamakura. Rather than assembling various bronze pieces cast in a distant pit, as sculptors of his time did, Chares cast his Colossus in place, level by level, by progressively raising the kilns with the help of an immense embankment of earth. He equipped it with an iron frame connecting the bronze walls to a stone pillar, which differentiated it from the Buddhas of Nara and Kamakura, two and three times smaller respectively. The exact opposite of the method used for the Statue of Liberty, the technique of casting by stages required an enormous quantity of bronze, which may have been in the order of 400 tonnes in the case of the Colossus. This technique dictated the representation of Helios with legs joined together and arms alongside the body, with no other attribute than a crown of rays.

The Colossus of Rhodes was thus the most perfect of the *kolossoí*, these motionless statues that Dorian people had long used to capture divine or mortal beings. It was shown as immobile and rendered as such by the technique used for its construction. It symbolized the Dorian origins of the city that managed to resist Demetrius' formidable assault. It was meant to definitively place Helios at the centre of the empire which this city had gained from the war. Thanks to its location and to its size, it was able to connect the two parts of this empire, the 'sea' (Rhodes) and the 'land' (the Peraea).

Because of its gigantic nature, the statue was worthy to be included in the list of the Seven Wonders of the World, which collected the monuments remarkable for their size. For this reason, '*kolossós*' came to designate an oversized statue.

The earthquake of 227 BC broke off the Colossus at the height of its knees, which probably corresponded to a join between two of the courses cast by Chares. An oracle forbade the reconstruction of the statue, whose ruins were still visible in the second century AD. We then definitely lose its tracks.

References

AA.VV. (1986). *La Statue de la Liberté: l'exposition du centenaire, organisée par le Comité officiel franco-américain pour la célébration du centenaire de la Statue de la Liberté et l'Union des arts décoratifs*. Paris.
AA.VV. (1999). *Ρόδος 2.400 χρόνια. Η πόλη της Ρόδου από την ίδρυσή της μέχρι την κατάληψη από τους Τούρκους (1523). Διεθνές επιστημονικό συνέδριο, Ρόδος 24–29 οκτωβρίου 1993*. Athens.
AA.VV. (2007). *15 χρόνια έργων αποκατάστασης στη μεσαιωνική πόλη της Ρόδου*. Athens.
Accame, S. (1947). 'Alceo di Messene, Filippo V e Roma', *RFIC* 75 [n.s. 25]: 94–105.
Adam, J.-P. and Blanc, N. (1989). *Les sept merveilles du monde*. Paris.
Adelson, C. J. (1994). *European Tapestry in the Minneapolis Institute of Arts*. Minneapolis.
Agusta-Boularot, S. (2006). 'Malalas épigraphiste? Nature, intégration et fonction des citations épigraphiques dans la *Chronique* de Jean Malalas', in S. Agusta-Boularot, J. Beaucamp, A.-M. Bernardi, and E. Caire (eds.), *Recherches sur la* Chronique *de Jean Malalas* II. Paris: 97–135.
Albertson, F. C. (2001). 'Zenodorus's "Colossus of Nero"', *MAAR* 46: 95–118.
Aleni, G. [艾儒略] (1623). *Zhifang Waiji* [職方外紀]. Beijing.
Allazi [Allatius], L. (1640). *Philo Byzantius de septem orbis spectaculis*. Rome.
Amari, M. (1880). *Biblioteca arabo-sicula* I. Turin, Rome.
——— (1881). *Biblioteca arabo-sicula* II. Turin, Rome.
Amelung, W. (1912a). 'Chaireas', in U. Thieme (1912): 331.
——— (1912b). 'Chares', in U. Thieme (1912): 389–390.
Ampolo, C., Erdas, D., and Magnetto, A. (eds.) (2014). *La gloria di Athana Lindia. ASNSP* [s. 5] 6.1. Pisa.
Angeli Bernardini, P. (1977). 'Le Halieia di Rodi e lo scolio a Pind. O.7, 146ab (p. 229 Dr.)', *Stadion* 3: 1–3.
Angiò, F. (2012). 'Nota sui composti in –βάμων. Da Eschilo ed Empedocle a Licofrone', *PP* 67: 269–276.
——— (2013). 'Il Nuovo Posidippo (2012)', *SEP* 10: 33–54.
——— (2016). 'Il papiro attribuito a Posidippo di Pella (*PMilVogl* VIII 309, *MP3* 1435.01, *LDAB* 3852) quindici anni dopo (2001–2016)', *PapLup* 25: 41–128.
Anniboletti, L. (2023). 'Il Colosso di Rodi. L'immagine di una delle Sette Meraviglie dell'Antichità al Museo Archeologico Nazionale di Civitavecchia', in F. Coarelli and E. Lo Sardo (eds.), *Alessandro Magno e l'Oriente*. Milan: 309–326.
——— (2024). *L'Apollo-Helios di Civitavecchia e il Colosso di Rodi. The Apollo-Helios of Civitavecchia and the Colossus of Rhodes*. Acquapendente.
Antonini, R. (2016). 'Sulla dedica arcaica ai Dioscuri da Cirene', in V. Purcaro and O. Mei (eds.), *Cirene greca e romana* II. Rome: 27–64.
Asheri, D. (2007). *A Commentary on Herodotus Books I–IV*. Oxford.
Ashton, R. H. J. (1988). 'Rhodian Coinage and the Colossus', *RN* 30: 75–90.
——— (2001). 'The Coinage of Rhodes 408–*c*. 190 BC', in A. Meadows and K. Shipton (eds.), *Money and Its Uses in the Ancient Greek World*. Oxford: 79–115.
Ashton, R. H. J., Kinns, P., and Meadows, A. (2014). 'Opuscula Anatolica IV', *NC* 174: 1–28.

Auclair, V. (2000). 'De l'exemple antique à la chronique contemporaine. L'*Histoire de la Royne Arthemise de l'invention de Nicolas Houel*', *Journal de la Renaissance* 1: 155–188.
―― (2007). 'Changement de programme: de *L'Histoire de la reine Artémise* de Nicolas Houel à la tenture d'Henri IV', in AA.VV., *À l'origine des Gobelins: la tenture d'Artémise. La redécouverte d'un tissage royal*. Paris: 19–26.
Auclair, V. (2010). *Dessiner à la Renaissance. La copie et la perspective comme instruments de l'invention*. Rennes.
Augé de Lassus, L. (1878). *Voyage aux Sept Merveilles du Monde*. Paris.
Aune, D. E. (1998). *Revelation 6–16*. Waco, TX.
Aurigny, H., and Durvye, C. (eds.) (2021). *Artémis dans les grands sanctuaires d'Apollon (Delphes, Délos, Claros, Didymes)*. Kernos Supplément 37.
Badoud, N. (2002). 'La Table claudienne de Lyon au XVIe siècle', *CCG* 13: 169–195.
―― (2003). 'Remarques sur la chronologie des éponymes amphoriques rhodiens', *REA* 105: 579–587.
―― (2011a). 'Les colosses de Rhodes', *CRAI*: 111–152.
―― (2011b). 'L'intégration de la Pérée au territoire de Rhodes', in Badoud (2011c): 533–565.
―― (ed.) (2011c). *Philologos Dionysios. Mélanges offerts au professeur Denis Knoepfler*. Geneva.
―― (2012). 'L'image du Colosse de Rhodes', *MMAI* 91: 5–40.
―― (2015). *Le temps de Rhodes. Une chronologie des inscriptions de la cité fondée sur l'étude de ses institutions*. Munich.
―― (2015–2016). 'Note sur trois inscriptions mentionnant des Rhodiens morts à la guerre. Contribution à l'étude des relations entre Rhodes et Rome à la fin du IVe s. av. J.-C.', *BCH* 139–140: 237–246.
―― (2017a). 'Deciphering Greek Amphora Stamps', *CHS Research Bulletin* 5.2, online.
―― (2017b). 'Deux fragments de boucliers votifs découverts en ville de Rhodes. Contribution à l'étude des esclaves publics', *ZPE* 204: 105–115.
―― (2017c). *Inscriptions et timbres céramiques de Rhodes. Documents recueillis par le médecin et explorateur suédois Johan Hedenborg (1786–1865)*. Stockholm.
―― (2018a). 'L'Apollon de Piombino', *JS*: 185–288.
―― (2018b). 'La Victoire de Samothrace, défaite de Philippe V', *RA*: 279–305.
―― (2019a). 'À propos d'un décret d'Argos pour les Rhodiens (ISE 40)', *MediterrAnt* 22: 77–96.
―― (2019b). 'Ce qu'étaient les timbres amphoriques grecs. Genre et statut dans l'industrie céramique rhodienne', in N. Badoud and A. Marangou (eds.), *Analyse et exploitation des timbres amphoriques grecs*. Rennes: 195–209.
―― (2019c). 'Early Explorers of Rhodes 1342–1853', in Schierup (2019): 35–50.
―― (2019d). 'Le déchiffrement des timbres amphoriques grecs', *CRAI*: 375–401.
―― (2019e). 'Le Laocoon et les sculptures de Sperlonga: chronologie et signification', *AK* 62: 71–95.
―― (2020a). '[Remarks on S. Damigos, O. Kaklamani, *From Thera to Cyrene: Early Society and Complex Networking in the Age of Colonization*]', in S. Ranieri and A. Roncaglia (eds.), *Ricerche a confronto. Dialoghi di Antichità classiche e del Vicino Oriente, Bologna 2015*. Zermeghedo: 339–341.
―― (2020b). 'Trois décrets de Camiros. À propos de la colonisation de Cyrène par les Rhodiens', *Ricerche Ellenistiche* 1: 153–168.
―― (forthcoming 1). 'Le premier temple d'Apollon à Délos'.
―― (forthcoming 2). 'Religion and Forgery. The Rhodian Cult of Alexander the Great'.
―― (forthcoming 3). 'The Rhodian Fleet'.
―― (forthcoming 4). 'Lysippus, Alexander, and the Chariots of Helios at Rhodes and Delphi'.

―― (forthcoming 5). 'The Victory of Samothrace: A Reset'.
Badoud, N., Fincker, M., and Moretti, J.-C. (2015–2016). 'Les monuments érigés à Délos et à Athènes en l'honneur de Ménodôros, pancratiaste et lutteur', *BCH* 139–140: 345–416.
Bairami, K. (2023). 'Sculpture from "Pantheon": An Open-Air Sanctuary at the Foothills of the Rhodian Acropolis', in Stefanakis et al. (2023): 93–104.
Baker, P., and Thériault, G. (2005). 'Les Lyciens, Xanthos et Rome dans la première moitié du 1er s. a.C.: nouvelles inscriptions', *REG* 118: 329–366.
Baltrušaitis, J. (1978). *Le Miroir: essai sur une légende scientifique. Révélations, science-fiction et fallacies*. Paris.
Bartholdi, F. A. (1885). *The Statue of Liberty Enlightening the World Described by the Sculptor*. New York.
Bastet, F. L. (1987). *De drie collecties Rottiers te Leiden*. Leiden.
Bastianini, G., and Gallazzi, C. (2001). *Papiri della Università degli Studi di Milano* VIII. *Posidippo di Pella: epigrammi (P.Mil.Vogl. 309)*. Milan.
Bayle, P. (1697). *Dictionnaire historique et critique. Tome premier, seconde partie*. Rotterdam.
Bean, G. E. (1962). 'Report on a Journey in Lycia 1960', *Anzeiger/Österreichische Akademie der Wissenschaften. Philosophisch-historische Klasse* 99: 4–10.
Beckby, H. (1965^2). *Anthologia Graeca. Buch I–VI*. Munich.
Becker, A. (1883). 'De Rhodiorum primordiis', *Commentationes philologae Ienenses* 2: 91–136.
Beekes, R. (2010). *Etymological Dictionary of Greek*. Leiden.
Bekker, I. (1826). *Platonis scripta Graeca omnia* V. London.
Belot, R., and Bermond, D. (2004). *Bartholdi*. Paris.
Benndorf, O. (1876). 'Bemerkungen zur griechischen Kunstgeschichte', *MDAI(A)* 1: 45–66.
Benveniste, É. (1932). 'Le sens du mot κολοσσός et les noms grecs de la statue', *RPh* 58: 118–135, 381.
Berges, D. (1996). *Rundaltäre aus Kos und Rhodos*. Berlin.
Bergk, T. (1882^4). *Poetae lyrici Graeci* III. *Poetas melicos continens*. Leipzig.
Bergmann, M. (1993). *Der Koloss Neros, die Domus Aurea und der Mentalitätswandel im Rom der frühen Kaiserzeit*. Mainz.
Bernand, A. (1995). *Alexandrie des Ptolémées*. Paris.
Bernand, A., and Masson, O. (1957). 'Les inscriptions grecques d'Abou-Simbel', *REG* 70: 1–46.
Bernardini, C. (2006). *I bronzi della stipe di Kamiros*. Athens.
Bernouilli, J. J. (1905). *Die erhaltenen Darstellungen Alexanders des Grossen. Ein Nachtrag zur griechischen Ikonographie*. Munich.
Bertheroy, J. [Le Barillier, B. C. J.] (1909). *Le Colosse de Rhodes. Roman antique*. Paris.
Berthold, R. M. (1978). 'A Historical Fiction in Vitruvius', *CPh* 73: 129–134.
―― (1984). *Rhodes in the Hellenistic Age*. Ithaca, London.
Beschi, L. (1986). 'La scoperta dell'arte greca', in S. Settis (ed.), *Memoria dell'antico nell'arte italiana* III. *Dalla tradizione all'archeologia*. Turin: 293–372.
Bettinetti, S. (2001). *La statua di culto nella pratica rituale greca*. Bari.
Biliotti, E., and Cottret (1881). *L'île de Rhodes*. Rhodes.
Biondo, F. [Blondus] (1510). *De gestis Venetorum*. Venice.
Björck, G. (1950). *Das Alpha impurum und die tragische Kunstsprache. Attische Wort und Stilstudien*. Uppsala, Wiesbaden, Leipzig.
Blaeu, W. J. (1606). *Nova totius terrarium orbis geographica ac hydrographica tabula*. Amsterdam.
Blinkenberg, C. (1912). *La Chronique du temple lindien*. Copenhagen.
―― (1913). 'ΡΟΔΟΥ ΚΤΙΣΤΑΙ', *Hermes* 48: 236–249.
―― (1915). *Die lindische Tempelchronik*. Bonn.

Blinkenberg, C. (1931). *Lindos. Fouilles de l'acropole (1902-1914)* I. *Les petits objets*. Berlin.

—— (1941). *Lindos. Fouilles de l'acropole (1902-1914)* II. *Inscriptions* […] *avec un appendice contenant diverses autres inscriptions rhodiennes*. Berlin, Copenhagen.

Blinkenberg, C., and Kinch, K.-F. (1905). *Exploration archéologique de Rhodes. Troisième rapport*. Copenhagen.

Boardman, J., and Hayes, J. W. (1966). *Excavations at Tocra, 1963-1965. The Archaic Deposits* I. *ABSA* Suppl. 4.

Bober, P. P., and Rubinstein, R. (2010). *Renaissance Artists and Antique Sculpture*. London.

Bodnar, E. W. (1998). 'Ciriaco's Cycladic Diary', in G. Paci and S. Sconocchia (eds.), *Ciriaco d'Ancona e la cultura antiquaria dell'Umanesimo. Atti del Convegno internazionale di studio (Ancona 6-9 febbraio 1992)*. Reggio Emilia: 49-80.

—— (2003). *Cyriac of Ancona. Later Travels*. Cambridge, MA.

Boeckh, A. (1821). *ΠΙΝΔΑΡΟΥ ΤΑ ΣΩΖΟΜΕΝΑ. Pindari opera quae supersunt* II.2. Leipzig.

Bollack, J. (1981). *L'Agamemnon d'Eschyle: Le texte et ses interpretations. Agamemnon 1, deuxième partie*. Lille.

Bommelaer, J.-F., and Laroche, D. (2015²). *Guide de Delphes. Le site*. Athens, Paris.

Bonfante, L. (1989). 'Nudity as a Costume in Classical Art', *AJA* 93: 543-570.

Borchardt, L. (1911). *Statuen und Statuetten von Königen und Privatleuten im Museum von Kairo* I. Berlin.

Bosworth, C. E. (1996). 'Arab Attacks on Rhodes in the Pre-Ottoman Period', *JAS* 6: 157-164.

Boussac, M.-F. (1982). 'À propos de quelques sceaux déliens', *BCH* 106: 427-446.

—— (1992). *Les Sceaux de Délos* I. *Sceaux publics: Apollon, Hélios, Artémis, Hécate*. Athens, Paris.

Bouzek, J. (1969). 'Die Anfänge des griechisch-geometrischen Symbolguts', *Eirene* 8: 97-122.

Boyxen, B. (2018). *Fremde in der hellenistischen* Polis *Rhodos. Zwischen Nähe und Distanz*. Berlin, Boston.

Brake, A. S. (2019). *Visions of the Lamb of God. A Commentary on the Book of Revelation*. Eugene, OR.

Bresson, A. (1979). *Mythe et contradiction. Analyse de la* VIIe *Olympique de Pindare*. Besançon, Paris.

—— (1980). 'Rhodes, l'Hellénion et le statut de Naucratis (VIe-IVe siècle a.C.)', *DHA* 6: 291-349 [reprinted in Bresson, A. (2000). *La cité marchande*. Bordeaux: 13-63].

—— (1991). *Recueil des inscriptions de la Pérée rhodienne (Pérée intégrée)*. Besançon.

—— (1994). *Recherches sur la société rhodienne (480 av. J.-C.-100 ap. J.-C.)*. Unpublished *thèse d'État*. Besançon.

—— (2001). 'Grecs et Cariens dans la Chersonèse de Rhodes', in Fromentin and Gotteland (2001): 147-160.

—— (2003). 'Les intérêts rhodiens en Carie à l'époque hellénistique, jusqu'en 167 av. J.-C.', in F. Prost (ed.), *L'Orient méditerranéen de la mort d'Alexandre aux campagnes de Pompée. Cités et royaumes à l'époque hellénistique. Colloque international de la SOPHAU, Rennes, 4-6 avril 2003*. Toulouse: 169-192.

—— (2006). 'Relire la *Chronique du temple lindien*', *Topoi* 14: 527-551.

—— (2007). 'Rhodes, Rome et les pirates tyrrhéniens', in P. Brun (ed.), *Scripta Anatolica. Hommages à Pierre Debord*. Paris: 145-164.

—— (2012). 'Painted Portrait and Statues. Honors for Polystratos at Phrygian Apameia', in K. Konuk (ed.), *Stephanèphoros. De l'économie antique à l'Asie Mineure. Hommages à Raymond Descat*. Bordeaux: 203-216.

——— (2016). *The Making of the Ancient Greek Economy. Institutions, Markets, and Growth in the City-States*. Princeton.
——— (2021a). 'Palmette Coins: An Update', in A. Meadows and U. Wartenberg (eds.), *Presbeus. Studies in Ancient Coinage Presented to Richard Ashton*. New York: 19–24.
——— (2021b). 'Rhodes Before the Synoecism and the Cult of Zeus Atabyrios', *VDI* 81.3: 663–672.
——— (2021c). 'Rhodes Circa 227 B.C.', in S. Fachard and E. Harris (eds.), *The Destruction of Cities in the Ancient Greek World. Integrating the Archaeological and Literary Evidence*. Cambridge: 189–227.
Bresson, A., Brun, P., and Varinlioğlu, E. (2001). 'Les inscriptions grecques et latines', in P. Debord and E. Varinlioğlu (eds.), *Les hautes terres de Carie*. Bordeaux: 81–311.
Brett, G. (1949). 'The Seven Wonders of the World in the Renaissance', *Art Quarterly* 12: 347–353.
Breydenbach, B. (1486). *Peregrinatio in terram sanctam*. Mainz.
Brieger, A. (1857). *De fontibus librorum XXIII, XXXIV, XXXV, XXXVI, naturalis historiae Plinianae, quatenus ad artem plasticam pertinent*. Greifswald.
Britannico [Britannicus], G. (1512). *Junius Juvenalis, opus quidem divinum, antea impressorum vitio tetrum, mancum et inutile, nunc autem a viro bene docto recognitum [...]*. Venice.
Brodersen, K. (1992). *Reiseführer zu den Sieben Weltwundern. Philon von Byzanz und andere antike Texte*. Frankfurt am Main, Leipzig.
——— (2004⁶). *Die Sieben Weltwunder. Legendäre Kunst- und Bauwerke der Antike*. Munich.
Bruneau, P. (1970). *Recherches sur les cultes de Délos à l'époque hellénistique et à l'époque impériale*. Paris.
Brunn, H. (1889²). *Geschichte der griechischen Künstler* I. *Die Bildhauer*. Stuttgart.
Bruson, J.-M., and Leribault, C. (1999). *Peintures du musée Carnavalet: catalogue sommaire*. Paris.
Bulliet, R. W. (1990²). *The Camel and the Wheel*. New York.
Burke, F. (2011). 'The Colossus of Rhodes', in L. Bayman (ed.), *Directory of World Cinema 6. Italy*. Bristol, Chicago: 179–181.
Bursian, C. (1863). 'Übersicht der neuesten Leistungen und Entdeckungen auf dem Gebiete der griechischen Kunstgeschichte', *Jahrbücher für classische Philologie* 9: 85–106.
Busdraghi, P., Chiabó, M., Dessì Fulgheri, A., Gatti, P., Mazzacane, R., and Roberti, L. (1996). *Osberno. Derivazioni*. Spoleto.
Büsing, H. (1982). 'Metrologische Beiträge', *JDAI* 97: 1–45.
Butcher, K., and Ponting, M. (2014). *The Metallurgy of Roman Silver Coinage. From the Reform of Nero to the Reform of Trajan*. Cambridge.
Cadwallader, A.H. (2023). *Colossae, Colossians, Philemon. The Interface*. Göttingen.
Cairns, F. (2005). 'Pindar. *Olympian* 7: Rhodes, Athens, and the Diagorids', *Eikasmos* 16: 63–91.
Calboli, G. (1993). *Rhetorica ad C. Herennium*. Bologna.
Caliò, L. M. (2001). 'Il santuario di Camiro. Analisi delle strutture e ipotesi di ricostruzione della grande stoà dorica', *Orizzonti. Rassegna di archeologia* 2: 86–107.
——— (2012). *Asty. Studi sulla città greca*. Rome.
Calmet, A. (1728). *Dictionnaire historique, critique, chronologique, géographique et littéral de la Bible* IV. Paris.
Cameron, A. (1993). *The Greek Anthology from Meleager to Planudes*. Oxford.
Campbell, D. A. (1991). *Greek Lyric* III. *Stesichorus, Ibycus, Simonides, and Others*. Cambridge, MA.

Cante, M. (1986–1987). 'Rodi: l'arco quadrifronte sul decumano massimo', *ASAA* 64–65 [n.s. 48–49]: 175–266.
Caoursin [Caorsin], G. (1496). *Obsidionis Rhodie urbis descriptio* […]. Ulm.
Carastro, M. (2012). 'Fabriquer du lien en Grèce ancienne: serments, sacrifices, ligatures', *Mètis* [n.s.] 10: 77–105.
Cartari, V. (1647). *Imagini delli dei de gl'antichi di Vencenzo Cartari Reggiano*. Venice.
Ceccarelli, P., and Steinrück, M. (1995). 'À propos de *schol. in Lycophronis Alexandram* 1226', *MH* 52: 77–89.
Chamoux, F. (1953). *Cyrène sous la monarchie des Battiades*. Paris.
Champlin, E. (2003). *Nero*. Cambridge, MA.
Chandezon, C. (2011). 'Particularités du culte isiaque dans la basse vallée du Céphise (Béotie et Phocide)', in Badoud (2011c): 149–182.
Chankowski, V. (2008). *Athènes et Délos à l'époque classique: recherches sur l'administration du sanctuaire d'Apollon délien*. Athens.
Chantraine, P. (1931). 'Grec *ΚΟΛΟΣΣΟΣ*', *BIAO* 30: 449–452.
—— (1970). *Dictionnaire étymologique de la langue grecque. Histoire des mots* II. Paris.
Chevreau, U. (1691). *Histoire du monde* II. Paris.
—— (1697). *Œuvres meslées* I. Paris.
Cioffi, C. (2014). 'Lo storico Xenagoras: una ricostruzione frammentaria', in Ampolo et al. (2014): 239–257.
Clark, T., and Gerstle, A. (2013). 'What Was *Shunga*?', in T. Clark, C. A. Gerstle, A. Ishigami, and A. Yano (eds.), *Shunga. Sex and Pleasure in Japanese Art*. London: 31–33.
Clay, D. (1977). 'A Gymnasium Inventory from the Athenian Agora', *Hesperia* 46: 259–267.
Clayton, P. A., and Price, M. J. (eds.) (1989). *The Seven Wonders of the Ancient World*. London, New York.
Clinton, K., Laugier, L., Stewart, A., and Wescoat, B. D. (2020), 'The Nike of Samothrace: Setting the Record Straight', *AJA* 124: 551–573.
Coarelli, F. (2001). 'Origo Sagunti. L'origine mitica di Sagunto e l'alleanza con Roma', in Fromentin and Gotteland (2001): 321–326.
—— (2016). *I mercanti nel tempio. Delo: culto, politica, commercio*. Athens.
Coates-Stephens, R. (2017). 'The Byzantine Sack of Rome', *AntTard* 25: 191–212.
Collins, J. J. (1993). *Daniel*. Minneapolis.
[Colonna, F. (?)] (1499) [1467]. *Hypnerotomachia Poliphili* […]. Venice.
Colvin, S. (1999). *Dialect in Aristophanes and the Politics of Language in Ancient Greek Literature*. Oxford.
Condello, F., and Floridi, L. (2023). *Pseudo-Filone di Bisanzio, 'Le Sette Meraviglie del Mondo'. Introduzione, testo critico, traduzione, note esegetiche e testuali*. Berlin, Boston.
Conrad, L. I. (1996). 'The Arabs and the Colossus', *JAS* 6: 165–187.
Constantakopoulou, C. (2005). 'Proud to Be an Islander: Island Identity in Multi-*Polis* Islands in the Classical and Hellenistic Aegean', *MHR* 20: 1–34.
—— (2007). *The Dance of the Islands. Insularity, Networks, the Athenian Empire, and the Aegean World*. Oxford.
Coppola, G. (2008–2011). 'Rodi eraclide tra Achei e Dori', *RAAN* [n.s.] 75: 27–50.
Cordano, F. (1974). '*Ῥόδος* prima del sinecismo e *Ῥόδιοι* fondatori di colonie', *PP* 29: 179–182.
Coulton, J. J. (1977). *Greek Architects at Work: Problems of Structure and Design*. London.
Courby, F. (1921). 'Notes topographiques et chronologiques', *BCH* 45: 174–241.
—— (1931). *Exploration archéologique de Délos* XII. *Les temples d'Apollon*. Paris.
Coutin, A. (2001). *Le monde des Sept merveilles*. Paris.

Currie, B. (2011). 'Epinician *Choregia*: Funding a Pindaric Chorus', in L. Athanassaki and E. Bowie (eds.), *Archaic and Classical Choral Song. Performance, Politics and Dissemination*. Berlin: 269–310.

Cusset, C., and Prioux, É. (2009a). 'Introduction', in Cusset and Prioux (2009b): 7–15.

—— (eds.) (2009b). *Lycophron: éclats d'obscurité. Actes du colloque international de Lyon et Saint-Étienne, 18–20 janvier 2007*. Saint-Étienne.

Dapper, O. (1703). *Description exacte des isles de l'Archipel et de quelques autres adjacentes; dont les principales sont Chypre, Rhodes, Candie, Samos, Chio, Negrepont, Lemnos, Paros, Delos, Patmos, avec un grand nombre d'autres […]*. Amsterdam.

Darblade-Audoin, M.-P., and Mille, B. (2008). 'Le pied de bronze colossal de Clermont-Ferrand', *MMAI* 87: 31–68.

Dawid, M. (1968). *Weltwunder der Antike. Baukunst und Plastik*. Frankfurt am Main, Innsbruck.

De Aguilón [Aguilonius], F. (1613). *Opticorum libri sex*. Antwerp.

De Beys, C. (1651). *Œuvres poétiques*. Paris.

Debord, P. (1999). *L'Asie Mineure au IVe siècle (412–323 a.C.): pouvoirs et jeux politiques*. Bordeaux.

De Bruijn, C. (1698). *Reizen van Cornelis de Bruyn door de vermaardste deelen van Klein Asia, de eylanden Scio, Rhodus, Cyprus, Metelino, Stanchio, etc. mitsgaders de voornaamste steden van Ægypten, Syrien en Palestina*. Delft.

De Callataÿ, G. (2006). 'The Colossus of Rhodes: Ancient Texts and Modern Representations', in C. R. Ligota and J.-L. Quantin (eds.), *History of Scholarship. A Selection of Papers from the Seminar on the History of Scholarship Held Annually at the Warburg Institute*. Oxford, New York: 39–73.

De Choiseul-Gouffier, M. G. F. A. (1782). *Voyage pittoresque de la Grèce*. Paris.

De Conihout, I., and Ract-Madoux, P. (2002). 'Veuves, pénitents et tombeaux: reliures françaises du XVIe siècle à motifs funèbres, de Catherine de Médicis à Henri III', in J. Balsamo (ed.), *Les funérailles à la Renaissance. XIIe colloque international de la Société française d'étude du seizième siècle (Bar-le-Duc, 2–5 décembre 1999)*. Geneva: 229–241.

De Fortia d'Urban, A. J. F. (ed.) (1826). *Histoire de Hainaut, par Jacques de Guyse, traduite en français avec le texte latin en regard* II. Paris, Brussels.

De Jonge, C. C. (2013). 'Longinus 36.3: The Faulty Colossus and Plato's *Phaedrus*', *Trends in Classics* 5: 318–340.

De Jonghe [Junius], A. (1598). *Poëmatum Hadriani Iunii Hornani medici liber primus continens pia & moralia carmina*. Leiden.

De la Vigenère, B. (1578). *Les images ou tableaux de platte-peinture de Philostrate Lemnien Sophiste Grec. Mis en françois par Blaise de Vigenere avec des Argumens & Annotations sur chacun d'iceux*. Paris.

Delrieux, F. (2008). *Les monnaies des cités grecques de la Basse Vallée de l'Harpasos en Carie (IIe s. a.C.–IIe s. p.C.)*. Bordeaux.

Delrieux, F., and Ferriès, M.-C. (2010). 'Le siège de Rhodes par C. Cassius Longinus en 42 av. J.-C., de la bataille de Myndos à la prise de la ville', in Faucherre and Pimouguet-Pédarros (2010): 175–199.

Demus-Quatember, M. (1981). 'Guglia di Babilonia', *Römische historische Mitteilungen* 23: 213–225.

—— (1986). 'Bemerkungen zur Chronologie des Kolosses von Rhodos', in O. Feld, U. Peschlow (eds.), *Studien zur spätantiken und byzantinischen Kunst Friedrich Wilhelm Deichmann gewidmet* III. Bonn.

Denoyelle, M., Descamps-Lequime, S., Mille, B., and Verger, S. (eds.) (2012). *Bronzes grecs et romains: recherches récentes. Hommage à Claude Rolley. Collections électroniques de l'INHA*, online.
De Pestels, A.-C. [Comte de Caylus] (1759). 'Réflexions sur quelques chapitres du XXXIVe livre de Pline, dans lesquels il fait mention des ouvrages de bronze', *Histoire de l'Académie royale des Inscriptions et Belles-Lettres. Mémoires de la littérature* 25: 335–367.
De Polignac, F. (1984). 'Al-Iskandariyya: œil du monde et frontière de l'inconnu', *MEFRM* 96: 425–439.
De Sanctis, G. (1923). *Storia dei Romani* IV.1. *La fondazione dell'Impero: dalla battaglia di Naraggara alla battaglia di Pidna*. Milan, Turin.
Descamps-Lequime, S. (2010). 'Couleurs originelles des bronzes grecs et romains. Analyse de laboratoire et patines intentionnelles antiques', in M.-T. Dinh-Audhouin, R. A. Jacquesy, D. Olivier, and P. Rigny (eds.), *La chimie et l'art. Le génie au service de l'homme*. Les Ulis: 115–128.
Detlefsen, D. (1873). *C. Plinii Secundi Naturalis historia V. Libri XXXII–XXXVII*. Berlin.
De Troia, P. (2009). *Geografia dei paesi stranieri alla Cina*. Brescia.
De Vaivre, J.-B. (2010). 'La forteresse de Kolossi en Chypre', *MMAI* 79: 73–155.
—— (2020). 'Désastres survenus à Rhodes et ayant entraîné la ruine de deux édifices insignes. Le témoignage de Johan Hedenborg', *Bulletin de la Société de l'histoire et du patrimoine de l'Ordre de Malte* 42: 25–46.
De Vaivre, J.-B., and Vissière, L. (2014). *Tous les deables d'enfer. Relations du siège de Rhodes par les Ottomans en 1480*. Geneva.
Dickie, M. W. (1996). 'What Is a *Kolossos* and How Were *Kolossoi* Made in the Hellenistic Period?', *GRBS* 37: 237–257.
Didi-Huberman, G. (1993). *Le Cube et le visage. Autour d'une statue d'Alberto Giacometti*. Paris.
Dignas, B. (2003). 'Rhodian Priests after the Synoecism', *AncSoc* 33: 35–51.
Dinsmoor, W. B. (1922). 'Structural Iron in Greek Architecture', *AJA* 26: 148–158.
Dittenberger, W. (1886–1887). *De sacris Rhodiorum commentatio* I–II. Halle.
Dobias-Lalou, C. (2011). 'Κολοσσός', in A. Blanc and C. de Lamberterie (eds.), 'Chronique d'étymologie grecque 13 (*CEG* 2013)', *RPh* 85: 352.
—— (2013–2014) [2016]. 'Une décennie de travaux épigraphiques en Cyrénaïque: bilan 2005–2014 et projets', *LibAnt* [n.s.] 7: 185–193.
—— (2014). 'Une inscription archaïque du temple des Dioscures à Cyrène', in M. Luni (ed.), *Cirene Greca e romana*. Rome: 31–37.
—— (2015). 'Les débuts de l'écriture en Cyrénaïque', in A. Inglese (ed.), *Epigrammata 3. Saper scrivere nel Mediterraneo antico. Esiti di scrittura fra VI e IV sec. a.C.* Tivoli: 59–80.
—— (2017). 'Sur quelques correspondances lexicales entre Cyrène, Rhodes et Cos', in A. Panayotou and G. Galdi (eds.), Ἑλληνικὲς διάλεκτοι στὸν ἀρχαῖο κόσμο. *Actes du VIe colloque international sur les dialectes grecs anciens (Nicosie, université de Chypre, 26–29 septembre 2011)*. Leuven, Paris, Bristol, CT: 157–172.
Dombart, T. (1970). *Die Sieben Weltwunder des Altertums*. Munich.
D'Onofrio, A. M. (1982). '*Korai* e *kouroi* funerari attici', *AION* [Sezione di archeologia e storia antica] 4: 135–170.
Donohue, A. A. (1988). *'Xoana' and the Origins of Greek Sculpture*. Atlanta.
—— (1997). 'The Greek Images of the Gods. Considerations on Terminology and Methodology', *Hephaistos* 15: 31–45.
Dörig, J. (1999). 'Der Helios Eleutherios des Chares von Lindos. Neues zum Koloss von Rhodos', in AA.VV. (1999): 185–192.

Doyen, C. (2012). *Études de métrologie grecque* II. *Étalons de l'argent et du bronze en Grèce hellénistique*. Louvain-la-Neuve.

Drew-Bear, T., and Fillon, J.-M. (2011). 'Honneurs pour un gymnasiarque d'Apamée', in L. Sumerer (ed.), *Kelainai—Apamée Kibôtos*. Bordeaux: 277–280.

Ducat, J. (1976). 'Fonctions de la statue dans la Grèce archaïque: *kouros* et *kolossos*', *BCH* 100: 239–251.

Du Choul, G. (1556a). *Discours de la religion des anciens Romains*. Lyon.

—— (1556b). *Discours sur la castrametation et discipline militaire des Romains*. Lyon.

Durbec, Y. (2014). *Lycophron et ses contemporains*. Amsterdam.

Durrell, L. (1953). *Reflections on a Marine Venus. A Companion to the Landscape of Rhodes*. London.

Dyggve, E. (1960). *Lindos. Fouilles de l'acropole (1902–1914 et 1952)* III. *Le sanctuaire d'Athana Lindia et l'architecture lindienne*. Berlin, Copenhagen.

Ebert, J. (1967). 'Epigraphische Miszellen', *Wissenschaftliche Zeitschrift der Martin-Luther-Universität Halle-Wittenberg* 16: 411–417.

Edson, Jr., C. F. (1934). 'The Antigonids, Heracles, and Beroea', *HSPh* 45: 213–246.

Ehrmann, J. (1968). 'Quatre pièces notariales sur Antoine Caron et sur les tapisseries de la suite d'Artémise', *Bulletin de la Société de l'histoire de l'art francais*: 1–7.

—— (1986). *Antoine Caron: peintre des fêtes et des massacres*. Paris.

Ekschmitt, W. (1996[10]). *Die Sieben Weltwunder. Ihre Erbauung, Zerstörung und Wiederentdeckung*. Mainz.

El-Tanbouli, M. A. L. (1975). *Garf Hussein* III. *La grande salle (E). Mur est—piliers et colosses*. Cairo.

Engelmann, H. (2007). 'Die Inschriften von Patara. Eine Übersicht', in C. Schuler (ed.), *Griechische Epigraphik in Lykien: eine Zwischenbilanz. Akten des int. Koloquiums München, 24–26 Februar 2005*. Vienna: 133–139.

Faber, J. (1528). *Oratio de origine, potentia ac tyrannide Thurcorum* […]. Cologne.

Fabricius, J. (1716). *Bibliothecae Graecae liber III. de scriptoribus qui claruerunt a Platone usque ad tempora nati Christi sospitatoris nostri. Accedunt Albini introductio in Platonem et Anatolii quaedam nunc primum edita, tum poeta vetus de viribus herbarum dii sacrarum, cum latina versione ac notis*. Hamburg.

Faraclas, N. (1968). 'Περὶ τῆς ὀνομασίας τῶν ἐλευθέρων στύλων τῶν ἱερῶν κορυφῆς', *AAA* 1.2: 210–211.

Faraone, C. A. (1991). 'Binding and Burying the Forces of Evil: The Defensive Use of "Voodoo Dolls" in Ancient Greece', *ClAnt* 10: 165–205.

Farnell, L. R. (1930). *The Works of Pindar* I. *Translation in Rhythmical Prose with Literary Comments*. London.

—— (1932). *The Works of Pindar* II. *Critical Commentary*. London.

Faucherre, N., and Pimouguet-Pédarros, I. (eds.) (2010). *Les sièges de Rhodes de l'Antiquité à la période moderne*. Rennes.

Feissel, D. (2003). 'Le Philadelphion de Constantinople: inscriptions et écrits patriographiques', *CRAI*: 495–523.

Fenaille, M. (1903). *État général des tapisseries de la manufacture des Gobelins depuis son origine jusqu'à nos jours, 1600–1900* I. *Les ateliers parisiens au XVIIe siècle (1601–1662)*. Paris.

Ferri, S. (2011[4] [1946[1]]). *Plinio il Vecchio. Storia delle arti antiche*. Milan.

Ffolliott, S. (1993). 'Once upon a Tapestry: Inventing the Ideal Queen', in C. J. Adelson and S. Ffolliott (eds.), *Images of a Queen's Power: The Artemisia Tapestries*. Minneapolis: 13–19.

Filimonos-Tsopotou, M. (2004). *Η ελληνιστική οχύρωση της Ρόδου*. Athens.

Filimonos, M., and Kontorini, V. (1989). "Ἕνα νέο γυμνάσιο στὴ 'Ρόδο καὶ ἡ μαρτυρία τοῦ Διοδώρου XX, 100, 3–4', *AC* 58: 128–177.
Filimonos-Tsopotou, M., and Marketou, T. (2014). 'Les fouilles grecques', in A. Coulié and M. Filimonos-Tsopotou (eds.), *Rhodes. Une île grecque aux portes de l'Orient (xve–ve siècle avant J.-C.)*. Paris: 63–75.
Finkielsztejn, G. (2001). *Chronologie détaillée et révisée des éponymes amphoriques rhodiens, de 270 à 108 av. J.-C. environ. Premier bilan*. Oxford.
Fischer, S. (2014). *Das Landschaftsbild als gerahmter Ausblick in den venezianischen Villen des 16. Jahrhunderts. Sustris, Padovano, Veronese, Palladio und die illusionistische Landschaftsmalerei*. Petersberg.
Fischer von Erlach, J. B. (1721). *Entwurff einer historischen Architectur, in Abbildung unterschiedener berühmten Gebäude, des Alterthums, und fremder Völcker, umb aus den Geschichtbüchern, Gedächtnüsz-Müntzen, Ruinen, und eingeholten wahrhafften Abriszen, vor Augen zu stellen*. Vienna.
Foley, E., and Stroud, R. S. (2019). 'A Reappraisal of the Athena Promachos Accounts from the Acropolis', *Hesperia* 88: 87–153.
Folin, M., and Preti, M. (2022). 'Da Anversa a Roma e ritorno', *Mitteilungen des Kunsthistorischen Institutes in Florenz* 64: 31–67.
Fontaine [Fontanus], J. (1524). *De bello Rhodio libri tres*. Rome.
Fraenkel, E. (1950). *Agamemnon*. Oxford.
Fraenkel, H. (1915). *De Simia Rhodio*. Göttingen.
Fraser, P. M. (1979). 'Lycophron on Cyprus', *RDAC*: 328–343.
Fraser, P. M., and Bean, G. E. (1954). *The Rhodian Peraea and Islands*. Oxford.
Frel, J. (1975). 'Games on the Rhodian Shore', *AAA* 8: 77–78.
Fromentin, V., and Gotteland, S. (eds.) (2001). *Origines gentium*. Bordeaux.
Frontisi-Ducroux, F. (1975). *Dédale. Mythologie de l'artisan en Grèce ancienne*. Paris.
Fuchs, W. (1967). 'Hellenistic Art', in J. Boardmann, J. Dörig, W. Fuchs, and M. Hirmer, *The Art and Architecture of Ancient Greece*. London: 499–524.
—— (1969). *Die Skulptur der Griechen*. Munich.
Fujisawa, A., and Hemuki, N. (2019). 'A Diagnostic Study of the Cast-Bronze Great Buddha Statue in the Kotoku-in Temple, Japan', in C. Chemello, L. Brambilla, and E. Joseph (eds.), *Metal 2019. Proceedings of the Interim Meeting of the ICOM-CC Metals Working Group (September 2–6, 2019, Neuchâtel, Switzerland)*. Neuchâtel: 17–25.
Fulvio [Fulvius], A. (1527). *Antiquitates Urbis*. Rome.
Gabriel, A. (1921). *La cité de Rhodes MCCX—MDXXII. Topographie. Architecture militaire*. Paris.
—— (1923). *La cité de Rhodes MCCX—MDXXII. Architecture civile et religieuse*. Paris.
—— (1932). 'La construction, l'attitude et l'emplacement du Colosse de Rhodes', *BCH* 56: 331–359.
Gabrielsen, V. (2000). 'The Synoikized Polis of Rhodes', in P. Flensted-Jensen, T. Heine Nielsen, and L. Rubinstein (eds.), *Polis & Politics. Studies in Ancient Greek History. Presented to Mogens Herman Hansen on His Sixtieth Birthday, August 20, 2000*. Copenhagen: 177–205.
Galle, P. (1572). *Octo mundi miracula*. Antwerp.
Garnier, R. (2006). 'Κολοφών', in C. de Lamberterie and J.-L. Perpillou (eds.), 'Chronique d'étymologie grecque 11', *RPh* 80: 355–356.
Gebauer, K. (1938-1939). 'Alexanderbildnis und Alexandertypus', *MDAI(A)* 63–64: 1–106.
Gernet, L. (1948-1949). 'Droit et prédroit en Grèce ancienne', *L'Année sociologique* [s. 3] 3: 21–119 [reprinted in Gernet, L. (1968). *Anthropologie de la Grèce antique*. Paris: 173–329 and Gernet, L. (1982). *Droit et institutions en Grèce antique*. Paris: 7–119].

Giangiulio, M. (2009). ' "Bricolage" coloniale. Fondazioni greche in Cirenaica', in M. Lombardo, F. Frisone (eds.), *Colonie di colonie: le fondazioni sub-coloniali greche tra colonizzazione e colonialismo*. Lecce: 87–98.

Giannikouri, A. (ed.) (2013). *Ὄλβιος Ἄνερ. Μέλετες στη μνήμη του Γρηγόρη Κωνσταντινοπούλου*. Rhodes.

Gibbon, E. (1788). *History of the Decline and Fall of the Roman Empire* V. London.

Ginzburg, C. (1991). 'Représentation: le mot, l'idée, la chose', *Annales ESC* 46: 1219–1234.

Giorgetti, D. (1977). 'Il faro di Alessandria fra simbologia e realtà: dall'epigramma di Posidippo ai mosaici di Gasr Elbia', *RAL* 33: 245–261.

Golvin, J.-C. (2005[2]). *L'Antiquité retrouvée*. Paris.

Golvin, J.-C., and Coutin, A. (2001). *Le Monde des sept Merveilles*. Paris.

Gow, A. S. F., and Page, D. L. (1965). *The Greek Anthology* I. *Hellenistic Epigrams*. 1: *Introduction, Text, and Indexes of Sources and Epigrammatists*. 2: *Commentary and Indexes*. Cambridge.

Grace, V. R. (1963). 'Notes on the Amphoras from the Koroni Peninsula', *Hesperia* 32: 319–334.

––––– (1965). 'The Commercial Amphoras from the Antikythera Shipwreck', *TAPhA* 55: 5–17.

––––– (1974). 'Revisions in Early Hellenistic Chronology', *MDAI(A)* 89: 193–200.

Graef, B. (1900). 'Helioskopf aus Rhodos', in AA.VV., *Strena Helbigiana*. Leipzig: 99–110.

Graham, A. J. (1960). 'The Authenticity of the ΟΡΚΙΟΝ ΤΩΝ ΟΙΚΙΣΤΗΡΙΩΝ of Cyrene', *JHS* 80: 94–111 [reprinted in Graham, A. J. (2001). *Collected Papers on Greek Colonization*. Leiden: 83–112].

Gualandi, G. (1976). 'Sculture di Rodi', *ASAA* 54 [n.s. 38]: 7–260.

Guérin, V. (1856). *Étude sur l'île de Rhodes*. Paris.

Guillon, P. (1936). 'La stèle d'Agamédès', *RPh* 62: 209–235.

Gutzwiller, K. (2002). 'Posidippus on Statuary', in G. Bastianini and A. Casanova (eds.), *Il papiro di Posidippo un anno dopo*. Florence: 41–59.

––––– (2019). 'Posidippus and Ancient Epigram Books', in C. Henriksén (ed.), *A Companion to Ancient Epigram*. Hoboken, NJ: 351–370.

Habicht, C. (2003). 'Rhodian Amphora Stamps and Rhodian Eponyms', *REA* 105: 541–578.

Hamiaux, M. (2006). 'La Victoire de Samothrace: construction de la base et reconstitution', *MMAI* 85: 5–60.

Hamilton, W. J. (1842). *Researches in Asia Minor, Pontus and Armenia* II. London.

Hargrove, J. (1986). 'La campagne américaine', in AA.VV. (1986): 170–183.

Harris, W. V. (2017). 'Rome at Sea: The Beginnings of Roman Naval Power', *G&R* 64: 14–26.

Haskell, F., and Penny, N. (1988). *Taste and the Antique. The Lure of Classical Sculpture 1500–1900*. New Haven, London.

Hassler, C. D. (1849). *Fratris Felicis Fabri evagatorium in Terrae sanctae, Arabiae et Aegypti peregrinationem* III. Stuttgart.

Haynes, D. E. L. (1957). 'Philo of Byzantium and the Colossus of Rhodes', *JHS* 77: 311–312.

––––– (1992). *The Technique of Greek Bronze Statuary*. Mainz.

Head, B. V. (1887[1], 1911[2]). *Historia Numorum. A Manual of Greek Numismatics*. Oxford.

––––– (1891). 'Archaic Coins Probably of Cyrene', *NC*: 1–11.

Hebert, B. (1989). *Schriftquellen zur hellenistischen Kunst. Plastik, Malerei und Kunsthandwerk der Griechen vom vierten bis zum zweiten Jahrhundert*. Graz.

Heffter, W. H. (1833). *Die Götterdienste auf Rhodus im Alterthume* III. Zerbst.

Helbig, W. (1896). 'Sopra un busto colossale d'Alessandro Magno trovato a Ptolemais', *MAL* 6: 73–88.

Held, W. (2003). 'Neue und revidierte Inschriften aus Loryma und der karischen Chersones', *EA* 36: 55–86.

Hermary, A. (1994). 'Les noms de la statue chez Hérodote', in M.C. Amouretti and P. Villard (eds.), *Eukrata. Mélanges offerts à Claude Vatin*. Aix-en-Provence: 21–29.
—— (1995). 'Rhodes et les statues colossales', *Dossiers d'archéologie* 202: 54–59.
Higbie, C. (2003). *The Lindian Chronicle and the Greek Creation of Their Past*. Oxford.
Higgins, M. D. (2023). *The Seven Wonders of the Ancient World. Science, Engineering, and Technology*. Oxford.
Higgins, R. (1989). 'The Colossus of Rhodes', in Clayton and Price (1989): 124–137.
Hijmans, E. A. (2024). *Sol. Image and Meaning of the Sun in Roman Art and Religion*. Leiden, Boston.
Hiller von Gaertringen, F. (1895). 'Inschriften aus Rhodos', *MDAI(A)* 20: 222–229.
—— (1931). 'Rhodos', *RE* Suppl. V: 731–840.
Hoepfner, W. (2000). 'Der Koloss von Rhodos', *AA*: 129–153.
—— (2003). *Der Koloss von Rhodos und die Bauten des Helios: neue Forschungen zu einem der sieben Weltwunder*. Mainz.
—— (2007). 'Rhodos und der Gott Helios/Ρόδος και ο θεός Ἥλιος', in AA.VV., *Αρχαιολογικές έρευνες και ευρήματα στα Δωδεκάνησα. Ρόδος, Ιαλυσός, Κως, Νίσυρος και Γυαλί/Archäologische Forschung und Funde in der Dodekanes. Rhodos, Ialysos, Kos, Nisyros und Giali*. Weilheim: 69–119.
Hoepfner, W., and Schwandner, E.-L. (1986[1], 1994[2]). *Haus und Stadt im klassischen Griechenland*. Munich.
Holleaux, M. (1903). 'Le prétendu traité de 306 entre les Rhodiens et les Romains', in *Mélanges Perrot. Recueil de mémoires concernant l'archéologie classique, la littérature et l'histoire ancienne*. Paris: 183–190.
—— (1921). *Rome, la Grèce et les monarchies hellénistiques au IIIe s. av. J.-C. (273–205)*. Paris.
—— (1923). 'Polybe et le tremblement de terre de Rhodes', *REG* 36: 480–498 [reprinted in Holleaux, M. (1938). *Études d'épigraphie et d'histoire grecques* I. Paris: 445–462].
Holtzmann, B. (2003). *L'acropole d'Athènes. Monuments, cultes et histoire du sanctuaire d'Athèna Polias*. Paris.
Hornblower, S. (1982). *Mausolus*. Oxford.
—— (2004). *Thucydides and Pindar. Historical Narrative and the World of Epinikian Poetry*. Oxford, New York.
—— (2015). *Lykophron*: Alexandra. *Greek Text, Translation, Commentary, and Introduction*. Oxford.
—— (2018). *Lykophron's* Alexandra, *Rome, and the Hellenistic World*. Oxford.
—— (2019). [Review of Marek and Zing (2019)], *Sehepunkte* 19.1, online.
How, W. W., and Wells, J. (1912). *A Commentary on Herodotus* I. Oxford.
Hoyland, R. G. (2011). *Theophilus of Edessa's Chronicle and the Circulation of Historical Knowledge in Late Antiquity and Early Islam*. Liverpool.
Huebner, S. R. (2013). 'Adoption and Fosterage in the Ancient Eastern Mediterranean', in J. Evans Grubbs, T. Parkin, and R. Bell (eds.), *The Oxford Handbook of Childhood and Education in the Classical World*. Oxford: 510–531.
Hurst, A. (2008). *Lycophron*: Alexandra. Paris.
—— (2012). *Sur Lycophron*. Geneva.
Icard-Gianoloi, N., and Lochin, C. (2004). 'Déplacements—transferts définitifs', *ThesCRA* II: 471–476.
Iossif, P. P., and Lorber, C. C. (2009a). 'Celestial Imagery on the Eastern Coinage of Antiochus IV', *Mesopotamia* 44: 129–146.
—— (2009b). 'The Cult of Helios in the Seleucid East', *Topoi* 16: 19–42.

Jacoby, F. (1955). *Die Fragmente der griechischen Historiker (*FGrHist*). Dritter Teil: Geschichte von Städten und Völkern (Horographie und Ethnographie). B: Kommentar zu Nr. 297*–607. Leiden.

Jacopi [Jacopich], G. (1926). 'Lavori del Servizio archeologico a Rodi e nelle isole dipendenti durante il biennio 1924–1925, 1925–1926', *Bolletino d'Arte* [s. II] 20: 324–328.

—— (1928). 'Esplorazione del santuario di Zeus Atabyrios', *Clara Rhodos* I. Rhodes: 88–91.

—— (1932a). 'Monumenti di scultura del Museo Archeologico di Rodi II (continuazione e fine)', *Clara Rhodos* V.2. Rhodes: 1–58.

—— (1932b). 'Nuove epigrafi dalle Sporadi meridionali', *Clara Rhodos* II. Rhodes: 169–255.

Jacquemin, A. (1995). 'Basamento del Carro del Sole', in Moreno (1995b): 181.

Jacquemin, A., and Laroche, D. (1986). 'Le char d'or consacré par le peuple rhodien', *BCH* 110: 285–307.

—— (2012). 'Regards nouveaux sur deux quadriges delphiques', in Denoyelle et al. (2012), online.

Jahn, L. (1860). *C. Plini Secundi Naturalis Historiae libri XXXVII. Vol. V: libb. XXXIII–XXXVII*. Leipzig.

Jakubiec, A. (2016). 'La nature de l'envoyeur du premier ΙΚΕΣΙΟΣ de la loi cathartique de Cyrène (*SEG* IX, 72, l. 111–121)', *ZPE* 197: 96–100.

Janin, R. (1964). *Constantinople byzantine. Développement urbain et répertoire topographique*. Paris.

Jeffery, L. H. (1990). *The Local Scripts of Archaic Greece. A Study of the Origin of the Greek Alphabet and Its Development from the Eighth to the Fifth Centuries B.C. Revised Edition with a Supplement by A. W. Johnston*. Oxford.

Jenkins, G. K. (1989). 'Rhodian *Plinthophoroi*. A Sketch', in G. Le Rider, G. K. Jenkins, N. Waggoner, and U. Westermark (eds.), *Kraay-Mørkholm Essays. Numismatic Studies in Memory of C. M. Kraay and O. Mørkholm*. Louvain-la-Neuve: 101–136.

Jeppesen, K. (1986). 'The Ancient Greek and Latin Writers', in K. Jeppesen and A. Luttrell, *The Maussolleion at Halikarnassos. Reports of the Danish Archaeological Expedition to Bodrum* II. *The Written Sources and Their Archaeological Background*. Aarhus: 8–113.

Jessen, O. (1912). 'Helios', *RE* XV: 58–93.

Jex-Blake, K., and Sellers, E. (1896). *The Elder Pliny's Chapters on the History of Art*. London.

Johnston, A. W. (1975), 'Rhodian Readings', *ABSA* 70: 145–167.

Johnston, S. I. (1999). *Restless Dead. Encounters between the Living and the Dead in Ancient Greece*. Berkeley.

Jones, K. R. (2014a). 'Alcaeus of Messene, Philip V and the Colossus of Rhodes: A Re-examination of *Anth. Pal.* 6.171', *CQ* 64: 136–151.

—— (2014b). 'Lycophron's *Alexandra*, the Romans and Antiochus III', *JHS* 134: 41–55.

Jones, M. W. (2000). 'Doric Measure and Architectural Design 1: The Evidence of the Relief from Salamis', *AJA* 104: 73–93.

Jordan, P. (2002). *The Seven Wonders of the Ancient World*. Edinburgh. London.

Jucker, I. (1956). *Der Gestus des* Aposkopein. *Ein Beitrag zur Gebärdensprache in der antiken Kunst*. Zurich.

Judet de la Combe, P. (1982). *L'Agamemnon d'Eschyle: Le texte et ses interprétations*: Agamemnon 2. Lille.

—— (2001). *L'Agamemnon d'Eschyle: commentaire des dialogues*. Lille.

Kahil, L. (1984). 'Artemis', *LIMC* II.1: 618–753.

Kansteiner, S., Lehmann, L., Hallof, K., Seidensticker, B., and Söldner, M. (2014). *Der Neue Overbeck* III. *Spätklassik. Bildhauer des 4. Jhs. v.Chr. DNO 1799–2677*. Berlin.

Kantzia, C. (1999). ''Ενα ασυνήθιστο πολεμικό ανάθεμα στο ιερό της οδού Διαγοριδών στη Ρόδο', in AA.VV. (1999): 75–82.

Kantzia, C., and Zimmer, G. (1989). 'Rhodische Kolosse. Eine hellenistische Bronzegusswerkstatt', *AA*: 497–523.

Kaplun, A. H. (2015). *Le Colosse de Rhodes. Un géant imaginaire?* Geneva.

Katori, T. [香取忠彦] (1981). *Nara no daibutsu: sekai saidai no chūzōbutsu* [奈良の大仏: 世界最大の鋳造仏]. Tokyo.

Kazhdan, A. P. (1991). 'Kosmas of Jerusalem 3. The Exegesis of Gregory of Nazianzos', *Byzantion* 61: 396–412.

Kebric, R. B. (2019a). 'Lighting the Colossus of Rhodes: A Beacon by Day and Night', *Athens Journal of Mediterranean Studies* 5: 11–32.

—— (2019b). 'The Colossus of Rhodes: Its Height and Pedestal', *Athens Journal of Humanities and Arts* 10: 1–40.

—— (2019c). 'The Colossus of Rhodes: Some Observations About Its Location', *Athens Journal of History* 5: 83–114.

Keesling, C. M. (2017). 'Greek Statue Terms Revisited: What does ἀνδριάς mean?', *GRBS* 57: 837–861.

Kerkhecker, A. (1999). *Callimachus' Book of 'Iambi'*. Oxford.

King, E. S. (1944-1945). 'A New Heemskerck', *JWAG* 78: 60–73.

Kinnard, R. and Crnkovich, T. (2017). *Italian Sword and Sandal Films, 1908-1990.* Jefferson, NC.

Kircher, A. (1679). *Turris Babel* II. Amsterdam.

Kleiner, G. (1957). 'Helios und Sol', in K. Schauenburg (ed.), *Charites. Studien zur Altertumswissenschaft E. Langlotz gewidmet.* Bonn: 101–104.

Knoepfler, D. (2008). 'Louis Robert en sa forge: ébauche d'un mémoire resté inédit sur l'histoire controversée de deux concours grecs, les Trophonia et les Basileia à Lébadée', *CRAI*: 1421–1462.

Konstantinopoulos, G. (1963). ''Επιγραφαὶ ἐκ Ρόδου', *AD* 18: 1–36.

—— (1967). ''Ροδιακά ΙΙ. Πύργοι τῆς ἑλληνιστικῆς Ῥοδιακῆς ὀχυρώσεως', *AEph*: 115–128.

—— (1969). 'Ἀρχαιότητες καὶ μνημεῖα Δωδεκανήσου', *AD* 24B: 451–485.

—— (1973). 'Ἀνασκαφαὶ εἰς Ῥόδον', *PAAH*: 127–136.

—— (1975). 'Ἀνασκαφαὶ εἰς Ῥόδον', *PAAH*: 238–248.

—— (1986). *Ἀρχαῖα Ῥόδος. Ἐπισκόπηση τῆς ἱστορίας καί τῆς τέχνης.* Athens.

—— (1994-1995). ''Έργα πλαστικῆς καὶ επιγραφές από το 'Διονύσιον' τέμενος της αρχαίας Ρόδου', *AD* 49–50A: 75–82.

—— (1997). *Ο ροδιακός κόσμος* II. *Η ροδιακή μυθολογία του VII Ολυμπιονίκου.* Athens.

Kontis, J. D. (1951). 'Ἀνασκαφικαὶ ἔρευναι εἰς τὴν πόλιν τῆς Ῥόδου', *PAAH*: 224–245.

—— (1952). *Ἀνασκαφικαὶ ἔρευναι εἰς τὴν πόλιν τῆς Ῥόδου* (II)', *PAAH*: 547–590.

—— (1954). *Συμβολὴ εἰς τὴν μελέτην τῆς ῥυμοτομίας τῆς Ῥόδου.* Rhodes.

—— (1958). 'Zum antiken Stadtbauplan von Rhodos', *MDAI(A)* 73: 146–158.

—— (1973). ''Επίμετρο', in C. I. Karouzou, *Ρόδος. Ἱστορία, μνημεῖα, τέχνη.* Athens: 118–127.

Kontorini, V. (1975). 'Les concours des Éréthimia à Rhodes', *BCH* 99: 97–117.

—— (1983). 'Rome et Rhodes au tournant du IIIe s. av. J.-C. d'après une inscription inédite de Rhodes', *JRS* 73: 24–32.

—— (1987). 'L'influence de Lindos sur le droit sacré de Cyrène: les suppliants de Cyrène à la lumière d'une inscription inédite de Lindos', in A. Mastino (ed.), *L'Africa romana. Atti del IV convegno di studio, Sassari, 12-14 dicembre 1986.* Sassari: 579–580.

—— (1989). *Ἀνέκδοτες ἐπιγραφές Ρόδου* II. Athens.

Kosmetatou, E., and Papalexandrou, N. (2003). 'Size Matters: Poseidippos and the Colossi', *ZPE* 143: 53–58.

Kowalzig, B. (2007). *Singing for the Gods. Performances of Myth and Ritual in Archaic and Classical Greece*. Oxford.
Kretzschmar, U. (1990). *Der kleine Finger der Bavaria. Entstehungsgeschichte der Bavaria von Ludwig von Schwanthaler anlässlich der Auflage 'Der kleine Finger der Bavaria'*. Offenbach am Main.
Kroll, W. (1941). 'Philon 49', *RE* XX.1: 54–55.
Kunze, M. (ed.) (2003). *Die Sieben Weltwunder der Antike. Wege der Wiedergewinnung aus sechs Jahrhunderten*. Mainz.
Lacroix, L. (1949). *Les reproductions de statues sur les monnaies grecques. La statuaire archaïque et classique*. Liège.
Lambin, C. (2005). *L'Alexandra de Lycophron*. Rennes.
Langlotz, E. (1976). 'Eine Nachbildung des Helios von Rhodos', *RPAA* 48: 141–150.
Łanowski, J. (1965). 'Weltwunder', *RE* Suppl. X: 1020–1030.
—— (1983). 'Les listes des Merveilles du monde "grecques" et "romaines"', in P. Oliva and A. Frolíková (eds.), *Concilium Eirene* XVI.2. Prague: 182–186.
—— (1985). 'Zum Werk des Philon von Byzanz "Über die Sieben Weltwunder"', *Eos* 73: 31–47.
Lapatin, K. (2014). 'Pair of Cups with Literary Figures', in K. Lapatin (ed.), *The Berthouville Silver Treasure and Roman Luxury*. Los Angeles: 142–145.
La Rocca, E. (2018). *La Nike di Samotracia tra Macedonia e Romani. Un riesame del monumento nel quadro dell'assimilazione dei Penati agli Dei di Samotracia*. *ASAA Supplemento* 1.
Larson, J. (2007). 'A Land Full of Gods: Nature Deities in Greek Religion', in D. Odgen (ed.), *A Companion to Greek Religion*. Oxford: 56–70.
Laumonier, A. (1958). *Les cultes indigènes en Carie*. Paris.
Laurenzi, L. (1938). 'Un'immagine del dio Sole rinvenuta a Rodi', *Memorie FERT* 2: 21–26.
—— (1939). 'Rilievi e statue d'arte rodia', *MDAI(R)* 54: 42–65.
—— (1959). 'Colosso di Rodi', *Enciclopedia dell'arte antica* II. Rome: 773–774.
Lazarus, E. (1889). *The Poems of Emma Lazarus* I. Boston.
Le Bonniec, H., and Gallet de Santerre, H. (1953). *Pline l'Ancien, Histoire naturelle. Livre XXXIV*. Paris.
Le Grand, L. (1895). 'Relation du pèlerinage à Jérusalem de Nicolas de Martoni, notaire italien (1394–1395)', *Revue de l'Orient latin* 3: 582–586 and 638–645.
Leblanc, C. (1980). 'Piliers et colosses de type "osiriaque" dans le contexte des temples de culte royal', *BIAO* 80: 69–89.
Lega, C. (1989–1990). 'Il Colosso di Nerone', *BCAR* 93: 339–378.
Léger, R. M. (2017). *Artemis and Her Cult*. Oxford.
Legrand, E. (1897). *Description des îles de l'Archipel par Christophe Buondelmonti. Version grecque par un anonyme publiée d'après le manuscrit du Sérail avec une traduction française et un commentaire*. Paris.
Legrand, P.-E. (1936). *Hérodote: Histoires II*. Paris.
Lehmann, K. (1973). 'The Ship-Fountain from the Victory of Samothrace to the Galera', in P. W. and K. Lehmann (eds.), *Samothracian Reflections. Aspects of the Revival of the Antique*. Princeton: 181–259.
Lemoine, B. (1986). *La Statue de la Liberté (The Statue of Liberty)*. Brussels, Liège.
Lemos, A. A. (1991). *Archaic Pottery of Chios. The Decorated Styles* I. Oxford.
Lenormant, F. (1867). *Chefs-d'œuvre de l'art antique. Deuxième série : Monuments de la peinture et de la sculpture* IV. Paris.
Lesbazeilles, E. (1876). *Les Colosses anciens et modernes*. Paris.
Lévêque, P. (1955). 'Lycophronica', *REA* 57: 36–56.
Linant de Bellefonds, P., Pouzadoux, C., and Prioux, É. (2017). 'Lycophron l'Italien?', in Linant de Bellefonds and Prioux (2017): 199–246.

Linant de Bellefonds, P., and Prioux, É. (2017). *Voir les mythes. Poésie hellénistique et arts figurés*. Paris.

Lippolis, E. (1988-1989). 'Il santuario di Athana a Lindo', *ASAA* 66-67 [n.s. 48-49]: 97-157.

―――― (2016). 'Gli scavi dell'acropoli di Rodi e il culto di Apollo e di Halios', *ArchClass* 67: 111-181.

Little, S. (1996). 'The Lure of the West: European Elements in the Art of the Floating World', *Art Institute of Chicago Museum Studies* 22: 74-93, 95-96.

Livadiotti, M. (1996). 'Lo stadio', in Livadiotti and Rocco (1996): 20-23.

Livadiotti, M., and Rocco, G. (eds.) (1996). *La presenza italiana nel Dodecaneso tra il 1912 e il 1948. La ricerca archeologica. La conservazione. Le scelte progettuali*. Catania.

―――― (1999). 'Il tempio di Athana Polias a Ialiso: un contributo alla conoscenza dell'architettura rodia', in AA.VV. (1999): 109-118.

Luce, J.-M. (2008). *Fouilles de Delphes* II. *Topographie et architecture* 13. *L'aire du Pilier des Rhodiens (fouille 1990-1992). À la frontière du profane et du sacré*. Athens.

Lüders, C. F. (1865). *Der Koloss von Rhodos*. Hamburg.

Lund, J. (2017a). 'Kolossen på Rhodos', in S. G. Saxkjær and E. Mortensen (eds.), *Antikkens 7 vidundere*. Aarhus: 131-147.

―――― (2017b). [Review of Badoud, N. (2015). *Le temps de Rhodes. Une chronologie des inscriptions fondée sur l'étude de ses institutions*. Munich], *AJA* 121.2, online.

Luni, M., Mei, O., and Cardinali, C. (2010). 'Cirene in età arcaica e tracce dell'insediamento pregreco', *RAL* [s. 9] 21: 569-605.

Luttrell, A. (1987). 'Greeks, Latins and Turks on Late-Medieval Rhodes', *ByzF* 11: 357-374.

―――― (2003). *The Town of Rhodes: 1306-1356*. Athens.

Ma, J. (2008). 'The Inventory *SEG* XXVI 139, and the Athenian Asklepieion', *Tekmeria* 9: 7-16.

―――― (2013). *Statues and Cities. Honorific Portraits and Civic Identity in the Hellenistic World*. Oxford.

Machaira, V. (2011). Ἑλληνιστικά γλυπτά της Ῥόδου I. Athens.

Madonna, M. L. (1976). '*Septem mundi miracula* come temple della virtù. Pirro Ligorio e l'interpretazione cinquecentesca delle meraviglie del mondo', *Psicon* 7: 25-63.

Maillot, S. (2009). 'Une association de sculpteurs à Rhodes au IIe siècle av. J.-C.: un cercle d'intégration à la société rhodienne', in L. Bodiou, V. Mehl, J. Oulhen, F. Prost, and J. Wilgaux (eds.), *Chemin faisant. Mythes, cultes et société en Grèce ancienne. Mélanges en l'honneur de Pierre Brulé*. Rennes: 39-57.

―――― (2015). 'Foreigners' Associations and the Rhodian State', in V. Gabrielsen and C. A. Thomsen (eds.), *Private Associations and the Public Sphere. Proceedings of a Symposium Held at the Royal Danish Academy of Sciences and Letters, 9-11 September 2010*. Copenhagen: 136-182.

Mair, A. W., and Mair, G. R. (1921). *Callimachus*: Hymns *and* Epigrams. *Lycophron*: Alexandra. *Aratus*: Phaenomena. Cambridge, MA.

Maiuri, A. (1918). *Rodi. Guida dei monumenti e del museo archeologico*. Rhodes.

―――― (1922). *Rodi*. Rome, Milan, Florence, Naples.

―――― (1925). *Nuova silloge epigrafica di Rodi e Cos*. Florence.

―――― (1928). 'La topografia monumentale di Rodi', *Clara Rhodos* I. Rhodes: 44-55.

―――― (1992). *Vita d'archeologo*. Milan.

Malkin, I. (1991). 'What Is an *Aphidryma*?', *ClAnt* 10: 77-96.

―――― (2011). *A Small Greek World: Networks in the Ancient Mediterranean*. Oxford, New York.

——— (2018). 'Returning Heroes and Greek Colonists', in S. Hornblower and G. Biffis (eds.), *The Returning Hero. Nostoi and Traditions of Mediterranean Settlement*. Oxford: 83–104.

Manesson Mallet, A. (1683). *Description de l'univers* II. Paris.

Männlein-Robert, I. (2007). *Stimme, Schrift und Bild. Zum Verhältnis der Künste in der hellenistischen Dichtung*. Heidelberg.

Manoussou-Ntella [Della], K. (2001). *Medieval Town of Rhodes. Restoration Works (1985–2000)*. Rhodes.

——— (2008). 'Ἀποκατάσταση-ανάδειξη μεσαιωνικού μόλου και φρουρίου Αγίου Νικολάου', in K. Manoussou-Ntella and G. Ntellas (eds.), *Μεσαιωνική πόλη Ρόδου. Ἔργα αποκατάστασης 2000–2008*. Rhodes: 204–210.

——— (2010a). 'Le paysage culturel et les monuments symboles disparus de la ville de Rhodes', *Europa Nostra. Scientific Bulletin* 64: 59–74 [French version of Manoussou-Ntella (2010b)].

——— (2010b). 'Το πολιτισμικό τοπίο και τα χαμένα μνημεία της πόλης της Ρόδου', *Δωδεκανησιακά Χρονικά* 24: 582–613 [Greek version of Manoussou-Ntella (2010a)].

——— (2017). 'Η πόλη της Ρόδου. Από την Αρχαιότητα στο Μεσαίωνα', *Δωδεκανησιακά Χρονικά* 27: 172–183.

Marcadé, J. (1953). *Recueil des signatures de sculpteurs grecs* I. Paris.

——— (1969). *Au musée de Délos: étude sur la sculpture hellénistique en ronde bosse découverte dans l'île*. Paris.

Marcadé, J., and Croissant, F. (1991). 'La sculpture en pierre', in J.-F. Bommelaer (ed.), *Guide de Delphes. Le musée*. Athens, Paris: 29–138.

Marek, C., and Zingg, E. (2018). *Die Versinschrift des Hyssaldomos und die Inschriften von Uzunyuva (Milas/Mylasa)*. Bonn.

Marengo, S. M. (2008). 'Dédicace aux Dioscures et d'autres graffiti', in M. Luni, 'Le Dioskourion de Battos découvert à Cyrène dans le quartier de l'agora', *CRAI*: 26–36 [reprinted in Laronde, A., and Leclant, J. (eds.) (2010a). *Journée d'hommage à François Chamoux (Mirecourt 1915–Paris 2007)*. Paris: 120–127].

——— (2010b). 'Segni e graffiti greci: proposte di lettura', in S. Antoli, A. Arnaldi, and E. Lanzilotta (eds.), *Giornata di studi per Lidio Gasperini*. Rome: 13–27.

Mariño Sánchez-Elvira, R. M. (2008). 'El Coloso de Rodas', in J. L. Arcaz Pozo and M. Montero (eds.), *Maravillas del mundo antiguo*. Madrid: 101–129.

Marlowe, E. (2006). 'Framing the Sun: The Arch of Constantine and the Roman Cityscape', *ABull* 88: 223–242.

Martelli, M. (1996). 'La stipe votive dell'Athenaion di Ialiso', in Livadiotti and Rocco (1996): 46–50.

Martin, G. R. R. (2011). *A Feast for Crows*. New York.

Maruyasu, T., and Oshima, T. (1965). 'Photogrammetry in the Precision Measurement of the Great Buddha at Kamakura', *Studies in Conservation* 10: 53–63.

Maryon, H. (1956). 'The Colossus of Rhodes', *JHS* 76: 68–86.

Mason, P. (2013). *The Colossal. From Ancient Greece to Giacometti*. London.

Massa-Pairault, F.-H. (2009). 'Lycophron et les Géants', in Cusset and Prioux (2009b): 487–505.

Masseti, M. (2002). 'The Fallow Deer on Rhodes (Τα πλατόνια στη Ρόδο)', in M. Masseti (ed.), *Το νησί των ελαφιών. Φυσική ιστορία του πλατονιού της Ρόδου και των σπονδυλωτών της Δωδεκανήσου/Island of Deer. Natural History of the Fallow Deer of Rhodes and of the Vertebrates of the Dodecanese (Greece)*. Rhodes: 139–158.

Masseti, M., Cavallaro, A., Pecchioli, E., and Vernesi, C. (2006). 'Artificial Occurrence of the Fallow Deer, *Dama dama dama* (L., 1758), on the Island of Rhodes (Greece): Insight fom mtDNA Analysis', *Human Evolution* 21: 167–175.

Masseti, M., Pecchioli, E., and Vernesi, C. (2008). 'Phylogeography of the Last Surviving Populations of Rhodian and Anatolian Fallow Deer (*Dama dama dama* L., 1758)', *Biological Journal of the Linnean Society* 93: 835–844.

Matern, P. (2002). *Helios und Sol. Kulte und Ikonographie des griechischen und römischen Sonengottes*. Istanbul.

Mattusch, C. C. (2014). *Enduring Bronze. Ancient Art, Modern Views*. Los Angeles.

Mayhoff, K. F. T. (1897). *C. Plinii Secundi Naturalis Historiae libri XXXVII. Vol. V: libri XXXI–XXXVII*. Leipzig.

McMullin, R. M. (2001). 'Aspects of Medizing: Themistocles, Simonides, and Timocreon of Rhodes', *CJ* 97: 55–67.

Meadows, A. (forthcoming). 'Dating the Nike of Samothrace: New Evidence'.

Megiser, H. (1606). *Propugnaculum Europae. Warhaffte/eigentliche und außführliche beschreibung der viel und weitberühmten Africanischen Insul Malta: Welche dieser zeit des hochlöblichen Johanniter Ritter Ordens Residens [...]: Sampt angehenckter gründlicher erklerung des ursprungs [...] ermeltes Hochwürdigen Ritterlichen Ordens der Johanniter [...]; Mit schönen newen Kupfferstücken gezieret/Alles zum theil aus eigener Erfahrung/zum theil aber auß glaubwürdigen Historicis mit sonderm fleiß zusammen gezogen [...]*. Leipzig.

Meiggs, R., and Lewis, D. (1969). *A Selection of Greek Historical Inscriptions to the End of the Fifth Century B.C.* Oxford.

Meinardus, O. F. A. (1973). 'Colossus, Colossae, Colossi: confusio colossaea', *Biblical Archaeologist* 36: 33–36.

Meliadò, C. (2019). 'Lycophron', *Lexicon of Greek Grammarians of Antiquity*, online.

Mellaart, J. (1959). 'The Royal Treasure of Dorak—A First and Exclusive Report of a Clandestine Excavation Which Led to the Most Important Discovery since the Royal Tombs of Ur', *Illustrated London News* 28, Supplements: 754–757.

Menegon, E. (1994). *Un solo cielo. Giulio Aleni S. J. (1582–1649). Geografia, arte, scienza, religione dall'Europa alla Cina*. Brescia.

Merker, G. S. (1973). *The Hellenistic Sculpture of Rhodes*. Göteborg.

Mexía [Messia], P. (1576). *Della selva di varia lettione*. Venice.

Meyer, E. (1925). *Die Grenzen der hellenistischen Staaten in Kleinasien*. Zurich.

—— (1937). 'Peraia 2', *RE* XIX.1: 566–582.

Michalaki-Kollia, M. (1999). 'Σημειώδες στωικό οικοδόμημα στις υπώρειες της ροδιακής ακρόπολης. Το τέμενος του Ηλίου ή δημόδιο κτίριο;', in AA.VV. (1999): 73–74.

—— (2007). 'Η ελληνιστική Ρόδος στα όρια της μεσαιωνικής πόλης και η ερηνευτική παρουσίαση των υπολειμμάτων της', in AA.VV. (2007): 71–80.

—— (2013a). 'À la recherche de l'ancienne Rhodes, que les Hospitaliers trouvèrent à leur arrivée', in AA.VV. *Rhodes et les chevaliers de Rhodes, 1310–2010. Actes du colloque (Rhodes, 28 et 29 mai 2010)*. Flavigny-sur-Ozerain: 7–29.

—— (2013b). 'Η ανάδειξη της ροδιακής ακρόπολης. Ένα μεγάλο αρχαιολογικό πάρκο της πόλης', in Giannikouri (2013): 79–106.

—— (2017). 'Ο κολοσσός της Ρόδου από τις αρχαίες πηγές και τις εικονογραφικές παραστάσεις ή "πως η φαντασία υποσκελίζει την ιστορία"', *Δωδεκανησιακά Χρονικά* 27: 130–155.

—— (2023). 'Temples, Sacred Places and Cults in the City of Rhodes: Revisiting the Evidence', in Stefanakis et al. (2023): 160–188.

Mille, B., and Darblade-Audoin, M.-P. (2012). 'Le pied colossal de bronze de Clermont-Ferrand et la question de l'atelier de Zénodore', in Denoyelle et al. (2012), online.

Mingazzini, P. (1974). 'Su una statua di Apollo rinvenuta a Santa Marinella', *MAL* [s. 8] 17: 49–57.

Moggi, M. (2009). 'Insularità e assetti politici', in C. Ampolo (ed.), *Immagine e immagini della Sicilia e di altre isole del Mediterraneo antico*. Pisa: 51–65.

Momigliano, A. (1936). 'Note sulla storia di Rodi', *RFIC* 64 [n.s. 14]: 49–63 [reprinted in Momigliano, A. (1975). *Quinto contributo alla storia degli studi classici e del mondo antico* I. Rome: 511–530].

—— (1942). 'Terra marique', *JRS* 32: 53–64 [reprinted in Momigliano, A. (1960). *Secondo contributo alla storia degli studi classici e del mondo antico*. Rome: 431–446].

—— (1945). 'The Locrian Maidens and the Date of Lycophron's *Alexandra*', *CQ* 39: 49–53 [reprinted in Momigliano, A. (1960). *Secondo contributo alla storia degli studi classici e del mondo antico*. Rome: 446–453].

Momigliano Lepschy, A. L. (1966). *Viaggio in Terrasanta di Santo Brasca, 1480. Con l'itinerario di Gabriele Capodilista, 1458*. Milan.

Monaco, M. C. (2023). 'Synecism as a Divide? Cults of the Rhodian Cities: Ancient Hypotheses, New Perspectives', in Stefanakis et al. (2023): 126–134.

Mooney, G. W. (1921). *The Alexandra of Lycophron with English Translation and Explanatory Notes*. London.

Moorhead, S. (2007). 'Small Colossus', *British Museum Magazine* 57: 40–42.

Morelli, D. (1959). 'I culti in Rodi', *SCO* 8: 1–184.

Moreno, P. (1973–1974). 'Cronologia del Colosso di Rodi', *ArchClass* 25–26: 453–463.

—— (1974). *Lisippo. Volume primo*. Bari.

—— (1977). 'Da Lisippo alla scuola di Rodi', in R. Bianchi Bandinelli (ed.), *Storia e civiltà dei Greci X. La cultura ellenistica. Le arti figurative*. Milan: 412–460.

—— (1990). 'La fase ellenistica della produzione di Lisippo ed il Colosso di Rodi', in *Akten des XIII. Internationalen Kongresses für klassische Archäologie, Berlin 1988*. Berlin: 343–344.

—— (1994a). 'Colosso di Rodi', *Enciclopedia dell'arte antica* II. Supplemento. Rome: 240–242.

—— (1994b). *Scultura ellenistica*. Rome.

—— (1995a). 'Colosso di Zeus a Taranto', in Moreno (1995b): 278–280.

—— (ed.) (1995b). *Lisippo: l'arte e la fortuna*. Milan.

—— (1999). 'La nuova ricostruzione del Colosso e la personificazione del Demo di Rodi', in AA.VV. (1999): 193–200.

—— (2004). 'Lysippos (I)', in Vollkommer (2004): 27–39.

—— (2013). 'Lisippo nell'ep. 62 AB del nuovo Posidippo', in Angiò (2013): 47–53.

Moretti, L. (1953). *Iscrizione agonistiche greche*. Rome.

—— (1957). '*Olympionikai*, i vincitori negli antichi agoni olimpici', *Memorie/Atti della Accademia Nazionale dei Lincei, Classe di Scienze Morali, Storiche e Filologiche* [s. 8] 8: 57–198 [reprinted in M. E. Barraco and I. Soda (eds.) (2014). *Luigi Moretti e il catalogo degli Olympionikai. Testimonianze epigrafiche, letterarie, papirologiche e numismatiche sui vincitori degli agoni olimpici panellenici (Ellade e Magna Grecia: 776 a.C.–393 d.C.)*. Rome: 23–166].

Morricone, L. (1949–1951). 'I sacerdoti di Halios. Frammento di catalogo rinvenuto a Rodi', *ASAA* 27–29 [n.s. 11–13]: 351–380.

—— (1965). 'Rodi', *Enciclopedia dell'arte antica* VI. Rome: 743–754.

Müller, H. P. (2001). 'Chaireas (I)', in Vollkommer (2001): 130–131.

Müller, K. O. (1848). *Handbuch der Archäologie der Kunst*. Breslau.

Muller-Dufeu, M. (2004). *La sculpture grecque. Sources littéraires et épigraphiques*. Paris.

Münster, S. (1545). *Cosmographia. Beschreibung aller Lender [...]*. Basel.

Münzer, F. (1897). *Beiträge zur Quellenkritik der Naturgeschichte des Plinius*. Berlin.
Musti, D., and Pulcini, B. (1996). 'La fiaccola della *Demokratia* e la statua della *Libertà*', *RCCM* 38: 289–308.
Neger, M. (2014). '*"Graece numquid" ait "poeta nescis?"* Martial and the Greek Epigrammatic Tradition', in A. Angoustakis (ed.), *Flavian Poetry and Its Greek Past*. Leiden, Boston: 327–344.
Neils, J. (2010). 'Colossus', in M. Gagarin (ed.), *The Oxford Encyclopedia of Greece and Rome*. Oxford: 264–265.
Nercessian, A. (2004). 'Offrandes alimentaires, encens, banquets', *ThesCRA* II: 438–439.
Neudecker, R. (1999). 'Kolossos', *Der Neue Pauly* VI: 670.
Newton, C. T. (1865). *Travels and Discoveries in the Levant* I. London.
Ng, S. F. (2019). *Alexander the Great from Britain to Southeast Asia. Peripheral Empires in the Global Renaissance*. Oxford.
Nielsen, T. H., and Gabrielsen, V. (2004). 'Rhodos', in M. H. Hansen and T. H. Nielsen (eds.), *An Inventory of Archaic and Classical 'Poleis': An Investigation Conducted by the Copenhagen Polis Centre for the Danish National Research Foundation*. Oxford: 1196–1210.
Nilsson, M. P. (1909). *Exploration archéologique de Rhodes (Fondation Carlsberg)* V. *Timbres amphoriques de Lindos, publiés avec une étude sur les timbres amphoriques rhodiens*. Copenhagen.
—— (1933). 'Sonnenkalender und Sonnenreligion', *ARW* 30: 141–173 [reprinted in Nilsson, M. P. (1952). *Opuscula Selecta* II. Lund: 462–504].
Nöth, M. (2019). 'Die Hafenfestung von Loryma', in W. Held (ed.), *Die Karische Chersones vom Chalkolithikum bis in die byzantinische Zeit. Beiträge zu den Surveys in Loryma und Bybassos*. Marburg: 177–295.
Ntantalia, F. (2001). 'Chares (II)', in Vollkommer (2001): 133–134.
Ntellas, G. (2007). 'Ἡ ἀρχιτεκτονική τῶν μεγάλων ιπποτικῶν ἐκκλησιῶν τῆς Ῥόδου. Παναγιά τοῦ Μπούργου, Παναγιά τοῦ Κάστρου, Ἅγιος Ἰωάννης', in AA.VV. (2007): 370–395.
Oliverio, G. (1928). 'Iscrizioni di Cirene', *RFIC* 56: 183–239.
—— (1933). 'La stele dei nuovi comandamenti e dei cereali', *Documenti antichi dell'Africa italiana* II. *Cirenaica* I. Bergamo: 7–94.
Omont, H. (1882). 'Les Sept Merveilles du Monde au Moyen-Âge', *BECh* 43: 40–59.
Osborne, G. R. (2002). *Revelation*. Grand Rapids, MI.
Osborne, R. (2009). *Greece in the Making: 1200–479 BC*. London, New York.
Overbeck, J. (1868). *Die antiken Schriftquellen zur Geschichte der bildenden Künste bei den Griechen*. Leipzig.
Pacht Bassani, P. (1993). *Claude Vignon: 1593–1670*. Paris.
Palagia, O. (2021). 'The Nike of Samothrace', in M. Lagogianni-Georgakarakos (ed.), *Known and Unknown Nikai in History, Art and Life*. Athens: 148–167.
Papachristodoulou, I. C. (1989). *Οἱ ἀρχαῖοι Ῥοδιακοί δῆμοι. Ἱστορική ἐπισκόπηση— Ἡ Ἰαλυσία*. Athens.
Papantonopoulos, C. (2006). 'Spanning Intervals: Towards Understanding the Ancient Greek Optimization Procedure for the Design of Horizontal Beams', in S. K. Kourkoulis (ed.), *Fracture and Failure of Natural Building Stones. Applications in the Restoration of Ancient Monuments*. Dordrecht: 257–268.
Papini, M. (2022). '*Inexplicabilis multitudo*: le statue in bronzo del IV-I. sec. a.C.', *ASAA* 100: 183–209.
Parker, R. (2004). 'New "Panhellenic" Festivals in Hellenistic Greece', in R. Schlesier and U. Zellmann (eds.), *Mobility and Travel in the Mediterranean from Antiquity to Middle Ages*. Münster: 9–22.

—— (2009). 'Subjection, Synoecism and Religious Life', in P. Funke and N. Luraghi (eds.), *The Politics of Ethnicity and the Crisis of the Peloponnesian League*. Washington, DC: 183–214.

Partida, E. (2017). 'Glorification of the Sun (Helios) at Delphi and Reflections on Some Architectural Remains on Mount Parnassos', in H. Frielinghaus and J. Stroszeck (eds.), *Kulte und Heiligtümer in Griechenland. Neue Funde und Forschungen*. Möhnesee: 207–231.

Patsiada, V. (2013). 'Η αρχιτεκτονική του τοπίου στην πόλη της Ρόδου', in Giannikouri (2013): 47–77.

Paul, S. (2015). 'Local Pantheons in Motion: Synoecism and Patron Deities in Hellenistic Rhodes', *CHS Research Bulletin* 2.3, online.

Perale, M. (2011). 'Simia e la testa del Sole: note esegetiche al fr. 4 Pow.', *Eikasmos* 22: 195–200.

Peter, H. W. G. (1906). *Historicorum Romanorum reliquiae* II. Leipzig.

Picard, C. (1933). 'Le cénotaphe de Midéa et les Colosses de Ménélas', *RPh* 59: 341–354.

—— (1936). 'Le rituel des suppliants trouvé à Cyrène et le champ des "colossoi" à Sélinonte', *RA* 8: 206–207.

—— (1943). 'Bulletin archéologique. Sculpture, statuaire: du IVe s. à la fin de l'ère hellénistique III. Époque hellénistique', *REG* 56: 169–234.

—— (1950). 'Un cénacle littéraire hellénistique sur deux vases d'argent du trésor de Berthouville-Bernay', *MMAI* 44: 53–82.

—— (1960). 'Les "Colossoi" de Dorak (Anatolie du Nord)', *RA*: 106–108.

—— (1963). *Manuel d'archéologie grecque. La sculpture* IV. *Période classique—IVe siècle (deuxième partie)*. Paris.

Piccolomini, E. S. [Pius II] (1534). *Cosmographia in Asiae et Europae descriptione*. Paris.

Picón, C. A., and Hemingway, S. (eds.) (2016). *Pergamon and the Hellenistic Kingdoms of the Ancient World*. New York.

Piel, T. (2010). 'À propos du Colosse de Rhodes: quelques considérations sur un monument commémoratif', in Faucherre and Pimouguet-Pédarros (2010): 135–156.

Piérard, C. (2000). 'Conclusions ou la signification de l'édition des *Chroniques de Hainaut* au milieu du XVe siècle', in P. Cockshaw and C. Van den Bergen-Pantens (eds.), *Les Chroniques de Hainaut ou les Ambitions d'un Prince bourguignon*. Turnhout: 169–175.

Piérart, M. (1990). 'Un oracle d'Apollon à Argos', *Kernos* 3: 319–333.

Pimouguet-Pédarros, I. (2011). *La cité à l'épreuve des rois. Le siège de Rhodes par Démétrios Poliorcète (305–304 av. J.-C.)*. Rennes.

Plassart, A. (1926). 'Fouilles de Thespies et de l'hiéron des Muses de l'Hélicon. Inscriptions', *BCH* 50: 383–462.

Pollitt, J. J. (1986). *Art in the Hellenistic Age*. Cambridge, London, New York, New Rochelle, Melbourne, Sydney.

—— (2000). 'The Phantom of a Rhodian School of Sculpture', in N. T. de Grummond and B. Sismondo Ridgway (eds.), *From Pergamon to Sperlonga. Sculpture and Context*. Berkeley, Los Angeles, London: 92–110.

Pouzadoux, C., and Prioux, É. (2009). 'Orient et Occident au miroir de l'*Alexandra* et de la céramique apulienne', in Cusset and Prioux (2009b): 451–485.

Powell, J. U. (1925). *Collectanea Alexandrina*. Oxford.

Préchac, F. (1919). 'Le Colosse de Rhodes', *RA* [s. 5] 9: 66–76.

Pressouyre, S. (1969). 'Les fontes de Primatice à Fontainebleau', *Bulletin monumental* 127: 223–239.

Prioux, É. (2007). *Regards alexandrins. Histoire et théorie des arts dans l'épigramme hellénistique*. Leuven, Paris, Dudley.

Prioux, É. (2017). 'Posidippe: l'évidence et l'occasion', in Linant de Bellefonds and Prioux (2017): 13–51.
Provoyeur, P. (1986a). 'Bartholdi et la tradition colossale', in AA.VV. (1986): 72–85.
—— (1986b). 'La construction', in AA.VV. (1986): 116–131.
—— (1986c). 'L'idée et la forme', in AA.VV. (1986): 86–109.
Pugliese Carratelli, G. (1939–1940). 'Per la storia delle associazioni in Rodi antica', *ASAA* 21–22 [n.s. 1–2]: 147–200.
—— (1950). 'Epigrafi rodie inedite', *PP* 5: 76–80.
—— (1951). 'La formazione dello stato rodio', *SCO* 1: 77–88.
—— (1952–1954). 'Supplemento epigrafico rodio', *ASAA* 30–32 [n.s. 14–16]: 247–316.
—— (1955–1956). 'Nuovo supplemento epigrafico rodio', *ASAA* 33–34 [n.s. 17–18]: 157–181.
—— (1967–1968). 'Supplemento epigrafico di Iasos', *ASAA* 45–46 [n.s. 29–30]: 437–486.
—— (1987). '*KYPHNAIKA*', *QAL* 12: 25–32.
Quantin, S., and Quantin, F. (2007). 'Le déplacement du temple d'Athéna Polias en Chaonie. Remarques sur les *cosiddetti* "temples voyageurs"', in D. Berragner-Auserve (ed.), *Épire, Illyrie, Macédoine... Mélanges offerts au professeur Pierre Cabanes*. Clermont-Ferrand: 175–196.
Queyrel, F. (2020). *La sculpture hellénistique. Royaumes et cités*. Paris.
Rackham, H. (1952). *Pliny: Natural History. Books 33–35*. Cambridge, MA.
Reinach, A. (1913). 'Notes tarentines I. Pyrrhus et la Niké de Tarente', *Neapolis. Rivista di archeologia, epigrafia e numismatica* 1: 19–29.
Reinach, S. (1905). 'Une statuette de bronze représentant Alexandre le Grand (Collection de M. Edmond de Rothschild)', *RA*: 32–43.
Reinach, T. (1897). [Review of Jex Blake, K. and Sellers, E. (1896). *The Early Pliny's Chapters on the History of Art*. London], *REG* 10: 119–120.
Rejna, I. (1823). *Memorie intorno il sagro monte e colosso di S. Carlo sopra Arona*. Novara.
Rice, E. E. (1993). 'The Glorious Dead. Commemoration of the Fallen and Portrayal of Victory in the Late Classical and the Hellenistic World', in J. Rich (ed.), *War and Society in the Greek World*. London, New York: 224–257.
Richter, G. M. A. (1960). *Kouroi. Archaic Greek Youths. A Study of the Development of the Kouros Type in the Greek Sculpture*. London.
—— (1968). *Korai. Archaic Greek Maidens. A Study of the Development of the Kore Type in Greek Sculpture*. London.
Rieger, N. F. (2004). 'Engineering Aspects of the Collapse of the Colossus of Rhodes Statue', in M. Ceccarelli (ed.), *International Symposium on History and Mechanisms. Proceedings HMM2004*. Dordrecht: 69–85.
Ringwood Arnold, I. (1936). 'Festivals of Rhodes', *AJA* 40: 432–436.
Robert, C. (1899). 'Chares 15', *RE* III.2: 2130–2131.
Roberts, S. (2016). 'From Crusade to Colossus: Rhodes in the Early Modern European Visual Imagination', in S. E. J. Gerstel (ed.), *Viewing Greece. Cultural and Political Agency in the Medieval and Early Modern Mediterranean*. Turnhout: 237–259.
Rocco, G. (1996a). 'Il tempio di Athana Polias e Zeus Polieus', in Livadiotti and Rocco (1996): 43–46.
—— (1996b). 'La città di Rodi. L'acropoli. Il tempio di Apollo Pizio. Il tempio di Artemide', in Livadiotti and Rocco (1996): 12–20.
Rocco, G., and Livadiotti, M. (2023). 'The Sanctuary of Zeus on Mt Atavyros, Rhodes: Some Preliminary Notes on Its Architecture', in Stefanakis et al. (2023): 220–231.
Roger, P. (1986). 'L'édifice du sens', in AA.VV. (1986): 282–289.

Rolley, C. (1981). 'Deux gorgones, deux problèmes. À propos de deux bronzes grecs du Louvre', *RLMF* 5/6: 323–330.

—— (2004). 'Les bronzes grecs et romains: recherches récentes', *RA*: 287–299.

Rollin, C. (1734). *Histoire ancienne des Égyptiens, des Carthaginois, des Assyriens, des Babyloniens, des Mèdes et des Perses, des Macédoniens, des Grecs*. Paris.

—— (1774). *De geschiedenis der waereld, vertoont in de lotgevallen der oude volken* IV. Amsterdam.

Romer, J., and Romer, E. (1995). *The Seven Wonders of the World. A History of the Modern Imagination*. New York.

Roosen, B. (1999). 'The Works of Nicetas Heracleensis (ὁ) τοῦ Σερρῶν', *Byzantion* 69: 119–144.

Rosamilia, E. (2014). 'Biblioteche a Rodi all'epoca di Timachidas', in Ampolo et al. (2014): 325–362.

—— (2018). 'From Magas to Glaukon. The Long Life of Glaukon of Aithalidai and the Chronology of Ptolemaic Re-Annexation of Cyrene (ca. 250 BCE)', *Chiron* 48: 263–300.

Ross, L. (1845). *Reisen auf den griechischen Inseln des ägäischen Meeres* III. Stuttgart, Tübingen.

Rottiers, B. E. A. (1830). *Description des monumens de Rhodes*. Brussels.

Roux, G. (1960). 'Qu'est-ce qu'un κολοσσός?', *REA* 62: 5–40.

Rowland, I. D. (2016). 'Three Seaside Wonders. Pharos, Mausoleum and Colossus', in M. M. Miles (ed.), *A Companion to Greek Architecture*. Chichester: 440–453.

Rutter, N. K. (2001). *Historia Numorum: Italy*. London.

Saiz Viadero, J. R. (2010). *Cuando Laredo fue Hollywood*. Santander.

Sassu, R. (2013). 'Culti primari e secondari nel santuario urbano di Metaponto', *Thiasos* 2: 3–18.

Scaliger, J.-J. (1606). 'Animadversiones in chronologica Eusebii', *Thesaurus temporum, Eusebii Pamphilii Caesareae Palaestinae episcopi, Chronicorum canonum omnimodae historiae libri duo, interprete Hieronymo*. Leiden: 1–278.

Schade, G. (1999). *Lykophrons 'Odysee'. Alexandra 648–819*. Berlin, New York.

Schedel, H. (1493a). *[Liber cronicarum]*. Nuremberg.

—— (1493b). *[Buch der cronicken und geschichten]*. Nuremberg.

Scheer, T. S. (2000). *Die Gottheit und ihr Bild. Untersuchungen zur Funktion griechischer Kultbilder in Religion und Politik*. Munich.

Schierup, S. (ed.) (2019). *Documenting Ancient Rhodes: Archaeological Expeditions and Rhodian Antiquities. Acts of the International Colloquium Held at the National Museum of Denmark in Copenhagen, February 16–17, 2017*. Aarhus.

Schmitt, H. H. (1957). *Rom und Rhodos. Geschichte ihrer politischen Beziehungen seit der ersten Berührung bis zum Aufgehen des Inselstaates im römischen Weltreich*. Munich.

Schott, H. (1891). *De septem orbis spectaculis quaestiones*. Ansbach.

Schreiber, T. (1903). *Studien über das Bildniss Alexanders des Grossen. Ein Beitrag zur alexandrinischen Kunstgeschichte mit einem Anhang über die Anfänge des Alexanderskultes*. Leipzig.

Schwartz, S. A. (1983). *The Alexandria Project*. New York.

Scrinzi, A. (1898–1899). 'Iscrizioni greche inedite di Rodi', *AIV* [s. 7] 57: 251–287.

Segre, M. (1935). 'Epigraphica I. Catalogo di libri da Rodi', *RFIC* 63 [n.s. 13]: 214–222.

Segre, M., and Pugliese Carratelli, G. (1949–1951). 'Tituli Camirenses', *ASAA* 27–29 [n.s. 11–13]: 141–318.

Seidensticker, B. (2015). '*Andriantopoiika* (62–70)', in Seidensticker et al. (2015): 247–282.

Seidensticker, B., Stähli, A., and Wessels, A. (eds.) (2015). *Der Neue Poseidipp. Text—Übersetzung—Kommentar*. Darmstadt.

Sekino, M. (1965). 'Restoration of the Great Buddha Statue at Kamakura', *Studies in Conservation* 10: 39–46.

Sekunda, N. (2004–2009). 'The Date and Circumstances of the Construction of the Fortifications at Phalasarna', *Horos* 17–21: 595–600.

Selivanov, S. A. [Селиванов, С. А.] (1892). *Ocherki drevnei topografii ostrova Rodosa* [Очерки древней топографии острова Родоса]. Kazan.

Sens, A., and Keesling, C. (2004). 'Posidippus on Rhodian Statue-Making (68.6 Austin-Bastianini; P.Mil.Vogl. VIII 309 XI 11), *ZPE* 148: 75–76.

Servais, J. (1965). 'Le "colosse" des Cypsélides', *AC* 34: 144–174.

Siebert, G. (1990). 'Hermes', *LIMC* V.1: 285–387.

Sillig, J. (1827). *Catalogus artificum sive Architecti statuarii sculptores pictores caelatores et scalptores Graecorum et Romanorum literarum ordine dispositi*. Dresden, Leipzig.

Simon, E. (1978). 'Apollo in Rom', *JDAI* 93: 220–227.

—— (1984). 'Apollo in Rom und Italien', *LIMC* II: 365–447.

Sinner, G. K. L. (1824). *Christophori Buondelmonti Florentini Liber Insularum Archipelagi*. Leipzig, Berlin.

Sismondo Ridgway, B. (1996) [Review of Moreno, P. (1994). *Scultura ellenistica*. Rome], *AJA* 100: 426–427.

—— (2001). *Hellenistic Sculpture I. The Styles of ca. 331—200 B.C.* Madison.

—— (2004). [Review of Hoepfner, W. (2003). *Der Koloss von Rhodos und die Bauten des Helios. Neue Forschungen zu einem der Sieben Weltwunder*. Mainz], *BMCRev* 2004.01.25.

Skaltsa, S. (2021). 'Building Projects in the Rhodian State: Local Dynamics and Interrelations', in B. Poulsen, P. Pedersen, and J. Lund (eds.), *Karia and the Dodekanese. Cultural Interrelations in the Southeast Aegean* II. *Early Hellenistic to Early Byzantine*. Oxford, Philadelphia: 155–173.

—— (2022). 'A First Overview of the Rhodian Stamped Handles from a Public Monumental Building in Rhodes: Context, Chronology and Function', in M. L. Lawall (ed.), *Archaeology and Economy in the Ancient World. Proceedings of the 19th International Congress of Classical Archaeology: Panel 6.6. Assemblages of Transport Amphoras: from Chronology to Economics and Society. Propylaeum* 36: 55–2371.

Smith, R. R. R. (1991). *Hellenistic Sculpture. A Handbook*. New York.

—— (2000). 'Nero and the Sun-God: Divine Accessories and Political Symbols in Roman Imperial Images', *JRA* 13: 532–542.

Spieser, M. (2017a). 'Réflexions sur l'abandon de la statuaire dans l'Antiquité tardive', in L. Canetti (ed.), *Rituali, scienza e magia dalla Tarda Antichità al Rinascimento*. Florence: 123–144.

—— (2017b). 'La "Renaissance macédonienne": de son invention à sa mise en cause', in B. Flusin and J.-C. Cheynet, *Autour du Premier humanisme byzantine et de Cinq études sur le* XIe *siècle, quarante ans après Paul Lemerle*. Paris: 43–52.

Sprague de Camp, L. (1963² [1960¹]). *The Bronze God of Rhodes*. New York.

Staffieri, G. M. (1996). '"ΕΙC ΖΕΥC CΑΡΑΠΙC" su una dramma alessandrina inedita', *Annotazioni numismatiche* 25: 255–269.

—— (1997). 'Il "Colosso di Rodi": un nuovo riscontro numismatico', *Annotazioni numismatiche* 27: 612–620.

Stark, K. B. (1864). 'König Maussollos und das Mausoleum von Halikarnass', *Eos. Süddeutsche Zeitschrift für Philologie und Gymnasialwesen* 1: 345–400 [reprinted in Stark, K. B. (1864). *Vorträge und Aufsätze aus dem Gebiete der Archäologie und Kunstgeschichte*. Leipzig: 174–217, 456–477].

Stefanakis, M. I., Mavroudis, G., and Seroglou, F. K. (eds.) (2023). *Religion and Cult in the Dodecanese during the First Millenium BC. Proceedings of the International Archaeological Conference.* Oxford.
Steiner, D. (1995). 'Eyeless in Argos: A Reading of *Agamemnon* 416-19', *JHS* 115: 175-182.
―― (2001). *Images in Mind. Statues in Archaic and Classical Greek Literature and Thought.* Princeton, Oxford.
Stendhal [Beyle, H.] (1817). *Histoire de la peinture en Italie* II. Paris.
Stewart, A. F. (1990). *Greek Sculpture. An Exploration.* New Haven, London.
―― (1993). *Faces of Power. Alexander's Image and Hellenistic Politics.* Berkeley, Los Angeles, Oxford.
―― (2005). 'Posidippus and the Truth in Sculpture', in K. Gutzwiller (ed.), *The New Posidippus. A Hellenistic Poetry Book.* Oxford: 183-205.
―― (2016). 'The Nike of Samothrace: Another View', *AJA* 120: 399-410.
Stritt, M. (2004). *Die schöne Helena in den Romruinen. Überlegungen zu einem Gemälde Maarten van Heemskercks.* Frankfurt am Main.
Strocka, V. M. (2007). 'Poseidippos von Pella und die Anfänge der griechischen Kunstgeschichtsschreibung', *Klio* 89: 332-345.
Stroud, R. S. (1984). 'An Argive Decree from Nemea Concerning Aspendos', *Hesperia* 53: 193-216.
Sturgeon, M. C. (1987). *Isthmia* IV. *Sculpture* 1: *1952-1967*. Princeton.
Sydenham, E. A. (1916). 'The Coinage of Nero. An Introductory Study', *NC*: 13-36.
Sztetyłło, Z. (1966a). 'Quelques problèmes relatifs à l'iconographie des timbres amphoriques. La représentation des statues', *Études et travaux* 3: 46-80.
―― (1966b). 'Quelques remarques en marge des études sur l'iconographie des timbres amphoriques grecs', in M. L. Bernhard (ed.), *Mélanges offerts à Kazimierz Michałowski*. Warsaw: 663-669.
Talansier, C. (1883). 'La statue de la Liberté éclairant le monde', *Le génie civil* 3.19: 461-471.
Themelis, P. (1998). 'Attic Sculpture at Kallipolis (Aitolia). A Cult Group of Demeter and Kore', in O. Palagia and W. Coulson (eds.), *Regional Schools in Hellenistic Sculpture. Proceedings of an International Conference Held at the American School of Classical Studies at Athens, March 15-17, 1996.* Oxford: 47-59.
Thevet, A. (1554). *Cosmographie de Levant.* Lyon.
―― (1575). *Cosmographie universelle* I. Paris.
Thieme, T. (1988). 'The Canon of Pliny for the Colossus of Rhodes and the Statue of Athena Parthenos', in S. Dietz and I. Papachristodoulou (eds.), *Archaeology in the Dodecanese.* Copenhagen: 164-168.
Thieme, U. (ed.) (1912). *Allgemeines Lexikon der bildenden Künstler* VI. Leipzig.
Thobie, J. (2004). *L'administration générale des phares de l'empire ottoman et la société Collas et Michel (1860-1960). Un siècle de cooperation économique et financière entre la France, l'Empire ottoman et les États successeurs.* Paris.
Thurn, J., Meier, M., Drosihn, C., Priwitzer, S., and Enderle, K. (2019). *Johannes Malalas, Weltchronik.* Stuttgart.
Toishi, K. (1965). 'Radiography of the Great Buddha at Kamakura', *Studies in Conservation* 10: 47-52.
Torr, C. (1885). *Rhodes in Ancient Times.* Cambridge.
―― (1887). *Rhodes in Modern Times.* Cambridge.
Trachtenberg, M. (1976). *The Statue of Liberty.* London.
Tréheux, J. (2023). *Études critiques sur les inventaires de l'indépendance délienne.* Athens.

Triantafyllidis, P. (2017). 'Η αρχαιολογική έρευνα στο παρροδιακό ιερό του Αταβυρίου', in P. Triantafyllidis (ed.), Το αρχαιολογικό έργο στα νησιά του Αιγαίο. Διεθνές επιστημονικό συνέδριο, Ρόδος, 27 Νοεμβρίου - 1 Δεκεμβρίου 2013 III. Mytilene: 553–563.
Triantafyllidis, P., Rocco, G., and Livadiotti, M. (2017). 'Il santuario di Zeus sul monte Atabyros a Rodi: note preliminari', Scienze dell'Antichità 23: 275–289.
Turner, W. (1820). *Journal of a Tour in the Levant*. London.
Uhlenbrock, J. P. (2015). 'Heirlooms, *Aphidrumata*, and the Foundation of Cyrene', in S. Huysecom-Haxhi and A. Muller (eds.), *Figurines grecques en contexte. Présence muette dans le sanctuaire, la tombe et la maison*. Villeneuve d'Ascq: 143–156.
Ullrich, K. H. (1898). *De Polybii fontibus Rhodiis*. Leipzig.
Urlichs, L. (1857). *Chrestomathia Pliniana*. Berlin.
Valavanis, P. D. (1999a). 'Βαλβίδες και ύσπληγες του σταδίου της Ρόδου', in AA.VV. (1999): 95–108.
—— (1999b). *Hysplex. The Starting Mechanism in Ancient Stadia. A Contribution to Ancient Greek Technology*. Berkeley, Los Angeles, London.
Valentini, R., and Zucchetti, G. (1940). *Codice topografico della Città di Roma*. Rome.
Van Bremen, R. (2009). 'Networks of Rhodians in Karia', in I. Malkin, C. Constantakopoulou, and K. Panagopoulou (eds.), *Greek and Roman Networks in the Mediterranean*. London, New York: 109–128.
Van Buren, A. H. (1972). 'New Evidence for Jean Wauquelin's Activity in the *Chroniques de Hainaut* and for the Date of the Miniatures', *Scriptorium* 26: 249–268.
Van de Passe, C. (1614). *Admiranda et prodigiosa antiquitatis opera, quae septem orbis miracula vulgo vocantur*. Utrecht.
Van Driessche, V. (2009). *Études de métrologie grecque I. Des étalons pré-monétaires au monnayage en bronze*. Louvain-la-Neuve.
Van Gelder, H. (1900). *Geschichte der alten Rhodier*. The Hague.
Van Grätz [Gratius] (1535). *Fasciculus rerum expetendarum ac fugiendarum* [...]. Cologne.
Van Hall, E. (1941). *Over den oorsprong van de grieksche grafstele*. Amsterdam.
Van Meurs [Meursius], J. (1675). *Rhodus*. Amsterdam.
Vedder, U. (1999–2000). 'Der Koloss von Rhodos. Mythos und Wirklichkeit eines Weltwunders', *Nürnberger Blätter zur Archäologie* 16: 23–40.
—— (2003). 'Der Koloss von Rhodos als Wächter über dem Hafeneingang', in Kunze (2003): 131–149.
—— (2006a). 'A Latin Grand Master, a Greek Philosopher, and the Colossus of Rhodes', in C. C. Mattusch, A. A. Donohue, and A. Brauer (eds.), *Common Ground: Archaeology, Art, Science and Humanities. The Proceedings of the 16th International Congress of Classical Archaeology*. Oxford: 151–153.
—— (2006b). 'Das kolossale Weihgeschenk aus der Kriegsbeute und das Heiligtum des Helios in Rhodos', in N. Kreutz and B. Schweizer (eds.), *Tekmeria. Archäologische Zeugnisse in ihrer kulturhistorischen und politischen Dimension: Beiträge für Werner Gauer*. Münster: 361–370.
—— (2010). 'Plinius der Ältere, die Zahl LVI und der Koloss von Rhodos', *AA*: 39–45.
—— (2015). *Der Koloss von Rhodos. Archäologie, Herstellung und Rezeptionsgeschichte eines antiken Weltwunders*. Mainz.
—— (2017). 'Was the Colossus of Rhodes Cast in Courses or in Large Sections?', in J. M. Daehner, K. Lapatin, and A. Spinelli (eds.), *Artistry in Bronze. The Greeks and Their Legacy. XIX*[th] *International Congress on Ancient Bronzes*. Los Angeles: 21–27.
Vernant, J.-P. (1965). *Mythe et pensée chez les Grecs: études de psychologie historique*. Paris [English translation: Vernant, A. (1983). *Myth and Thought Among the Greeks*. London, Boston, Melbourne, Sydney].

—— (1990). *Figures, idoles, masques*. Paris.
Vine, B. (2006). 'Autour de sud-picénien qolofítúr', in G.-J. Pinault and D. Petit (eds.), *La langue poétique indo-européenne. Actes du colloque de travail de la Société des études indo-européennes (Indogermanische Gesellschaft/Society for Indo-European Studies), Paris, 22-24 octobre 2003*. Paris: 499–515.
Vollkommer, R. (ed.) (2001). *Künstlerlexikon der Antike* 1. Munich, Leipzig.
—— (2004). *Künstlerlexikon der Antike* 2. Munich, Leipzig.
Von Hammer-Purgstall J. (1811). *Topographische Ansichten gesammelt auf einer Reise in die Levante*. Vienna.
Von Wilamowitz-Möllendorff, U. (1883). 'Phaeton', *Hermes* 18: 396–434.
—— (1922). *Pindaros*. Berlin.
—— (1925). 'Grammatische Erscheinungen', in Ferri (1925): 38–40.
—— (1927). 'Heilige Gesetze: eine Urkunde aus Kyrene', *Sitzungsberichte der Preussischen Akademie der Wissenschaften. Philosophisch-historische Klasse* 19: 155–176.
—— (1931). *Der Glaube der Hellenen* I. Berlin.
Walbank, F. W. (1942). 'Alcaeus of Messene, Philip V, and Rome', *CQ* 36: 134–145.
Weitzmann, K. (1984² [1951¹]). *Greek Mythology in Byzantine Art*. Princeton.
West, S. (1984). 'Lycophron Italicised', *JHS* 104: 127–151.
Wiemer, H.-U. (2001). *Rhodische Traditionen in der hellenistischen Historiographie*. Frankfurt am Main.
—— (2002). *Krieg, Handel und Piraterie. Untersuchungen zur Geschichte des hellenistischen Rhodos*. Berlin.
—— (2010). 'Structure and Development of the Rhodian Peraia: Evidence and Models', in R. van Bremen and J.-M. Carbon (eds.), *Hellenistic Karia. Proceedings of the First International Conference on Hellenistic Karia—Oxford, 29 June-2 July 2006*. Bordeaux: 415–434.
—— (2011). 'Early Hellenistic Rhodes: The Struggle for Independence and the Dream of Hegemony', in A. Erskine and L. Llewellyn-Jones (eds.), *Creating a Hellenistic World*. Swansea: 123–146.
—— (2013). 'Zeno of Rhodes and the Rhodian View of the Past', in B. Gibson and T. Harrison (eds.), *Polybius and His World. Essays in Memory of F. W. Walbank*. Oxford: 279–306.
Will, É. (1979²). *Histoire politique du monde hellénistique (323–30 av. J.-C)* I. *De la mort d'Alexandre aux avènements d'Antiochos III et de Philippe V*. Nancy.
Williamson, G. (2005). 'Mucianus and a Touch of Miraculous: Pilgrimage and Tourism in Roman Asia Minor', in J. Elsner and I. Rutherford (eds.), *Pilgrimage in Graeco-Roman and Early Christian Antiquity*. Oxford: 219–252.
Winkel, M. (2005). 'A Flier for the Aphrodisiacal Ointment *Chōmeigan*', in C. Uhlenbeck and M. Winkel, *Japanese Erotic Fantasies. Sexual Imagery of the Edo Period*. Amsterdam: 199–201.
Wittek, M. (2000). 'L'inscription du Colosse de Rhodes: essai de déchiffrement et d'interprétation', in P. Cockshaw and C. Van den Bergen-Pantens (eds.), *Les Chroniques de Hainaut ou les ambitions d'un prince bourguignon*. Turnhout: 57–60.
Witulski, T. (2011). 'Implizite Polemik durch Parallelisierung. Der ἄλλος ἄγγελος ἰσχυρός (Apk 10,1 f.5), der Gott Helios und der Koloss von Rhodos', in O. Wischmeyer and L. Scornaienchi (eds.), *Polemik in der frühchristlichen Literatur. Texte und Kontexte*. Berlin: 543–575.
Woods, D. (2016). 'On the Alleged Destruction of the Colossus c. 653', *Byzantion* 86: 441–451.

Wriedt Sørensen, L. (2019). 'The Colossus of Rhodes: A Powerful Enigma', in Schierup (2019): 15-34.
Wuilleumier, P. (1939). *Tarente, des origines à la conquête romaine*. Paris.
Wujewski, T. (2018). 'Kolos Rodyjski: gdzie stał I jak był wykonany', *Artium quaestiones* 29: 289-320.
Zangger, E. (2018). 'James Mellaart's Fantasies', *Talanta* 50: 125-182.
Zervoudaki, I. (1975). '"Ηλιος και Ἁλίεια', *AD* 30: 1-20.
Zielinski, S., and Weibel, P. (eds.) (2015). *Allah's Automata. Artifacts of the Arab-Islamic Renaissance (800-1200)*. Ostfildern.
Zimmer, G. (1990). *Griechische Bronzegusswerkstätten. Zur Technologieentwicklung eines antiken Kunsthandwerkes*. Mainz.
Zimmer, G., and Bairami, K. (2008). Ροδιακά εργαστήρια χαλκοπλαστικής. Athens.
Żybert, E. (2016). [Review of Hornblower, S. (2018). *Lykophron's* Alexandra, Rome, and the Hellenistic World. Oxford], *Eos* 103: 381-384.

INDEXES

Literary Sources

[Aeschines] *Epistulae* 10 104
Aeschylus *Agamemenon* 282 33
    404–419 21–24, 26, 28, 31–34, 46, 50
    689 33
Agapius *Kitāb al-'unwān* (Vassiliev) p. 482 69
Alcaeus Messenius, Gow–Page, *HE*, I 97–103,
    105, 107–108, 120, 222
Al-Masʿūdī *Murūj aḏ-Ḏahab wa-Maʿādin
    al-Jawhar* (De Meynard and De
    Courteille) II, pp. 433, 435 171
Alpheus *apud Anth. Pal.* 9.526 98
Ampelius *Liber memorialis* 8.19 73
Anastasius Bibliothecarius *Historia tripertita*
    (De Boor) p. 216 69, 72
Androtion *FGrH* 324, F46 12
Anthologia Palatina 16.6 (Anonymous) 98
    6.171 (Anonymous) 92, 96–108, 126, 151,
        153, 157, 168, 200–202
    8.177 (Gregorius Nazianzenus) 94
    9.58 (Antipater) 94
    9.518 (Alcaeus Messenius) 98, 107
    9.526 (Alpheus) 98
    9.656 (Anonymous) 95
    9.682 (Anonymous) 25
Anthologia Planudea 82 53–54, 63, 73, 78,
    93, 99, 101
Antipater, Gow–Page, *GP*, XCI 94
[Apollodorus] 1.2.2 9
    3.2.1 7
Appianus Ἀννιβαϊκή 31 113
    Μιθριδάτειος 103–104 7
Aristophanes Byzantius frag. (Slater) 19 113
Aristotle frag. (Rose) 569 11
Aristides *Orationes* (Behr) 24.27 6
    25.53 67, 132–133
Arrianus *Anabasis* 2.20.2 58
Athenaeus 2.30 59
    7.47 14
Athenaeus Mechanicus 27 107
Aulus Gellius 15.31 14

[Beda Venerabilis] *De septem miraculis huius
    mundi* 73, 78

Callimachus *Aetia* frag. (Pfeiffer / Massimilia)
    106–107 / 209–210 115
    Iambi 53
Cassius Dio 47.33.6 59, 77, 141
    65.15.1 68
    73.22.3 68
    frag. 41 115
Chronicon Paschale I (Dindorf) p. 331 65
    p. 464 67
    p. 476 68
    p. 492 68
Clemens Alexandrinus *Stromateis* 5.50.2 116
Codex Theodosianus 16.1.2 67
Constantinus Porphyrogenitus,
    CIG IV, 8703 25
    De administrando imperio 20 69
        21 54, 73, 78, 93, 99, 210
Cosmas Hierosolymitanus, *Commentarii in
    Gregorii Nazianzeni carmina* (Lozza)
    p. 216 22, 71
    p. 226 22
Curtius Rufus, Q. 4.5.9 58
    4.8.12 58
Cyrillus *Adversus Iulianum* (Brüggemann,
    Kinzing, and Riedweg) 3.22 7

Daniel 2:31–45 70–71, 73, 94, 220
Dio Chrysostomus 31.86 47
Diodorus Siculus 1.46.1 21, 51
    5.59.2–3 7
    9.19.1 87
    11.72.2 21, 51
    13.38.5 6, 12
    13.45.1 12
    13.75.1 7
    16.33.1 21
    18.8.1 58
    19.45.4 145
    20.83.4 104
    20.91.4 107
    20.91.5 107
    20.100.2–4 66
    20.100.3–4 162

Dionysius Halicarnassensis *Antiquitates Romanae* 20.14 115
  20.15 119
Dionysius Rhodius *FGrHist* 511 T1 161

Epistle to the Colossians 156
Epitoma rerum gestarum Alexandri magni cum Libro de morte testamentoque Alexandri (Thomas) 107–108 108
Etymologicum Magnum, s.v. Ἠλύσιον πεδίον 144
Eusebius *Chronica* II (Schoene) pp. 87–88 19
  p. 118 94
  pp. 122–123 21, 65
  p. 158 67
  p. 159 78
  p. 174 68
Eustathius *Commentarii ad Homeri Odysseam* 6.266 161
  12.350 113
  Commentarii in Dionysium Periegetem 504 67, 73, 156
Eutropius 2.15 115
Excerpta Vaticana (Festa) p. 89 73

Georgius Cedrenus *Compendium historiarum* I (Bekker) p. 377 67, 73
  p. 755 54, 69, 73, 78
Georgius Monachus *Chronica* (de Boor) p. 285 156
Georgius Syncellus (Mosshammer) p. 417 67
  p. 433 68
Gregorius Nazianzenus *Epigrammata* (*PG* XXXVIII) 1 22, 94
  50 94
  Orationes (Bernardi) 43 22, 94, 163
  Scholia Alexandrina in orationes Gregorii Nazianzeni (Brodersen) 73, 167
Gregorius Turonensis *De cursu stellarum ratio* (Arndt and Krusch) p. 859 93

Hellenica Oxyrhynchia (Bartoletti) 15.2 12
Herodianus 1.15.9 68
Herodotus 1.144 10
  2.130–131 21, 28–30
  2.131 29
  2.132 29
  2.143 21, 28–30
  2.149 21, 28–30
  2.153 21, 28–30
  2.175 24, 28–30, 50
  2.176 21, 28–30
  2.178 10
  4.152 23, 28–30, 35

  4.159 36
  7.99 176
  8.68–69 176
  8.87–88 176
  8.93 176
  8.101–103 176
  8.107 176
Hero Mechanicus *Definitiones* 135.13 50
Hesiodus *Theogonia* 956–957 9, 11
Hesychius s.v. Ἄβαντες 22–23, 26, 44, 46
  Onomatologus 115–116
Hieronymus frag. (Wehrli) 48 59
Historia Augusta, Commodus, 17.9–10 68
  Hadrianus, 19.12 68, 72, 74
Homerus *Ilias* 2.653–656 6
  2.655–656 41
  2.657–670 6
  2.668 41
  2.668–670 7
  2.669 6, 9
  5.336 112
  Odyssea 10.135–139 11
  11.109 14
  11.312 102
  12.132–133 11
  20.71 102
[Hyginus] *Fabulae* 223 73

Isidorus *Etymologiae* 14.6.22 73
Isigonus *FHG* IV, p. 435, no. 4 7

Joannes Malalas (Dindorf) p. 149 71, 156
  p. 279 68, 205, 220
Josephus *Bellum Judaicum* 1.413–414 50
  1.424 143, 145, 147
Justinus *Epitome* 11.11.1 58
  18.2.9 115
Juvenalis 8.230 168

Lactantius *Divinae institutiones* 1.22 7
Landolfus Sagax *Historia miscella* 19.4 69
Liber Pontificalis 137.3 (Duchesne I, p. 346) 71
Livius 9.30.3–4 119
  21.48.9 113
  24.45.1 113
  26.38.6 113
  Per. 14 115
[Longinus] 36.3 94
Lucianus *Amores* 8 145
  Gallus 24 88
  Icaromenippus 12 210
    12 (*scholia*) 56
  Juppiter tragoedus 11 89
  Verae historiae 1.8 131

Lycophron *Alexandra* 592–631 112
  615 24
  615 (*scholia*) 45
  615–618 45–46
  1226 (*scholia*) 111
  1226–1280 44, 108
  1435–1450 44, 108
  1441 109
  1444 109
  1446 109
  Telegonus 116

Manuel Philes *Carmina* (Miller) p. 23,
    XLIV 156
Martialis 1.70 78
Menecles Barcaeus *FGrHist* 270 F6 37
Michael the Syrian *Chronicle* IV (Chabot),
    p. 430a 69
  p. 526b 69
Mnaseas Patarensis *FHG* III, p. 151, no. 12 14

Nicephorus Gregoras *Historia Romana* 22.6
    (Bekker III, pp. 13–18) 157
Nicetas Heracleensis *Commentarii in XVI
    orationes Gregorii Nazianzeni*
    (Constantinescu) 67 22, 73, 167
[Nonnus] *Scholia mythologica in orationes
    Gregorii Nazianzeni* (Nimmo
    Smith) 18 163–164

Paulus Diaconus *Historia
    Langobardorum* 5.11 71
  5.13 71
Pausanias 2.31.5 202
  2.36.4 11
  3.14.3 37
  3.23.2–5 33
  4.24.2 11
  5.17.4 62
  5.20.10 62
  6.7.1–3 11
  6.7.2 11–12
  6.7.4 12
  6.7.6 12
  10.9.9 14
Philo *De Josepho* 39 51
  De Opificio Mundi 6 51
  Legatio ad Gaium 118 51
    203 51
    306 51
    337 51
[Philo Byzantius] (Brodersen) pp. 20–36 94
  p. 30 21, 42, 73, 90, 92–93
  pp. 30–32 80–82

p. 32 25, 75, 88, 92, 107, 129, 132, 143, 145,
    147, 159, 161, 172, 202
p. 34 92
Philostratus *Vita Apollonii* 5.21 68
Photius *s.v.* Κυψελιδῶν ἀνάθεμα ἐν Ὀλυμπίᾳ 22
Pindarus *Olympian Odes* 5.10 (*scholia*) 38
  5.124 (*scholia*) 38
  7 inscr. 11
  7.13–14 11
  7.15–17 11
  7.19 6
  7.21 11
  7.35–53 14
  7.36 (*scholia*) 11, 13
  7.39–76 11
  7.58 15
  7.73–74 14
  7.77–80 13
  7.78 103
  7.80–87 11
  7.87–88 7, 12
  7.101 (*scholia*) 11
  7.146 (*scholia*) 11
  7.147 (*scholia*) 11, 159
  7.159 (*scholia*) 9
  7.160 (*scholia*) 7
  Pythian Odes 4 and 5 37
Plato *Phaedrus* 236b 22
  Philebus 15 (*scholia*) 153
Plinius *Naturalis Historia* 1.34a 50
  2.62 187
  5.31 172
  7.126 14
  34.39 50, 77, 91
  34.40 75, 77
  34.41 1, 54, 64–65, 77, 89, 92, 106, 133, 165
  34.42–43 50
  34.44 83
  34.45 50
  34.45–47 77
  34.46 91
  34.51 61
  34.63 59
  34.75 61
  35.104 14
  36.26 187
Plutarchus *De daedalis Plataeensibus*
    frag. 10 33
  Moralia
    Ad principem ineruditum 2 779F 50
      779F–780A 127
      780A 82, 127
    *An vitiositas ad infelicitatem
      sufficiat* 498E 50

Plutarchus (*cont.*)
　Vitae parallelae
　　Aemilius Paulus 32.4 50
　　Alexander 32.6 59
　　Demetrius 20.9 101, 133
　　　21.1.4 107
　　　22 14
　　Fabius Maximus 22.8 50
　　Lucullus 37.4 50
　　Themistocles 21 6
Polybius 3.21–27 118
　3.30.1 119
　5.70.6 7
　5.88.1 21, 65, 145, 153, 155
　5.88.1–2 46–47
　5.88.3 90
　5.88.8 132–133
　5.88–89 153
　9.27 9
　15.23.3 139
　16.8 107
　16.15.8 139
　18.16.2 50
　20.5.7 65
　21.24.10 6
　29.11.6 139
　30.5.6 117
　31.4.4 50, 86
Posidippus *Epigrams* (AB) 62 44, 196
　68 43–44, 52–53, 56, 87, 93

Revelation 10:1 73
　10:1–8 68, 208
Rhetorica ad Herennium 4.9 55

[Scylax] 99 104
Sextus Empiricus *Adversus mathematicos*
　7.107–108 63
Simias frag. (Powell) 4 93, 210
Sopater frag. (Kaibel) 1 24, 47
Stephanus Byzantius *s.v.* Ἀταβύριον 7, 9
　s.v. Κρητινία 7
Strabo 1.1.23 51
　4.4.5 50
　5.2.5 118
　6.3.1 47, 50, 56
　7.6.1 50
　12.5.2 50
　14.1.14 51
　14.2.5 53, 67, 78, 92, 155
　14.2.12 7
　14.18 87

　14 [*Chr.* 18] 53, 73
Suda, *s.v.* Διονύσιος Μουσωνίου 161
　s.v. Κολοσσαεῖς 96
　s.v. Κολοσσαεύς 66, 92
　s.v. Λύκος 115–116
　s.v. Λυκόφρων 110
　s.v. Ῥόδος 156
　s.v. Σεβαστιανός 94
　s.v. Φάρος 94
Suetonius *Nero* 31 74, 78
　Divus Vespasianus 18 68

Theocritus *Idylls* 22.47 22
Theophanes Confessor *Chronographia* (De Boor)
　p. 345 69
Thucydides 1.94 6
　1.98.4 12
　1.100–101 12
　2.14.4 104
　2.62.2 104
　3.8.1 12
　7.57.6 6
　8.35.1 12
　8.44 6, 12
　8.84.2 12
Timachidas *FGrH* 532 F1.17 36
Timaeus *FGrH* 566 F39a 7, 9
Timocreon *PMG* 727 6
Tzetzes *Ad Lycophronem* (Scheer)
　p. 4 115
　Historiarum variarum Chiliades
　4.392–396 7
　4.703–705 7
　8.474 115

Valerius Maximus 1.5.8 59, 77
　4.3.9 115
Vibius Sequester, *Appendix* 73
Vitruvius *De architectura* 2.8.14–15 176
　7, *praef.* 14 62
　10.16.4 101, 107
　10.16.8.3–5 133

Xenophon *Hellenica* 1.1.2 12
　1.5.19 12
Xenophon Ephesius 1.12.2 161
　5.10–11 161
　5.10.6 161
　5.11.2–5.12.2 161–162

Zonaras *Annales* 8.6 115
　14.19 69

Papyri

P. Berol. 13044 94
P. Lond. VII 1986 115
P. Mil. Vogl. VIII 309 43, 77

P. Oxy. 2.222 (*FGrH* 415 F2) 11
P. Oxy. 5.842 (*FGrH* 66 F1.1) 12

Other Manuscripts

Bamberg, Staatsbibliothek
   Msc. Class. 42 66–67, 78
Brussels, Bibliothèque royale (KBR)
   9242–9244 164–165

Florence, Biblioteca Medicea Laurenziana
   Codex Laurentianus IV 13 167
   Codex Laurentianus VII 8 167

Jerusalem, Greek Patriarchal Library
   Codex Taphou 14 163–164, 166, 171–172

Munich, Bayerische Staatsbibliothek
   Codex Monacensis Graecus 204 167

Paris, Archives nationales
   Minutier central, XIX 176
Paris, Bibliothèque nationale de France
   Dupuy 255 128
   Français 306 176

Français 312 165
Français 11333 122
Latin 6067 125, 127
Réserve, AD–105 176

Rhodes, Ephorate of Antiquities
   KK 5090–5094 142

Turin, Biblioteca Nazionale Universitaria
   Codex Taurinensis B I 4 167
Turin, Biblioteca Reale
   Varia 212 170

Valletta, National Library of Malta, Archives of the Order of Malta
   411–412 171
   417 171
Vatican City, Biblioteca Apostolica Vaticana
   Codex Vaticanus Graecus 305 73
   Codex Vaticanus Latinus 4929 73

Inscriptions

AER II, 1 41–42
    53–62 135, 137
    53–84 135, 137
    55 138
    63 137, 139
    63–69 137
    64 137
    65 137
    66–69 137
    71 137
    73 135
    74 137
    75 137
    76 137

Badoud (2011) 563–565, Appendix 2 104
Badoud (2017c) 40–42, no. 59 142
Badoud (2019a) 80 6, 105
Badoud (2019c) 49, no. 1 14
Bean (1962) 7, no. 5 7
Berges (1996) 144, no. 224 36
Bernand and Masson (1957) 10–14, no. 2 41
Boardman and Hayes (1966) 169, no. 976 38
Bresson (2021b) 670 7

CIG IV, 8703 25

Drew-Bear and Fillon (2011) 277 51

Ebert (1967) 411–412, no. 1 48
Engelmann (2007) 157, no. 1 51

FD III, 4, 229 62

Held (2003) 55–58, nos. 1–2 7
Hiller von Gaertringen (1895)
        228, no. 2 14
HTC 20 7

I. Délos 1709 143
I. Didyma 217 50
IG I³, 435 91
  II², 1081/5 51
    1424a 35
    1425 35
  XI, 2, 145 22, 28, 33

XI, 4, 1100 98
    1101 98
XII, 1, 2 140, 152, 161
    23 138
    25 142–143, 145, 147
    31 7
    61 15
    64 152
    73 138
    155–156 139
    161 7
    162 143
    437 36
    438 36
    677 13
    786 7, 15
    891 7
    937 7
    1195 42
    1303 42
XII, 3, 1015 27–28
XII, 3, suppl., 1269 14
XII, 4.2, 654 7
IGCyr 011000 19, 27–29, 34
    016700 17–19, 27–29, 34, 42, 46
    118100 39–40
IGR IV, 292 51
IGUR I, 227 6
IK 5–Kyme 13 51
IK 28–Iasos 2 65
IK 38–Rhodische Peraia 8 36
    155 36
    555 13
IK 41–Knidos I, 111 87
I. Milet 735 50
I. Olympia 151 11
    152 11
    153 12
    159 11
IOSPE I², 670 7
I. Sardis I, 27 51
I. Thespies 333 48–49

Konstantinopoulos (1963) 1–2, no. 1 135
    1–8, nos. 1–12 135
    7, no. 11 135

Konstantinopoulos (1967)
    124–128 145
Konstantinopoulos (1969) 482, β, 1 7
Kontorini (1975) 99–103 66
Kontorini (1983) 24–32 117

Lemos (1991) 242, nos. 236–237 38
Lindos 1 14
    2 6, 13, 35–36, 58–59
    16 7, 10
    37 87
    44 36
    50 57–59
    51 58
    84 87
    117 139
    119 87
    134 142, 146
    137 87
    183 14
    219 14
    222 6
    281a 139
    281b 139
    323 61–62
    339 7
    391 7
    392 7
    441 13
    482 13
    707 6

Marcadé (1953) 11 62
    12 62
Marek and Zingg (2018) 1–139 116
Moretti (1953) 51–56, no. 21 12
    57–60, no. 23 12
Moretti (1957) 56, no. 201 12
    73, no. 322 12

NESM 9 15
    10 15
    31 87, 104
    59 152
    144–217 7
NS 3 139
    14 152
    18 14
    19 6
    46 139
    174 36
NSER 3 143–144

Papachristodoulou (1989) 171, no. 7* 139
    197, no. 8 7
Pérée 5 13
    128 36
    195 36
Piérart (1990) 329–330, no. 1 23, 28, 34
Plassart (1926) 460–461, no. 116 47
PSA 15 13
    19 7, 36
Pugliese Carratelli (1950) 80, no. 17 7
Pugliese Carratelli (1967–1968) 445–453, no. 2 65

Scrinzi (1898–1899) 259–260, no. 2 139
SEG XXVII, 481 10
    XXVIII, 737 50
    XXXIII, 1037 51
    XLVI, 989 13
    LV, 1503 51
Segre (1935) 214–222 116
SER 8 7
    17 7
    18 6
    19 6
    51a 87
Stroud (1984) 195 6
*Syll.*³ 82 12

TAM V.2, 1308 50
TC 31 130
    38 7
    40 130
    41 87
    63 6
    86 139
    92 87
    105 9, 36, 42
    147 9
Themelis (1998) 55–56 62
TRI 1 11, 14
    2 138
    9 14, 159
    12 14
    15 58
    16 47
    28 138, 160
    34 135, 137
    35 139
    37 143
    38 135
    66 7, 15
    67 9, 148
    128 160

Greek Index

This index is limited to words whose etymology, geographic distribution, or meaning is discussed.

ἄβαντες (*ábantes*) 22
ἄγγαρος (*ággaros*) 33
ἀναδασμός (*anadasmós*) 13
ἀνατίθημι (*anatíthēmi*) 100, 102
ἀνδριάς (*andriás*) 21, 51, 163
ἀνίστημι (*anístēmi*) 95
ἀφικετεύω (*aphiketeúō*) 42
δέκομαι (*dékomai*) 42
ἕδος (*hédos*) 50
εἰκών (*eikṓn*) 51
ἑλένας (*helénas*) 33
ἐργάζομαι (*ergázomai*) 143
ἐρείδω (*ereídō*) 23
ἐσχάζοσαν (*escházosan*) 113
ἱδρύω (*hidrúō*) 100, 102
ἴχνος (*íchnos*) 175
κατασκευάζω (*kataskeuázō*) 143
κίων (*kíōn*) 21–22, 25, 167–168
κοιρανία (*koiranía*) 97, 105
Κολοσσαί (*Kolossaí*) 16, 151, 213
κολοσσιαῖος (*kolossiaîos*) 50
κολοσσικός (*kolossikós*) 50

κολοσσοβάμων (*kolossobámōn*) 24, 45–46, 116
κολοσσός (*kolossós*) 4, 16–51, 56, 77, 88, 92, 95, 103, 105, 116–117, 151, 162, 196, 220–223
Κολοφών (*Kolophṓn*) 16, 151
κυπάρισσος (*kupárissos*) 16
λάχος (*láchos*) 11, 14–15
Λίνδιος (*Líndios*) 52–54
μακύνομαι (*makúnomai*) 100, 102
μοχλός (*mochlós*) 88, 90, 92
νάρκισσος (*nárkissos*) 16
ξόανον (*xóanon*) 33–34, 50
ὁρίζω (*horízō*) 63
ποιέω (*poiéō*) 87
πολύλλιστος (*polúllistos*) 93
Ῥόδιος (*Rhódios*) 41, 52
σήκωμα (*sḗkōma*) 88, 92
συνεργάζομαι (*sunergázomai*) 143
σχεδία (*schedía*) 88, 92
ὑποδέκομαι (*hupodékomai*) 42
φέγγος (*phéggos*) 201, 210
χαλκουργέω (*chalkourgéō*) 87

General Index

Abu Simbel 39
Accame, Silvio 99–100, 102, 104–105
Achaia Polis 13
Aegae 213
Aetolians 112–113
Agamedes, stele of – at Lebadeia 24
Agasias of Ephesus 57
Agias, son of Daochos (statue at Delphi) 61
Agios Fokas 150
Aigospotami 14
Ajax, son of Oileus 113
Al–Balādhurī, ʾAḥmad ibn Yaḥyā 71–72
Aleni, Giulio 184
Alexander III the Great 58–60, 62, 92, 99, 103, 108, 116
   Portraits 61, 92, 211–212
   Statue of –, with the lance 211–212
   see Coins
Alexandra (Cassandra) 44, 110–114, 117
Alexandria 95, 98, 115–116, 119–120, 130, 211
   Column of Diocletian ('Pompey's pillar') 211
   Library 112, 116
   Lighthouse 94–95, 131, 164, 171, 173, 210, 217
   Musaeum 116
Alka 14
Altars, from Pergamon and Rhodes 148–149
Althaimenes 13
Amasis II 10, 29
Amastris 213
Amenemhat III 28
Amphora stamps, Rhodian – 4, 42–43, 47, 51, 200–201
   Sinopean – 201
Androcles (historian) 112
Angel of the Revelation 68–69, 73, 205, 209, 220
Angelion (sculptor) 22, 33
Antigonus II Gonatas 104, 113
Antioch, Library of – 112
Antiochus II Theos 70
Antiochus III the Great 70
Antiochus IV Epiphanes 70
Antisthenes (priest of Helios) 138, 160
Apameia (Phrygia) 51
Aphídruma 37, 161

Aphrodite 112
Apolakkia 150
Apollo 67, 93, 138, 142, 213
   at Apollonia Pontica (statue) 75–77, 91
   at Argos 23
   Belvedere (statue in Rome) 179–181, 206–207, 219
   Caelispex 207
   Cytharoedus 189, 191–192, 204, 210
   at Delos (statue) 22–23, 33
   at Delphi 59, 67
   Katharsios 207
   Lycian (statue at Athens) 189
   Pythios at Rhodes 134, 139–151, 221
      Priest of – 146
   from Santa Marinella (statue) 126, 205–210, 212
   Strangford (statue) 215
Apollonia Pontica: see Apollo
Apollonia Salbace 213
Apollonios of Rhodes 112
Arabs 1, 69–72, 94, 124, 151, 171, 184, 220
Aradus 213
Argos 6, 11, 23, 28, 33–34, 45–46, 103
   see Krater
Aristotle 22, 167
Arona 75
Arpi 112–113
Artemis 134, 140, 144–151, 221
Artemisia (I and II) 176–178
Arverni: see Mercury
Ashton, Richard 66, 90–91, 212–213
Atabyron, Mount 7, 12, 15
   Sanctuary of Zeus Atabyrios 7, 15
Athena
   at Athens 145
   Polias at Ialysos 14–15
     at Kamiros 14–15, 159
     at Rhodes 15, 50, 86, 143, 145–146, 151, 157, 162
     Priest of – 146
   Lindia at Lindos 9, 14–15, 35, 59, 61, 64
   Promachos (statue at Athens) 90–91
Athens 6, 43, 51, 85
   Temple of Athena 145
     of Olympian Zeus 145
   see Apollo; Athena

GENERAL INDEX 263

Attalus (statue at Sicyon) 50
Augé de Lassus, Lucien 126, 195, 201
Augustus 53, 91
Aune, David 68

Babylon, Hanging Gardens of – 94, 186
    Walls 94, 186
Barboutis, George 216
Barsine 99
Bartholdi, (Frédéric) Auguste 82, 198–200, 205,
    208–209, 219
Bases, naturalistic – from Rhodes 129–130
Basil the Great 163, 167
Basíleia of Lebadeia 48
Baskánia, from Rhodes 148
Battos I 35–39, 41
Battos II 36
Bavaria (statue in Munich) 75, 210
Benndorf, Otto 97, 126
Benveniste, Émile 2, 16, 21–24, 26, 29, 32–33
Berenice, daughter of Ptolemy II 92
Berlin Adorant (statue from Rhodes) 145
Bernier, Louis 195–196
Bernouilli, Johann Jacob 211
Berthouville, treasure of – 114
Biliotti, Édouard 129, 142
Biondo, Flavio 72
Blaeu, Willem 184
Blake, William 205, 208–209
Blinkenberg, Christian 14, 36, 39, 42,
    57–59, 61
Borghese Gladiator (statue) 57
Bosse, Abraham 186–187
Brasca, Santo 122
Britannico, Giovanni 168
Briula 213
Bruneau, Philippe 22–23
Bruttium 119
Buddha, statue of – at Kamakura 83–84, 87,
    89–90, 223
    at Nara 80, 82–83, 86, 89–90, 92, 223
Buondelmonti, Cristoforo 170–171
Busts from Cyrene 24

Cabinet, Bohemian 186
Cadwallader, Alan 213
Calamis (sculptor) 75–77, 91
Callimachus of Cyrene 53, 115–116
Calyx with Rhodian inscription in
    Cyrene 38–39
Camels 69, 72–73, 90, 184–185
Caoursin, Guillaume 124–125, 127, 129
Caron, Antoine 176–179
Carthage 99, 113, 118–119

Cassius Longinus, Caius 59, 77, 129, 141,
    145, 184
Caylus, Anne-Claude de Pestel, Count of – 1, 68,
    82, 86, 126–127, 131, 172, 189
Chaereas (sculptor) 61, 211
Chalcedon, Council of – 70
Chalcis 113, 115–116
Chamoux, François 19, 30, 35–36
Chantraine, Pierre 2, 16–17, 21–22, 30, 50
Chares of Lindos 1–2, 4–5, 17, 21, 25, 27, 33,
    42–44, 46–47, 50–56, 59, 61–63, 69,
    71, 73–77, 79, 82–83, 86–92, 95, 107,
    122, 127, 130, 161, 163, 191, 196, 201,
    205, 207, 211, 214, 223
Charias (engineer) 62
Charles Borromeo, Saint (statue at Arona) 75
Charles IX of France 176
Cidrama 213
Clairvoyants 131
Cleobulus 36
Cleopatra I Syra 70
Coins
    with Alexander the Great as Heracles (various
        cities) 100–101
    with Apollo (Apollonia Pontica) 75–76
    with Helios head (Rhodes) 173, 175,
        210–214, 221
    with Helios or Sol (various
        cities) 179, 211–213
    Pseudo-Byzantine 51
    with Rhodos (Rhodes) 200–201
Collachium 156
Colonization 6, 19, 33–42, 103, 222
Colossensis 132–133, 156
Colossus of Rhodes, The – (movie) 213–215
Colossus of the Cypselids (statue in
    Olympia) 22, 24, 28, 33, 48, 222
'Colossus' of the Naxians (statue in Delos) 33
Columns, Minoan – 24
Commodus 67–68
Conrad, Lawrence 67–70, 72, 78, 90
Constans II 71, 220
Constantinople 25, 71–72, 184
    Obelisks in the Hippodrome 25,
        167–168, 200
Corinth 28, 33–34, 213, 222
Corinthian bronze 94
Cornelius Lentulus, Publius 61–62
Courby, Fernand 22
Crete 28
Cyrene 17–24, 26–28, 31–32, 34–42, 46–47, 112
    Sanctuary of the Dioscuri 38–39
    see Busts; Calyx; Figurines; Tile
Cyriac of Ancona 167–168, 173, 210

Daedalus 50
Dali, Salvador 204
Damascus 213
Dankbaar, Ann 131
Dapper, Olfert 131
Dasii 112
D'Aubusson, Pierre 124
Daunia 112–113, 115
De Beauvais, Vincent 164
De Beys, Charles 186
De Bruijn, Cornelis 122–123
De Caullery, Louis 184
De Comans, François 176, 178
Deer, fallow 148–150
De Guyse, Jacques 164
De Jode, Gerard 184
De Jonghe, Adriaen 179
De la Condamine, Charles Marie 122–123
De la Planche, Marc 176, 178
De la Vigenère, Blaise 148
Delos 22, 28, 50, 98, 143
   see Apollo; 'Colossus' of the Naxians
Delphi 12, 67, 142
   Rhodian pillar 59–60, 140–141
   Votive monument of Daochos 61
   see Agias; Helios
De Martoni, Nicola 121–123, 127–129
De' Medici, Catherine 175–176, 178
De' Medici, Marie 176
Demetrius of Phaleron 116
Demetrius Poliorcetes 1, 58, 64–66, 89, 96–97, 99, 101, 103–107, 116, 129, 133, 155, 157, 162, 201, 221–223
Demus-Quatember, Margarete 70–71, 172
De Passe the Elder, Crispin 184
De Rycke, Josse 184
De Sanctis, Gaetano 98, 105
De Vauzelles, Georges 170–171
De Vignay, Jean 164–165
De Vos, Maarten 184
Diagoras, son of Damagetos 11–14
Diagorids: see Eratids
Dickie, Matthew 2, 23–24, 26–27, 30, 45, 74, 79, 82
Didyma 50
Dinnus (mercenary) 115
Diocletian 78, 211
Diognetos (engineer) 133
Diomedes 24, 45–46, 112–113, 115
Dionysus 145, 162
   Head of – 208
Dioscuri 38–39, 137
Dobias-Lalou, Catherine 17, 27, 38–39, 42

Dombart, Thomas 66, 74, 126–127, 131, 156, 201, 210
Donato, Pietro 167
Dorian dialect, Dorians 6, 9–10, 12–13, 21, 26, 33–35, 43, 46, 49–50, 96–97, 103, 105, 221–223
Dorieus, son of Diagoras 11–12
Doryphorus (statue) 94
Dotis 14
Ducat, Jean 2, 22–24, 26–27
Du Choul, Guillaume 131, 170–173, 175, 187
Duoviri navales 99, 118
Dürer, Albrecht 166

Earthquake (c. 227 BC) 1, 46–47, 50, 64–66, 87, 132, 145, 153–154, 161, 164, 185, 189, 206, 223
   (c. AD 141/2) 67
Ebert, Joachim 48
Edson, Charles 2, 97, 103–105
Egypt Carrying the Light to Asia (statue in Port Said) 198
Ekschmitt, Werner 66, 82, 95, 156–157, 204, 208, 210
Elektryone 13
Elephants 72
Emesa (Homs) 64, 71
Ephesus, Temple of Artemis at – 82, 94
Epirus 94
Eratids 10–12, 14, 161
   Statues of the – at Olympia 11
Eratosthenes of Cyrene 112
Erethimiázontes 143
Erysichthon 33
Etruscans 118
Euphorion of Chalcis 112, 116
Euripus 65

Faber, Johann 72
Fabius Verrucosus, Quintus 77
Fabri, Felix 122
Faraklas, Nikolaos 24
Faraone, Christopher 24
Figurines from Dorak 24
   from Rhodes (?) in Cyrene 37–38
Fischer von Erlach, Johann Bernhard 187–188, 200, 210
Fokke, Simon 189
Fontaine, Jacques 128, 156, 171
Fontainebleau 179
Franco, Francisco 214
Fraser, Peter 10, 14, 66, 104, 112
Frel, Jiří 10
Fulvio, Andrea 168

Gabriel, Albert 2, 75, 82, 88–89, 93, 107, 124, 127–130, 133, 156, 201–202, 208, 210, 217
Gaius (soldier) 115
Galle, Philippe 182
Gaugamela 59
Gelon II of Syracuse 133
Gerf Hussein 29–30
Gibbon, Edward 72
Glaucon, son of Eteocles 142
Golvin, Jean-Claude 201
Gómez, Ramiro 215
Gortyn 50
Guérin, Victor 123, 126, 148, 150, 189
Guillon, Pierre 24

Hadrian 68, 71, 74, 91, 205–206
Haliádai 139
Haliastaí 136, 138–139, 143
Halicarnassus 176–177
   Mausoleum 94, 195
Halíeia 10–11, 137, 139, 143–144, 159, 162
Hamilton, William 123, 126, 189
'Hand of the Colossus' 131–132
Harris, William 118
Haynes, Denys 2, 82–83, 88, 90, 107
Head, Barclay 36, 210–211
Hecate 148
Hedenborg, Johan 142–143
Helbig, Wolfgang 61, 211
Helen 21, 32, 168–169
Helepolis 64, 106–107, 133
Helios
   at Delphi (chariot) 59–61, 140–141
   Eleutherios at Troezen 202
   at Rhodes 1, 4–5, 9–16, 42, 52, 67, 70, 81, 105, 137, 141–142, 144, 146, 148, 150, 153, 161–162, 164, 201, 204, 210, 219, 223
      Chariot of – 59–61, 93, 140–141, 195, 223
      Cult statue of – 93
      Heads of – 154, 205, 207–208
      Herm of – on amphora stamps 42–43
      Kolossós of – on amphora stamps 42–43
      Priests of – 65, 135, 137–139, 142, 146, 152–153, 158–161
      Prophets of – 139
   see Coins
Henry II of France 176
Henry IV of France 176
Henry VIII of England 72
Heracles 6, 35–36, 97, 100–101, 103
   Statue of – at Tarentum 55
Heracles, son of Alexander III 99, 113
Heraclids 97–98, 100–101, 103

Hercules, Capitoline – (statue in Rome) 168–169, 179
Herm 22, 26, 42–43
Hermary, Antoine 33, 42, 201
Hermes 143
Herod the Great 145
Hexapolis, Dorian – 10
Hieron II of Syracuse 133
Hiller von Gaertringen, Friedrich 27, 42, 59, 152, 160, 208
Hipparchus 26
Hitler, Adolf 98
Hoepfner, Wolfram 2, 55, 66, 68–69, 75, 88, 90, 124, 127, 129–130, 132, 136–137, 140–141, 144–145, 147, 156, 195–197
Hof, Gert 216
Holleaux, Maurice 65, 118–119
Houel, Nicolas 175–178
Hugo, Victor 184
Huguccio of Pisa 164
Huguenots 178
Hydria, from Rhodes 10
Hyperion 9
Hypnerotomachia Poliphili (book) 165
Hyrkanis 50
Hyssaldomos, son of Eirenaios 116

Ialysos 6–7, 9–15, 36, 38, 41, 87, 139, 143, 145, 147, 158
   Sanctuary of Athena Polias and Zeus Polieus 14–15
      of Elektryone 13
      of Kerkaphos 13
Ialysos, son of Kerkaphos (painting) 14
Iasos 65
Ikarakuri 87
Isthmia 32
Isthmian Games 12, 138
Ivory, Byzantine – 164

Jacopi, Giulio 145, 149, 203–204
Jason and the Argonauts (film) 215
Jerome (saint) 65
Jewish merchant 69, 71–73, 124, 184, 220
Jones, Kenneth 2, 45, 54, 99–105
Julius II 179
Jupiter 184

Kalche 105
Kamiros 6–7, 9–15, 38, 41, 87, 129–130, 139, 145, 148, 158–159
   Sanctuary of Athena Polias and Zeus Polieus 14–15
Kamiros, son of Kerkaphos 11, 14

Karpathos 105
Kasara 14
Kekoia 150
Kerkaphos 11, 13–14
Kerkaphos, father of Philonikos 14
Kirchhoff, Adolf 38
Knoepfler, Denis 48
Kolophon 16, 151
Kolossai 16, 151, 213
Kolossi 156
Konstantinopoulos, Grigoris 10–11, 15, 135–136, 145, 152–153, 155
Kontis, Ioannis 15, 135, 145, 152
Kontorini, Vassa 41, 117–118, 135, 153, 162
Korai 23, 26, 50
Kos 7
Kotziamanis, Nikolaos 216
Kouroi 23, 26, 33, 50, 215
Krater, Argolic – at Samos 28, 30–31, 34–35
Kunitora, Utagawa 193–194
Kupka, František 195, 197
Kyme 51

Laches 54, 63
Lade 98, 107
Lafrery, Antoine 179–180
Laocoon (statue in Rome) 101
Laodicea ad Mare 213
Laredo 214–215
La Rochelle 178
Lartos 59, 130
Laurenzi, Luciano 61, 88, 92–93, 107, 129, 148, 210–211, 213
Lazarus, Emma 200
Le Brun, Charles 141
Lebadeia 24, 48
Lenormant, François 200
Leochares of Athens 62
Leone, Sergio 213–215, 217
Lerambert, Henri 176
Lesbazeilles, Eugène 126, 200–201
Liberty Enlightening the World, The – (statue in New York) 75, 79, 82, 88–89, 129, 189, 192, 195, 198–202, 205, 209, 214, 217–219, 223
Licinus Mucianus, Gaius 64, 73, 101
Licymnios 6
Lindos 6–7, 9–15, 35–39, 41–43, 52–53, 57, 59, 61, 64, 74, 87, 122, 139, 145, 158
    Sanctuary of Artemis Kekoia 150
    of Athena Lindia and Zeus Polieus 14–15, 59
Lindos, son of Kerkaphos 11, 14

Lippolis, Enzo 9, 14, 59, 136–137, 139–141, 144–145, 147–148, 153
Locrian Maidens 113
Loryma 104, 157–158
Louis XIII 177
Lüders, Carl Ferdinand 1, 54, 68, 82, 127
Lycophron of Chalcis 44, 98–99, 108–116, 120, 222
Lycos of Rhegium 115–116
Lygdamis 176
Lysippus of Sicyon 4, 43–44, 47, 54–63, 76–77, 92, 195, 210–211, 214, 223

Maiuri, Amedeo 145, 150, 152
Malkin, Irad 9, 19, 36, 161
Manesson Mallet, Allain 186, 188
Manoussou-Ntella, Katerina 69, 124, 129, 153–154, 157, 160
Manutius, Aldus 168
Marengo, Silvia 38
Martin, George R. R. 215
Maryon, Herbert 2, 82, 89–90, 156, 202–205
Masseti, Marco 150
Mausolus 176
Mellaart, James 24
Memphis, Palace of Amasis II at – 29–30
    Pyramids 94
    Temple of Ptah 29
Menedemus of Eretria 114
Menelaus 21, 31–32
Mercouri, Melina 131
Mercury (statue of – commissioned by the Arverni) 91–92
Mexía, Pedro 184
Michalaki-Kollia, Maria 69, 126, 136, 139, 146, 148, 152–153
Michelangelo 69
Midea, statues menhirs from – 24
Miletus 50
Minoans 24
Mithridates VI Eupator 129
Momigliano, Arnaldo 2, 9, 42, 44, 97–100, 103–105, 112–113, 115, 118
Mopsos 211
Moreno, Paolo 2, 42, 44, 47, 54–56, 58–59, 61–62, 65–66, 68, 70, 73–74, 76, 92, 94, 107, 126, 151, 155–157, 200–201, 205–212
Morricone, Luigi 65, 152, 158–160
Muñoz Degraín, Antonio 191, 193, 204
Münster, Sebastian 122, 166
Mussolini, Benito 214–215
Muʿāwiya ibn ʾAbī Sufyān 69, 71–72, 151, 184–185, 220

GENERAL INDEX

Mycenaeans 6, 9, 24, 46
Mykerinos 29

Naucratis, Hellenion of – 10
Naxos 12, 33
Neaira 11
Neapolis (Scythia) 7
Nebuchadnezzar 70–71, 73
Nemean Games 12, 48, 138
Nero, Colossus of – (statue in Rome) 5, 68, 72–79, 91, 146, 153, 205, 220, 222
Newton, Charles 126, 128–129, 137–138
Newton, Isaac 129
Nicaea Cilbianorum 213
Nike (statue at Samothrace) 107–108, 141, 222
Nikopolis 211
Nilsson, Martin 9, 42, 200–201

Olympia: *see* Colossus of the Cypselids; Eratids; Philipp II of Macedonia; Zeus
Olympic Games 11–12, 37, 215, 216
On Her Majesty's Secret Service (movie) 217
Oracle 36, 67, 206, 223
Osbern of Gloucester 164
Osiris (statues of – in Egypt) 28–29
Ouranos 9
Oxen, bronze – from Mount Atabyron 7

Padovano, Gualtiero 168
Palmara, Mimmo 214
Panels, painted – from a hotel in Paris 186
Pankis, children of – 35–36
Paris 21, 32
Patara 51
Patmos 68
Paul the Apostle 156
Peisistratus, son of Hippocrates 33
People of Rhodes being crowned by the People of Syracuse (statue at Rhodes) 132–133
People of Rome (statue at Rhodes) 86
Peraea 7, 98, 104–108, 120, 157–158, 162, 222–223
Perale, Marco 93
Pergamon 51, 108
  Great Altar 209
  Library 116
  see Altars
Pericles, son of Xanthippus 104
Perirrhantêrion 30–32
Perse(is) 11
Peucetians 115
Phalasarna 118
Pharsalus 61
Pheidias of Athens 53, 91
Philip II of Macedonia, portraits of – 61, 211
  Statues of – and his family at Olympia 62

Philip V of Macedonia 97–98, 100–101, 103–104, 107–108, 244
  Statue of – at Samothrace 108, 110–111
Philip the Good of Burgundy 164
Philo of Byzantium (engineer) 79–80
Philo of Byzantium, Pseudo- (paradoxographer) 24, 79, 82–83, 85–87, 219–221, 223
Philostephanos of Cyrene 112
Picard, Charles 24, 58, 114–115, 208
Piel, Thierry 69, 73, 129, 133
Pillars, Egyptian – 29–30
Piracy 116, 118, 120
Pius II 72
Plassart, André 47
Polyclitus of Argos 43
Polyperchon 99
Pornography 192
Poseidon Amoibeus 45–46
  Hippios at Rhodes, priest of – 146
Powell, John 93
Préchac, François 63, 132, 155, 171, 208, 210
Primaticcio, Francesco 179
Protogenes (painter) 14
Psammetichus II 39
Ptolemy I Soter 66, 94–95, 116, 162
Ptolemy II Philadelphus 44–46, 94, 98–99, 108, 111, 115
Ptolemy III Euergetes 67, 90, 155
Ptolemy V Epiphanes 70
Pugliese Carratelli, Giovanni 9, 12, 14, 24
Pyrrhus I 94
Pythia 36
Pythian Games 138

Qasr, mosaic at – 163–164

Relief, funerary – from Rhodes 202–204
Remiet, Perrin 164–165
Rhamnous: *see* Themis
Rhegium 115–116
Rhodes
  Acropolis (Monte Smith) 15, 83, 86, 122, 133, 137–140, 144–146, 150–152, 157–158, 160–162, 173, 211–214, 219
  Agora 132–133
  Bouleutêrion 139
  Church of Saint John 133, 152, 156–157
    of Saint Nicholas 121–122, 127
  Clock tower, Ottoman 134, 157
  Deîgma 132–133, 145
  Dungeon, Byzantine 152, 153, 156
  Eghrì-limàn 124

Rhodes (*cont.*)
  Fortifications, Hellenistic 66, 124, 128–129, 168, 220
  Fort Saint Nicholas 127–129, 131, 156
  Foundries 83, 85–86
  Halíeion pedíon 144
  Harbours 1, 68, 89, 122–131, 153, 168, 171–173, 176, 178, 185, 187, 189, 191, 193, 195, 200–201, 205, 214, 216, 219–221
  Hippodrome 143–144
  'Iron Mosque' 158
  Kástro, Byzantine 153, 157, 222
  Palace of the Hospitallers' Grand Master 56–57, 134, 136, 152–153, 162, 222
  'Pantheon' 133
  prutaneîon 139
  Sanctuary of Apollo Pythios 134, 139–151, 221
    of Artemis 86, 134, 140, 146–151, 221
    of Athena Polias and Zeus Polieus 15, 50, 86, 145–146, 151, 157, 162
    of Dionysus 145, 162
    of the Dioscuri 137
    of Helios 136, 138, 140–142, 144–146, 148, 152, 157–158, 160–162, 219
    of Ptolemy I Soter 162
    of Zeus Atabyrios 7
  Soichan-Minetou plot 134–139, 152–153, 160–162
  Süleymaniye school 134, 157
  see Apollo; Altars; Amphora stamps; *Baskánia*; Berlin Adorant; Calyx; Helios; Hydria; People of Rhodes being crowned by the People of Syracuse; People of Rome; Relief; Tile
Rhodos 11, 13, 137, 200–201
Rice, Ellen 82, 135
Ridpath, John Clark 189, 204, 209–210
Rigaud, Georges 214
Rollin, Charles 187, 189
Rome
  Capitoline 64, 77, 117–118, 223
  Colosseum 74–75
  Domus Aurea 72, 74
  Meta Sudans 74
  see Hercules; Laocoon; Nero
Roseo, Mambrino 184
Ross, Ludwig 123, 126, 189
Rottiers, Bernard Eugène Antoine 56–57, 123–124, 126, 133, 189–191, 204, 215, 217
Rousselet, Gilles 186–187
Roux, Georges 2, 21–24, 26–27, 30, 32, 42, 87, 167–168
Rubens, Peter Paul 184

Sagunto 119
Salamis (Attica) 176
Samos: *see* Krater
Samothrace: *see* Nike; Philip V of Macedonia
Sardis 184
Scaliger, Joseph Justus 66
Schedel, Hartmann 165–168
Schreiber, Theodor 61, 211
Seleukos I Nikator 66
Selinus: *see* Stelae
Selivanov, Sergey 132
Semiramis 186
Servais, Jean 22
Seven Wonders of the World, list of the – 51, 94–95
Shakespeare, William 184, 191
Sicyon: *see* Attalus
Siege of Rhodes (305–304 BC) 1, 58, 64–66, 89, 99, 103–108, 133, 162, 201
  (88 BC) 129
  (42 BC) 59, 77, 129, 141, 145
  (AD 1480) 127
  (AD 1522) 127
Simonides of Keos 54, 171
Sinope: *see* Amphora stamps
Smith, Sidney 122
Socles, father of Lycophron 115
Sol 163, 179, 219
  Statue of – from Chalon-sur-Saône 195–196
  from Montdidier 195–198
  see Coins
Sparta 6, 12, 23, 37
Spirit 17
Staffieri, Giovanni Maria 211–212
Stelae from Selinus 24
Stendhal 47
Storck, Abraham 184
Suleiman the Magnificent 168
Suppliants 17, 19, 21, 41–42
Sura (Lycia) 7
Syme 14
Syme, daughter of Ialysos 14
Synoecism 7, 9–14, 41, 104, 141
Syracuse 71–72, 132–133, 220

Tabor, Mount 7
Tarentum 99–100, 119
  see Heracles; Zeus
Tektaios (sculptor) 22, 33
Tempesta, Antonio 184–185
Terentius Varro Lucullus, Marcus 77
Theagenes 186–187
Thebes (Egypt) 29
Themis (statue at Rhamnous) 62
Theocritus 22, 24, 48, 50, 114

Theodosius I 25
Theon of Alexandria 111, 115
Theophanes the Confessor 69
Theophilus of Edessa 69–72, 90, 93–94, 210, 220
Theoxenía 23, 26
Thera 19, 21, 27–28, 31, 34–37
Thespiae 47–50
Thessalonica, Edict of – 67
Thevet, André 121–123, 173–174, 176, 178, 182, 201, 210
Tigrini, Orazio 172
Tile from Cyrene mentioning a Rhodian (?) 39–41
Timothy of Ephesus 156
Tlapolémeia 11, 13
Tlepolemos 6, 11–13, 15
Torr, Cecil 132, 156
Tourists 131, 191, 205, 218
Trajan 68
Tralles 213
Tréheux, Jacques 23
Trianta 13
Tripolis 213
Troezen 202
Troy 6, 21, 45, 112–113
Tsunami 65
Tuby, Jean-Baptiste 141
Turks 56–57, 72, 185
Turner, William 123–124
Tyre 58
Tyrrhenians 118

Uhlenbrock, Jaimee 37
Urania 114
Urlichs, Ludwig 66, 78, 90

Valavanis, Panos 143–145
Van Gelder, Hendrik 7, 9, 68, 104, 126, 139, 144, 152
Van Heemskerck, Maerten 137, 168–169, 179, 181–182, 184–185, 193, 195–196, 201, 207, 209, 219
Van Meurs, Johannes 63, 72

Vedder, Ursula 2, 66, 69, 73, 82–83, 85–86, 107, 127, 136, 142–143, 145–148, 166, 172–173, 182, 185–186, 208, 210
Verbiest, Ferdinand 183–184
Vernant, Jean-Pierre 2, 23, 26, 32
Vespasian 67–68
Vicenza, Villa Godi Malinverni at – 138
Video games 4, 215–217
Vignon, Gilles 186–188
Von Breydenbach, Bernhard 122, 178, 182
Von Hammer-Purgstall, Josef 122–123
Von Wilamowitz-Moellendorf, Ulrich 9, 21, 24, 47–48, 51, 93
Voodoo dolls 24

Walbank, Frank 2, 97–98, 102
Wauquelin, Jean 164–165
Weitzmann, Kurt 163
West, Stephanie 45, 112
Wiemer, Hans-Ulrich 10, 13, 54, 102–105
Will, Édouard 65
Witdoeck, Pierre-Joseph 190
Witulski, Thomas 68
Wolgemut, Michael 166
Women, statues of nude – in Egypt 29
Wujewski, Tomasz 68–69, 82, 140, 151, 155

Xanthos 51
Xenagoras (historian) 36–37

Zenodorus (sculptor) 74, 77, 79, 86, 91
Zenon (historian) 13
Zeus 28–29, 81
    Atabyrios on Rhodes 6–9, 12, 15
    Melichios at Selinus 24
    Olympios at Athens 145
    at Olympia (cult statue) 53, 94
        (*kolossós*) 22, 28–29, 33–34, 222
    Polieus on Rhodes 15, 134, 145, 151, 157, 162
        Priest of – 146
    at Tarentum (statue) 4, 55–56, 76–77